Lotus in a Sea of Flames

Ryuei Michael McCormick

Table of Contents

Table of Contents

Illustrations

Preface

At the age of 18 I was introduced to Nichiren Buddhism. Since that time I have voraciously read everything I could find in English translation connected to Buddhism, Mahayana Buddhism, the *Lotus Sutra*, the teachings of Tiantai, and the life and writings of Nichiren Shōnin, the founder of the school of Buddhism that I am ordained in as a minister. So this book is the product of my 30 years of research, some might say obsession. However, it would not have begun at all had not my sensei, the Ven. Ryūshō Matsuda, asked me to write a book about Nichiren Shōnin's life using as my primary source the seven volumes of the *Writings of Nichiren Shōnin* put out by the Nichiren Shū Overseas Propagation and Promotion Association. To get me started, I was handed two very thick sheaves of notes. One was a collection of passages from the aforementioned seven volumes pertaining to events in Nichiren's life, and the second consisted of my sensei's outline of Nichiren's life based on those passages and other sources. He also provided me with his own translation of the booklet that accompanies a documentary DVD on the life of Nichiren Shōnin by Dr. Takashi Nakao. Provided with these materials, I began to marshal my own resources and set to work. The end result is the present book. This book is my attempt, given my own limitations, to present a historical novelization of the life of Nichiren Shōnin in order to understand him in the context of his own time and place. I hope that I have at least partially succeeded in conveying some of his spirit so that others will come to appreciate his life, teachings, and sacrifices as I have.

I should also say that this book, for me, is also very much about the passing of my mother, Carolyn McCormick. She died of cancer on January 26th, 2013. In a way, as a student and practitioner of Buddhism, I have been contemplating mortality and impermanence since I was 18. However, such abstract meditations don't really impact a person the way the death of a parent does. Especially someone who had given me so much love and support, and a patient sympathetic ear, for my whole life until just a couple of years ago. My thoughts and feelings about death and the manner of her death are very much a part of this book. I think that is only appropriate, since Nichiren Shōnin himself said that from a young age he had "determined to study the matter of the last moment of life before all else."

It is my hope that this book will not only interest Nichiren Buddhists, but also those who may not be familiar with Nichiren Shōnin, or even with Buddhism at all. The Kamakura period of Japanese history is of great historical interest in my opinion. I also think that the religious issues that Nichiren Shōnin and his contemporaries were concerned with are actually still relevant. If one takes the trouble to look past the foreign terms and unfamiliar imagery one will, I believe, see that these issues and concerns touch upon universal questions and longings.

Finally, I would just like to alert the reader to a few things. I have used diacritical marks for most words in Sanskrit and Japanese with the exception of those that appear in English dictionaries (e.g. nirvana, Hinayana, and Mahayana). Unfamiliar terms and names appear in the glossary if they appear in more than one passage or if there is some information (including dates) that cannot be told in the narrative. I have also provided notes at the end in order to show exactly what sources I used in each chapter and also to explain anything that I could not in the narrative. I have adapted just about all the passages I have used from my sources in order to cater to the needs of this kind of novelization and also to suit my own translation preferences, though I have endeavored not to change the intent or meaning. Also, I have used American, rather than Japanese, conventions of counting age and periods of time, as this is less confusing to an English-speaking reader.

Ryūei Michael McCormick
San Francisco, CA

Acknowledgments

Nichiren always stressed the importance of requiting one's debts of gratitude. So here I wish to express my gratitude to my sensei, the Ven. Ryūshō Matsuda for his copious notes and the translation of Dr. Nakao's DVD booklet, without which this project would not have gotten off the ground. I am also grateful to Rev. Shinkō Arnold Matsuda, the head minister of the Myōkakuji Betsuin, San Jose Nichiren Buddhist Temple. Without his support and the support of the temple, this publication would not have been possible.

I especially want to thank Dr. Jacqueline Stone, for graciously giving of her time and expertise to fact check this novelization of Nichiren's life. She also suggested many helpful revisions, esp. in connection with the translations of passages from Nichiren Shōnin's writings and the *Lotus Sutra*. I want to make it clear that she is not responsible for any mistakes, oversights, or inaccuracies. Those would be mine. In addition, her constant encouragement kept me from giving up on the project during those times when I was feeling overwhelmed by it.

I am also thankful to Rhea Adri for the beautiful cover art and the five illustrations that accompany the story in order to help bring it to life.

I am also thankful to Marcus Moreno for his last minute contribution of the back cover art.

I am also thankful to J. de Salvo for his edits and revisions.

I am also thankful to Robert Louis Henry for formatting this sizeable tome.

Finally, as always, I am thankful to Yumi Moriguchi and my daughter Julie for their patience during the many months when I was preoccupied with this project.

At the End

The old monk accepted that he was dying. A constant chill gripped his body. There were sharp pains in his bowels that never abated. Gradually, they were becoming worse, it was undeniable. He shifted uneasily on his futon and glanced up at the small wooden statue of Śākyamuni Buddha. He had carried it with him for more than 20 years, and now it gazed down on him from the table with warm regard and a serene smile; right palm up and left palm down, as if to say, "Have no fear." Behind the Buddha hung the mandala the monk had composed a few years before. Down the middle of the mandala, in Chinese calligraphy, he had inscribed "Devotion to the *Sutra of the Lotus Flower of the Wonderful Dharma*" in seven characters pronounced by the monk and the people of his land as *Na*, *Mu*, *Myō*, *Hō*, *Ren*, *Ge*, and *Kyō*. Their lines radiated out like shafts of light, embracing and illumining all the names arranged around the center; names representative of every realm that came together in this one: the awakened, the blessed, the confused, the damned, humans, beasts, spirits, and creatures heard of but rarely if ever seen. These seven characters, called the *daimoku* or "sacred title," were a paean to the *Lotus Sutra*, the culmination and flowering of all the teachings of Śākyamuni Buddha. The monk had spent 29 years, almost half his life, promoting faith in the *Lotus Sutra* through the practice of the *daimoku*. He had assured all who would listen that anyone who received and kept the *daimoku* in their hearts and minds, and who chanted it with their lips and tongues, would know peace in their present lives and be reborn in good places. Not merely that, but those who defied the corrupt world of the Latter Age of Degeneration and upheld the *daimoku* without compromise would be embraced by the Eternal Śākyamuni Buddha and find that those seven characters had become like seeds of buddhahood, "perfect and complete spiritual awakening," planted within the soil of their lives. It took great courage and determination however, for between the sowing of the seed and the harvesting of the fruit, one still had to face the hatred

1

and jealousy directed towards the *Lotus Sutra*, and those who upheld it, by the confused and the corrupt. They also had to endure the suffering of their world's deterioration, and this could be as hazardous as waking in the middle of the night to realize that one's house is aflame on all sides.

Still, the monk did have his followers and supporters. They surrounded him now – his six senior disciples, other monks and nuns, the samurai Ikegami Munenaka, his younger brother Munenaga, their households, attendants, servants, retainers, men, women, and even children - all chanting the *daimoku* and passages from the *Lotus Sutra* with moist eyes and quivering chins. This gentle susurration had a calming effect and helped him keep his own mind centered on Namu Myōho Renge Kyō and away from his mounting pain and discomfort.

He reflected that it was the fifth year of the Kōan era (1282). He was 60 years old, a fairly long life, considering the hardships he had faced. On the 28th day of the fourth month of the fifth year of Kenchō (1253) he had begun his mission. By this accounting, he had now endured 29 years of fire and ice, swords and starvation, beatings, exile, the murder of friends and adherents, and all other manner of abuse and slander. Yet, he kept resentment at bay and everything he did was for the sake of gratitude. After all, those who study and practice Buddhism must never forget the kindness shown them by their parents, teachers, and ruler, not to mention their debt to the Three Treasures of Buddha, Dharma, and Sangha. His parents had brought him into this world, fed and clothed him, and even secured for him the opportunity to study with Master Dōzen-bō at the temple Seichōji near his home village. Would he see them again in the Pure Land of Eagle Peak? Master Dōzen-bō had taught him to read and write, had opened up for *him*, the son of a fisherman with no standing, the civilizing teachings of the Chinese classics and the scriptures, called sutras or "threads of discourse," of Śākyamuni Buddha. Master Dōzen-bō had passed away some years ago, would he too make it to the Pure Land of Eagle Peak despite his slanders of the Buddha's teaching? The ruler, whether regarded as the emperor in Kyōto or the shogun and his regents in Kamakura, upheld the laws of the land, oversaw the orderly progression of sowing and harvest, and guarded the frontiers. Unless there was a ruler to uphold the moral and universal order life would become impossible for all, from court noble of the highest rank to the lowliest peasant, and even for those who lived on the margins of society and were considered *hinin* or "nonhuman" – the most menial servants, butchers, tanners, beggars, lepers, street performers, and prostitutes. The Three Treasures were above everything else, for they alone provided not just life, education, and order but a path to liberation from life's torments and anguish. Only through them was it possible to awake to the true wondrous nature of all beings and things. There was the Buddha, the "Awakened One" who more than 2,000 years ago in the distant land of India had awakened to the true nature of reality; his Dharma, the teaching and practice found in the sutras that enabled others to also awaken as the Buddha had; and finally the Sangha, the community of monks, nuns, and laypeople who upheld, practiced, realized, and passed on the Buddha's teaching so that it would remain in the world for all people. By taking refuge in the Three Treasures one could attain liberation and lead others to liberation, and thereby repay one's debts of gratitude in full. In fact it was the only way to do so. Sometimes one even had to defy one's parents, teachers, and ruler, or even denounce provisional forms of the Three Treasures in order to attain liberation and repay one's debts. One had to appear ungrateful in order to be truly grateful. If one's benefactors clung to false views, one had a duty to expound the true teaching though it provoked their scorn and wrath. One had to weather exile and all manner of deadly persecutions, even be willing to give up one's life, in order to truly express the depths of one's gratitude. By forthrightly confronting them with the truth of the *Lotus Sutra* one's benefactors might very well turn against it and fall into hell, but they would still have formed a relationship to it and in the fullness of time that connection would enable them to attain buddhahood. For 29 years the monk had done what he could, endured all that had to be endured, given body and mind until now his body lay wasted, his mind fragmented by waves of pain. He suffered also from the debilitating effects of age, hunger, and dehydration. Had he done enough? Would the seeds of correct faith he had tried most of his adult life to sow germinate? Would the couple dozen or more people gathered here be enough to pass on what he had taught and save Japan, or perhaps, eventually, the world? Had he, Nichiren, been able to repay his debts in full? What more could he give? And there was no time left. Life was measured in short gasping breaths.

Zennichi-maro

He cast his mind back to the time when he was the "Splendid Sun," for his childhood name until the age of eleven had been Zennichi-maro. He had been born on the 16th day of the second month of the fourth year of the Jōkyū era (1222) and was raised among the rough and uncultured people of the fishing village of Kominato in the Tōjō District of Nagasa County, in Awa Province, a remote region on the southeastern shore of the main island of Japan. His father was a fisherman by trade. Far from being a simple peasant, though, he was a man both educated and refined. He held a position of responsibility over the other fishermen, and answered to the lady known as the Nun Proprietress whose estate their village was on. It was said by some that he must have been of samurai stock, his fortunes somehow fallen. Whatever the truth of the matter was, Zennichi-maro and his family and neighbors were tainted, one and all, by the ongoing slaughter of sentient beings: the fish and other sea life that they caught, consumed, and bartered to survive. In India, the land of the Buddha, they would be considered *chandālas*, "untouchables." Still, life along the sunny shore of the bay beneath the pine clad hills seemed idyllic to Zennichi-maro. He never forgot the foamy waves, the streamers of seaweed glimpsed through the transparent waters of a calm day, the cries of the gulls and plovers, the salty tang of the sea breeze, the weight of a net full of squirming red sea bream, even the sight of the laver growing on the rocks along the shore. It didn't matter to him that he was an untouchable living on a small island nation in the Latter Age of Degeneration, a time and place far removed from the land and age of Śākyamuni Buddha. He was blessed to live in the land of the *kami*, the "gods" manifest in the awe one felt in the presence of boulders, trees, birds, beasts, mountains, oceans, wind, rain, lightning, thunder, the sun, moon, and stars, and even such as the emperor. Even the dead could be *kami* and make their wishes known through blessings bestowed and curses wrought upon the living. The rays of Amaterasu Ōmikami, the Sun Goddess who was the greatest of them all, shone first upon the shores of Awa. While they lived, the people would enjoy the beauty and bounty of the sea and the protection of the gods. When they died, Amitābha, the Buddha of Infinite Light, along with his attendants, the bodhisattvas World Voice Perceiver and Great Power Obtainer would come to greet them and escort them to his Pure Land of Utmost Bliss in the western region of the universe. All must have seemed safe, orderly, and blessed as Zennichi-maro spent his days enjoying the quiet unassuming joys of life. When did he first come to know that things had gone horribly wrong, even before he had first opened his eyes to the world?

The blind lute playing monk made his way into the temple hall, led by the hand of a young novice. The blind had long lodged and been cared for in Buddhist temples throughout the land. They shaved their heads and wore the black robes and patchwork ochre mantle or *kesa* of the monks, but they were not necessarily ordained. They earned their living playing the Chinese lute and telling tales at crossroads or in the halls of Shinto shrines or Buddhist temples where the rites for the dead were performed. People of all classes gathered to hear their stories. The blind monk plucked the strings of his lute to introduce each passage of his tale. He sang of the Genpei War, fought almost half a century ago. His whitened pox-scarred eyes gazed into the netherworld. His song called out to the fallen warriors of the samurai clans known as the Taira, or Heike, and the Minamoto, also called Genji, to pacify their uneasy spirits. His audience, their emotions aroused by his singing, covered their faces in the long sleeves of their kimonos and wept.

The Genpei War ended when the Minamoto forces finally caught up with the Taira clan at Dan-no-ura near the Straits of Shimonoseki at the southwestern tip of the main island, in the second year of the Genryaku era (1185). In the final battle of the conflict, thousands of ships engaged one another.

6

With the Taira was the child emperor, Antoku. They also had with them the imperial regalia that had been bequeathed by the Sun Goddess to her descendants as symbols of their divinity and right to rule. The monk Nichiren recalled how, long ago, when he was only a child, he had pondered the outcome of this battle. When, in fact, had he first heard this tale? Was it from one of the lute-monks? As the boy Zennichi-maro, was he too spellbound by the quavering ghostly tones that evoked the fall of the Heike and with them the child emperor, Antoku?

In his mind's eye, Zennichi-maro imagined the last of the Taira leaders, Taira no Tomomori vault up from his small boat onto the emperor's ship. In a frenzy, he began sweeping the deck from fore to aft, even as the ships of the Minamoto samurai closed in. "This is it! We have reached the end!" he cried. "Everything overboard! Get rid of this clutter! This ship must look presentable for our guests!"

The court ladies gaped at him. In voices quivering with fear, they asked him how the battle was going. With bitter sarcasm Tomomori laughed in their faces and told them, "Let's just say you'll soon be intimately familiar with the bold warriors of the eastern provinces."

Desperately trying to fend off the hysteria that threatened to render them helpless, the ladies began to shriek as they cowered away from him. "How can you joke like that?" spat back one young woman in disgust.

Tomomori's mother, Taira no Tokiko, the widow of the late Taira no Kiyomori, who was now known as the Nun of the Second Rank, was not about to waste time with black humor or trading barbs. Garbed in the simple gray robes and white headdress of a Buddhist nun, she was a calming presence among the court ladies and attendants. She could see well enough that the doom of the Taira had come. All around them the other Taira boats were adrift upon the waves. Such of these as had avoided being capsized or overturned appeared all the more disarming for it. Their decks strewn with corpses, stained with blood. The very waves were crimson. The Minamoto clan ships, fast approaching from all sides as far as the eye could see, would be upon them in moments.

Tokiko could see the Minamoto warriors, led by the bold young General Minamoto no Yoshitsune, gripping their swords and preparing to board. There was no time to hesitate. She would see to it personally that they would not get what they were coming for. Draping her dark-gray under-robes over her head so she would not trip on them, she hitched up her silk skirts, tucked the imperial jeweled necklace under one arm, the sword that was another part of the imperial regalia into her belt, and pulled her eight year old grandson, the Emperor Antoku, to her side. Next to her stood one of the emperor's nurses, bearing a Chinese chest containing the last of the three parts of the imperial regalia, the sacred mirror. A sudden inspiration seizing her, Tokiko shot the nurse a look that said all that was needed for the woman nodded back at her, her face set like stone. She betrayed no feeling or concern, only stoic acknowledgment of her apparent duty.

"Where are we going, grandmother?" asked the emperor. He looked anxiously at the enemy boats and then to his mother, who stood nearby surrounded by Taira samurai.

Tokiko's chin quivered but she mastered herself and said, "You don't understand do you? Dear child, you were born to be an emperor because in a past life you followed the ten courses of wholesome conduct. You did not kill, or steal, or take the wives of other men. You did not lie, or speak abusively, or maliciously, or gossip. You did not give in to greed, hatred, or foolishness. Still, we have all lived innumerable lives in the past, and you must also have committed transgressions as well. Now the fruit of past good deeds has been consumed and we must reap the retribution for evil deeds sown in the past. There are none who can escape the outcome of karma, our past

8

actions – not so long as we bind ourselves to this world. The Buddha has told us that this world is called Sahā, the world of Endurance, because here we must endure so much suffering. But there is a better world. So now we must say goodbye to this one."

Emperor Antoku nodded. Being a child as well as an emperor he could only partly understand what was being said, but the emperor accepted that which the child could not comprehend. Tears slipped down his cheeks. Turning her body to the east, Tokiko continued: "We must say goodbye to Amaterasu Ōmikami, the Sun Goddess who is the ancestress of all the emperors, even you." She bowed deeply to the distant grand shrine in Ise, the earthly dwelling of the goddess. Emperor Antoku also joined his palms together and bowed.

Tokiko turned again, this time to the west. With a gentle hand she turned the child emperor with her into the light of the setting sun. "There, off in the west beyond the sun is the Pure Land of Amitābha Buddha, the Buddha of Infinite Light and Life. According to his vows, anyone who calls his name will be reborn in his land. Therefore, let us chant his name so that he and his host of bodhisattvas, the awakening beings who strive for buddhahood, will escort us to that happy land!" Grandmother and grandchild together joined hands and entrusted themselves to Amitābha Buddha. "Namu Amida Butsu, Namu Amida Butsu, Namu Amida Butsu..."

Even as they chanted the *nembutsu*, the name of the Buddha, the Minamoto samurai began leaping aboard. Tokiko snatched up the young emperor and whispered in his ear, "We must go! Look! Beneath the waves! See, there is a new capital where you can rule in peace..." With the boy in her arms she leapt overboard. His mother wailed as they sank beneath the waters.

After casting their nets out of their small boat into the waters of the bay one peaceful spring day, Shigetada looked to his son, Zennichi-maro, and saw that once more he was lost in thought. Shigetada shook his head at this. His son was only eleven, but already so earnest and thoughtful. Maybe he was still thinking about the story of the fall of the Heike that they had heard only a few nights before.

"Son, we must pull up the nets soon. What are you so concerned about?"

"Father, do you think Emperor Antoku and his grandmother, and all those other people who drowned or killed themselves were reborn in the Pure Land? Are they really with the Buddha now?" asked Zennichi-maro.

His father, Shigetada, replied, "Who can say? We can only hope that this is true."

"Father, I thought the emperors are the divine descendants of the Sun Goddess, Amaterasu. Why didn't she protect Emperor Antoku?" Zennichi-maro looked into the waters of the bay, peering at them as if he could see for himself Emperor Antoku's palace under the waves. "He was younger than I am... Who became emperor after him?"

"Emperor Antoku's younger half-brother became Emperor Go-Toba. Currently, Emperor Shijō is the emperor. He would be about two years old now. He is the grandnephew of the Retired Emperor Go-Toba who left the throne many years ago and now lives in exile on Oki Island far away from here."

"Exiled?! But who would dare to exile an emperor?"

Shigetada grimaced. He looked out over the waters, sighed. "The emperors reign, but they no longer rule. They preside over the imperial court in Kyōto, the capital city, and perform the annual rites for the *kami*, the gods of our land, but it is the *bakufu*, the "bivouac government" of the shogun, the barbarian subduing general, that rules the land from its own city, Kamakura."

10

"So this general, the shogun, exiled an emperor? How could a general dare to exile an emperor?"

"Well, actually at the time Go-Toba was a retired emperor, and it was not the shogun who exiled him but the *shikken*, the shogunal regent."

Zennichi-maro shook his head and frowned. "This is confusing. Who actually rules our country?"

Shigetada laughed ruefully. "That is indeed the question. Listen carefully, and I will try to explain what has happened. Then you will know what dark times we are living in:

"Our country, Japan, consists of 66 provinces and the two islands of Iki and Tsushima. Of the 66 provinces, five of them are central, and the others are found along the seven circuits or main roads. This, our land, is a small island kingdom to the northeast of the Middle Kingdom, China, but it is from our land that the sun rises and the gods and buddhas watch over it. The first human emperor of Japan was Jimmu, the descendant of the sun goddess Amaterasu Ōmikami. Only her direct descendants may ascend the Chrysanthemum Throne. The Sun Goddess entrusted the sacred sword, mirror, and jeweled necklace to them. "

Zennichi-maro almost leaped up, but quickly sat back down as the boat rocked beneath him. "Isn't the shrine in our village the home of the Sun Goddess now? That's what the shrine attendants tell us!"

"Yes. That is true. Now, sit still, you're rocking the boat. Don't interrupt."

"Sorry father."

"But you are right. For a long time, however, the Sun Goddess lived in Ise province; but when the emperor devoted himself to Great Bodhisattva Hachiman and the Kamo shrines and slackened in his devotion to her, she became angry. At that time, Minamoto no Yoritomo wrote a pledge ordering that she be moved to the outer shrine of Ise and that satisfied her. Maybe it was because he so pleased the goddess that he was able to defeat the Taira, become shogun, and rule Japan. He later decided that the home of the Sun Goddess should be here in the Tōjō District of Awa."

"So she allowed Emperor Antoku to drown? And what about the imperial regalia? The Nun of the Second Rank took the sword and the jeweled necklace with her into the sea and the nurse meant to follow after with the mirror. Does that mean the Sun Goddess has withdrawn her favor for good?"

"It is hard to know the will of the gods. Still, as I told you, the imperial lineage did not end with Emperor Antoku. Also, the regalia were recovered. The Minamoto samurai caught the nurse before she could jump overboard and they took back the mirror. Divers later found the jeweled necklace. As for the sword, some say it was a only replica that was lost and that the original is still kept at Atsuta Shrine..." Shigetada shrugged.

"What about Great Bodhisattva Hachiman? Why didn't he save the emperor? Isn't a bodhisattva more powerful than a goddess?"

"So many questions! I am neither a monk nor a Shinto priest, so I don't know if a bodhisattva is stronger than a god or goddess or not. I have heard that the gods of our land are the shadows cast by the buddhas and the bodhisattvas but you will have to ask the monks about this. Great Bodhisattva Hachiman, however, is or was a god as well. In this life he was Emperor Ōjin, the 16th emperor, and later he became the protector of the temple Todaiji in Nara, the ancient capital. That is when he was declared a "great bodhisattva," so I guess he is both a god and a bodhisattva. I have also heard that he vowed to protect 100 rulers of our country, and yet Emperor Antoku, the 81st emperor, was still carried off by the Taira and drowned. The Minamoto consider Great Bodhisattva Hachiman to be the tutelary god of their clan, since they are descendants of the Emperor Ōjin. Minamoto no Yoritomo established the Tsurugaoka Shrine for him in Kamakura, and now all the warriors in Japan worship him as the god of the samurai. He is the protector of our country but he seems to have turned away from the imperial family.

"The samurai like the Taira and the Minamoto and their vassals were originally the warriors who served the nobles in the countryside. Minamoto no Yoritomo turned this upside down. He forced the imperial court to serve him and the samurai who were his vassals. Right after the defeat of the Taira, in the first year of the Bunji era (1185), he began to fear the ambitions of his younger brother, Yoshitsune. Yoritomo declared Yoshitsune a rebel and hunted him throughout Japan. At the end of that year he 'requested' that the court allow him to appoint his vassals as constables over each province and as stewards over each estate in order to root out the 'rebel' Yoshitsune and his allies, collect taxes to pay for the campaign, and maintain peace and order. In the fifth year of the Bunji era (1189), after four years on the run, Yoshitsune finally committed *seppuku* in order to escape the dishonor of surrender or capture. He slashed open his own abdomen and a trusted retainer swiftly decapitated him. Even after that, Yoritomo, the Lord of Kamakura, kept the power he had gained over the provinces and estates. In the third year of the Kenkyū era (1192), Yoritomo was granted the title shogun by the imperial court. As the shogun, Yoritomo ruled from Kamakura until his death in the tenth year of the Kenkyū era (1199) when he was thrown from a horse. He was only 52.

"That is when Yoritomo's wife and father-in-law took over. Prior to his uprising against the Taira, Yoritomo had been an exile in Izu province under the watchful eye of the Hōjō clan, a branch family of the Taira. He married Masako, the daughter of Tokimasa, the head of the Hōjō clan. After Yoritomo's death, she became a nun and was thenceforth known as the Nun Shogun. Yoritomo's oldest son Yoriie was finally appointed the second shogun in the second year of the Kennin era (1202) but he soon became mortally ill. Yoriie's chief supporter, his father-in-law Hiki Yoshikazu, wished for Yoriie's infant son, Ichiman, to be designated the third shogun; but Masako overheard him trying to convince her son Yoriie to turn against his brother Sanetomo. Masako told her father and Tokimasa soon had Yoshikazu assassinated. Other Hiki conspirators were later massacred at the orders of Tokimasa and the infant Ichiman died with them when the Hiki mansion was consumed by flames during the fighting. Yoriie then tried to convince other vassals to turn against his grandfather but his plots came to nothing. He was found out and deposed in favor of his younger brother Sanetomo in the third year of the Kennin era (1203). Sanetomo was only eleven at the time, the age you are now. Because of Sanetomo's youth, Tokimasa was declared the regent who would rule until Sanetomo was old enough to rule himself. As for Yoriie, he was assassinated at his home in Izu the following year, some say by the orders of his grandfather. Yoriie had two other sons who could have been eligible to succeed him, but the middle son Yoshinari was adopted by his uncle Sanetomo and sent away to be trained as a Buddhist monk at the age of six a year after his father's murder. He was given the Buddhist name Kugyō and he later became the head monk to perform Buddhist rites at the Tsurugaoka Shrine of Hachiman. In the years that followed, other factions among the Minamoto vassals conspired to overthrow Sanetomo and install Yoriie's third son, Senju-maru, as shogun. Their plots failed and Senju-maru, who was only 13 at the time, was killed along with his supporters in the first year of the Kenpō era (1214). Tokimasa also plotted to depose Sanetomo in favor of another Minamoto samurai, who was the son-in-law of his second wife. When Masako learned of this plot against her son she exposed her father Tokimasa and forced him to retire from public life. He took the tonsure as a monk and retired to Izu where he died in the second year of the Kenpō era

14

(1215). Masako's brother, Yoshitoki, became the second regent, but it was Masako who was the true head of the Hōjō family, and therefore of the shogunate. The third shogun, Sanetomo, met his end at the hands of his nephew and adopted son, Kugyō, who murdered him on the steps of the Tsurugaoka Shrine in the first year of the Jōkyū era (1219). Kugyō, the last of the Minamoto line, was caught and beheaded later that same day. After that there was no shogun for a time. The Hōjō regents and the so-called Nun Shogun Masako became the real rulers of our country."

Zennichi-maro was stunned. "Brother hunted brother, family members plotting against one another and even killing each other? How could the gods permit this? And what about the emperors?"

"Ah, now I can tell you what happened to the Retired Emperor Go-Toba and his successors. Emperor Go-Toba, seeing that he was powerless as emperor, retired in the ninth year of the Kenkyū era (1198). His two sons in turn became emperors and then retired, these being Emperor Tsuchimikado and Emperor Juntoku. In the third year of the Jōkyū era (1221), the year before you were born, Retired Emperor Go-Toba tried to restore the rightful rule of the emperors. His first act was to appoint the three-year old son of Retired Emperor Juntoku to be the next emperor without consulting the shogunate. He assembled warriors in the five central provinces and throughout the seven circuits and declared Hōjō Yoshitoki a rebel. On the 15th day of the fifth month, the imperial forces attacked and killed the shogunal constable of Kyōto. This was reported to the shogunate at Kamakura on the 19th day of the same month. Masako rallied the vassals and reminded them of their indebtedness to her late husband the first shogun, Yoritomo, who had bestowed on them the lands, wealth, and rank they currently enjoyed. Two days later, the son of the regent, Hōjō Yasutoki, rode swiftly with a cavalry troop towards Kyōto along the Tōkaidō, the Eastern Sea Road; while the Minamoto in Kai Province advanced on the Tōsandō, the Eastern Mountain Road; and a third army marched along the Hokurikudō, the Northern Land

Road. On the fifth day of the sixth month, the Kamakura forces routed the imperial force defending Ōtsu, the capital of Ōmi province to the north of Kyōto. Fighting began at the outskirts of Kyōto on the 13th of the sixth month but on the 14th day the Kamakura forces broke through the defense line at the Uji Bridge. They at once captured the Retired Emperor Go-Toba and the other two retired emperors who were his sons and set fire to the imperial palace and razed it. Retired Emperor Go-Toba's efforts had all been in vain. The shogunate's army had defeated the imperial army in little less than a month. On the seventh day of the seventh month, Retired Emperor Go-Toba was exiled to Oki Island where he lives to this day; Retired Emperor Tsuchimikado was exiled to Shikoku where I heard that he passed away a few years ago; and Retired Emperor Juntoku was exiled to Sado Island where he still lives. Seven of Retired Emperor Go-Toba's courtiers were beheaded. The son of Retired Emperor Juntoku was dethroned a couple of months later and thereafter known as the Kujō Dethroned Emperor."

Shigetada shook his head. "I still do not know how Retired Emperor Go-Toba could have been defeated so thoroughly. For a ruler like himself to conquer Yoshitoki, his own subject, should have been just like a hawk capturing a peacock or a cat grabbing a mouse, but instead it was as if the mouse ate the cat or the peacock caught the hawk. Such a disgrace has never been equaled in history." He fell silent, frowning in thought and glaring at the bottom of the boat, and then resumed his tale. "Thousands of estates were confiscated from those who had fought for the Retired Emperor Go-Toba and given to the vassals of the shogunate as a reward. Yasutoki was made shogunal deputy and remained in Kyōto in the Rokuhara district with a garrison to keep watch over the imperial court. His father died three years later and his aunt, the Nun Shogun Masako, died the year after that. Hōjō Yasutoki returned to Kamakura after his father's death and he is now the regent. The shogun is now a nine-year-old boy from the Fujiwara family, a distant relative of the first shogun, and he is of course nothing but a puppet of the Hōjō clan. To this day, the emperors and

16

the imperial court have no choice but to follow the dictates of the Hōjō regents who control the shogunate, even in the matters of the abdication or enthronement of emperors." He sighed. "Well, it can't be helped. That is just the way things are in this world."

Agitated, Zennichi-maro tugged at the lines that held the fishnets. "I still don't understand why the gods and buddhas did nothing to safeguard the emperors and retired emperors. Don't they have any power at all?"

Shigetada shrugged. "I am not a god or buddha. All I know is that they turned away from the emperors and chose to bestow their favors upon Yoritomo and his successors for reason of their own. Or perhaps because it is *mappō*, the Latter Age of Degeneration, they can no longer help us in this world. But that is something that you will have to ask the monks about."

"When will I get a chance to do that?"

"Sooner that you think." Shigetada smiled with pride at his son. "I have been speaking with the Nun Proprietress of your eagerness to learn and how well you've been doing in your studies at home. She knows that there is only so much I am able to teach you however, and she believes, as your mother and I do, that you have the ability to become a great scholar. She has spoken with Master Dōzen-bō of Seichōji temple and he has agreed to take you on as his attendant. He and the other monks will become your teachers. If you do well you might even be able to secure a position as an official in Kamakura and thereby restore the fortunes of our family. Would you like that?"

Zennichi-maro's eyes widened as he turned from the lines back to his father. "Really? Yes, of course I would!" He looked to the pine clad hills and the peak of Mt. Kiyosumi where the temple was located. "When do I go?"

Shigetada smiled, "In a week. We will walk up to the temple together. There you may find the answers to your questions."

Yakuō-maro

Early in the morning on the twelfth day of the fifth month of the first year of the Tenpuku era (1233), Zennichi-maro said a tearful goodbye to his three older brothers, and to his mother, Umegiku. Shaded by pines, he and his father were traveling along the path that would take them to Mt. Kiyosumi. Though it was a hot and humid day, the shade of the trees provided some relief. Despite the heat, they walked on, listening to the sounds of the birds and, more loudly, chirring of the cicadas.

"Look, a cicada fell on the path!" said Zennichi-maro. "It must have died already." He bent to pick it up but the cicada rattled and twitched. "Oh, it's not dead yet. I'll move it off the path so no one will step on it."

Shigetada nodded. "That is very kind of you. It is sad. They come up out of the ground, leave their shells in the trees, and for only a week or two they are able to fly, sing, mate, and lay their eggs. When they stop singing you will know they have all died."

"Oh!" Zennichi-maro replied. He looked at the cicada again. Now it was still. What could life be like for them if it was so short? Did human life seem that short to the gods and those who live in the pure lands for hundreds of thousands or even millions of years? Were humans like these noisy bugs to them? The last four years had been an especially difficult time all over the countryside. There was famine. There was not enough rain, there was too much rain, or else it rained at the wrong time. Also, there were unseasonable chills and frost. Pestilence followed starvation. All too many times the monks had to be called down from the mountains to perform services for the dead, especially for the young and elderly. Yes, to the gods, human life must seem as absurdly brief as that of the cicadas.

By noon they reached the summit of the mountain. Here, nestled within the landscape, was Seichōji, the Temple of Clear Luminosity. First they passed beneath the temple's Two Kings Gate. A tower gate, usually two-storied, marked the entrance to the compounds of large temples. The upper stories of the gates were merely decorative and often vacant. Some of the larger temples even had a double-roof. This too, was more ornamental than practical.

In the bays on either side of the gate's first story were enshrined statues of two scowling muscle bound giants wrapped in sarongs with their hair tied back in chignons. The one on the right was a blazing red. This guardian was open-mouthed with his teeth bared as though shouting, "Ah!" His right hand was held down with fingers spread out while in his upraised left was a *vajra* or "diamond pounder," a kind of club made of prongs curling in on each other and merging into a ball-shaped top. The one on the left was a deep blue. His mouth was firmly shut as though to make the sound "Hum!" His left hand was held down in a fist while his right hand was upraised with a *vajra* poised to strike. Together the two kings ensured that no evil influences passed the gate into the temple grounds.

Passing through, Shigetada and Zennichi-maro found themselves in the middle of a great complex of buildings including the residence hall for the monks, the dining hall, the lecture hall, the bell-tower, a two-storied pagoda, a sutra repository that had been commissioned by the Nun Shogun only three years before Zennichi-maro was born, and of course the main worship hall. Seichōji had been founded in the second year of the Hōki era (771) when a monk known only as Fushigi (Mystery) first carved an oaken statue of Space Repository Bodhisattva and enshrined it as the *honzon* or "focus of devotion." The temple later fell upon hard times but was restored in the third year of the Jōwa era (836) by the third abbot of the head temple of the Tendai school, Great Master Jikaku. Since that time, Seichōji had become a major temple in Awa Province and a regional center for the study of Tendai teachings and esoteric practices as well as the ubiquitous pieties of Pure Land Buddhism centered on faith in Amitābha Buddha.

A young monk greeted Shigetada and Zennichi-maro and asked if he could help them. Like the other monks his head was shaved to a glossy sheen, his inner robe was white and his outer robe was black, and over that he wore a *kesa*. Once Shigetada told them of their business at the temple the young monk brought them to the quarters of the current abbot, Dōzen-bō. As greetings and pleasantries were exchanged, Zennichi-maro was relieved to see that the abbot was not at all as he had imagined. He had pictured an elderly monk with bushy white overhanging brows, a long wispy beard, glaring eyes flashing like lightning, lips pressed together and drawn down in a frown of stern disapproval. Instead, what he saw was an ordinary looking monk certainly no older than his father. He was clean-shaven, his bare scalp shining in the daylight. He smiled happily at them. Instead of a stick with which to rain blows upon the foolish, his right hand held Buddhist prayer beads called *juzu*. Even as Dōzen-bō conversed with his father, he never ceased thumbing through the beads. "Click, click, click," sounded the *juzu* as the abbot's thumb pressed each bead down in turn, the outward sign of an unceasing inner prayer.

"I think you will find that Zennichi-maro will be as good a student as you could ever hope to have. He is a fine worker as well," Shigetada was saying.

Dōzen-bō looked appraisingly at Zennichi-maro. "Yes, I have been told good things about him by the Nun Proprietress." Then he addressed Zennichi-maro directly. He smiled and said, "She has told me that you have great promise. She will have need of someone who can read and write and help her maintain the estate's records. With her patronage you could do quite well for yourself."

"Thank you, Master Dōzen-bō, I will do my best."

"Ha, ha. I am sure you will. Well, now that you will be my attendant and taking up the scholarly life you should be given a new name. Let's see... In the *Lotus Sutra* there is a great bodhisattva named Medicine King, who we call Yakuō. Śākyamuni Buddha told him that if he heard and rejoiced at even a verse or phrase of the *Lotus Sutra* he would attain buddhahood. That bodhisattva then vowed to keep and share the sutra and provided protective spells, called *dhāraṇīs*, for other teachers of the Dharma. There is even a story that he and his brother, Medicine Superior, in a previous life were able to convert their father, a king, to the Dharma and enabled him to attain awakening and become a great bodhisattva as well. So I will name you Yakuō-maro, and hopefully you too will learn at least a verse or a phrase, rejoice in it, and requite your debts of gratitude to your teachers and parents."

Zennichi-maro, now Yakuō-maro, beamed with pride to be given such an exalted name. "Thank you, Master Dōzen-bo." He bowed low in gratitude, touching his forehead to the floor. Upon arising Yakuō-maro asked, "Please excuse me, what exactly is a bodhisattva?"

"Now is not the time to be asking such questions," warned Shigetada.

"It's okay. He is already showing his thirst for knowledge. How wonderful!" said Dōzen-bo. He turned again to the boy. "Well, I will answer your question if you first tell me what a buddha is."

"Oh, well, a buddha is like a god, I think. Don't buddhas live in the pure lands that we can be reborn in after death if we call upon them in this life. Don't they watch over and protect us like the gods? So are bodhisattvas just their assistants or attendants?"

"Ah, you have so much to learn." Dōzen-bo smiled indulgently. "The word 'buddha' means 'awakened one.' Buddhas are also known as the 'teachers of gods and men.' So they are actually greater than the gods in wisdom and even power. Through their awakened wisdom they have cut off the selfish craving, hatred, and ignorance that bind people, beasts, spirits, and even the gods to the cycle of birth and death. They are no longer compelled to be born in any land or as any creature, but they appear through their miraculous powers in order to help others break the chains of suffering. So even the gods look to the buddhas for help and for the wisdom to overcome suffering; for even gods will someday exhaust their merit and then they too will die and be reborn into some other, most likely, less exalted state. The buddha of this world, Śākyamuni Buddha, was born a prince in the land of India far to the west. It was Śākyamuni Buddha who taught the sutras, the Buddhist scriptures that we recite, study and copy. This was more than 2,000 years ago. It was he who told us about Amitābha Buddha and his Pure Land of Utmost Bliss.

"Now, bodhisattvas are 'awakening beings.' They are not yet fully awakened but are on the path to awakening. Bodhisattvas hear the teachings of the buddhas but they do not follow those teaching in order to immediately escape the cycle of birth and death. They have so much compassion for other suffering beings that they can't bear the thought of leaving them behind. They voluntarily remain in the realms of suffering to help others, serve the buddhas, and teach the Dharma. They do this in order to accumulate merit and wisdom so that someday they will completely awaken and as buddhas be able to more fully liberate others from suffering."

A growing warmth spread out from Yakuō-maro's heart and filled up his whole body as he listened to Dōzen-bo's explanation. He hadn't realized that buddhas and bodhisattvas were not just spirits or gods living in some other world but could be people living in this world, kind and gentle people doing their best for others. "I would like to be such a person," he said to Dōzen-bō. "Will you teach me how?"

Dōzen-bō and his father laughed. Dōzen-bō replied, "I have not even made much progress myself, so I will be a sorry teacher for you. But I promise to teach you what little I do know."

Yakuō-maro bade a solemn farewell to his father. Dōzen-bo then introduced him to Gijō-bō, the monk who had first greeted them upon their arrival at the temple, and to another young monk named Jōken-bō. "These two are my disciples. They will be your tutors while you are here. They will show you how to perform your duties as my attendant and will help you in your studies."

"It is very good to meet you both. Please take good care of me," said Yakuō-maro. As he spoke he bowed low to the two monks in the expected formal greeting.

The two monks showed Yakuō-maro to the small cell he would be staying in near Dōzen-bō's quarters. Inside it were a futon, a writing table, and a small chest for his clothes and other personal items, such as his brush and ink-stone. As an attendant, Yakuō-maro did not shave his head or wear black robes or a *kesa* as the monks did. Instead, he kept his hair in the long ponytail appropriate for children and wore colorful kimonos and a matching *hakama* or divided skirt. Though Yakuō-maro did not feel he qualified, he knew that temple attendants should be beautiful, for they were viewed as "divine children" and as earthly incarnations of bodhisattvas such as Medicine King, Yakuō-maro's namesake. It was the duty of attendants to wait upon their masters from morning till evening. In particular they laid out and later folded and put away their master's robes, received their master's guests, served meals for their master and his guests, participated in religious ceremonies and processions, entertained at banquets by singing, dancing, or playing music, and generally saw to all their master's needs. Attendants came to be very dear to their masters and were most often treated with great affection.

Over the next few years, Seichōji became Yakuō-maro's home, Dōzen-bō was like his second father, and his tutors Gijō-bo and Jōken-bō became his elder brothers. There were also dozens of other monks within the grounds of the temple – some in the residence halls, some scattered in hermitages on the mountainsides and in the valleys. Every morning, hours before sunrise, a monk would walk around the grounds beating a small handheld *mokugyō*, a hollow wooden percussion instrument carved like a fish. At the sound of its *"Tok, tok, tok"* the monks would all awaken, perform their morning ablutions, and then gather in the main hall for the early morning service. Chores would follow and then breakfast. The monks would gather again in the main hall before noon to present rice and other food offerings brought to the monastery to the buddhas and bodhisattvas. They then moved to the dining hall for the noon meal, though actually it was completed before noon as per the Buddha's monastic regulations wherein the monks of India did not eat in the afternoon. Nevertheless there would be a supper in the late afternoon, which was referred to as "medicine." This would be followed by the evening service. A few hours later the monks would extinguish their lamps and sleep for about six hours before the "tok, tok, tok" of the *mokugyō* awakened them once more.

At his family home Yakuō-maro had always enjoyed praying and presenting offerings to the gods and buddhas. At Seichōji, he immediately fell in love with the beautiful and haunting solemnity of the various services held morning, noon, and evening. In these services, the assembled monks praised and took refuge in the Three Treasures of Buddha, Dharma, and Sangha, invoked the presence of the buddhas, bodhisattvas, and protective deities, repented of their transgressions in thought, word, and deed; implored the buddhas to remain in the world and impart the Dharma, their holy teaching; rejoiced in the meritorious works of others, dedicated their own meritorious deeds to the awakening of all sentient beings, and pronounced the four great vows of the bodhisattvas: to save all beings, quench the fires of greed, hatred, and delusion, master all the

Buddha's teachings, and attain the Buddha Way. Yakuō-maro especially liked to lose himself in the sound of the assembled monks as they recited the sutras in Chinese translation. It wasn't exactly a recitation in Chinese, but a Japanese approximation of the sounds of the Chinese characters. He could not yet understand the passages that they chanted but there was a power and driving energy to it that he found invigorating. He also enjoyed the plaintive sound of *shōmyō*, the singing of short verses and phrases. Likewise, he looked forward to the staccato declamation of the *dhāraṇī*, protective spells composed of "seed syllables" whose power was in their sound and not their meaning. These were never translated, but rather transliterated, with Chinese characters used to represent only the sound of the original Sanskrit incantations. These kinds of recitations, hymns, prayers, and dedications would be repeated throughout the day, punctuated by the sounding of gongs, the beating of drums and other percussion instruments, and the ringing of various small and large bells that were shaped like metal bowls. Incense was always offered to the buddhas and bodhisattvas at these services and its scent pervaded not just the temple but the robes of the assembly as well. All of these things stirred a great desire in Yakuō-maro to become a monk himself. He wished to be peaceful and wise like Master Dōzen-bō and live in such a beautiful way forever, dispensing wisdom and the teachings of the Buddha to all people.

In the meantime, he had his studies. When the monks and other attendants at Seichōji were not conducting services, eating, or sleeping, they each went their own way to engage in meditation, esoteric rites, private devotions, repentance ceremonies, or study. Yakuō-maro spent his days with either Gijō-bō or Jōken-bō. Yakuō-maro's father and mother had already taught him the two Japanese syllabaries (the *hiragana* for Japanese words and the *katakana* for foreign words) and also several hundred of the thousands of Chinese characters that the Japanese called *kanji*. His tutors at Seichōji taught him the rest of the characters that he would need to know as well as how to understand the grammar of the Chinese classics and the sutras.

They showed him different styles of calligraphy and guided him in developing power and elegance in his brushwork. In time, his teachers came to praise his skills. As part of his studies he copied and memorized countless passages from the classics of China, such as the teachings of Confucius and other Chinese sages that were the basis of civilized life. From them he learned of the fundamental importance of filial piety and the five constant virtues of benevolence, righteousness, propriety, wisdom, and trustworthiness. By cultivating filial piety and the five virtues people were able to live in a harmonious and dignified way and rise above the level of thoughtless beasts.

The Triple World

Yakuō-maro also learned of the greater world, or rather ocean of worlds, of which Japan was just a small part. According to the Buddhist teachings the known world was part of a vast continent called Jambudvīpa, the "Island of the Jambu Tree." A *jambu* or "rose-apple" was a kind of black plum. On Jambudvīpa were the countries of Korea, China -- the Middle Kingdom, and far off in the west India, the land of the setting sun where Śākyamuni Buddha had lived. Jambudvīpa was the southern continent wherein lived humans, beasts, and spirits of diverse kinds, including the hungry ghosts who haunted wastelands and other desolate places. Deep below Jambudvīpa, in vast caverns, were the hell-dwellers and their ox and horse-headed tormentors distributed among the eight hot hells, eight cold hells, and countless multitudes of peripheral and even individualized hells with the worst of them all being the Avīci or Hell of Incessant Suffering, which was the last and deepest of the eight hot hells. Three other continents lay to the north, east, and west of Mt. Sumeru, the mountain at the center of the world. On those continents lived giants who lived complacent lives of ease for hundreds or thousands of years. Surrounding these four continents and the four seas that separated them was the ring of the Iron Mountains.

Surrounding Mt. Sumeru at the center of the world were seven concentric mountain ranges composed of gold with freshwater oceans separating them. Beneath those oceans were the cities of the many-limbed and multi-eyed hulking monstrosities known as the *asuras*. Cast down from the heavens by the gods these "fighting demons" had not died but lay in wait for the age in which they would arise from the ocean depths and reclaim what they felt was their rightful place as lords of all creation. In the meantime, days and nights succeeded each other as the chariots of the gods of the sun, moon, and stars coursed around Mt. Sumeru. Halfway up the slopes were the palaces of the four heavenly kings who guarded the cardinal directions with their spirit legions, ever watchful for any resurgence of the *asuras*. At the top of Mt. Sumeru was the Heaven of the 33 Gods. Śakra Devānām Indra, god of thunder and lightning, was the chieftain of these gods who presided over Mt. Sumeru and the world below.

Above Mt. Sumeru were other grander and more refined heavens, one above the other. There was the Heaven of Time where King Yama, the chief judge of the dead, resided and from whence he commuted to his underworld court. Above that was the Heaven of Contentment where Maitreya Bodhisattva resided, awaiting his turn to be reborn in Jambudvīpa billions of years in the future in an age when the Buddha Dharma was completely forgotten. At that time he would attain buddhahood and preach the Dharma anew. Above that heaven was the Heaven of Joy in Transformations where the dwellers could magically create anything they needed for their own pleasure, and over them the Heaven of Free Enjoyment of Transformation by Others whose dwellers were able to control and enjoy what the dwellers in the previous heavens had made. In the Heaven of Free Enjoyment was the palace of Māra, the evil one, who regarded everything from the heaven he lived in down to the Hell of Incessant Suffering as his domain, the realm of desire. Māra zealously worked to ensure that no one acted in such a way as to escape his domain and be reborn in the heavens above that were outside his jurisdiction, or even worse to escape the cycle of rebirth altogether, or worst of all to escape the cycle of rebirth and proceed to teach others how to do so as the buddhas and bodhisattvas did.

Above the realm of desire were the heavens of the realm of form, a vast region of tranquil contemplation where the inhabitants had, for the time being, overcome sensual craving, hostility, nervous agitation, torpidity, and debilitating doubts. In place of such unwanted feelings they had instead cultivated boundless loving-kindness, compassion, sympathetic joy, and equanimity in regard to all beings. Here were the palaces of Brahmā, who claimed to be the creator of the world, and his heavenly court. Above and beyond the heavens of Brahmā and his court were other even vaster and more refined heavens. These heavens hung suspended over not just one Mt. Sumeru world but thousands and millions of such worlds. The highest of these heavens was the home of the god Maheśvara, the Great Freedom God, who was the most sublime and aloof of all the gods of the realm of form.

Finally there was the realm of formlessness, where the heavens of boundless space, consciousness, nothingness, and neither-perception nor non-perception stretched out without end. Here material form was transcended and even self-consciousness was left behind at the last, though again only temporarily, a mere billions or trillions of years. After that, even those heavenly beings must fade and be reborn elsewhere to take up again the restrictions of bodily forms, passions, and vulnerabilities. This was the last part of what was known as the triple world, the worlds of desire, form, and formlessness, in which hapless sentient beings were reborn again and again, driven ever on by the three poisons of their greed, hatred, and delusion.

Everything within the ring of the Iron Mountains, from the deepest hells to the highest heavens was the world named Sahā or "Endurance." Outside of the Sahā world was the etheric ocean upon which floated 1,000 million such world-disks with their own Mt. Sumerus, four continents, world-oceans, and Iron Mountains, though these others had more pleasant names and the sufferings that abounded within them were said to be of a more subtle kind. It was taught that the best horse would run at even the shadow of the whip, while the worst was the horse that only ran when the whip had broken the flesh and the pain penetrated to its very marrow. Those reborn in the Sahā world were those who did not run from the cycle of birth and death until suffering had become truly unbearable. Desperately they tried to find permanent happiness by murder, theft, gratifying their lusts, deceptions of all kinds, and resort to drink and other forms of intoxicants. They slandered and abused others, gave in to their cravings and every violent impulse, and refused to recognize the law that one had to sow what one reaped, if not in the present lifetime than in future ones. Doing all this they sank down into the lowest parts of the realm of desire to become hell-dwellers, hungry ghosts, or animals. Others tried to live virtuously to earn a favorable rebirth. They refrained from killing, stealing, sexual misconduct, lying, and intoxication and cultivated the five constant virtues. Some of these were reborn as proud and self-righteous *asura*. Others were able to be reborn among humans. Others went so far as to perform the ten good acts and to support spiritual strivers with food, clothing, shelter, and medicine and by their virtue and generosity they generated the karma to be reborn in the heavens of the realm of desire. Others cultivated meditation and so were able to be reborn in the heavens of the realms of form and formlessness. But in none of those states was there ever any permanent happiness, all who were born had to eventually die and be reborn elsewhere, and the permutations of karma were unfathomable and even maddening to any but a fully awakened buddha. It was therefore all but impossible to know whether the karma about to ripen in the present or future life would be of a happy or harmful nature. Such were the wanderings of birth and death in the Sahā world, and in time the suffering did cause some to wonder how to escape it altogether, and eventually some did, such as Śākyamuni Buddha and those who followed him.

Yakuō-maro also learned to think of time differently. The ordinary way of reckoning time was in terms of the twelve periods of the day, each with its associated animal of the Chinese zodiac. Sunrise was at the time of the rabbit, noon was the time of the horse, sunset the time of the rooster, and midnight the time of the rat, and so on. Each such time period was divided into four half-hour periods. A year was divided by the four seasons and cycles of the moon. Larger periods of time were reckoned in terms of the reigns of emperors or eras consisting of a handful of years. The imperial court changed the name of the era when new emperors were enthroned or whenever a fresh start was needed in the wake of large scale or multiple disasters. The Buddhist way of reckoning time took in vaster scales and also more precise divisions. Buddhism spoke in terms of *kalpas*, or ages. A *kalpa* was said to be as long as it would take for a celestial maiden to wear away a mountain by brushing it with a silken cloth once every 100 years. There were various kinds of *kalpas*. The small *kalpa* was said to last for roughly 16 million years. An intermediate *kalpa* was 20 small *kalpas* long. A great *kalpa* was four intermediate *kalpas*. Long enough for the formation, continuation, dissolution, and reduction to nothingness of countless Mt. Sumeru worlds. Buddhism, however, did not only speak of vast periods but also very miniscule moments of time such as the *ksana*, 60 of which would pass in the time it would take to snap one's fingers. Ninety such moments would pass in the time it took to have a single thought. In that time hundreds of changes could occur, too swift and subtle to be noticed let alone comprehended. Whether on vast cosmic scales or miniscule moments all conditioned things were arising and ceasing, all sentient beings were either being born or passing away.

The Awakening of Śākyamuni Buddha

Yakuō-maro's mind reeled to think of 1,000 millions of Mt. Sumeru worlds, each laid out as a mandala of pleasure and pain; coming to be and passing away over periods of time that he could scarcely grasp. All of the beings in those realms, even the gods, were passing away and constantly becoming something other than they had been. Contemplating his own life, he realized how uncertain it was. In exhaling one moment there was no guarantee that one could draw a new breath in the next. Life was as transient as dew before the wind and its end occurred suddenly to everyone, the wise and the ignorant, the aged and the young. Thinking of these things he determined to study the matter of the last moment of life before all else. In order to do this, he would have to delve even deeper into the life and teachings of Śākyamuni Buddha, who had lived in India more than 2,000 years ago. For to awaken to the true nature of birth and death, what other teacher could one look to, if not to the Buddha, the "Awakened One"? With the help of his tutors, Yakuō-maro found every passage about the life of the Buddha that could be located in the sutras and commentaries stored in the sutra repository of Seichōji. Using oil lamps he would read in his small cell late into the night after he had finished with his formal studies and duties as an attendant. Often he tried to imagine what the Buddha's life had been like. What he wondered about most was that moment when the Buddha awakened. What was it that enabled him to finally resolve the great matter of birth and death? With works such as the *Record of Wonders in the Book of Zhou* and Nāgārjuna's *Treatise on the Great Perfection of Wisdom*, Yakuō-maro learned all he could about Śākyamuni Buddha. With those and other works as his sources he tried to imagine the Buddha's life:

Before he attained buddhahood, Śākyamuni had also been a bodhisattva. Like Maitreya presently, Śākyamuni Buddha had lived in the Heaven of Contentment awaiting the right circumstances for his final rebirth. When the right conditions arose he appeared in a dream to Queen Māyā of Kapilavastu in India as a six-tusked white elephant holding a white lotus flower in its trunk. The white elephant circled around her three times and then entered into her womb. At that moment she conceived the bodhisattva. Nine months later, Queen Māyā gave birth painlessly while standing up and holding onto the branch of a śāla tree while visiting the Lumbinī Garden near Kapilavastu in the 24th year of the reign of King Zhao of the Zhou dynasty (1029 BCE) on the eight day of the fourth month. Immediately upon entering the world, the infant crown prince took seven steps and then pointed to the skies above his head and the ground beneath his feet. He announced, "I alone am the most honored one in all the heavens above and on the earth below. For the good of the world I am born for awakening; this is my last birth in the phenomenal world." His mother passed away a week after his birth, so his aunt, Mahāprajāpati, was the one who raised him. King Śuddhodana named him Siddhārtha, which means "Aim Accomplished." He grew up in luxury, but at 19 he was struck by the inescapable fact that no matter how pleasant or easy life seemed it could only end in old age, sickness, and death. One night, in order to find a way to transcend the world, the young prince rode away from the palace, leaving behind his father King Śuddhodana, his wife Yaśodharā, and his son Rāhula. He set aside his jeweled ornaments, shaved his head, and traded in his fine court robes for the ochre patchwork robe of a forest ascetic. He turned over his crown and the jewel that had been in his topknot to his servant, whom he sent back to the palace with his horse.

After Siddhārtha left the palace he met two great masters of the yogic meditation tradition of India. His first instructor, Ārāda Kālāma, believed that he had attained liberation by cultivating a state wherein one experiences nothingness. Siddhārtha rapidly achieved this state as well under Ārāda Kālāma's instruction, but he found that it was not the final end of suffering but only a temporary state of mind. He then studied with Rudraka Rāmaputra, who was able to enter into a state wherein there is neither perception nor non-perception. This was also temporary. Siddhārtha saw that these states of mind brought about by yogic discipline had not brought any new insight or freed him from impermanence and death. By the same token, the heavenly realms that one might be born into by cultivating these meditative states were also only temporary, though those born into them as the fruit of their spiritual practice might reside in those heavens for millions of years in worldly terms. Eventually even the mightiest of gods would realize that they could not escape the signs of decay that signaled the end of their heavenly terms. In time, whether short or long, the fruits of their merit were consumed and darker deeds from their past lives began to germinate. The end result of this was that they too were finally reborn among the evil realms of the hells, of hungry ghosts, and of animals.

Finished with yoga as taught by these masters, Siddhārtha traveled north and entered the penance groves of Mt. Dandaloka. He lived a very austere and reclusive life in the hope that self-denial and severe discipline would provide the answer he sought. He was joined there by a band of five ascetics. The ascetics hoped that by foregoing pleasure and punishing their bodies in the present they could win their way to a heavenly rebirth. Some thought that by overcoming bodily needs they could even liberate the spirit and attain awakening. To accomplish their aims they turned their backs on all luxuries and even civilization itself. Many of them lived naked in the forest like beasts. Others bathed three times a day in the Ganges River, even in the middle of winter. Some pulled out their hair by the roots, or jumped off rocks, or sat in the midst of bonfires under the blazing summer sun. Siddhārtha chose to take up the practice of fasting. He perfected this discipline to the point where he was eating only one grain of rice a day. After twelve years of this, he was so weakened from fasting that he was close to death. He was killing himself, and still no closer to finding a way to end life's suffering. In the end, he left the penance groves. He passed out by the side of the Nairañjanā River while trying to get some water. A village woman named Sujātā was stirred to compassion when she saw him sprawled upon the riverbank. She nursed him back to health with rice-gruel, saving him from death. Upon reviving, Siddhārtha realized that the self-denial practiced by the ascetics had come close to killing him. Far from helping, it was as much of a hindrance to achieving spiritual awakening as self-indulgence. He would not return to the ease of the palace life, but no longer would he deny the basic needs of body and mind for adequate food, clothing, medicine, shelter, and rest. Spiritual practice must be neither too severe nor too easygoing, just as lute strings must be neither too taught nor too slack. From that moment on, Siddhārtha determined to follow the middle way between self-indulgence and self-denial.

The time had come for Siddhārtha to realize his ultimate aim. He recalled a day in his youth when he sat beneath a rose-apple tree in a state of calm abiding and clear awareness. He decided to again sit in the shade of a tree and reflect upon life in such a state of calm centeredness. After regaining his health he went to the base of a fig tree near the town of Gaya. There he sat upon a mat made of grass. He crossed his legs in the full lotus posture, with each foot resting upon the opposite thigh. His hands rested in his lap, left hand atop the right with both palms up and thumb tips lightly touching. He held his body erect and his head straight so that nose and navel were aligned. He set an unwavering gaze upon the ground before him. Then he spoke the following vow, "Even if the flesh and blood in my body dries up, and only my skin, sinews, and bones remain; I will not arise from this seat of meditation until I attain supreme awakening."

Siddhārtha's bold declaration aroused the ire of Māra, the Devil King of the Sixth Heaven, for he knew this was no idle boast. Siddhārtha was no longer seeking the attainment of heavenly bliss or the acquisition of supernatural powers such as the other yogis sought. Instead, he was using the power of his years of yogic discipline to sit upright in direct awareness of the actual state of conditioned phenomena, beginning with his own mind and heart. If not stopped,

Māra knew that the bodhisattva who was Siddhārtha would soon achieve his aim.

Māra quickly summoned his beautiful daughters to tempt the bodhisattva back to a worldly life of sensual pleasures. As Siddhārtha sat they each danced in turn while those who were not dancing accompanied with drum and flute. They wore black silk caps and their hair hung down to the ground in a ponytail. They were the models of courtly beauty, with white powdered faces, rouged lips, and blackened teeth. They had even plucked and shaven their eyebrows and smudged in new ones on their foreheads. They wore bright red baggy trousers, white over-robes with long sleeves, and jeweled swords hung at their sides. In their hands they carried fans to gesture with as they danced. They danced with languid graceful motions and sang of midnight trysts in darkened rooms, whispered secrets, passionate embraces, and the longing of hermits for lost loves and opportunities that may never come again. After the dancing and singing they sat by Siddhārtha and chatted quietly. Coy glances and inviting smiles were cast in his direction, but the bodhisattva did not respond. Growing bolder they sat around him. Offered him tea. Brushed him with their sleeves in passing. They used every artifice they knew to entice the prince turned ascetic into rising up from his grass cushion to embrace them. Siddhārtha was not moved. He had seen all this before while living in the palace. Yes, there might be some pleasure to be had with these heavenly maidens, but he saw it as nothing more than a lure, and behind the lure the hook that once embedded would drag him back into the world where all ended in the infirmity of old age, debilitating sickness, and ultimately the funeral pyre. He did not even look up at the daughters of Māra as they began to weaken, sag, and transform into wrinkled hags. Their delicate songs turned into sneers and shouts of outrage and bitter scorn. They withered, died, and fell in heaps upon the ground. Flesh decayed and fell away, leaving only dry scattered bones. These turned to dust that the wind carried away. Not a trace was left.

Māra resorted to brute force. His army rode in from all sides in full battle regalia. They wore full lamellar armor. Their helms bore golden horns or antlers while their facemasks bore the visages of fierce beasts with whiskers, manes, snouts, tusks, and fangs. The expressions of these beasts were myriad – faces full of craving and lust, doubt and deceit, wrath, outrage, arrogance, confusion, fear, and even boredom, and torpidity. Māra's demons carried long bows taller than themselves and arrowheads for disemboweling foes filled their quivers. At their sides hung long gently curving swords for closer fighting. The legion of demons surrounded the bodhisattva for as far as the eye could see. Once again, Siddhārtha was unmoved. Even when the demons shot clouds of arrows at him, or brought forth catapults and hurled boulders or balls of flame at the bodhisattva, he remained still. As they hit the shade of the tree the missiles transformed into flowers and floated harmlessly to the ground. The army vanished, leaving behind only fallen cherry blossoms.

Out of desperation Māra himself appeared and challenged Siddhārtha, saying, "Who are you to think that you can leave my realm of desire?" Siddhārtha did not speak or even look up. He simply reached out to place one hand upon the ground. The earth itself was his witness that there was nowhere in present and past existence where he had not sacrificed himself in previous lifetimes for the sake of the liberation and awakening of all sentient beings. Māra could do no more. He faded from sight.

Now that all of his distractions, doubts, and unconscious inhibitions were cleared away, Siddhārtha just sat beneath the fig tree with a clear yet alert mind. Memories came unbidden into the field of his awareness. In the first watch of the night, he recollected all of the events in his present life that had enabled him to just sit beneath that fig tree on that particular night. Then more memories came, swimming up from the depths of his mind - memories of other lives, not all of them human. These seemed to him to be memories from countless prior lifetimes when he had cultivated the qualities of

38

generosity, morality, patience, energy, meditation, and ultimately wisdom that every bodhisattva must perfect in order to attain buddhahood. Reviewing these memories he saw how his life was shaped by the flow of causes and conditions, the most direct and important being those causes he himself had sown, nurtured, and brought to fruition.

In the second watch of the night, Siddhārtha's awareness took in the lives of all sentient beings. He saw them dying and being reborn only to age and die and be reborn again; treading the same ground over and over as they traveled on the paths of suffering. He saw hell-dwellers burning in their own rage and self-destruction, hungry ghosts tormented by their own unreasoning craving, beasts thoughtlessly devouring and being devoured, *asura* demons submerged in their own pride and pettiness, humans undergoing birth, aging, sickness, and death; inevitably meeting the agreeable with attachment and the disagreeable with aversion, longing for what is ever out of reach, and finding in every moment transition without surcease. And finally, the gods, complacent and serene until the day when their celestial robes become soiled, their garlands begin to wilt, beads of sweat appear, the stink of mortality rises up around them, and in a deadly gloom they fade from the heavens to be reborn in the lower realms. The bodhisattva became a silent witness to the suffering of all these beings as they were driven by their deeds to express their natures in each and every one of these six paths of suffering – whether the obvious pains of the hells or the false promises of the heavens.

Finally, in the third and final watch of the night, the bodhisattva contemplated the chain of causation itself, whereby all things come into existence and all beings forge their own destiny. He saw that all sentient beings were suffering within samsara, the cycle of birth and death; trapped by their ignorant pursuit of selfish desires. Siddhārtha realized that all suffering was due to a misapprehension of the nature of reality. In the constant flux of conditioned phenomena there was no one and nothing to hold on to. Grasping at anything, even trying to find a fixed being standing apart to do the grasping, was nothing but an exercise in futility. It made no sense to demand of life what it could never give. So – he let it all fall away. Free of selfish craving and the ignorance that it was based on, Siddhārtha knew that he would no longer be subject to the mental anguish of the paths of suffering again. As the night came to an end and the morning star rose into the dawn sky on the eighth day of the twelfth month, Siddhārtha awakened to the true nature of reality. From that moment on he was Śākyamuni, the "Sage of the Śākya Clan." As one who could now come and go from the realm of Truth, he would also henceforth be known as the "Tathāgata," meaning both "Thus Come One" and "Thus Gone One."

The Buddha considered, 'Who can be so wretched as to not show gratitude? Who in the present deserves praise and reverence for enabling me to attain perfect and complete awakening?' For innumerable lives he had attended on hundreds of thousands of billions of past buddhas, but in the present life there was no one who had been the equal of the bodhisattva in wisdom and merit. Therefore he concluded, 'Very well, I will praise the Wonderful Dharma itself, for that has always and ever been my guide.'

Brahmā, the god who believed he was the creator of the world, appeared, coalescing from the dawn light. A heavenly entourage that included the four heavenly kings, Śakra Devānām Indra, and the gods of the sun, moon, and stars accompanied him. Even Maheśvara, the Great Freedom God from the highest of the heavens of the realm of form, came to observe. Brahmā praised Śākyamuni Buddha, saying, "All the buddhas of the past, present, and future who remove the sorrows of sentient beings abide in devotion to the Wonderful Dharma. This is as it should be. Any who desire the highest good and aspire to awakening should reflect on the Buddha's teaching and likewise devote themselves to the Wonderful Dharma."

For three weeks after that fateful morning of his awakening, the Buddha stayed by the fig tree, which would later come to be known as the Bodhi Tree, the "Tree of Awakening." Most often he just sat and gazed upon the roots of the tree. Other times he walked about reflecting to himself, 'The wisdom I obtained is most wonderful and excellent. The living beings wandering among the six paths of suffering are too dull, attached to their own pleasures, and blinded by stupidity to be able to understand or appreciate it. How can I possibly share what I have awakened to with them?'

Brahmā and the rest of the heavenly host were still present. They joined their hands together palm to palm and bowed respectfully. Brahmā, speaking for them all, said, "Venerable sir, let the Blessed One teach the Dharma; let the Fortunate One teach the Dharma. There are beings with little dust in their eyes that are falling away because they do not hear the Dharma. There will be those who will understand the Dharma."

Of course, every bodhisattva vows at the outset of their taking up the path to buddhahood, "I will cause all living beings to attain the same awakening that I aim to attain." Śākyamuni Buddha had done the same. Upon hearing Brahmā's request he looked upon all beings with compassion. He thought to himself, 'How sad and strange, all these beings already have the nature of buddhas but they do not see it because they are blinded by their greed, hatred, and ignorance. Yet, there are some with only a little dust in their eyes. Some beings are submerged by delusion, others are about to emerge from it, and others have already begun to emerge. These beings are like a pond of red, white, and blue lotus flowers. Some of the flowers are still submerged in the pond, others are just below the surface, and yet others have risen above the muddy waters and are about to bloom.' The Buddha determined that he would teach all of these beings using his vast store of skillful means to mature them and enable them, also, to realize buddhahood. To Brahmā and the heavenly host he responded, "I have appeared in this defiled world just like all the other buddhas. I will expound the Dharma according to the capacities of all living beings. Now is the time to do this."

Considering the Buddha's life, Yakuō-maro realized that the worldly hopes that his parents had for him were as nothing compared to the new ambition welling up in his heart. What good would it do to become a mere scholar, a clerk in a remote estate, or even an official in Kamakura? Resolving the great matter of birth and death was the most important thing. To do that he would have to follow the Buddha Way, become a monk, and master the Buddha Dharma himself. Then he could truly repay his parents, teachers, and many benefactors.

Renchō

Master Dōzen-bō ordained Yakuō-maro at the age of 15 on the eighth day of the tenth month of the third year of the Katei era (1237). The ceremony of "attaining the way and bestowing the precepts" was held in the abbot's quarters of Seichōji. In addition to Dōzen-bō and Yakuō-maro, several other monks were present to assist and witness to the ordination, including Gijō-bō and Jōken-bō. Together they sung the *shōmyō* of the "Place of Practice." The verses affirmed that the present location reflected all things, just as the jewels caught in the vertices of the net of the god Indra were said to each reflect every other jewel. In the reflection of that present place and time gathered all the Three Treasures of the universe: all buddhas, all their teachings, all their assemblies. As they sang the last verse they all bowed low in homage, touching their foreheads to the floor and lifting their hands, palms up, over their heads as though to raise up the buddhas by their feet. In this way they showed that they had lowered the mast of ego and exalted the awakened ones.

Dōzen-bō then led them in an invocation expressing their devotion to the buddhas, bodhisattvas, and the Buddha Dharma taught in the sutras. They called to Vairocana, the buddha representative of the ineffable true nature of reality that is the Dharma-body; to Lochana Buddha, one of the enjoyment-body buddhas like Amitābha who abide in the pure lands where they enjoy the fruition of their virtue and the realization of the true nature; to Śākyamuni Buddha, who had appeared in India as one of the myriad transformation-body buddhas emanated by the enjoyment-bodies for the sake of all sentient beings in need of the Buddha Dharma; to Maitreya, the bodhisattva destined to be born in a future age as the next buddha of this world; and to all buddhas throughout space and time. They invoked the *Sutra of the Lotus Flower of the Wonderful Dharma of the Mahayana.* They invoked Mañjuśrī, the bodhisattva of great wisdom; Universal Sage, the bodhisattva of great activity; World Voice Perceiver, the bodhisattva of great compassion; all honored ones, all the bodhisattvas. They invoked Mahāprajñāpāramitā, the "great perfection of wisdom," regarded as the mother of all buddhas and the name of a class of sutras that conveyed the Buddha's teachings for bodhisattvas.

Dōzen-bō then announced to the assembly, "Here is a good man, who is undertaking the ceremony of crossing over and receiving the precepts before the Buddha and the Three Treasures. His name is Yakuō-maro. Since he was born in this world, spring and fall have passed 15 times. His previous good roots have now met with opportune conditions so that he has finally made the determination to leave home and accept the Mahayana precepts and wear the black robe. He is taking Śākyamuni Buddha's saving vow and activities as his own, thereby inheriting the seed of the Buddha to spread throughout the ages so that he can requite one ten thousandth of the beneficence of the Buddha. May the buddhas and bodhisattva and ancestors of our lineage place their hands upon his head and certify this crossing over and reception of the precepts with joy. May the great vow of happiness in this world and the next be accomplished."

Dōzen-bō gave the signal, and Yakuō-maro rose to face him. Palms joined in reverence, he bowed, then lowered himself into a full prostration. When he again sat upright, his palms still joined, Dōzen-bō asked, "May I shave your hair for you?"

Yakuō-maro responded, "My sincerest hope is to have it shaved."

Gijō-bō, standing to Dōzen-bō's left said, "Very well, good man! Seeing that nothing is permanent in this world, leave the secular life and seek the Way of Awakening."

Joken-bō, standing to Dōzen-bō's right said, "Devote yourself to the World Honored One, leave suffering behind, and make the truth of your faith the purpose of your life for the sake of all people."

In unison, all of his tutors said to him, "Leave the material world, stand by your determination, concentrate on seeking the Way of the Buddha, and arouse the thought of saving all sentient beings."

Once he was given the tonsure by Dōzen-bō, the other monks helped Yakuō-maro exchange his kimono and *hakama* for the simple white under-robe he wore from then on under his monastic robes.

Dōzen-bō said, "If you wish to receive the Mahayana precepts, you should first repent of all your past transgressions. Repeat after me: I now fully repent of all my past wrongful deeds, born from beginningless greed, hate, and delusion, through body, speech, and mind."

Having repeated these words of repentance, Yakuō-maro prostrated himself once more and again sat upright with palms joined.

Dōzen-bō said, "Now that you have purified yourself by repenting of your past transgressions it is time for you to take refuge in the Three Treasures." He then led Yakuō-maro in repeating three times: "I take refuge in the Buddha, I take refuge in the Dharma, I take refuge in the Sangha." Each time Yakuō-maro bowed and prostrated himself. Many times over the past four years he had recited these words or sung verses with the other monks to praise or take refuge in the Three Treasures. This time was different, as he was not only saying these words together with others, as part of a regular ceremony. This time he was saying them to show that he himself had made the decision to take refuge and follow through, regardless of what trials this decision might lead to.

When he had raised himself up from his last prostration, his teacher announced: "Now is the time to take the three pure precepts." Yakuō-maro knew from his studies that now he would be accepting the precepts that spelled out the heart of the bodhisattva way of life, the way of life that would lead to buddhahood. The most all-encompassing were the three pure precepts that would be given first.

Dōzen-bō asked him, "Until you attain buddhahood, will you uphold the precept to put an end to all that is evil?"

Yakuō-maro responded, "Yes, I will."

"Until you attain buddhahood, will you uphold the precept to cultivate all that is good?"

"Yes, I will."

"Until you attain buddhahood, will you work to save all beings?"

"Yes, I will."

Once Yakuō-maro accepted the three pure precepts, Dōzen-bō conferred the ten major and 48 minor precepts for bodhisattvas as found in the *Brahmā Net Sutra*. These were the precepts that were taken by the monks of the Tendai school founded by the Great Master Dengyō on Mt. Hiei more than 400 years ago. Before this, Buddhist monastics took the precepts of the Hinayana, or pre-Mahayana teachings. Lay Buddhists commonly took the five precepts: not to kill, not to steal, not to engage in sexual misconduct, not to lie, and not to indulge in intoxicants, but monastics took many more to regulate every aspect of their lives and keep them from being entangled in worldliness. Initially they would take the novice precepts that reiterated the five taken by laypeople but also included not to adorn or perfume themselves, not to sleep on luxurious elevated beds, not to eat after noon so as to not disturb their supporters by begging for food or accepting meals throughout the day, not to waste time listening to or watching worldly entertainments, and not to possess gold or silver. The complete disciplinary rules included 250 precepts for monks and 348 for nuns. These hundreds of monastic precepts were still followed in Korea and China, and there were some who were trying to revive them in Japan, but for the most part all the monks and nuns of Japan had become disciples of Great Master Dengyō, as their lives were now guided by the Mahayana precepts for bodhisattvas who aimed to attain buddhahood for the sake of all beings, rather than the Hinayana precepts for those who simply wanted to end samsara, the cycle of birth and death, for themselves alone.

"First is the precept against taking life," Dōzen-bō stated. "Will you uphold this precept against taking life?"

"Yes, I will," Yakuō-maro affirmed.

Dōzen-bō went through the rest of the ten major precepts in turn, and Yakuō-maro dutifully accepted them all: the precepts against stealing, against sexual misconduct, against lying, against dealing in intoxicants, against talking about other bodhisattva's faults, against praising oneself and disparaging others, against being miserly with possessions or the Dharma, against hatred and refusal to accept apologies, and finally the precept against slandering the Three Treasures. To break any of these ten was to be considered expelled from the Sangha of bodhisattvas until one had sincerely repented of the transgression – for which the Mahayana teachings had provisions in the form of repentance ceremonies meant to rehabilitate fallen bodhisattvas.

Dōzen-bō next conferred the 48 minor precepts that Yakuō-maro also accepted. Many of these precepts were the same as, or similar to, the precepts and codes of conduct of the Hinayana monastics, but presented in the *Brahmā Net Sutra* in the context of Mahayana aspirations and ideals. Among these were precepts against drinking intoxicants oneself, eating meat or pungent herbs, stocking weapons, and so forth. There were precepts enjoining the bodhisattva to teach the Dharma, to correct the errors of others, to take care of the sick, and to save the lives of animals. Other precepts enjoined the bodhisattva against pride, self-seeking, using their wiles to gain patronage, or turning away from the Mahayana to seek the lesser way of individual liberation. A bodhisattva must always be motivated by compassion for others and strive for the liberation of all beings.

Once he had taken all the bodhisattva precepts, Gijō-bō and Jōken-bō brought forth the black garment known as the "Dharma-robe" and the *kesa* that Yakuō-maro would wear as a monk. Before helping him put on the robes the two monks said together, "This *kesa* and Dharma-robe are the armor of the practice of the Buddha Way. Put them on, bear all hardships, uphold the precepts of the Buddha, and lead the people."

Before putting on the *kesa*, Yakuō-maro held it over his head and recited the Verse for Donning the *Kesa*: "Great is the robe of liberation / An incomparable field of merit! / Wearing it, take on Buddha's conduct / Thereby, freeing all sentient beings!" As the final knot was tied, allowing the *kesa* to hang from his left shoulder, Yakuō-maro couldn't help but swell with pride as he stood forth in his new robes. Just like Prince Siddhārtha more than 2,000 years ago he had taken the tonsure and put on the ochre patchwork mantle. Now he was no longer a child but a man who could follow in the Buddha's footsteps.

Dōzen-bō said, "Now I will establish your Dharma name. Change from your worldly name, Yakuō-maro, to your new name Renchō, "Lotus Eternal." From now on, let us together make efforts to spread the Buddha Dharma as the Buddha's disciples.

Gijō-bō then said, "If you come upon teachers of the Dharma, you will be able to complete the Way of the Bodhisattva quickly."

Jōken-bō added, "If you practice as a good master teaches, you will be able to find the straight path to attain awakening."

The new monk Renchō beamed at his master and his tutors and responded, "I swear to practice strenuously with the Wonderful Dharma in my heart and to never slacken."

With both hands Renchō accepted the certificate upon which his Dharma-name was written. He bowed once more holding up the paper in grateful acknowledgment, after which he turned in the direction of his home village and recited the words of taking leave from the life of a householder: "Insofar as we transmigrate in the triple world, we cannot cut off the bonds of love and affection. Entering the unconditioned by disregarding favors is the true way of repaying them." As he recited he thought of his last visit to Kominato. His mother and father had been pleased that he would be accepted as Dōzen-bō's disciple, as the merit of becoming a monk would be shared with the entire family. They had asked him to discover for them the surest way to attain rebirth in the Pure Land. Was it really as simple as just chanting the name of Amitābha Buddha? Renchō was not sure if they were asking just to humor him or if they were in earnest. Fishermen, like his father, knew that they were destined for rebirth in the lower realms, as they made their living through the slaughter of living creatures. As for his mother, she knew, as did all the women of the village, that according to the Buddha's teachings they could not hope to attain buddhahood in their present forms, but would have to find a way to be reborn as a male in the pure lands. For his mother and father and all the villagers, the question of how to attain rebirth in the Pure Land of Amitābha was a grave concern.

Now a monk and no longer a child, Renchō sat with the other monks, at the lowest position, being the most junior among them. Together they recited the Verses for Opening the Sutra: "The most profound and wonderful Dharma is presented in this sutra / This sutra is difficult to meet even once in thousands and millions of eons / Now we have been able to see, hear, receive and keep this sutra / May we understand the most excellent teaching of the Tathāgata!" These verses were recited prior to the chanting of the sutras in order to acknowledge the rare opportunity of encountering and being able to uphold the Buddha's teachings.

The passage they recited was not one of the usual ones. It was from the 27th chapter of the *Lotus Sutra*, "King Wonderful Adornment as the Previous Life of a Bodhisattva." The chapter describes how in a past life the bodhisattvas Medicine King and Medicine Superior were the sons of a king. Their father was at first opposed to the teachings of the buddha of that time and place, but by displaying miraculous powers gained by cultivating the Buddha Dharma the sons persuaded him to visit that buddha and hear his teachings. In the passage recited the two brothers request the permission of their parents to renounce the world.

"The two sons said to their parents, 'Excellent, Father and Mother! Go to the Buddha, see him, and make offerings to him because to see a Buddha is as difficult as to see an *uḍumbara* flower that only blooms once every 3,000 years or as for a one-eyed tortoise to find a hole in a floating piece of wood that it can rest in! We accumulated so many merits in our previous existence that we are now able to meet the teachings of the Buddha in this life of ours. Allow us to renounce the world because it is difficult to see a Buddha, and also because it is difficult to have such a good opportunity as this to see him.'"

The passage ended with the assertion that all the people in the household of King Wonderful Adornment became able to keep the *Sutra of the Lotus Flower of the Wonderful Dharma*. 'May I also find myself able to lead people to the Buddha's teachings, just as my former namesake did,' thought Renchō.

The ordination ceremony came to a close as Dōzen-bō spoke the final dedication of merits, led the recitation of the four great vows of the bodhisattvas, and together they sang a last *shōmyō* to reverently send off all the buddhas, bodhisattvas, and guardian deities who had gathered to witness the ceremony, and to express the wish that, though returned to their own abodes, they would continue to watch over them all.

The ceremony concluded, Dōzen-bō smiled proudly at his disciple. He said to Renchō, "So now you are a disciple of the Buddha, an inheritor of the Tendai lineage that has come down to us from the Great Master Tiantai in China and Great Master Dengyō here in Japan. Do not slacken in your studies now that you are a monk. Strive ever harder, for you are quite a smart young man. Who knows? Maybe you will someday be the wisest man in Japan." He chuckled and turned away.

The Teachings of the Buddha

Renchō had no intention of slackening in his studies. He spent even more time delving deeply into the sutras, as well as the commentaries on them that were available in the sutra repository of Seichōji. He did not want to disappoint his parents, Master Dōzen-bō, his tutors, or even the Three Treasures themselves. He would do everything he could to learn and practice the way to awakening.

The Buddha's teachings, however, were vast and subtle. They could be said to have begun right after his perfect and complete awakening at the age of 30, during the three weeks that he sat beneath the Bodhi Tree conversing with Brahmā and a cloudlike assembly of gods and celestial bodhisattvas. During that time he appeared to these celestial beings as Vairocana Buddha in the Lotus Matrix World. Most of the expounding of the Dharma was done at that time by those bodhisattvas who celebrated and discoursed on the glory and wonder of the Buddha's awakening as he reflected upon the harmonious interfusion of all phenomena. The bodhisattvas asserted, "There is no distinction among the mind, the Buddha, and ordinary beings." They also stated that "mind is the ultimate reality" that it is "like a skilled painter" creating all the worlds. Vairocana Buddha himself taught the *Brahmā Net Sutra* and its precepts for bodhisattvas, and that too was considered to have happened as Śākyamuni Buddha sat beneath the Bodhi Tree. Renchō had a hard time following or even visualizing what was taught in the many fascicles of the *Flower Garland Sutra* that recorded these teachings. It was evident that they were intended for advanced bodhisattvas and not beginners in the Dharma.

After three weeks, Śākyamuni Buddha got up from beneath the Bodhi Tree and went to seek out the five ascetics who had been his former companions on Mt. Dandaloka. He found them at a place called the Deer Park in the town of Vārānasī. They were reluctant to greet him at first, but once the Buddha was among them they could not help but be impressed by the great change in his demeanor. He was no longer a gaunt and driven youth striving for an unattainable goal. The person they now saw before them was a man who was in full health, though still weathered and lean. Here was a man, or more than that, perhaps, who was at complete ease with himself, with everyone, with everything. He no longer viewed the world and its beings as prizes to be won, nor did he view them as threats or disappointments. He had overcome anguish and suffering, though his heart still recognized sorrow and his body was still vulnerable to the pains of hunger, exhaustion, illness, and injury. He looked upon the ascetics with a joyful glimmer in his eyes and the slightest of smiles. The five wanted to know, in spite of themselves, what their former companion had come to tell them. They reverently offered him a seat and then they too sat down, to listen. He spoke to them of the middle way, the course between extremes that was the path to awakening. He taught them what would become known as the "four noble truths," which were as much a guide to what one must do as they were an explanation of what was. The first truth was that all the suffering throughout the triple world must be completely understood; the second was that the causes of suffering, selfish craving and the underlying ignorance that sought from conditioned things what they could never give, were to be rooted out and abandoned; the third was that the cessation of suffering was to be realized so that one could awaken to the bliss of the unconditioned beyond samsara; and the fourth was that to bring suffering to an end the middle way consisting of right view, right intention, right speech, right action, right livelihood, right effort, right mindfulness, and right concentration was to be cultivated.

The middle way of the eightfold path described the way of life for and of those who wished to overcome samsara. Right view meant to view life in terms of the four noble truths. Right intention meant to let go of possessiveness and ill-will. Right speech was to abstain from lying, abusive speech, spreading stories to divide people against one another, and also idle senseless talk that did not lead to liberation.

Right action was to abstain from killing, stealing, and sexual misconduct (anything involving rape, incest, violence, coercion, deception, or the breaking of vows and commitments - for monastics it meant a life of celibacy). Right livelihood meant to live in a way that did not exploit, harm, or cheat others. Right effort was to make efforts to prevent the arising of unwholesome states, overcome unwholesome states already arisen, generate wholesome states not yet arisen, and maintain wholesome states already arisen. Right mindfulness meant to reflect upon forms, feelings, mental states, and phenomena generally in their arising and ceasing according to the interplay of causes and conditions. Right concentration meant to cultivate a clear and focused mind. The practitioner first had to overcome sensual craving, ill-will, dullness and drowsiness, restlessness and remorse, and debilitating doubt regarding the teachings or one's own capabilities. This was done by stilling body and mind while focusing the attention on the subject of meditation (such as one's breath). The result would be the attainment of deeper and deeper states of meditative absorption in which every extraneous thought and feeling fell away until only one-pointedness of mind and equanimity were left. With one-pointed equanimity the practitioner of the eightfold path would see that forms, feelings, mental states, and all conditioned phenomena were impure, ultimately unsatisfying, impermanent, and without a fixed, independent, abiding self. In conditioned things there was no pure, blissful, eternal self that could be found or grasped.

In the Buddha's early teachings he analyzed all the components and elements that make up human life in order to show that there was no abiding self to be found anywhere. Life was an ever-shifting composite of five aggregates: forms, feelings, perceptions, mental formations, and consciousness. Forms perceived by the eyes, and other sense objects as perceived by the appropriate senses, gave rise to feelings of pleasure or pain leading to perceptions of self, others, and the world. These in turn gave rise to mental formations of attachment and aversion. This whole process was informed by conscious awareness of one's life and circumstances, which it served also to perpetuate. This process never rested for a moment and in it there could be found no abiding self. The Buddha also spoke of how experience arose through the meeting of six sense bases, the five physical senses and mind, with their objects: forms, sounds, odors, flavors, tangibles, and mental objects (concepts and emotions). Six different kinds of consciousness arose from the meeting of a particular sense with its object. Altogether there were 18 elements of the process of experience, comprised of the six sense bases, their respective objects, and the respective types of consciousness that arose from the meeting of sense and object. By contemplating these things, it could be observed that it was not just the body that was impermanent and composed of parts, for consciousness too was an interdependent process arising and ceasing moment-to-moment and therefore empty of an abiding self.

The five ascetics at the Deer Park in Vārāṇasī were the first to hear and realize for themselves the truth of the Buddha's teachings. In the years that followed the Buddha wandered from town to town, gathering about him other ascetics and spiritual strivers who had left the household life. He taught them the Dharma and then he sent them forth, saying, "Monks, I am free from all shackles whether human or divine. You too are free from all shackles whether human or divine. Go now and wander for the welfare and happiness of many, out of compassion for the world, for the benefit, welfare, and happiness of gods and men. Teach the Dharma that is good in the beginning, good in the middle, and good in the end, both in meaning and in letter. Explain the holy life that is utterly perfect and pure."

To those who wished to become his followers he bid them take refuge in the Three Treasures. Of these there were many who did not wish to leave the household life, so they became lay supporters who observed the five precepts and gave material support to the monks and nuns of food, clothing, medicine, and shelter. By doing this they generated merit so they could be reborn in the heavens and/or have the opportunity to become monks in future lifetimes. Those who joined the Sangha as monks or nuns committed themselves to following the monastic precepts and to memorizing and putting into practice the Buddha's teachings. They wandered from town to town subsisting on alms, except during the rainy season retreat when they stayed in monasteries and deepened their practice.

Among the first to become monks were two friends called Śāriputra and Maudgalyāyana who became the Buddha's chief disciples, known to be foremost in wisdom and supernatural power respectively. The austere Mahākāśyapa later joined the Sangha and he was known as foremost in the cultivation of the various ascetic disciplines sanctioned by the Buddha for those who wished to strengthen their self-discipline and live as simply as possible. These disciplines included using only cast-off rags instead of accepting donated robes, eating only by begging door-to-door instead of accepting invitations to dinner, eating only once a day, sleeping outdoors, and other such practices which were austere but not harmful given the climate in sub-tropical India. Śākyamuni Buddha eventually returned to Kapilavastu, and there his son Rāhula joined the Sangha at the bidding of his mother Yaśodharā. Rāhula would become foremost in inconspicuous practice. Many other Śākya nobles also joined, including the Buddha's cousin Ānanda, who would in time become the Buddha's personal attendant and foremost in hearing the Buddha's discourses. Another Śākya noble who became a monk was Aniruddha, who became foremost in the development of the divine eye, by which he could see as the gods did. He was able to look at things in far away places and to see the doings of beings in the lower and higher realms. The Śākya clan's barber, Upāli, also became a monk and would become foremost in observing the precepts. Later, the Buddha's aunt and foster mother, Mahāprajāpati, followed the Sangha in its wanderings until the Buddha allowed her to become the first nun. At that time the Buddha's wife, Yaśodharā, also became a nun. Other monks who were foremost in the Sangha were Subhūti, foremost in understanding that all things are empty of a self-nature;

Mahākātyāyana, foremost in explaining the Dharma; and Pūrṇa, who was foremost in expounding the Dharma.

All of these monks and nuns would become known as "voice-hearers," because they heard the Dharma directly from the Buddha and put into practice the eightfold path in order to attain nirvana, the extinguishing of the inner fires of greed, hatred, and ignorance. Attaining nirvana, they were no longer subject to mental anguish or even agitation, though they were far from immune to life's pains and tragedies. Those voice-hearers who had done this were known as arhats or "worthy ones," who had achieved the goal of the Buddha's teachings as given at the Deer Park. Upon death, so they believed, they would no longer be reborn among the six paths of suffering in the triple world, or anywhere else. Their bodies would be cremated and reduced to ashes and their consciousness would be annihilated. For them, death was the attainment of "final nirvana" because, for them, there would never again be any experience of physical pain or mental suffering.

The Buddha acknowledged that in places and times when the Buddha Dharma had been lost and a new buddha had not yet appeared to teach there were some who awakened to the interdependent flow of causes and conditions on their own by observing the transience of worldly phenomena. They might observe the scattering of cherry blossoms in the spring or the falling of leaves in autumn. By deeply contemplating causality on their own these "private-buddhas" or "cause-knowers" eliminated within themselves all greed, hatred, and ignorance and had cut off the cycle of birth and death, but unlike buddhas they had no wish or ability to involve themselves in attempting to teach others. For those inclined to take up the contemplative practices of the cause-knowers the Buddha taught the twelve-fold chain of dependent origination. The twelve links of the chain were all the different aspects of life that were bound up in one another and composed the round of suffering. The first link was ignorance, out of which arise willful acts of attachment and aversion.

Out of these acts arises conscious awareness. Consciousness identifies itself with a name and form. Name and form have the six senses. The six senses allow for contact with physical and mental stimuli. Contact gives rise to pleasurable and painful feelings. Feeling leads to craving. Craving leads to clinging. Clinging leads to perpetuating the process of becoming a sentient being. Becoming leads to birth in the triple world. Birth inevitably leads to the sufferings of aging and death. Death, however, is not the end for it leads back to ignorance. Samsara continues interminably until ignorance is finally eradicated. With the eradication of ignorance all these other relations are likewise eliminated, including birth and death. Like the arhats, the cause-knowers realized nirvana in life and upon death their bodies were likewise reduced to ashes and their minds annihilated, never to be reborn among the six paths in the triple world.

The teachings given to the voice-hears and the private-buddhas became known as the two vehicles that carried those who embarked on them to nirvana. Together the two vehicles comprised what would be known as the Hinayana or Small Vehicle because, like a raft that could only carry one person across to the far shore of a river, the vehicles for voice-hearers and private-buddhas carried only the individual practitioner to the far shore of liberation from suffering. Those who followed the Hinayana teachings had no aspirations to help others escape samsara. They felt that it was hard enough to win their own liberation and that helping others was beyond their abilities. There were, however, those who did aspire to attain buddhahood and for them the Buddha taught a third vehicle, the bodhisattva vehicle. Those who aspired to the bodhisattva vehicle took up the four great vows and cultivated the six perfections of generosity, morality, patience, energy, meditation, and wisdom. Wisdom in particular was emphasized because not only did it guide and inform all the others, it was also the final goal of each. The bodhisattva vehicle came to be called the Mahayana or Great Vehicle because it emphasized the attainment of buddhahood for the sake of liberating all beings. For this reason it was considered to be like a large ship that could carry multitudes of beings across from the shore of suffering to the far shore of liberation.

Scholars, such as the Great Master Tiantai, believed, based on a close reading of the sutras, that the Buddha taught the Āgamas or "scriptures" of the Hinayana teaching for twelve years as a concession to those who would at least understand the need to be liberated from samsara. After that the Buddha introduced the more challenging Mahayana teachings. He criticized the voice-hearers for their limited aspirations and conversely praised the bodhisattvas for their compassion and determination to bring about the liberation of all beings. He encouraged everyone to arouse the "awakening mind" that aspires to buddhahood. He warned his listeners not to fall into the trap of taking up either of the two vehicles because those who did would lose their awakening mind, cut themselves off from the triple world by attaining "final nirvana," and thereby be unable to practice the bodhisattva vehicle that necessitated continued rebirth in the triple world for many *kalpas* in order to accumulate the wisdom and meritorious deeds that would come to their fruition in buddhahood. In these Expanded discourses of the Mahayana the Buddha revealed that even after his passing there would still be buddhas in the pure lands of the ten directions where aspiring practitioners could be reborn and advance in their progress under the guidance of a buddha among fellow bodhisattvas in a world designed to be conducive to the rapid attainment of buddhahood. Furthermore, the Buddha taught that all things are creations of the mind, so that the difference between a pure land and an impure land is really the difference between a pure and an impure mind. The duality between subject and object, between self and other, between a foolish being caught up in suffering and a perfectly and completely awakened buddha was all generated by impurities within the mind. If one could overturn the impurity within the mind then one would experience the buddha-nature within oneself, the true nature of all reality. This was the promise of the Mahayana teachings.

It did not end there, however. After the Expanded teachings the Buddha introduced the Perfection of Wisdom discourses. In these discourses the Buddha taught that all things were empty of self-nature, even mind. Bodhisattva practice aimed at the insight that all phenomena are ungraspable and without a fixed or independent selfhood. All the categories of the Hinayana teachings were shown to be empty: the five aggregates, the 18 elements, the four noble truths and its eightfold path, the twelve-fold chain of dependent origination, even nirvana, the unconditioned. There were no aggregates, elements, truths, links, or even a liberation that could be grasped as though it were an object to be clung to. All of these teachings were just skillful methods of freeing oneself of attachment and aversion and a way to see reality more clearly. Just as one cast aside a raft when reaching the far shore of a river, so too these teachings should not become objects of clinging. Even non-attachment should not become an object of attachment. To have no attachments whatsoever, to further realize that there was nothing to be attached to and that ultimately there was no one who could even have attachments, and yet to remain compassionately engaged with an insubstantial world to save insubstantial beings was what it meant to be a bodhisattva according to the Perfection of Wisdom discourses.

Even that was not the end of the Buddha's teachings. After instructing his followers with the Expanded and Perfection of Wisdom discourses of the Mahayana for a total of 30 years the Buddha began to teach the *Lotus Sutra*. In that sutra he revealed that all of his teachings, from the beginning, were for the purpose of enabling all beings to attain buddhahood. He taught that the two vehicles of the Hinayana and the bodhisattva vehicle of the Mahayana were really just One Vehicle wherein all could swiftly attain buddhahood. In addition, his buddhahood had no real beginning or end. He had been teaching all beings since the unimaginably distant past in various forms using innumerable skillful means and would continue to teach them on into the unimaginably distant future. As the Eternal Buddha, he would always be present, constantly thinking of ways to help sentient beings quickly attain buddhahood. On the last day of his life the Buddha reiterated this teaching in the *Nirvana Sutra*. In this last discourse, given on his deathbed, he also stated that all beings possess the buddha-nature and that unlike conditioned phenomena that are impure, lead to suffering, impermanent, and lacking self-nature, the buddha-nature can be said to be the pure, blissful, eternal, true self.

The Buddha passed away at the age of 80 under the twin śāla trees near the town of Kuśinagara in the 52nd year of the reign of King Mu of the Zhou dynasty (949 BCE) on the 15th day of the second month according to the *Record of Wonders in the Book of Zhou*. Three months after his "final nirvana," a council of 500 arhats presided over by Mahākāśyapa gathered outside the town of Rājagriha. At that first council Ānanda recited all the sutras he had heard. This is why every sutra begins with the words spoken by Ānanda, "Thus have I heard." Upāli recited the precepts and regulations for the monastic Sangha. According to some sources Mahākāśyapa recited the systemization of the Buddha's teachings known as the abhidharma or "higher Dharma." These three collections of the discourses, the precepts, and the higher Dharma were thereafter known as the "three baskets." The successive patriarchs who led the Sangha after the final nirvana of Śākyamuni Buddha made sure that the three baskets were faithfully passed down to future generations of practitioners.

Thus began the three ages of the Dharma. According to the *Great Assembly Sutra*, the Buddha had predicted how things would go for the Sangha and his teachings in the future. According to the Buddha, during the first 500 years after his death there would be many who practiced in the true spirit of his teachings and attained awakening. During the second 500 year period there would be many who learned the teachings and practiced meditation but very few if any were able to attain awakening in their lifetimes. The first 1,000-year period would be known as the Age of the True Dharma.

The third 500 years would be the time in which people read the sutras extensively and increased their knowledge though few if any actually put them into practice. The fourth 500 years would be the time when people would not even bother to learn the contents of the sutras but instead they would try to earn merit by building temples and pagodas. This second 1,000-year period would be known as the Age of the Semblance Dharma.

The fifth 500 years would be a time of increasing disputes and quarrels that would tear the Sangha apart as the monks, nuns, and lay followers lost sight of the Buddha's true intentions. This would eventually result in the destruction and loss of all the teachings. This would be the beginning of the Latter Age of Degeneration. After that, the world would be bereft of the Buddha Dharma until Maitreya Buddha was born into the world in a far distant time, perhaps 5,670 million years in the future, to begin a new cycle of teaching.

The Buddha had transmitted the Dharma to the first patriarch Mahākāśyapa, who spread the Buddha's teachings for 20 years. After that, the Dharma was transmitted successively to the patriarchs Ānanda, Śanavāsa, Upagupta, and Dhritaka, each of whom taught for 20 years each. There was also Madhyāntika who was given transmission along with Śanavāsa and taught at the same time. During these 100 years they spread only Hinayana teachings without even mentioning the names of the Mahayana sutras. They were succeeded by the patriarchs Mikkaka, Buddhanandi, Buddhamitra, Pārśva, and Punyayaśas, who for the most part spread only the Hinayana during the first 500 years of the Age of the True Dharma. It was not that they did not teach the Mahayana at all, but they did not emphasize it.

During the latter half of the Age of the True Dharma, namely between 500 and 1,000 years after the final nirvana of the Buddha, a dozen or so patriarchs transmitted the Dharma: Aśvaghoṣa, Kapimala, Nāgārjuna, Kānadeva, Rāhulata, Sanghānandi, Sanghayaśas,

Kumārata, Jayata, Vasubandhu, Manorhita, Haklenayaśa, and Āryasimha. These dozen or so patriarchs at first studied non-Buddhist schools before studying the Hinayana sutras, the latter of which they refuted completely when they turned to the Mahayana sutras. With the beheading of the 24th patriarch Āryasimha by a king hostile to Buddhism the time of the patriarchs came to an end.

Buddhism spread eastward to China in the 15th year of the Age of the Semblance Dharma (67 CE). 500 years or so after the beginning of the Age of the Semblance Dharma, all the sutras of Buddhism together with a wooden statue of the Buddha as well as monks and nuns were sent from the kingdom of Paekche to Japan. This was in the 13th year of the reign of Emperor Kimmei (552 CE), the 30th ruler of Japan counting from Emperor Jimmu. Later, Prince Shōtoku, the first son of Emperor Yōmei, who was a son of Emperor Kimmei, not only spread Buddhism but also designated the *Lotus Sutra*, the *Vimalakīrti Sutra*, and the *Śrīmālā Sutra* to be the fundamental teachings that would ensure the peace of the country.

Eventually eight schools of Buddhism were brought to Japan: the Abhidharma Treasury, Completion of Reality, Precepts, Dharma Characteristics, Three Treatises, Flower Garland, Mantra, and Tendai schools. Sometimes the list was extended to ten to include the appearance of the Pure Land and Zen schools within the last half-century or so. The first three were Hinayana schools. The Abhidharma Treasury and Completion of Reality schools focused on the systematic commentaries that formed the abhidharma basket of the three baskets. The Precepts school promulgated the precepts for monks and nuns, and also precepts for laypeople and bodhisattvas. The other seven were Mahayana schools. The Dharma Characteristics school focused on the Mahayana teachings concerning consciousness and the mind created nature of experience, especially as taught by the patriarch Vasubandhu. The Three Treatises school focused on the Perfection of Wisdom teachings, especially as taught in two treatises by Nāgārjuna and one treatise by his disciple Āryadeva. The Flower

Garland school focused on the teachings of the *Flower Garland Sutra*. The Mantra school focused on the esoteric practices of the three secrets of body, word, and thought: the gestures called mudras, the recitation of mantras, and the concentration of the mind by visualizing images from the Womb Realm and Diamond Realm mandalas. A practitioner of the three secrets was said to be able to attain buddhahood in their present lifetime by uniting with the physical, verbal, and mental characteristics of Mahāvairocana Tathāgata or one of the many buddhas, bodhisattvas, or gods who were his emanations. Esoteric rites could also be used for worldly benefits such as averting disaster, attracting prosperity, and even subduing enemies. The Tiantai school upheld the *Lotus Sutra* as the Buddha's highest teaching. It was Great Master Tiantai Zhiyi who established the school on Mt. Tiantai in China. In Japan it was called the Tendai school. Tendai differed from its Chinese counterpart by also specializing in its own version of the esoteric practices of the mantra teachings. The Pure Land and Zen schools had arisen only in the last 50 years since the rise of the shogunate. Of course, the practice of *nembutsu* was taken up by nearly all Mahayana Buddhists; similarly meditation practice for the calming of body and mind and contemplation practice to attain liberating insight were known to all Buddhists. The new Pure Land and Zen schools, however, practiced *nembutsu* and meditation respectively to the exclusion of all else.

Renchō's teachers assured him that each of those schools was like a mirror faithfully reflecting the teachings of the Buddha. By studying them and practicing their teachings one would be able to understand the heart of the Buddha Dharma. The problem was that there were too many teachings and practices. Which one was the most important? Which one was the most efficacious? Most importantly, which teaching or practice could guarantee the attainment of buddhahood? This is what Renchō needed to discover, not just for his own sake, but also for the sake of his parents, teachers, brothers, his fellow monks, the villagers, in fact all beings.

The Secret Method for Seeking, Hearing, and Retaining

One summer day, the year following his ordination, Renchō sought out Dōzen-bō to ask for guidance in his studies. He found him sitting beside a cedar tree near the temple's well. He was sitting on a large round stone and carving a hollowed out block of cypress. Renchō could see that he was working on the hands for a statue of Amitābha Buddha. He could tell because the fingers of both hands were back to back and the tips of the index fingers and thumbs of both hands touched so that they formed two circles side by side. This was the concentration mudra of Amitābha Buddha.

Dōzen-bō's eyes glanced up and then back to the delicate work of carving out the fingers. "Yes, Renchō, did you need to see me about something?"

"Pardon master, but I had a question."

"Go ahead, ask." Dōzen-bō carved out another notch of wood and then set aside the block and his knife. He gave his disciple his full attention.

"When I came here I hoped to learn the Buddha's teachings, but now that I am here I have found that I am not sure what that is. Of course we all hope to be reborn in the Pure Land and chant *nembutsu* and dedicate our merit to rebirth there, but now I am wondering if that is really what Śākyamuni Buddha intended for us. After all, according to the Tendai and mantra teachings we should be able to attain buddhahood in our very bodies. Doesn't that mean we should be able to attain buddhahood in this lifetime and not just after death? If that's so, then shouldn't we be practicing those teachings instead of *nembutsu*?"

Dōzen-bō nodded his head. "Hmm, yes, it is said that the esoteric mantra practices can enable us to do that. Still, they are very complex and not easily mastered. Also, you do know we are living in the Latter Age of Degeneration. It began in the seventh year of Eishō (1052) almost 200 years ago. That means that it may be that none of us born at this time have enough of a karmic connection with the Buddha to truly benefit from his teachings. We are the people who failed to sow enough good deeds in the past. So now we are born into this corrupt age. It may be there are some who can still practice and perhaps attain buddhahood in this life, but as for me I will just have to trust in the vows of Amitābha Buddha. He promised that any who call his name will be born in his pure land. You should just set your mind at rest. Have faith in Amitābha Buddha. He has taken care of everything for all of us, so why should you worry yourself?"

"I can't help but wonder, master. Here we still chant the *Lotus Sutra*, and the *Heart of the Perfection of Wisdom Sutra*, not just the *Amitābha Sutra*. We also follow the bodhisattva precepts and I know some of you practice meditation or perform the *goma* fire ceremony and other esoteric rites. Why do we do any of this if we only need to chant *nembutsu*?"

Dōzen-bō grimaced and nodded slowly. "Yes, I could see why you might wonder that. All of these practices do generate merit for us, for our families and ancestors, and for the protection of the nation. So it is important to continue to do them, even as we put all of our hopes for our future rebirth into the hands of Amitābha Buddha."

Renchō stared at the ground, the lines on his forehead folding themselves into deep creases. He thumbed the beads of his *juzu*, then looked up and asked, "If all of these other practices are still able to generate merit..." He worked his jaw but was not sure he could continue. He flushed, "I mean no disrespect master, but I have long been wondering..."

Dōzen-bō looked with kindness upon his disciple. He gestured for him to continue. "It is okay Renchō. I know you are sincere. Go on."

"Why, if we have these teachings and practices to protect the nation do they not seem to work? Is it because it is the Latter Age? Before I came here I heard about what happened to Emperor Antoku and to the Retired Emperor Go-Toba and his sons and grandson. How could this have happened? Didn't they use the Buddha's teachings to protect themselves and bring peace to the country?"

Dōzen-bō sighed. "Yes, Renchō. They did. I too have wondered about these things. When the war began between the Minamoto and Taira clans, Taira no Kiyomori, Emperor Antoku's grandfather, and more than 20 of his clan members put their names on a written pledge stating their promise to respect Enryakuji, the head temple of the Tendai school on Mt. Hiei, as their clan temple. They then donated 24 estates in Ōmi Province. In response the 3,000 monks on Mt. Hiei had a prayer service performed using the rites of the mantra teachings presided over by the Head Abbot Myōun for the defeat of the Minamoto. They also directed the warrior-monks to fight against the Minamoto clan. However, Kiso Yoshinaka, Yoritomo's cousin, leading several of his retainers, climbed up Mt. Hiei, dragged Head Abbot Myōun down from the platform of the prayer service in the main hall, tied him up, rolled him down the western slope as if he were a huge rock, and beheaded him. Two year later the whole Taira clan was destroyed in one stroke, and Emperor Antoku with them.

"When the Retired Emperor Go-Toba tried to overthrow Hōjō Yoshitoki, the imperial court commissioned the performance of esoteric rites for the purpose of chastising the country's enemies, killing them, and sending their spirits to the Pure Land of Mystic Glorification, where Mahāvairocana Tathāgata resides. Tendai chief priest Bishop Jien, an elder of the Mantra school, the abbot of Ninnaji temple, the abbot of Onjōji temple, and the abbots of the seven and 15 great temples in Nara, whose wisdom and observance of the precepts shone like the sun and moon, all prayed with blood, sweat, and tears from the 19th day of the fifth month until the 14th day of the sixth month using 15 fire altars for the secret Dharma of the mantra teachings established by the Great Master Kōbō, founder of the Mantra school in Japan, and Great Master Jikaku and Great Master Chishō, who were the successors of Great Master Dengyō, the founder of the Japanese Tendai school. Finally, the Omuro, the abbot of Ninnaji who was an imperial prince, performed in the main hall of the imperial palace a great Dharma rite beginning on the eighth day of the sixth month, a prayer that has never been repeated as many as three times. Then, on the 14th day of that month, the Kamakura army broke through the defense line in spite of everything. Tens of millions of people who depended upon these esoteric rites were either dead or wished they were. The samurai even forced their way into the Omuro's palace and captured and beheaded Seitaka, the prince's beloved attendant. The Omuro could not bear the tragedy and died in anguish, as did Seitaka's mother. It was all so pitiful. Even though Hōjō Yoshitoki had not been aware of these ceremonies nor did he resort to any prayers himself, it was as though the curses had recoiled upon their originators, as it says in chapter 25 of the *Lotus Sutra*." Tears collected in Dōzen-bō's eyes as he related the last part of his tale and he wiped them away with his sleeve.

"Renchō, these things are beyond us. Who can say why the gods and buddhas did not listen to the pleas of the emperors? Yes, perhaps it is because it is the Latter Age. Perhaps the imperial court angered them? Perhaps the monks were lacking in virtue? Or perhaps they found Minamoto no Yoritomo and the Hōjō clan more virtuous and worthier to rule the country?" He shrugged hopelessly. "We can only do our best to practice the teachings and have faith in the Three Treasures."

"That's just it," Renchō responded. "I wish to do my best, but I need to know what is the best teaching and practice to follow. If it is chanting *nembutsu*, then I will do it wholeheartedly. If it is to practice the rites of the mantra teachings, then I will do that. But how can I be sure which teaching to follow?"

"Very well, Renchō. I see that you are determined. In this case you had better perform a special prayer to Space Repository Bodhisattva. I know you have been praying to him for wisdom all these years, but I can teach you a particularly powerful practice that may help you. It will not be easy, however. It is extremely rigorous. There will be little to no time for sleep, food will be minimal, and you will have to concentrate your mind as never before. Are you sure you wish to do this?"

Renchō bowed deeply, excited and grateful. "Yes, Master Dōzen-bō. Please teach me this practice. I will not fail."

"I will teach it to you then. May you succeed and gain the wisdom you seek to find the true heart of the Buddha's teachings."

The practice Renchō was initiated into by Dōzen-bō had been brought to Japan over 500 years ago and had been practiced by the Great Master Kōbō. It was called the *Gumonji-hō*, which meant the "Method for Seeking, Hearing, and Retaining." Its successful performance would enable the practitioner to recall and understand anything they had seen or heard. Renchō hoped that it would give him the ability to resolve his doubts and discern which of the Buddha's teachings was really supreme and to be followed by an ordinary person such as himself in the Latter Age. For this practice he had to isolate himself in a ten-foot square hut on the peak of Mt. Kiyosumi. Large pines overshadowed it on the north side, but the space around it was clear on the other three sides so that the stars would be visible. He entered the hut hours before dawn and returned hours after sunset, coming and going up a steep and narrow path under the pines, bearing a torch to light his way and a bucket of well water for offerings and purifications. Before entering the hut he would perform ritual ablutions to wash his hands and face while visualizing himself purified of all defilements. The ablutions were accompanied by the mantra particular to Space Repository Bodhisattva: *"Nō bō akyashakyarabaya on ari kyamari bori sowaka!"* As far as it could be translated it meant, "In the name of Space Repository, Om! Flower garlanded lotus crowned one, may my wish be accomplished!" He entered the hall wearing a white mask over his lower face. On the east side of the hut was an open window through which the starry skies could be viewed, especially the morning star. Below that was a painting covered in a white cloth. Beneath the painting there was a small altar, in front of which stood a table with bowls for the offerings and a small oil lamp. Renchō lit the lamp, prostrated himself once and then sat in a half-lotus posture with one foot resting on the opposite thigh. With a specially consecrated stick he raised the cloth covering the painting of Space Repository Bodhisattva. The golden bodhisattva sat upon a lotus throne within a white moon disk. On his head was a crown bearing the images of the five conquerors who were the five buddhas of the zenith and four directions and representative of the five great types of wisdom: Mahāvairocana Tathāgata for the zenith and the wisdom of pure awareness, Akṣobhya Tathāgata for the east and the mirror-like wisdom that reflects reality just as it is, Amitābha Tathāgata for the west and the wisdom of equality that transcends the duality of self and other, Ratnasambhava Tathāgata for the south and the distinguishing wisdom that discerns the best skillful means to use in every situation for the liberation of all beings, and Amoghasiddhi Tathāgata for the north and the all-performing wisdom whose actions embody the life of one who has realized nirvana. In Space Repository Bodhisattva's left hand he held the stem of a pink lotus flower on which rested a blue wish-fulfilling gem radiating yellow flames. His right hand was held out on his lap, palm forward and fingers pointing down and slightly bent in the mudra of bestowing wishes.

When the painting was revealed, Renchō removed his mask. He performed the esoteric methods of protection with a series of mudras and mantras, beginning with the purification of his thoughts, words, and deeds, and ending by pressing the Armor Mudra to the five concentration points of the belly, heart, mouth, left shoulder, right shoulder, and forehead while reciting "Om! *Vajra* fire, protect me, Svaha!" As he did this he envisioned himself becoming one with Space Repository Bodhisattva and all the buddhas. He melded into their warm embrace and felt all his defilements vanish away like melting snow.

Renchō then recited the mantra to empower the water in a small bowl and sprinkled it on the offerings, the altar, and the floor. He took a pinch of powdered incense from a small box and rubbed it into his hands. He touched another pinch of incense to his lips and another to his chest, chanting yet another mantra. Quickly, precisely, Renchō ritually empowered the offerings and the altar, invoked the protection of the buddhas, bodhisattvas, gods, and other guardian spirits, performed further purification of thoughts, words, and deeds, paid homage to all the buddhas, bodhisattvas, and gods of the esoteric mandalas. As he did all of this he envisioned all of these beings before him. He called upon them to join him in his vows, rid the world of evil, produce all good, grant protections, blessings, health, peace and prosperity for all. Finally he pronounced the five vows of the bodhisattvas used in esoteric Buddhist practice: "All sentient beings, I vow to save. All wisdom and blessings I vow to practice. All Dharma paths I vow to follow. All Tathāgatas I vow to serve. The highest awakening, I vow to fulfill. Help me, children of the Buddha, to accomplish these vows."

On the first day of the practice, Renchō made a particular vow to discover which of the ten schools taught as the Buddha truly intended: "I will not favor any particular school; I will adopt whichever school provides evidence of being the true teaching of the Buddha and is reasonable. I will be guided solely by the sutras, not by the commentators in India, or the translators and great masters in China. I will not be afraid, regarding the doctrines of Buddhism, of being punished by a king; not to mention persecutions by the people below him. I will not follow instructions against the Buddha's teachings even if they were given by my parents, teacher, or elder brother, and I will speak up honestly, as was taught in the sutras, regardless of whether or not people believe me."

When the preliminary purifications, invocations, and vows were completed, Renchō performed another complex series of mudras accompanied by mantras while envisioning an impenetrable wall of *vajra* flames forming a perimeter around himself, the altar, and the image of Space Repository Bodhisattva. With *vajra* fire crackling around him he used mudra and mantra to send chariots forth to carry Space Repository Bodhisattva back as a guest to the sublime place of practice within the protected sphere inside the *vajra* flames. In his mind's eye, Renchō saw Space Repository Bodhisattva physically before him. He welcomed his guest by ringing a *vajra*-handled bell and visualized the washing of the guest's feet. From the bowls on the table before him he offered water, incense, leaves to represent flower garlands, uncooked rice, and a final mudra to represent the offering of fire and light. This would be followed by further homage and symbolic offerings using mudra and mantra to all the buddhas, bodhisattvas, and gods throughout the universe.

Then came the core practice of the ritual. Renchō contemplated his essential unity with Space Repository Bodhisattva as he recited the bodhisattva's mantra. "*Nō bō akyashakyarabaya on ari kyamari bori sowaka!*" He counted off each recitation with a *juzu* of 54 oak beads held in his left hand. His right hand formed the mudra of the bodhisattva that he held in front of his heart. The goal was to recite the mantra one million and 80,000 times over the next several weeks. In his mind's eye he saw a moon disk imprinted with the syllables of the mantra in Siddham (an Indian script for Sanskrit mantras) within the breast of the bodhisattva who sat before him. The golden characters of the mantra flowed from the bodhisattva's mouth and into the crown of Renchō's head, coursed throughout his body and then poured out of his own mouth as he recited it as swiftly as he

72

could without slurring the syllables. The mantra reentered the bodhisattva through his feet and returned to his breast completing the circuit. Over the course of hours the mantra flowed on as Renchō and Space Repository Bodhisattva mutually empowered one another. During this time, the moon disk and its Siddham script expanded until it engulfed the whole universe. As each session drew to a close, the moon disk contracted back to its original size, enclosed within the breast of Space Repository Bodhisattva. The session ended with another complex series of offerings, homages, dedications of merit, and vows, and also the dismissal of Space Repository Bodhisattva and all the other buddhas, bodhisattvas, and gods who were envisioned as present.

Renchō performed these sessions several times a day, each lasting for at least two hours. He stopped only to eat one meal of rice gruel in the morning and for two hours of sleep each night. He kept this routine up for three weeks during the cool autumn months. Despite hunger, drowsiness, and eventually a cold and persistent cough he continued on, refusing to be daunted by bodily weakness. According to the sutras, bodhisattvas of the past had used their flesh for paper, their blood for ink, and shards of their own bones for writing when no other materials were available to record the teachings. In the 23rd chapter of the *Lotus Sutra*, the Buddha told the story of how Medicine King Bodhisattva in a previous life had set himself alight as a living stick of incense for 1200 years and illumined a number of worlds 8,000 million times the grains of sand in the Ganges River as an offering to all the buddhas of those worlds. Such acts of self-sacrifice were beyond human understanding. No one Renchō knew had ever actually seen such a thing, but the point was that bodhisattvas were constantly offering their lives for the sake of the Dharma and the welfare of all beings. How could he do any less?

On the 21st day of practicing the *Gumonji-hō*, as Renchō made his way at dawn down the narrow path from the peak to the main hall of Seichōji after the day's first practice session, he was overcome by a fit of coughing. As he was about to pass by a grove of bamboo near the main hall, he stumbled and sank to his knees in front of it. His lungs felt as if on fire, but however hard he tried, he couldn't stop coughing and wretching. The stalks of bamboo and the ground before him were spattered with pinkish phlegm. The ground lurched beneath him and he rolled over onto his back. After some time, the coughing finally subsided. He stared up at the waxing moon and Venus. Everything was so sharp and clear! He heard the crunching of sandals on gravel. Looking up, he saw that they belonged to an old monk that he had never seen before. He thought he knew all the monks at Seichōji and the nearby lodging temples. The elder bent over and smiled down at him as though pleased. He held out a large gem, glittering like the morning star, in his right hand. He kneeled, then reached out and tucked the gem into the right sleeve of Renchō's black robe. Then the old monk stood up and walked away. Renchō could hear someone shouting nearby. It sounded like Gijō-bō. He tried to hold his head up to see where the monk had gone. He was too weak. His head fell back as he sank into a warm darkness.

The Pure Land of Utmost Bliss

In time Renchō recovered from the illness brought on by his practice of the *Gumonji-hō*. Dōzen-bō had been anxious, and had seen that he was given the best care. Gijō-bo and Jōken-bō watched over him day and night, as did other monks whose names he could not recall. They chanted *dhāraṇīs*, burned paper amulets and had Renchō drink the ashes in water. They gave him moxibustion treatments - the burning of dried mugwort cones at certain important acupuncture points. This was intended to stimulate the circulation of blood and spiritual power, and to restore his body's balance of yin and yang energy. Dōzen-bō himself checked in on Renchō as often as he could. He could often be found sitting by his side, thumbing his *juzu* murmuring the *nembutsu*, keeping watch over his young, overzealous disciple. "You took it too far," he would say to Renchō. "You did too many hours in a day. You tried to do in a quarter of the time what others would have spent months practicing. You recklessly endangered your health. I should have said something to you earlier. I blame myself for not telling you to pace yourself. Remember, Śākyamuni Buddha taught us the middle way; to forego both luxury and painful austerities. Furthermore, he taught us to hope for rebirth in the Pure Land through *nembutsu*. We do not have to kill ourselves trying to attain awakening in this life when we have been assured of rebirth and attaining buddhahood in the next by simply calling Amitābha Buddha to mind while chanting his name."

Renchō considered this. After taking up the middle way the Buddha *had* abandoned the practice of painful austerities. Pain and hardship, he had taught, did not need to be sought out. They came of themselves. Between the time he set out from the Bodhi Tree to teach the Dharma to his final nirvana under the twin śāla trees, the Buddha had experienced several ordeals. There were occasions when he was offered spoiled food by servants and mocked for it by the priestly caste. There were times when the only available food was horse fodder. There was a time when a local ruler forbade his subjects from providing offerings or listening to the Buddha's teachings. There were times when the Buddha and his monks had to endure bitterly cold winter winds blowing down from the Himalayas, clad only in their patchwork robes. Those who felt hatred and jealousy towards the Buddha convinced a woman named Sundarī to slander him by claiming to be his paramour. For similar reasons a woman named Ciñchā later maligned the Buddha by tying a tub to her belly and claiming he had impregnated her. Towards the end of his life, King Virūdhaka, who bore a grudge against the Śākya clan, massacred many members of his family. The Buddha faced all of these hardships and tragedies with equanimity.

There were many, even among the monks and nuns, who found that they were not yet able to maintain their own equanimity and peace of mind when life proved unstable, callous, and cruel. For those followers who were still householders, immersed in worldly desires, pressures, expectations, and ambitions, it was practically impossible to cultivate a stable and serene mind with which to view conditioned phenomena and overcome attachment and aversion. They were unable to obtain the light of the Buddha's wisdom to penetrate the darkness of old age, sickness, and death. Also, there were other, more unforeseeable, dangers such as the indifferent fury of the elements and the calculated cruelty of the ruthless and ambitious princes, kings, and warlords who struggled for supremacy over one another.

Queen Vaidehī of the city of Rājagriha, the capital of the kingdom of Magadha, was one of those who despaired of the world. She and her husband, King Bimbisāra, were dedicated followers and supporters of the Buddha. She had believed her life was blessed, the result of past good karma, and that her support of the Buddha would guarantee further protection and good fortune in the years ahead. This belief was shattered by the jealous scheming of the Buddha's cousin, Devadatta, and the ruthless ambition of her own son, Prince Ajātaśatru.

Devadatta had joined the Sangha along with several other Śākya nobles, at the time when the Buddha had first returned to Kapilavastu. For a long time, Devadatta was a respected member of the Sangha. Unfortunately, the jealousy and envy he felt prevented him from attaining any genuine insight or liberation, and his arrogance only increased as he cultivated meditation and austere living. For a time Devadatta split the Sangha by convincing several monks to practice more stringent forms of asceticism under his guidance, forms that the Buddha had refused to make mandatory or had rejected outright. This period ended when the schismatic monks heard the teaching of the True Dharma from Śāriputra and Maudgalyāyana and returned to the Sangha of the Buddha. After that, Devadatta turned to the patronage of Prince Ajātaśatru. The Buddha then publicly denounced Devadatta. He made it clear that Devadatta's actions were his own, and not condoned by the Buddha or the Sangha. Soon after that, Devadatta prompted Prince Ajātaśatru to overthrow King Bimbisāra. The prince imprisoned his father in the palace dungeons, and ordered his death, by starvation.

After the palace coup, Devadatta, with the help of the newly crowned Ajātaśatru, tried to have the Buddha killed so that he could take over the Sangha. First he sent assassins, but in the actual presence of the Buddha they found they could not lift their weapons against him; instead they ended up taking refuge in the Three Treasures. Devadatta then attempted to kill the Buddha himself by rolling a boulder down upon him. On that occasion the boulder split in half as it rolled down the hill and only a shard flew off and injured the Buddha's foot, causing him to be bedridden for a time. When the Buddha had recuperated and began once again to beg his morning alms, Devadatta made another attempt on his life by convincing King Ajātaśatru to release a drunken elephant upon the street the Buddha was walking down in the hopes that it would trample him. The Buddha, however, tamed the elephant with his calm presence. These incidents occurred when the Buddha was 72 years old and had been teaching the Dharma for 42 years.

Back in the palace, Bimbisāra's wife, Vaidehī, had found a way to keep her husband alive. She smuggled food and drink to him by mixing honey with flour and roasted barley and smearing it on her body and by filling hollow ornaments that she was wearing with juice before visiting him in the dungeon. Eventually, the usurper Ajātaśatru caught on to what was happening and, enraged, drew his sword with the intention of killing her. The physician Jīvaka, a lay follower of the Buddha, and another minister dissuaded him from such a heinous act. They told him that no on would follow a man so dishonorable that he would murder both his father and his mother. Ajātaśatru relented but he confined Vaidehī in a private palace so that she could no longer smuggle food into the dungeon to keep Bimbisāra alive.

In hope of receiving consolation, Vaidehī desperately called out to the Buddha, who was staying outside the city of Rājagriha on Eagle Peak. In response to her plea, the Buddha himself came to visit her. In anguish Vaidehī tore away her necklace and flung herself down upon the floor weeping miserably. She cried out, "O World Honored One, what bad karma did I create in former lives that I have given birth to such an evil son? I wonder what karmic relations could have made you a relative of Devadatta? I beseech you to reveal to me a land of no sorrow and no affliction where I can be reborn. I do not wish to live in this defiled and evil world where there are hells, realms of hungry ghosts, animals, and many vile beings. I wish that in the future I shall not hear evil words or see wicked people. I now kneel down to repent and beg you to take pity on me. I entreat you, O sun-like Buddha, to teach me how to visualize a land of pure karmic perfection."

For Vaidehī and other suffering people whose lives had become so broken, the Buddha provided a skillful means whereby they could see that their suffering and pain was itself impermanent and ephemeral.

He taught them that they were each encompassed by an infinite light and life that could overcome all evils, even those within their own hearts and minds. He gave them a vision of hope by describing a land free of suffering where it would be easy to attain buddhahood. He told them they could be reborn into that Pure Land of Utmost Bliss merely by being mindful of the name of its presiding buddha: Amitābha, the Buddha of Infinite Light and Life. For prior to attaining buddhahood, Amitābha Buddha had made 48 vows that had indeed come to fulfillment and the 18th of these vows stated: "If, when I attain buddhahood, sentient beings in the lands of the ten directions who sincerely and joyfully entrust themselves to me, desire to be born in my land, and think of me even ten times, should not be born there, may I not attain perfect complete awakening. Excluded, however, are those who commit the five grave offenses and slander the True Dharma." Later Buddhists regarded this 18th vow as the most important of all 48 vows. It came to be known as the Original Vow.

In Amitābha Buddha's Pure Land of Utmost Bliss there was no pain, only pleasure of the purest kind. Men and gods dwelled there among gardens filled with ponds, pavilions, and decorative nets adorned with precious gold, silver, beryl, crystal, sapphire, rose pearls, and carnelian. The ponds were filled with fragrant lotuses radiating red, white, blue, and yellow lights. The ground itself was gold and there were no mountains, and so no valleys, nor any rivers to obstruct travel. Six times a day māndārava flowers rained down from above. These were gathered by the people of that land and offered to the buddhas of the ten directions. The air was filled with the melodious singing of rare and beautiful birds, which never ceased. These birds were not born as animals from the effect of their past misdeeds, but were manifested by Amitābha Buddha so that their songs could proclaim the Dharma and cause the people to be mindful of the Three Treasures. Even the soft breezes wafting through the trees and jeweled nets produced a heavenly music to accompany the singing of the birds. In that land no one was ever reborn as a hell-dweller, a hungry ghost, or an animal. Nor was anyone so unfortunate as to be born in a female form, for a woman's freedom was always restricted. She had to obey her father in youth, her husband in marriage, and her sons in old age. Furthermore, it was said, a woman could not become a powerful deity like Brahmā, Indra, or Māra, or an emperor like the wheel-turning kings who were able to peacefully unite the world. Most importantly, a woman could not attain buddhahood. This is what was taught in both Buddhist and non-Buddhist teachings. The men and gods of the Pure Land of Utmost Bliss were not born from the womb; they simply appeared upon lotus pedestals with beautiful and unblemished golden bodies. They were free of all hindrances, and able to study and practice the Dharma with ease. In that land they were able to attain the stage of non-retrogression and quickly attain buddhahood.

Bimbisāra eventually died in the dungeons and Vaidehī died shortly afterwards. According to the *Sutra of Meditation on the Buddha of Infinite Life*, when she died it was without any doubt that she would be reborn in the Pure Land of Utmost Bliss. As for King Ajātaśatru, he began to realize the enormity of what he had done. This realization made him so ill that he feared for his life. His physician Jīvaka convinced him to talk to the Buddha. Upon hearing Śākyamuni Buddha's teachings on the law of causation he acknowledged his misdeeds and repented. From that time on he disavowed Devadatta and instead took refuge in the Three Treasures and became a supporter of the Buddha. Devadatta, however, only became more envious and destructive. Learning he had been barred from the palace, he became furious, and in his anger he beat to death a nun named Utpalavarnā who happened to be walking out of the palace gates that day. This nun was an arhat, and by murdering her Devadatta had committed yet another of the five grave offenses, crimes so heinous that, after death, the one who commits them is inevitably drawn into the Hell of Incessant Suffering. He had previously committed two other such offenses, first when he caused a schism in the Sangha, and then when he caused the Buddha to be injured. The five grave offenses also included the killing of one's father and the killing of one's mother. Devadatta had not committed those acts himself, but he had influenced Ajātaśatru, who had starved his father to death and was only barely restrained from becoming his mother's murderer. Devadatta came to be known as the prime example of a type of person called *icchantika*, "incorrigible disbelievers" who refused to believe in the Buddha Dharma and rejected all moral authority. These were people who were shameless and were utterly lacking in integrity or empathy for their fellow beings. Such people were said to be forever incapable of attaining buddhahood, regardless of how many lifetimes they spent wandering the six paths of the cycle of birth and death. They were likely to be reborn in the three lower realms as hell-dwellers, hungry ghosts, or animals. Only under very rare circumstances might they accrue enough worldly virtue to be reborn as an *asura*, human, or god, but their egoism prevented them from breaking free of the shackles of samsara.

Renchō wondered if perhaps there was a teaching that could save even the *icchantika*? And was it true that women could only attain buddhahood if they were first born as men in a pure land? And could the Buddha's disciples such as Śāriputra and Maudgalyāyana and the nun Utpalavarnā ever attain buddhahood if in becoming arhats they would never be reborn anywhere and so could not spend incalculable lifetimes as bodhisattvas cultivating wisdom and merit or even be reborn in a pure land themselves?

To resolve his doubts, Renchō resumed his studies soon after his recovery and undertook no further strenuous practices other than those that were part of the daily routine at Seichōji. His master gave him permission to begin reading and copying more esoteric writings, even those that were to be held in the strictest secrecy and not passed on to any who were not qualified. In this, Dōzen-bō showed his confidence in his young protégé. These texts, however, raised further questions for Renchō. They promised that one could attain buddhahood in one's very body, in one's present lifetime. All that was necessary was to awaken to the reality that one's true nature and the nature of the buddhas was no different. This could be realized through the practice of mantras. And yet, all the monks and nuns of Japan, not to mention the laity, entrusted themselves almost without exception to the vows of Amitābha Buddha and aspired to rebirth in the Pure Land of Utmost Bliss after death, assuming that it was unlikely if not impossible to attain buddhahood through one's own efforts in the present life. What was more, the Tendai school taught that Śākyamuni Buddha's highest teaching was expressed in the *Lotus Sutra*, so how did one come to realize the truth of that teaching? In their daily services the Tendai monks recited *dhāraṇīs* taken from various sutras, the *Heart Sutra* that affirmed the emptiness of all phenomena, and the *Amitābha Sutra* that described the wonders of the Pure Land of Utmost Bliss. They also recited several chapters from the *Lotus Sutra*: the second chapter wherein Śākyamuni Buddha taught the reality of all things in terms of ten suchnesses and spoke of the One Vehicle whereby all beings are led to the attainment of buddhahood; the 14th chapter on the peaceful practices of bodhisattvas; the 16th chapter wherein Śākyamuni Buddha revealed the incomprehensible duration of his life as a buddha; and the 25th chapter that spoke of the miraculous assistance and protection one could receive from World Voice Perceiver Bodhisattva, who was one of the attendants of Amitābha Buddha. That last chapter was especially revered, and there were many who chanted the name of that bodhisattva, though the practice was not as popular as the chanting of Amitābha Buddha's name. In all of this, what was the Buddha's true intention? What should be the real focus of study and practice?

Renchō thought about the gem he had been given. Of course he had found no physical gem in his sleeve. The old monk and the gem must have been a vision sent to him by Space Repository Bodhisattva. The bodhisattva appeared in that guise to give him, in the form of the wish-fulfilling gem, the wisdom to discern the truth. With the clarity he had received, Renchō took to heart the ancient Indian teaching that knowledge is arrived at by means of the testimony of a trusted authority (in this case the Buddha's words in the sutras), clear headed reasoning, and most importantly the evidence of actual events. These "three proofs" would enable him to distinguish the true teachings from the false ones and to discover which sutra is superior and which is subordinate. Renchō also realized that the Buddha had left clear instructions in the *Nirvana Sutra*, his final teaching, concerning what one can rely upon in one's search for the truth. The "four reliances" were that practitioners should rely on the Dharma as taught by the Buddha and not the opinions of ordinary people, rely on the inner meaning of the Dharma and not the words used to express it, rely on the wisdom of the Buddha and not on discursive knowledge, and rely on the sutra that is definitive and not those sutras whose meaning is indeterminate. Armed with the three proofs and four reliances, Renchō renewed his determination to study the Buddhist canon in breadth and depth to find out for himself what the true teaching was. To do that, he would have to leave Master Dōzen-bō and Seichōji.

The Exclusive Nembutsu

In the spring of the first year of the En'ō era (1239), Renchō made the journey to Kamakura in order to further his study of the Pure Land and Zen movements that had taken root there. He hoped to hear, from the exponents of those schools, why they believed that their practices were the best or perhaps even the only way to attain buddhahood. Bordered by mountains on three sides, and by Sagami Bay on another, Kamakura was a natural fortress. The only way into the city was either by sea or though one of a small handful of easily blocked passes. Tens of thousands of people lived there at that time, perhaps as many as 100,000. Renchō, who had grown up in a small fishing village and a mountain monastery thought that it must be one of the largest cities in the world. Here he found merchants, artisans, craftsmen, and scholars all plying their various trades along the twisting avenues and pine-clad hills. Despite their apparent freedom, the watchful eyes of the samurai were never far away. There were also visiting nobles from Kyōto in their brocade robes and silk caps carried along in lacquered palanquins by sweaty bearers dressed only in loincloths. Bands of armed retainers made way for them, dispersing the commoners to allow the procession to continue its progress along the roads of the town. Down along the beach samurai raced up and down on horseback firing their longbows at straw targets, honing their skills at mounted archery to be ready for the next conflict between rival samurai clans and political factions. At the eastern end of the beach was a small artificial island built of stone that served as Kamakura's harbor. Here hundreds of porters toiled ceaselessly, their backs laden down like those of mules or oxen with the heavy weight of goods traveling to and from ships soon to depart and those just arrived. Those who could not even work such menial jobs wandered through the city begging for alms or starved to death in the streets or in tiny shacks built in the narrow valleys of the wooded hills around the main city. At the western end of the beach were those even worse off than the beggars, condemned criminals arrested for such heinous crimes as murder, arson, or treason. These convicts were sealed up behind wooden bars in caves where they could only stare in resignation at their future place of execution. This point on the coast was known as Tatsunokuchi, the "Dragon's Mouth." There they would be decapitated, their heads displayed on pikes outside the prison as a lesson to others. Truly it seemed as though all the hells and heavens and everything in between that Renchō had read about in the Buddhist sutras and commentaries could be found elbow to elbow in Kamakura, the seat of power of the Hōjō regents, the true rulers of Japan.

As a Buddhist monk, Renchō was able to gain access to the sutra repository at the Tsurugaoka Shrine of Hachiman. This particular shrine was also a temple complex of the Tendai school. It was located at the northern end of "Young Prince Avenue," the sacred road that ran through the heart of the city, from the beach to the shrine itself. Spanning 100' in width, the avenue was lined with pine trees and flanked on both sides by deep canals. One entered the avenue at its southern terminus by passing beneath the Great Beach Torii, a large vermillion ceremonial gateway composed of two enormous pillars crossed by a curved lintel. Beyond this marker, the sands of the shore receded, and the avenue itself began. Continuing along it one passed by bridge over a river that branched out from the sea. At this point, those who were traveling on horseback had to dismount and proceed on foot towards the shrine, out of deference to the Great Bodhisattva Hachiman. A second torii gate would be passed at the midpoint between the beach and the shrine. A third torii gate marked the entrance to the main shrine complex itself. Common traffic was not permitted upon Young Prince Avenue, as it was used only for sacred processions and the visits of important dignitaries. To its east were the mansions of the Hōjō regents, and their chief vassals. Several of the most important government buildings also dotted this eastern side of the avenue. Across the great street, to the west, were assembled the more humble structures which served as the homes of persons of lesser standing. Only the mansions of the Hōjō rulers were allowed to have entrances facing the avenue. The Tsurugaoka Shrine of Hachiman, the tutelary deity of the shogunate, and the sacred avenue leading to it were clearly the centerpiece of Kamakura, and all roads led to one or the other.

Renchō quickly discovered that the people of Kamakura were more than usually concerned about the life to come. The *nembutsu* was chanted by nearly all he passed in his meanderings around the great city, regardless of their station. The chant could be heard issuing forth from the lips of noble, samurai, merchant, porter, prostitute, and beggar alike. Pure Land piety seemed to hang in the very air of the streets, becoming one with the clouds of incense spilling out from the various temples and practice halls dedicated to Amitābha Buddha. At the Pure Land temple called Kōtoku-in, a giant wooden statue of Amitābha Buddha seated in meditation was busily being carved and assembled inside a vast hall. Upon completion it was said that it would be well over 40 feet tall. Work on this statue had begun the year before Renchō's arrival and would continue for several more years. At Kōtoku-in, monks taught the practice of the exclusive *nembutsu*. These were the teachings that Renchō was eager to hear. All of his life Renchō had practiced *nembutsu* and he wished to gain a deeper understanding of how it could enable him to attain buddhahood and resolve the great matter of birth and death.

One day, a monk who was a preacher of the Pure Land way said to Renchō, "Your diligence in reciting the *Lotus Sutra* and practicing the mantra teachings is indeed admirable. I too used to do these practices, but unfortunately I seemed to have no good roots from past lives and I was unable to get any benefit from them. Then I came across a treatise entitled *A Collection of Passages on the Nembutsu Chosen in the Original Vow* written by the sage Hōnen about 40 years ago in which he advocated only the practice of the *nembutsu* for ignorant people like myself in this Latter Age. After reading his words I realized that the Tendai practices based on the *Lotus Sutra* and the esoteric sutras are like a gateway to awakening for the holy but they are too profound to be suitable for these times and for those like us whose spiritual capacities have not yet developed. I learned that all these many difficult practices should be cast aside in favor of the Pure Land gate of the easy and correct practice of *nembutsu* preached in the three Pure Land sutras: the *Buddha of Infinite Life Sutra* that tells us of Amitābha Buddha's Original Vow, the *Meditation on the Buddha of Infinite Life Sutra* that contains Śākyamuni Buddha's teachings to Queen Vaidehī, and the *Amitābha Sutra* that describes the Pure Land of Utmost Bliss. Those who mire us in practicing sutras that can no longer help are like bandits trying to tempt us to leave the safe path to rebirth in the Pure Land. Śākyamuni Buddha states in the *Buddha of Infinite Life Sutra*, 'In the future, the Buddhist scriptures and teachings will perish. But out of pity and compassion, I will especially preserve this sutra and maintain it in the world for a 100 years or more. Those beings who encounter it will attain deliverance in accord with their aspirations.' According to this passage, it is clear that in this Latter Age, when the holy way teachings taught by Śākyamuni Buddha in the other sutras are no longer able to help us, the teaching of the *nembutsu* alone will remain responsive to our prayers. Truly, the sage Hōnen was an emanation in this world of Great Power Obtainer Bodhisattva, Amitābha Buddha's attendant, sent to teach people like ourselves in this Latter Age to let go of our own futile self-powered efforts to attain buddhahood and to take hold of the Other-power of Amitābha Buddha so that we can be assured of rebirth in the Pure Land of Utmost Bliss."

"I have never heard of such a thing before!" exclaimed Renchō in surprise. "Certainly many sutras recommend rebirth in Amitābha Buddha's Pure Land of the West because it is relatively close to this Sahā world and accessible even to the most ignorant. Also, since the sun rises in the east and sets in the west, it is most natural to think of the west as the abode of the dead. Even the great patriarchs of the Tiantai school in China, the Great Master Tiantai and the Great Master Miaole, preached this teaching on occasion. In India, the patriarchs Nāgārjuna and Vasubandhu also believed in such rebirth.

Never yet, though, have I heard that we should abandon all other teachings and practices, even the *Lotus Sutra* and the mantra practices, and only chant *nembutsu*. Surely Hōnen's teachings could not be in accord with the True Dharma."

"Ah but this is not a new doctrine preached only by the sage Hōnen. This is the same doctrine preached in China by the three masters of Pure Land Buddhism: Tanluan, Daochuo and Shandao. Again, it was not an arbitrary idea of these Chinese masters; it stemmed from the previous teachings of the Indian patriarchs Nāgārjuna and Vasubandhu. It is not that we are denigrating sutras such as the *Lotus Sutra*, which were preached primarily for wise bodhisattvas and only secondarily for us, the ignorant. We are just saying that while it is true that those sutras preach profound doctrines to eliminate defilements and attain awakening, if we, the ignorant in the Latter Age, attempt to practice them, none of us will have the capacity to understand or practice the doctrines they teach. Besides, many lay people are illiterate, so how could they be expected to even know of the teachings let alone understand them? Do you have no compassion for them? Under the circumstances, the Pure Land school maintains that if only we, the ignorant, chant the six-character *nembutsu* of Amitābha Buddha, the Buddha will dispatch bodhisattvas to this Sahā world to protect us, the practitioners, surrounding us thick and fast as the shadow follows the body. Therefore, so long as we chant the *nembutsu*, we will be free of disasters and gain ease and happiness before we die. At the last moment of life Amitābha Buddha will never fail to welcome us, taking us upon the lotus pedestal of World Voice Perceiver Bodhisattva promptly to the Pure Land, where lotus flowers bloom according to our karma. There we can listen to the *Lotus Sutra* and become awakened to the truth of all phenomena. Why should we bother with paths that are difficult to practice in this impure world? What good could come of it? Instead, we should concentrate on calling the name of Amitābha Buddha, putting aside everything else."

Renchō, not quite convinced but eager to learn more, devoted himself for a time to the *nembutsu* and studied Hōnen's *A Collection of Passages on the Nembutsu Chosen in the Original Vow*. In that work he found citations from all the past teachers of Pure Land Buddhism and Hōnen's understanding of what they meant for the benighted people of the Latter Age. Again and again he considered a few key passages that seemed to sum up the teaching of the Pure Land school according to Hōnen:

"Now the reason why Daochuo, in his *Collection of Passages on the Land of Peace and Bliss* set up the distinction between the two gates of the holy way and the Pure Land way was to teach people to reject the gate of the holy way in favor of entering the gate of the Pure Land. There are two reasons for this preference: one is that the passing away of the Buddha has now receded far into the distant past, and the other is that the ultimate principle is profound while human understanding is shallow."

...

"First the gate of the holy way is divided into two parts: one is the Mahayana and the other is the Hinayana. The Mahayana is further divided into exoteric and esoteric, as well as the provisional and the true teachings. In the *Collection of Passages on the Land of Peace and Bliss* only the exoteric and provisional teachings of the Mahayana are treated. Hence the holy way teachings refer to the circuitous or gradual forms of practice, which require many *kalpas* to attain buddhahood. From this we can infer that the holy way teachings also include the esoteric and the true teachings. It follows then that the teachings of all eight contemporary schools – the Mantra, Zen, Tiantai, Flower Garland, Three Treatises, Dharma Characteristics, Ten Stage Discourse, and Summary of the Mahayana should all be included in the holy way, which should be discarded."

...

"To begin with Meditation Master Tanluan, we see that he stated in his *Commentary on the Treatise on Rebirth in the Pure Land*: 'Let us reverently reflect on what Bodhisattva Nāgārjuna said in his *Treatise*

Explaining the Ten Stages. He declared that there are two ways by which the bodhisattva may seek the stage of non-retrogression: one is the way of difficult practice and the other is the way of easy practice.' In this context, the way of difficult practice is the gate of the holy way, and the way of easy practice is the gate of the Pure Land."

...

"He who would learn of the Pure Land school should first of all understand the import of the above passages. Even though a man may have previously studied the gate of the holy way, if he should feel an inclination toward the gate of the Pure Land, he should set aside the holy way and take refuge in the Pure Land."

...

"Shandao says in the fourth book of his *Commentary on the Meditation Sutra*: 'As to establishing faith in practice, we should first note that practice is of two kinds: right and miscellaneous. The right consists in performing only the kinds of disciplines derived from the sutras on rebirth in the Pure Land, hence the name 'right practices.'

"Further within these right practices there are two types. The first is to concentrate single-mindedly and wholeheartedly on the name of Amitābha Buddha, whether walking or standing still, whether seated or lying down, without considering whether the time involved is long or short and without ceasing even for an instant. This is called the 'rightly established act.' It is so called because such a practice agrees with the intent of Amitābha Buddha's vow. Other practices, such as doing reverence to Amitābha Buddha and chanting the Pure Land sutras, are called the auxiliary acts. Besides these two – the rightly established and the auxiliary practices – all other good practices are collectively called miscellaneous practices.'"

...

"I believe that anyone who reads these words ought to cast aside the miscellaneous and take up the exclusive practice. Why should anyone cast aside the exclusive and right practice, by which a 100 out of a 100 attain rebirth, and stubbornly cling to the miscellaneous practices, by which not even one out of a 1,000 attain rebirth? Practitioners ought seriously to ponder this."

...

"One ought to clearly understand that Śākyamuni Buddha first opened the gate to the two ways of practicing meditation with a concentrated mind and performing meritorious deeds with a scattered mind in response to the wishes of the people. He later closed this gate in accordance with his own wish. The only gate that, once opened, will remain unclosed forever is that of *nembutsu*. Practitioners should know this is the intent of Amitābha's Original Vow and of Śākyamuni's act of entrusting it to Ānanda."

...

"In the *Meditation on the Buddha of Infinite Life Sutra* it is said: 'If there are sentient beings who desire rebirth in the Pure Land they must awaken in themselves the three kinds of mind. Then they will be reborn. What are the three minds? The first is the sincere mind; the second is the deep mind; the third is the mind that is determined to transfer all merits toward rebirth. If one possesses these three minds, one will unquestionably attain rebirth in the Pure Land.'"

Hōnen then cited a long passage from the *Commentary on the Meditation on the Buddha of Infinite Life Sutra* in which Shandao explained the three minds. He taught that the sincere mind is the truly authentic mind that does not "outwardly appear to be wise, good, and diligent while inwardly nourishing falsehood." He taught that the deep mind is the mind of deep faith with two aspects. "The first is firmly and deeply to believe that now in this present body one is an ordinary sinful being who has been for countless *kalpas* always sunk tumbling in the stream of samsara, unable to find the karmic conditions for escape. The second aspect is firmly and deeply to believe that Amitābha Buddha's 48 vows enfold sentient beings in their embrace and that those who without doubt or apprehension entrust themselves to the power of these vows will certainly attain rebirth in the Pure Land." He taught that the mind that is determined to transfer all merits towards rebirth is the mind that desires rebirth in

91

the Pure Land above all else and mentally dedicates all meritorious deeds performed by themselves or even others to that end. Shandao also provided a response for Pure Land practitioners to give to those who might criticize them. They should say that each person should practice that teaching with which they have a particular affinity and that in this way everyone will attain liberation from suffering. He then told a parable of a traveler who comes upon a river blocking his way. It was a singularly dangerous river in that flames roared in from the south and wild rapids poured in from the north, the fire and water crashing into one another directly before the traveler. Only a narrow white pathway stretched across to the other shore between the surging waves and roaring flames. The traveler was then alarmed to see a band of robbers and a horde of wild beasts coming after him. He knew he must cross, even though he was afraid of falling off the path into the flames or rapids. The traveler then hears a voice on his side of the river encouraging him to cross and another voice on the other shore calling him to come over. The traveler resolves to cross over and continues on even though the bandits tell him they mean no harm and that if he continues on he will surely fall into one or the other side of the river and thus drown or be burned to death. The traveler maintains his single-minded resolve and refuses to turn back. In the end he reaches the safety of the far shore. Shandao explains that the traveler is of course ourselves, the flames and rapids are our greed and anger, the white path is the pure mind that seeks rebirth in the Pure Land, the voice on the near bank represents the teachings of Śākyamuni Buddha while the voice on the other shore represents Amitābha Buddha expressing his intention to save all beings through his Original Vow, and the bandits and savage beasts represent defilements and wrong views that tempt one to leave the path.

...

In his concluding chapter Hōnen wrote: "When I consider the matter carefully, I wish to urge that anyone who desires to escape quickly from the cycle of birth and death should decide between the two types of the excellent Dharma, lay aside the holy way for awhile, and choose to enter through the gate of the Pure Land. If such a person should desire to enter through the gate of the Pure Land, he or she should decide between the right practices and the miscellaneous practices, abandoning for a while the various miscellaneous practices, and choose to take refuge in the right practices. If one desires to exercise oneself in the right practices, one should decide between the one right practice and the auxiliary right practices, setting aside the auxiliary practices and resolutely choosing the act of right assurance and follow it exclusively. This act of right assurance is uttering the name of Amitābha Buddha. Those who utter the name will unfailingly attain rebirth because it is based on Amitābha Buddha's Original Vow."

In the end, however, Renchō found that he could not give himself wholeheartedly to the *nembutsu*. He found Hōnen's teaching to be too extreme. And despite all their talk of being assured of rebirth in the Pure Land through the exclusive practice of *nembutsu*, Renchō did not see that the deaths of any of the *nembutsu* devotees that he knew of or heard about was necessarily any gentler or less anguished than that of those who did not follow Hōnen's teachings. Furthermore, why should one have to wait until after death to take up the study of the *Lotus Sutra* or the practice of the mantra teachings that claimed it was possible to attain buddhahood in one's very body, in this very lifetime? Didn't Śākyamuni Buddha say in the 16th chapter of the *Lotus Sutra*, "In reality I shall never pass away. I always live here and expound the Dharma"? Surely this meant that the Buddha was still present and still providing a way for the suffering people of the world to attain perfect and complete awakening in their present lives. Though he felt great sympathy for their aspirations, Renchō felt that Hōnen and his followers were greatly misled and were even grossly misrepresenting the Buddha's teachings. Therefore he left them to see if the Zen practitioners of Kamakura could provide a more direct way to resolve the great matter of birth and death and attain buddhahood.

The Way of Zen

At that time the Zen teachings that had recently been brought over from China had aroused the interest of the Hōjō regents and others in the samurai class as they provided them with a new form of Buddhism that seemed simple and direct and not involved with the court intrigues of the Tendai school and Mantra school establishment back in the imperial capital of Kyōto. It attracted those samurai who needed more than just an assurance of rebirth in a pure land in the afterlife. They required a more immediate way to attain liberation so they could serve their lords selflessly and maintain their resolve even in the face of certain death. One of the first of the Hōjō clan to become a patron of the Zen teachings was the Nun Shogun, who had received the precepts for nuns from a leading disciple of Eisai. Eisai had been a Tendai monk who had travelled to China and there received authorization as a teacher in the Rinzai lineage of Zen. As a memorial for her late husband the first shogun, the Nun Shogun established the temple Jufukuji in Kamakura and made Eisai its founding abbot in the second year of the Shōji era (1200). Officially it was a Tendai temple, but it was also a place where one could go to learn and practice Zen as it was currently being taught on the mainland in China and Korea. Kamakura had also become home to the elderly disciples and the younger grand-disciples of another Tendai monk named Dainichi Nōnin who had preceded Eisai in teaching Zen in Japan. Unlike Eisai, Dainichi had not gone to China or studied under a Zen master. He claimed to have self-awakened without a teacher, though he later dispatched two of his disciples to China with a letter expressing his realization to a Zen master in the fifth year of the Bunji era (1189). That master sent back a certificate authorizing Dainichi as a teacher. Also, unlike Eisai, Dainichi did not teach Zen as one among many practices of the Tendai school but rather established what he called the Bodhidharma school, named after the first patriarch of Zen in China. Until that time, Zen in Japan had been part of the Tendai school, as its founder Great Master

Dengyō had received transmission of the teachings of the Ox-head lineage, but now Zen, as taught by Dainichi and his successors, was being established as a separate school in its own right. Its popularity, at least in Kamakura, seemed to be ever on the rise.

Renchō, curious to find out for himself what Zen had to offer, sought out one of the successors of Dainichi Nōnin and asked, "Since I became a monk I have studied the sutras in an attempt to discover the Buddha's true teaching. Some regard the *Lotus Sutra* as the highest teaching of Śākyamuni Buddha but others say it is too profound and that we should entrust ourselves to the Other-power of Amitābha Buddha by chanting *nembutsu* as is taught in the three Pure Land sutras so we can be reborn in the Pure Land of Utmost Bliss and only there will we be able to awaken to the truth. What is the view of the Zen school?"

The Zen master shook his head and smiled. He said, "All the sutras are like a finger pointing to the moon, which is useless after seeing the moon itself. Those who attach themselves to mere words are like a hunter who once caught a rabbit when it collided with a stump and who then keeps watch over that same stump hoping that it will happen again. Instead of being caught up in words you should look directly into the mind. Such things as heaven, earth, the sun and moon all stem from the mind's delusions. The pure lands throughout the universe are just shadows of your greedy mind. Śākyamuni Buddha and his emanations manifested in the worlds throughout the universe are just variations of your awakened mind. Our Great Master Bodhidharma, without using words or other skillful means, transmitted this Dharma of Zen which is 'A special transmission outside the sutras, not founded upon words and letters; by pointing directly to mind it lets you see into the true nature and thereby attain buddhahood.' Even sutras such as the *Lotus Sutra*, to say nothing of the Pure Land sutras, do not reveal the true intent of the Buddha. If you want to truly awaken to the truth, do not cling to mere words and doctrines."

95

Renchō still had doubts however. "Do you really mean to say that I should disregard the sutras, even the *Lotus Sutra*?"

"Even the *Lotus Sutra* is a no more than a finger pointing to the moon while Zen is the moon itself. After grasping the moon there is no need for the finger to point it out. Zen is the heart and mind of the Buddha while the *Lotus Sutra* is merely his words. When the Buddha finished preaching all the sutras, including the *Lotus Sutra*, he held up a flower and Mahākāśyapa alone understood and smiled in response. The Buddha said, 'I have the treasury of the eye of the True Dharma, the wondrous mind of nirvana, the gate of the Wonderful Dharma that in its true form is formless. Without setting up scriptures, as a separate transmission apart from the teachings, I pass it on to Mahākāśyapa." As proof of this transmission of the Zen teaching the Buddha further entrusted Mahākāśyapa with his *kesa*, which was then handed down through the 28 patriarchs of Buddhism in India and to the first six patriarchs of Zen in China."

"Twenty-eight patriarchs? I had heard there were only 24 patriarchs in India. The last was Āryasimha. Why do you say there were 28?"

"Oh yes, there were actually four others. Bodhidharma was the last Indian patriarch, and it was he who came to China in order to bring the practice and teaching of Zen during the reign of Emperor Wu of the Liang dynasty."

"Well, that may or may not be, but still, I do not understand how you can presume to be a teacher of Buddhism if you reject the sutras. Apart from the sutras how else can you come to know and practice the teachings of the Buddha? If you reject the sutras you are rejecting Śākyamuni Buddha."

"It is not that we reject the sutras, for we too recite and study the *Descent into Lanka Sutra* brought to us by Bodhidharma, as well as the *Diamond Sutra*, the *Heart Sutra*, the *Heroic March Sutra*, the *Perfect Awakening Sutra*, and others. However, we know that all they can do is indicate the truth. Mere words and letters cannot hope to contain it. Trying to grasp the truth through words, thinking that the answer is in some verbal formulation, is as futile as a dog barking to drive away a thunderstorm or a monkey trying to grasp the reflection of the moon in a pond. Without the guidance of a Zen master the sutras will only mislead you. The words of the Buddha are like a wisteria vine hanging on the branch of a pine tree. What happens after the pine falls and the wisteria withers away? Śākyamuni Buddha entered nirvana more than two millennia ago and his teachings are disappearing and have long been misunderstood. What then shall people do? What we can do is look into the direct source of the Buddha's words, this very mind and body that are none other than the One Mind of the Buddha."

"So you are saying that the Buddha's teachings can no longer help us, that Śākyamuni Buddha is no longer present to assist us?"

The Zen master chuckled and gestured to a statue of Mañjuśrī Bodhisattva in the center of the meditation hall before which were offerings of water, rice, incense, and candlelight. "We practitioners of Zen also take refuge in the Three Treasures and present offerings to the buddhas and bodhisattvas, we recite the sutras, *dhāraṇīs*, and mantras, but we do not look to these things for awakening. We do not look to anything or anyone but our own direct realization of mind, for that alone is the way to meet the true Buddha. To come to know the true Buddha behind all the appearances of Buddha one must be able to walk on the head of Vairocana Buddha, the Dharma-body."

More than a little put off by such irreverence, Renchō nevertheless continued to question the Zen master. "Very well, let us say I wished to learn the Zen teaching. How should I begin?"

97

"Well, if you are a practitioner of the highest capacity then you would know that there is nothing to seek, nothing to cultivate, nothing to gain, and nothing to lose. You could abide in non-abiding and know the true nature of mind, which is no-mind. Most, however, are of lower capacities or they are beginners who have not even fully cultivated virtues such as generosity, morality, and patience, let alone the ability to sit still and allow, even if for a moment, the delusions of their own false thinking to subside. For these, such as many of the samurai who come here to take the precepts and become lay practitioners, we use the words of the sutras and provide straightforward instruction in how to sit upright and maintain awareness of the breath. For those of intermediate capacity who have progressed beyond such preliminary guidance or who have some innate ability, we advise them to contemplate one of the kōans or precedents of the past Zen masters. By contemplating these stories one can get beyond all words and false thinking and awaken to one's true nature. For instance, a monk once asked Zen Master Zhaozhou, 'What is the meaning of Bodhidharma's coming to China?' Zhaozhou responded, 'The oak tree in the garden.' There, you may sit with that one in fact and so begin your own practice."

Renchō was nonplussed. "That's ridiculous. You say the sutras cannot communicate the Buddha's teaching, but then you say I should contemplate 'the oak tree in the garden'? Why should I cling to those words instead of the words of Śākyamuni Buddha? I am sorry, but I do not think this can be right. I do thank you for your time." Renchō bowed and hastened away from the presence of the Zen master. The strange riddles and outrageous impieties of the followers of Dainichi Nōnin could not possibly be the right way to discover the true meaning of Śākyamuni Buddha's teachings, he thought to himself.

Studies in Kyōto

Renchō returned to Seichōji in the spring of the third year of the Ninji era (1242). It was a relief to be back home, away from the frantic crowds of Kamakura. When he had first arrived in Kamakura he had been taken in by the tangible scent of Pure Land piety, but in time he had grown weary of the underlying stench of so many people and animals crowded together and the constant haze of thousands of cooking fires. With joy he breathed in the clean clear air of Mount Kiyosumi with its scent of spring blossoms and sandalwood incense from its halls and shrines. At the first opportunity he found Master Dōzen-bō to tell him that he had returned.

"Did you get a chance to study the teachings of the sage Hōnen?" inquired Dōzen-bō after the initial pleasantries and small talk were out of the way.

"I did, but I am convinced that he must have been possessed by a devil to teach the things he did, and the people who follow him have become devils as well. He led people away from all the Buddha's teachings, both Hinayana and Mahayana. They seek a pure land apart from this world and an awakening apart from this body and mind, ignoring the fact that the *Lotus Sutra* and mantra teachings assure us that this world is the true pure land and that we can attain awakening in our own bodies."

"That is quite a harsh condemnation. I think you had better keep such views to yourself so that you do not needlessly antagonize others. Don't forget that even the patriarchs of India as well as the patriarchs of the Tiantai school in China and the Tendai school here in Japan have all aspired to rebirth in the Pure Land of the West. I know you have read the *Essential Collection Concerning Rebirth in the Pure Land* by the Venerable Genshin, who was a revered monk of our

Tendai school on Mt. Hiei. He too advocated *nembutsu* as the easy practice for ignorant people such as us in the Latter Age."

"Yes, I have read that work. Yet even the Venerable Genshin never taught that the other sutras should be discarded in favor of the *nembutsu*. On the contrary, it seems that it was entirely for the purpose of spreading the *Lotus Sutra* that he produced his many works. Even in the *Essential Collection* he taught that while the *nembutsu* was the most reliable of all practices leading to rebirth in a pure land, a single moment of faith in the *Lotus Sutra* was still tens of thousands of times more meritorious than the practice of *nembutsu*. So Genshin's true purpose for writing the *Essential Collection* was to guide people to take faith in the *Lotus Sutra*. Twenty years later he wrote the *Essentials of the One Vehicle Teaching* and in that work he expressed his faith in the One Vehicle of the *Lotus Sutra*."

Dōzen-bō nodded. "That is true. You should remember, however, that the Venerable Genshin was humble enough to admit that he himself did not have the wisdom or diligence for more difficult forms of practice, and that is why he relied upon the *nembutsu* as a practice within the One Vehicle. So, what is your intention now?"

"If you please, Master Dōzen-bō, I would like to continue my study of the sutras and cultivation of the mantra practices. I do not know if I have even a 16th of the wisdom or determination of someone like the Venerable Genshin, but how can I give up on my studies now before I have barely begun?"

Dōzen-bō chuckled. "Yes, that is a good attitude to have. I see that you are quite an earnest student. I will see if I can make arrangements for you to visit Enryakuji on Mt. Hiei so that you can deepen your studies there, at the head temple of our Tendai school."

In the second year of the Kōji era (1243), at the age of 21, Renchō made his way to Kyōto. There he launched himself upon a course of

100

study that would occupy him for the entirety of the next decade. He examined the exoteric and esoteric doctrines and practices of Tendai Buddhism at Enryakuji on Mt. Hiei and at Onjōji, head temple of the Jimon branch of Tendai at the mountain's foot. He pondered the mantra teachings of the Great Master Kōbō at Kongōbuji on Mt. Kōya. He considered exhaustively the doctrines of all the various schools at other temples throughout Kyōto, Nara, and the central provinces at the oldest and most prestigious temples in Japan. Yet, after all these studies were ended, he had still not cleared up all the doubts that were troubling him. In fact, what he saw was unsettling. Hundreds of years before, the court had established these temples so that the monks therein could pray for the spirits of the deceased emperors, the longevity and happiness of the current emperors and the imperial family, and for the tranquility and peace of the nation. The ranking official monks who had received full ordination upon the precept platforms at Enryakuji, Tōdaiji, and elsewhere were almost all members of the imperial family or other noble families. They studied the teachings, practiced the esoteric rites, and through subordinates managed the extensive estates granted to the temples by the court. Their concerns rarely extended to the anguish and misery of the common people such as Renchō's family and the villagers he grew up with. Aside from the aristocratic monks, Mt. Hiei was home to the so-called "evil monks" who were really just warriors in clerical garb. They wore helmets and armor and wielded sword, spear, staff and bow to defend the temples and their estates. Bands of militant monks from rival temples were known to fight with each other and even to commit arson against the temples and dwellings of those they perceived as their enemies. It was known that such monks all too often marched into the capital bearing inviolable portable shrines, to intimidate the court into doing their bidding. The warrior-monks of Mt. Hiei were so unmanageable that a former emperor had been known to say, "Three things refuse to obey my will: the floodwaters of the Kamo River, the fall of backgammon dice, and the monks of Enryakuji."

Renchō was a person of no consequence in the eyes of the aristocratic monks and the warrior-monks who served them. He lacked courtly manners and he had no connections with the nobility. His provincial accent instantly set him apart from such types when he encountered them. He considered himself lucky to be able to secure a small space at the back of the lecture halls where he had to squeeze himself in and listen. The lectures and debates, however, did not provide the definitive answer he was hoping for. Again he was faced with a bewildering array of claims and counterclaims concerning the true meaning of the Buddha's teaching and how one should best go about the realization of that truth in practice. The more he heard of these competing interpretations, some of which seemed clearly to be no more than thinly veiled slander of the Dharma, the more Renchō began to think to himself that in the Latter Age of Degeneration the only "good friend," in the sense of a wise mentor or guide, that one could find would be the sutras themselves. Only through them could one approach the words of the Buddha directly.

There were many sutras, however. Which expressed the most direct way to buddhahood for all beings? Which taught the most efficacious practice? He knew that the greatest sages of the past, particularly those in the Tiantai lineage, had regarded the *Lotus Sutra* as the true king of sutras. The patriarch Nāgārjuna had taught, "The teaching of the *Lotus Sutra* enabled the men of the two vehicles, voice-hearers and private-buddhas, to attain buddhahood even though they had been regarded as those who had no chance to do so. It is like a great physician who knows how to turn poison into medicine." The patriarch Vasubandhu had likened the *Lotus Sutra* and the *Nirvana Sutra* to *ghee*, or clarified butter, the most refined of milk products. The Great Master Tiantai Zhiyi had based his teachings on the *Lotus Sutra*. The Great Master Miaole, the sixth patriarch of the Tiantai school in China, wrote commentaries on Great Master Tiantai's teaching further developing them and emphasizing the primacy of the *Lotus Sutra*. When Great Master Dengyō established the Tendai school in Japan on Mt. Hiei he wrote the *Outstanding Principles of the Lotus Sutra* to make it clear that there should be no doubt that the *Lotus Sutra* was the Buddha's supreme teaching, in that it opened the gate to buddhahood for all people. Who would dare to contradict these teachings of the great sages of the past? And yet, many did, arguing instead for the greater profundity and power of other sutras such as the three Pure Land sutras, the *Flower Garland Sutra*, the *Nirvana Sutra*, or the three most important esoteric sutras: the *Mahāvairocana Sutra*, the *Act of Perfection Sutra*, and the *Diamond Peak Sutra*. Renchō, however, had already vowed before Space Repository Bodhisattva to be guided directly by the sutras and not mere commentaries. As the *Nirvana Sutra* taught, he would follow the Buddha's Dharma and not the opinions of scholars. So he looked to what the Buddha actually said to determine if the *Lotus Sutra* was indeed the king of sutras.

The Sutra of the Lotus Flower of the Wonderful Dharma

Śākyamuni Buddha had taught the *Lotus Sutra* on Eagle Peak outside the city of Rājagriha during the last eight years of his life. As King Ajātaśatru was present among the assembled hosts of bodhisattvas, arhats, gods, spirits, demons, monastics, and householders, the teaching must have begun sometime after the usurper had repented of his misdeeds, disavowed Devadatta, and taken refuge in the Three Treasures. Before the *Lotus Sutra* itself was taught the bodhisattvas present asked how they should practice in order to quickly attain buddhahood. In response, the Buddha taught the *Infinite Meanings Sutra*, in which he explained that all phenomena are tranquil and empty and without duality; but in order to respond to the innumerable desires of living beings the buddhas and bodhisattvas expound the Dharma in infinite ways with infinite meanings in order to enable them to realize the truth so that their suffering will be removed and they can know true happiness and joy. In the course of that teaching the Buddha said, "For more than 40 years I have expounded the Dharma in all manner of ways through adeptness in skillful means, but the final truth has still not been revealed." He recounted how he taught the four noble truths for the voice-hearers and the twelve-fold chain of dependent origination for the cause-knowers beginning with the teaching at the Deer Park and how he then taught the *kalpas* long bodhisattva practices in the Expanded sutras, the Perfection of Wisdom sutras, and the *Flower Garland Sutra* – to put them in order of increasing profundity. In response, the bodhisattvas praised the Buddha's teaching of the "infinite meanings" and stated that it was the great direct way to awakening, while those who had not heard it would be unable to attain perfect and complete awakening even after innumerable *kalpas*. The Buddha agreed saying of that teaching, "Because of it all living being will travel the great direct way with no hardships to detain them." He then entered into a state of *samādhi* or deep concentration. Flowers rained down from the sky, the earth quaked, and all assembled put their palms together and bowed to the Buddha, who then emitted a ray of light from the white curl between his eyebrows and illuminated all the worlds before him in the east, from the lowest hells to the highest heavens and all those within from the most miserable hell-dweller up to the buddhas of those worlds and their own assemblies. Maitreya Bodhisattva asked Mañjuśrī Bodhisattva the meaning of this and was told that the Buddha was about to expound the *Sutra of the Lotus Flower of the Wonderful Dharma*.

The Buddha then emerged quietly from his *samādhi* and said to Śāriputra, "The wisdom of the present buddhas is profound and immeasurable. The gate to it is difficult to understand and difficult to enter." He told Śāriputra that the wisdom of the buddhas was beyond the understanding of any but buddhas, and that he, like all other buddhas, had resorted to various skillful means in order to guide living beings. "Only the buddhas attained the highest truth, that is, the reality of all things in regard to their appearances as such, their natures as such, their entities as such, their powers as such, their activities as such, their causes as such, their conditions as such, their effects as such, their recompense as such, and their equality as such despite these differences." He also said, "As a rule, the world-honored ones expound the true teaching only after a long period of expounding expedient teachings." Śāriputra wished to hear more but had to ask three times before the Buddha consented to continue teaching. Even then the Buddha waited for 5,000 arrogant monastics and householders to leave the assembly, for they believed they had nothing more to learn from the Buddha. Once those people had gone the Buddha taught the one great purpose for which the buddhas appear in the worlds. "The buddhas, the world-honored ones, appear in the worlds in order to cause all living beings to open the gate to the insight of the buddha, and to cause them to purify themselves. They appear in the worlds in order to show the insight of the buddha to all living beings. They appear in the worlds in order to cause all living beings to obtain the insight of the buddha. They appear in the worlds in order to cause all living beings to enter the way to the insight of the buddha. This is the one great purpose for which the buddhas appear in the worlds." The Buddha further stated that buddhas really only teach One Vehicle leading to buddhahood. The previous teaching that there were separate vehicles for voice-hearers, private-buddhas (or cause-knowers), and bodhisattvas were just expedients, skillful means used to develop those who might otherwise turn away from the lofty goal of buddhahood if presented with it at the start. In the One Vehicle, even those who for a time had believed that they followed the two vehicles for voice-hearers and private-buddhas would obtain buddhahood through the Buddha's teachings. The Buddha said, "If I lead even a single person by the Hinayana, I shall be accused of stinginess," and "I am now joyful and fearless, I have laid aside all expedient teachings. I will expound only unsurpassed awakening to bodhisattvas."

Next the Buddha began giving predictions of buddhahood to Śāriputra, the other arhats, his aunt who had been his foster-mother, his wife, and his son. Ultimately all in the assembly were assured of buddhahood simply by virtue of having heard and taken faith in the *Lotus Sutra*. In order to make sure that everyone was able to understand and trust in his pronouncements the Buddha told several parables to get the point across. He told a parable about a wealthy man whose children were playing in a burning house. In order entice them out of the house he promised them sheep-carts, deer-carts, and ox-carts according to their inclinations. When they came out he gave all of them something far better than he had promised – a great white ox-cart. In the same way the Buddha had taught the three vehicles for voice-hearers, private-buddhas, and bodhisattvas but really he bestows the One Vehicle leading to buddhahood upon all his disciples. In response, the four arhats Subhūti, Mahākātyāyana, Mahākāśyapa, and Maudgalyāyana told a parable of a boy who ran away from his father and became desperately poor. Many years later the father saw and recognized his son but the young man was too afraid to approach and did not realize the wealthy man was his father.

The father then sent his servants to hire the young man to perform menial labor for him. In time the son was given greater responsibilities and became more dignified and at ease. When the son had sufficiently matured in his outlook and aspiration, the wealthy man revealed that the young man was in fact his heir. In the same way the Buddha teaches using skillful means for those who aspire to lesser vehicles but in the end he reveals that his purpose all along was to help them develop their ability to attain buddhahood. The Buddha responds to this parable with another in which he compares his teachings to a cloud that rains upon a variety of grasses, herbs, and trees which each benefit from the water in a way appropriate to itself. The Buddha also told his disciples that in a past life, more than 3,000 dust-particle *kalpas* ago, he had been one of the 16 sons of a previous buddha. At that time he had begun teaching the *Lotus Sutra* to those who, in the present life, were now his disciples. So in actuality the Buddha had been teaching those present in the assembly the One Vehicle of the *Lotus Sutra* for an immensely long period of time, though they had doubted the teaching, eventually forgetting it entirely, and had now to be reminded once more. The Buddha followed this with yet another parable. He compared himself to the leader of a caravan traveling a long and dangerous road. When the merchants became discouraged and wished to turn back the leader conjured an illusory city where they could rest. After the merchants had rested they were able to go on and reach the place of treasures that they had been seeking. In the same way the Buddha taught the attainment of the nirvana of the two-vehicles for the timid who needed to rest halfway into their spiritual development, but the true goal was buddhahood itself. In response to receiving predictions of buddhahood, 500 arhats compared themselves to a poor man whose rich friend revealed that he had once placed a priceless jewel inside his clothes when they were drinking. The poor man had forgotten about the gift but was overjoyed to discover that he had been carrying a fortune around all along. In the same way the Buddha had given them all the jewel of buddhahood but they had neglected it and were filled with joy to discover it once again.

The Buddha recognized that this new and unprecedented teaching, whereby all could obtain buddhahood, would not be immediately accepted. He said, "I have expounded many sutras. I am now expounding this sutra. I also will expound many sutras in the future. The total number of sutras will amount to many thousands of billions. This *Sutra of the Lotus Flower of the Wonderful Dharma* is the most difficult to believe and the most difficult to understand." Even Śāriputra confessed to being frightened and confused, thinking, "The Buddha troubles me. Isn't he Māra in the form of a buddha?" To those who refused to trust his teachings in the *Lotus Sutra* the Buddha warned, "Those who do not believe this sutra but slander it will destroy the seeds of buddhahood of all living beings of the world." The awful punishments and retributions such slanderers would suffer for denigrating the *Lotus Sutra*, turning people from it, and persecuting its devotees were then recounted, starting with falling into the Hell of Incessant Suffering. Slander of the *Lotus Sutra* was clearly a transgression even worse than the grave offenses committed by Devadatta and Ajātaśatru.

To assure those who might still harbor doubts, a buddha of the past named Many Treasures Buddha appeared within a stūpa made of treasures that sprang up from underground and hung in the sky. From within the stūpa Many Treasures Buddha said, "Excellent, excellent! You, Śākyamuni, the World Honored One, have expounded to this great multitude the *Sutra of the Lotus Flower of the Wonderful Dharma*, the Teaching of Equality, the Great Wisdom, the Dharma for Bodhisattvas, the Dharma Upheld by the Buddhas. So it is, so it is. What you, Śākyamuni, the World Honored One, have expounded is all true." Śākyamuni Buddha explained that Many Treasures Buddha had vowed to appear whenever the *Lotus Sutra* would be taught so that he could praise the buddha who is teaching it. Those assembled wished to see Many Treasures Buddha. In order to open the stūpa, however, Śākyamuni Buddha had to purify the Sahā world and recall the buddhas in the worlds of the ten directions, who were actually his emanations. With the world purified and all the buddhas assembled, Śākyamuni Buddha rose up into the sky and opened the door of the stūpa to reveal Many Treasures Buddha. The latter buddha then invited Śākyamuni Buddha to enter the stūpa and sit beside him. Once seated inside the stūpa, Śākyamuni Buddha enabled the whole assembly to rise up into the air as well. So began what would be known as the Ceremony in the Air.

Śākyamuni Buddha then asked who among the assembly would be able to uphold the *Lotus Sutra* after his final nirvana. He warned them that it would be very difficult but those who did so could attain buddhahood. He told them, "It is difficult to keep this sutra. I shall be glad to see anyone keeping it even for a moment. So will all the other buddhas. He will be praised by all the buddhas. He will be a man of valor, a man of endeavor. He should be considered to have observed the precepts and practiced austerities. He will quickly attain the unsurpassed awakening of the buddha. Anyone who reads and recites this sutra in the future is a true son of mine. He shall be considered to live on the stage of purity and good. Anyone, after my final nirvana, who understands the meaning of this sutra, will be the eyes of gods and men. Anyone who expounds this sutra even for a moment in this dreadful world, should be honored with offerings by all gods and men."

But what would become of *icchantikas*, like King Ajātaśatru and Devadatta? Here the *Lotus Sutra* resolved the questions Renchō had about their ultimate fate. The Buddha said to Medicine King Bodhisattva that anyone in the assembly, which included King Ajātaśatru, who rejoiced even for a moment at hearing even so much as a verse or phrase of the *Lotus Sutra* would be assured of attaining buddhahood. Devadatta, however, was absent from the assembly. Probably he had already died and fallen into the Hell of Incessant Suffering by the time the Buddha was teaching the *Lotus Sutra*. Nevertheless, a whole chapter was named for him. In it the Buddha revealed that Devadatta had been his teacher in a past life and had

109

enabled him to hear a previous version of the *Lotus Sutra*. In the future, Devadatta would eventually be able to obtain buddhahood as well. In the latter half of that chapter the eight-year old daughter of the dragon king Sāgara emerged from the ocean in the company of Mañjuśrī Bodhisattva. The bodhisattva attested that this young girl, the daughter of a dragon and not even a human being, was capable of quickly attaining buddhahood. A bodhisattva named Accumulated Wisdom and Śāriputra found this hard to believe but the dragon girl demonstrated her ability and transformed herself into a buddha presiding over a world to the south leaving the entire assembly speechless. So the sutra provided proof that even the most evil of men like Devadatta and Ajātaśatru, could attain buddhahood; and even women like the dragon king's daughter, despite all the teachings that denigrated their ability and restricted their freedom, could attain buddhahood. It had already been said that even arhats like Śāriputra, who had supposedly cut off any possibility of returning to the world and taking up bodhisattva practice, were to attain buddhahood. The Buddha's teaching in the *Lotus Sutra* made it explicitly clear that all beings could attain perfect and complete awakening.

The chapter concerning Devadatta was then followed by a chapter wherein the bodhisattvas vowed to uphold the *Lotus Sutra* in the world after the Buddha's final nirvana despite all the hardships that would have to be faced, and then a chapter in which the Buddha instructed them on the peaceful deeds, words, thoughts, and vows they should cultivate in order to teach the sutra. The Buddha also told another parable in which he compared himself to a king who bestowed all manner of gifts upon his soldiers for their service but withheld the brilliant gem in his top-knot until he was able to give it to a soldier of extraordinary merit. In the same way, the Buddha had reserved the *Lotus Sutra* but now was at last ready to bestow his most excellent and profound teaching upon those who had shown themselves ready to receive it.

Ultimately, however, the Buddha declined the offer of the bodhisattvas already assembled. He told them that there were other bodhisattvas-mahāsattvas (great beings) who would protect, keep, read, recite, expound, and copy the *Lotus Sutra* after his final nirvana. To the amazement of the assembly, the ground of the Sahā world quaked and cracked and innumerable bodhisattva-mahāsattvas and their equally countless attendants sprang up from underground from where they had lived in the empty space below the world. Their bodies were golden, possessed the 32 special marks of great men and gods, and rays of light shone from them. They had four leaders named Superior Practice, Limitless Practice, Pure Practice, and Steadily Established Practice. It took 50 small *kalpas* for them to emerge and praise the Buddha, but to the assembly it only seemed to take half a day. On behalf of the whole assembly, Maitreya Bodhisattva asked who these bodhisattvas were. The Buddha explained that he had been teaching these bodhisattvas who lived in the sky beneath the Sahā world for innumerable *kalpas*. Maitreya Bodhisattva asked how this could be since the Buddha had only attained buddhahood some 40 years prior beneath the Bodhi Tree. What the Buddha was saying was as strange as a young man of 25 claiming to be the father of an old man of 100. Maitreya Bodhisattva said to the Buddha, "Those who doubt this sutra and do not believe it will fall into the evil regions. Explain all this to us now! How did you teach these innumerable bodhisattvas in such a short time, and cause them to aspire to awakening and not falter in seeking awakening?"

In chapter 16 of the *Lotus Sutra*, the Buddha responded saying, "Listen to me attentively! I will tell you about my secret and supernatural powers. The gods, men, and *asuras* in the world think that I, Śākyamuni Buddha, left the palace of the Śākyas, sat at the place of awakening not far from the City of Gayā, and attained perfect and complete awakening 40-some years ago. To tell the truth, good men, it is many hundreds of thousands of billions of *nayutas* of *kalpas* since I became the Buddha." The Buddha then gave an analogy to convey the inconceivable span of time since he attained awakening, a period of time referred to in shorthand form as the five hundred million dust-particle *kalpas* by later commentators though it was in fact an unquantifiable period of time. The Buddha explains that in his view his awakened life span has no beginning or end, and neither does anything. "All that I say is true, not false, because I see the triple world as it is. I see that the triple world is the world in which the living beings have neither birth nor death, that is to say, do not appear or disappear, that it is the world in which I do not appear or from which I do not disappear, that it is not real or unreal, and that it is not as it seems or as it does not seem. I do not see the triple world in the same way as the living beings of the triple world do." The Buddha, therefore, has been the Buddha all along, and though it seems as though he would soon enter final nirvana, he will actually remain in the world expounding various teachings to all living beings in a way most fitting for each. He compares himself to a physician whose many sons become sick from accidentally drinking poison. In order to cure the sons he makes an antidote for them having a good color, taste, and smell. When some sons refuse to take it, the physician leaves them and has a messenger tell his sons that he has died; so that out of desperation those who were holding out would finally take the medicine. In the same way, the Buddha seems to enter final nirvana but in reality never passes away but always remains compassionately engaged with the world. The Buddha stated, "I am always thinking: 'How shall I cause all living beings to enter into the unsurpassed way and quickly become buddhas?'"

The Buddha proceeded to speak of the incomparable merits of those who take faith and rejoice, even for a moment, in what he just taught about his attaining of buddhahood in the remotest past. He also spoke of a bodhisattva known as Never Despising whose sole practice was to bow to all the monastics and householders he met and praise them saying, "I respect you deeply. I do not despise you. Why is that? It is because you will be able to practice the way of bodhisattvas and become buddhas." He did this even when the people refused to believe him and became abusive and even attacked him with rocks and sticks. Because of his perseverance, Never Despising was eventually able to achieve supreme awakening and enabled countless others to do the same. In fact, he is revealed to have been none other than the present Śākyamuni Buddha. The bodhisattvas who emerged from the earth then promised to expound the *Lotus Sutra* in the ages after the Buddha's apparent final nirvana. In response, the Buddha and all his emanation buddhas who had gathered from the ten directions of the universe displayed their supernatural powers by stretching out their tongues to touch the heavens of Brahmā and emitting rays of light with an immeasurable variety of colors by way of verifying that all that had been said was true. Thereupon the Buddha specifically transmitted the Wonderful Dharma to Superior Practice Bodhisattva and all the bodhisattva from underground saying, "To sum up, all the teachings of the Tathāgata, all the unhindered supernatural powers of the Tathāgata, all the treasury of the secret lore of the Tathāgata, and all the profound achievements of the Tathāgata are revealed and expounded explicitly in this sutra. Therefore, keep, read, recite, expound and copy this sutra, and act according to the teachings of it with all your hearts after my final nirvana! In any world where anyone keeps, reads, recites, expounds, or copies this sutra, or acts according to its teachings, or in any place where a copy of this sutra is put, be it in a garden, in a forest, under a tree, in a monastery, in the house of a person in white robes, in a hall, in a mountain, in a valley, or in the wilderness, there should a stūpa be erected and offerings be made to it because, know this, the place where the stūpa is erected is the place of awakening. Here the buddhas attained perfect and complete awakening. Here the buddhas turned the wheel of the Dharma. Here the buddhas entered into final nirvana." After that the Buddha gave a more general transmission to all present in the assembly. Many Treasures Buddha and the emanation buddhas all returned to their places, the assembly rejoiced, and the Ceremony in the Air came to close.

Even then the *Lotus Sutra* continues on for six more chapters dealing with the transmission of the *Lotus Sutra* for the future. In chapter 23

113

the story of Medicine King Bodhisattva setting himself ablaze out of devotion to the Dharma in a past life is told. In that chapter the Buddha says, "The person who keeps this sutra is superior to any other living being. Just as bodhisattvas are superior to voice-hearers and private-buddhas, this sutra is superior to any other sutra. Just as the Buddha is the king of the Dharma, this sutra is the king of all the sutras." The Buddha also specifically says that chapter (and by implication the sutra as a whole) should be propagated throughout the world in the Latter Age so that it will not be lost. In chapters 24 and 25 the miraculous powers and transformations of bodhisattvas Wonderful Voice and World Voice Perceiver is featured. In chapter 26, *dhāraṇīs* for the protection of the teachers of the *Lotus Sutra* are offered by Medicine King Bodhisattva, Brave-in-Giving Bodhisattva, two of the four heavenly kings, and finally the Mother-of-Devils and her ten daughters. The Mother-of-Devils and her daughters were all reformed *rākṣasī*, a type of malevolent spirit known to cause illness, but after taking refuge in the Three Treasures they had repented of their evil ways. They were now guardians of the Dharma and worked to protect children and prevent illness. In chapter 27 the past life story of the bodhisattvas Medicine King and Medicine Superior's efforts to convert their father King Wonderful Adornment in a prior life is told. Finally, in chapter 28, Universal Sage Bodhisattva appears and promises to assist and protect the teachers of the *Lotus Sutra* and he too offers a *dhāraṇī*.

The Buddha's expounding of the *Lotus Sutra* was followed by a discourse known as the *Meditation on Universal Sage Bodhisattva Sutra*. This was taught at the Great Forest Monastery in Vaiśālī three months before the Buddha's final nirvana. In this discourse the Buddha taught a method of repentance involving the recitation of the Mahayana sutras, by which it was understood that the Buddha specifically meant the *Lotus Sutra* that he had just taught. By doing this practice one would be able to see and contemplate Universal Sage Bodhisattva, Many Treasures Buddha within the stūpa of treasures, the emanation buddhas of the ten directions, and

Śākyamuni Buddha who is stated to be none other than Vairocana Buddha of the Pure Land of Eternally Tranquil Light. This sutra was understood to be the final part of the teaching of the *Lotus Sutra*. In it the Buddha said, "This expansive teaching is the eye of the buddhas, it is the means by which buddhas perfect the five kinds of eyes, and, from it, the Buddha's three bodies arise." Renchō knew that the five kinds of eyes meant the physical eye of ordinary people, the heavenly eye that sees the deaths and rebirths of all beings in the triple world, the wisdom eye that sees the emptiness of all phenomena, the dharma-eye that sees the attainments of noble beings and bodhisattvas, and the buddha-eye that sees the true nature of all things. The three bodies were the three bodies or aspects of buddhahood: the Dharma-body, which is reality itself; the enjoyment-body, which the buddha receives as the fruition of his own merit and wisdom and that can only be perceived by advanced bodhisattvas; and the transformation body, which interacts with and teaches ordinary people in the world. The *Meditation on Universal Sage Bodhisattva Sutra*, the closing part of the threefold *Lotus Sutra*, was asserting that all the powers and aspects of buddhahood originated in the teaching of the *Lotus Sutra*.

In the *Nirvana Sutra* the Buddha declared, "The many benefits accruing from the fruit realized when this sutra appears in the world means peace and joy for all, enabling living beings to see their buddha-nature just as the 8,000 voice-hearers were able to realize the fruit of their received predictions of buddhahood in the *Lotus Sutra*. In the fall one harvests and in the winter one stores, as nothing more is produced at that time." In other words, the teaching that all can attain buddhahood had already been given in the *Lotus Sutra*, and the *Nirvana Sutra* that followed it was simply restating that teaching for those, like the 5,000 arrogant people who had left the assembly, who had still not heard it. The *Nirvana Sutra* was like the gleaning that occurs after the main harvest.

The Three Thousand Realms in a Single Thought-Moment

It seemed obvious to Renchō that Śākyamuni Buddha, as well as Many Treasures Buddha and the buddhas of the ten directions who were the emanations of the Original and Eternal Śākyamuni Buddha, was asserting that the *Lotus Sutra* was indeed the king of all sutras and that one attained buddhahood only through this teaching. But what did it mean? Certainly it taught the One Vehicle whereby the people of the two vehicles could obtain buddhahood, but neither Renchō nor anyone he knew considered themselves followers of the vehicles for voice-hearers or private-buddhas in the first place. Certainly it clarified that Śākyamuni Buddha had attained buddhahood in the remote past and was in some way still presently teaching, but neither Renchō nor anyone he knew had encountered this Eternal Buddha as anything other than a brief vision or a dream, so how did it help to know this? To find the answer Renchō delved into the three major writings of the Great Master Tiantai: *Words and Phrases of the Lotus Sutra* that was a line-by-line commentary on the *Lotus Sutra*, *Profound Meaning of the Lotus Sutra* that used the five Chinese characters of the title of the *Lotus Sutra* (*myō*, *hō*, *ren*, *ge*, and *kyō*) as a framework to expound the true meaning of all the Buddha's teachings, and *Great Calming and Contemplation* that described the way of meditation based on the *Lotus Sutra*. He also studied the annotations and further commentaries written on those three works by the Great Master Miaole. In studying these writings in-depth, Renchō was most impressed by the teaching of the "3,000 realms in a single thought-moment" that Great Master Tiantai only fully expressed in the seventh and final chapter of the *Great Calming and Contemplation*. According to Great Master Miaole, this was Great Master Tiantai's ultimate and supreme teaching. Great Master Zhang'an, the successor to Great Master Tiantai, wrote in his preface to the *Great Calming and Contemplation* that it explained the approach to the Dharma that Great Master Tiantai practiced within his own mind. It seemed to Renchō that the "3,000 realms in a single thought-moment" truly expressed the inner meaning of the *Lotus Sutra*.

According to Great Master Tiantai the Dharma-realm consisted of ten Dharma-realms. There were the six paths or realms of suffering within samsara and then there were the realms of the voice-hearers, the private-buddhas, the bodhisattvas, and the buddhas. All of these realms had in common the ten suchnesses enumerated by the Buddha at the beginning of chapter two of the *Lotus Sutra*: appearance, nature, entity, power, activity, causes, conditions, effects, consequences, and the equality of all phenomena despite apparent differences. The ten realms were, therefore, not substantially distinct or separate from one another. Each realm embraced within itself the other nine. Each realm made itself felt in terms of three categories: the five aggregates of beings (forms, feelings, perceptions, mental formations, and consciousness), the lives of sentient beings as nominal individuals who interact with other individuals, and the environments of those beings. All of these realms are always to be found within a single moment of thought. Great Master Tiantai taught, "A single moment of thought contains ten realms within itself. Each realm also contains ten realms within itself. Therefore, there are 100 realms altogether in one thought. Each realm has 30 aspects (the three categories multiplied by the ten suchnesses). Therefore, there are actually 3,000 included in 100 realms. These 3,000 realms are in a single thought-moment. Where there is no thought, there is nothing. Where there is any thought at all, there are 3,000 realms altogether therein. But we cannot say that a thought-moment comes first and that all phenomena comes after, nor can we say that all phenomena come first and that the thought-moment comes after. It is just that thought is all phenomena and all phenomena is thought. ... That is why one thought-moment is called an object of contemplation beyond our comprehension. This is what I mean to say."

According to Great Master Tiantai's exegesis of the *Lotus Sutra*, the first half of the sutra comprised the Trace Gate, in which the transformation-body or historical aspect of Śākyamuni Buddha, the trace of the Original Buddha, taught the One Vehicle. In this half, the beings of the ten realms assembled to hear the Wonderful Dharma and the Buddha expounded on the ten suchnesses and the true reality of all phenomena. In this half through direct teaching, parables, and past life stories, the historical Buddha revealed that in principle all beings contain within themselves the realm of buddhahood. The latter half of the sutra comprised the Original Gate, in which Śākyamuni Buddha revealed in chapter 16 that he was the Original Buddha whose awakened lifespan had no beginning or end. The Original Śākyamuni Buddha, according to Great Master Tiantai, was not just representative of one or another of the three bodies of a buddha but embodied all three aspects of buddhahood, and all other types of buddhas were his emanations. The teaching of the Original Buddha in the Original Gate was that his buddhahood did not reject the lower nine realms of the un-awakened but continued to embrace them. His buddhahood was the actualization of the 3,000 realms in a single thought-moment. Unlike un-awakened beings, the Original Buddha fully realized the workings of all the 3,000 realms in every thought-moment and skillfully utilized them to awaken others. The Trace Gate and Original Gate of the *Lotus Sutra*, therefore, showed that the nine realms all contain the seed of buddhahood and that the realm of buddhahood always embraces the lower nine realms.

Renchō now wondered how he could practice Buddhism in accordance with the actuality and not just the principle or theory of the 3,000 realms in a single thought-moment. Just as importantly, how could the common people, who lacked education and wisdom, practice it? From the time of its founding there were two methods of practice taught at Enryakuji on Mt. Hiei. One method was the practice of the perfect and sudden calming and contemplation as taught in the *Great Calming and Contemplation*. This was the way of contemplating the 3,000 realms in a single thought-moment while practicing one of the four kinds of *samādhai* or meditative concentration: silent sitting, walking while chanting *nembutsu* and visualizing Amitābha Buddha and his pure land, engaging in repentance ceremonies involving both walking and sitting, or by maintaining mindfulness of one's thoughts in the midst of all activities regardless of whether or not one was sitting or walking.

The other method was through the mantra practices as taught in the three esoteric sutras. After the time of Great Master Dengyō the mantra practices had been increasingly emphasized. It had even been taught by the successors to Great Master Dengyō at Enyrakuji that while the esoteric sutras were equal to the *Lotus Sutra* in terms of the principles they taught they were superior in terms of the efficacy of esoteric practice involving the use of mudras, mantras, and mandalas. Renchō now questioned this. Upon reading the *Mahāvairocana Sutra* and the other esoteric sutras, he found nothing that guaranteed that even the arhats could attain buddhahood. Neither did these sutras reveal that Śākyamuni Buddha had actually attained buddhahood in the remote past and therefore had been a buddha all along while traversing the triple world, thereby showing that buddhas do indeed retain the nine realms within their lives and can manifest them to teach others. Aside from the mantra practices, the principles taught in these sutras did not seem to go beyond those taught in the other sutras of the Expanded period of the Buddha's teachings, taught prior to the Perfection of Wisdom sutras. The mantra teachings were also very complex. They required a lot of time and dedication to learn and practice and so were not the kind of practices that common people could perform, including most samurai or other busy officials. Could such an exclusive way of practice truly be the Mahayana way that would enable all beings to attain buddhahood? Another thing that disturbed Renchō about the mantra practices was that some of the initiations involved the initiate entering into mandalas by walking and sitting on mats with images symbolizing Vairocana Buddha and his emanations. Wasn't this symbolically to walk upon the head of Vairocana Buddha? The Zen Buddhists had said this as a kind of

119

kōan to contemplate, but the mantra teachings actually had one do it, at least symbolically. More and more, Renchō began to doubt whether the mantra teachings were really the practices that were in accord with the *Lotus Sutra*.

Despite Rencho's misgivings about the mantra teachings there were esoteric practices that did make a deep and lasting impression on him, such as the esoteric rites based on the *Lotus Sutra*. These held much in common with the exoteric Repentance Ritual of the Lotus Samādhi based on the *Meditation on Universal Sage Bodhisattva Sutra*. The Lotus Samādhi was one of the ways of meditation practice described in the *Great Calming and Contemplation* that involved alternating between periods of sitting silently and walking while chanting the *Lotus Sutra* for 21 days. Both the exoteric repentance ritual and the esoteric rites involved enshrining a copy of the *Lotus Sutra*, though sometimes a mandala depicting Śākyamuni Buddha and Many Treasures Buddha sitting together in the stūpa of treasures and surrounded by concentric rings of bodhisattvas, protective deities, and other beings from the sutra would be used instead. These rites would also, like the Lotus Samādhi, involve the invocation and praise of the buddhas, bodhisattvas, and other beings in the sutra, including the *daimoku* or sacred title of the sutra itself in the form of "Namu Myōhō Renge Kyō" meaning "Devotion to the Sutra of the Lotus Flower of the Wonderful Dharma." The esoteric Lotus rites even featured a mantra expressing the gist of the *Lotus Sutra*. It was said that Nāgārjuna found it and the other mantra teachings in an iron stūpa in India and it was thereafter transmitted to India, China, and Japan by his successors.

Nōmakusammandabodanan samyak sambuddhānām
on a an aku
sarubaboda kino sakishubiya
gyagyanōsanshaba arakishani
satsuridaruma fudarikya sotaran
ja un ban koku bazara rakishaman

un sowaka!

Which meant:

Hail to the all-pervading three-bodied buddhas!
Open, show, cause all living beings to obtain, and enter the way to
The insight of the buddhas!
Like the crisp-clear sky be rid of all delusions and defilements!
Accept the teaching of the Sutra of the Lotus Flower of the Wonderful
     Dharma!
Live with joy, firmly upholding the teaching!

After ten years, Renchō decided that he had learned what he could at Mt. Hiei and the other temples of the various schools of Buddhism in and near Kyōto. He had studied Hinayana and Mahayana Buddhism, exoteric and esoteric sutras, provisional teachings and the *Lotus* and *Nirvana* sutras that expound the True Dharma. He had practiced the contemplation of the 3,000 realms in a single thought-moment according to the *Great Calming and Contemplation* and the esoteric rites of the *Lotus Sutra*. He had thought deeply about the true intention of Śākyamuni Buddha and considered what could be the most efficacious practice for all people in the Latter Age of Degeneration. Now it was time to repay his debts to his parents, his teachers, the ruler, and to the Three Treasures. Now it was time to return home and declare the True Dharma of *Myōhō Renge Kyō*, the *Sutra of the Lotus Flower of the Wonderful Dharma*.

Nichiren

Renchō returned to Kominato and Seichōji early in the fifth year of the Kenchō era (1253). To his parents, brothers, fellow monks, and even Master Dōzen-bō, he seemed tense, yet quiet. It was as if he was holding back something of great importance, a great revelation perhaps, but was not sure how to express himself to others quite yet. Renchō was no longer a young man anymore. He was 31. It was expected that at his age, after so many years of study at the most prestigious temples in the empire, he should be able to give a talk on the Dharma.

Renchō knew they were all waiting for him to speak. He had returned, had he not, specifically to expound the True Dharma? Despite his silence, he knew inside himself that this was the only way to repay his debts owed to his parents, his teacher and tutors, and also Space Repository Bodhisattva who had bestowed upon him the great gift of the gem of spiritual discernment so many years ago in response to his prayers, and to express the gratitude he felt towards them all so deeply. Still he hesitated.

The 28th day of the fourth month of the fifth year of the Kenchō era (1253) was the day he finally gave his talk. The night before he was sleepless, lost in contemplation, considering whether to speak the truth without holding back. He knew that if he did so his life would be in jeopardy. He thought to himself, 'What a dilemma! What should I do? The Pure Land and Zen teachings are leading people astray, and in particular causing them to turn away from the *Lotus Sutra*, the king of sutras. It seems in all of Japan I alone realize this. And yet if I speak out I am sure to be challenged and abused. I may even face persecution from the authorities. They may have me exiled or even executed. My parents, brothers, and teachers might also be punished. And yet, if I do not speak out against those who slander the Dharma I cannot escape Śākyamuni Buddha's condemnation. The Buddha says in the *Nirvana Sutra*: "If a good monk sees someone acting in a way that is injurious to the Dharma and decides to leave him be, rather than taking steps to have him reprimanded by temporary removal or censure, understand that the monk who observes the bad behavior and does nothing is an enemy within the Dharma of the Buddha. If you can reprimand the violator by temporary expulsion or censure, then you will be a disciple of mine, for you have heard my true voice." If I keep silent, I will be betraying the Buddha's admonition not to hide the True Dharma even at the cost of my life, for he also teaches in the *Nirvana Sutra*, "Consider the analogy of an imperial envoy with expertise in diplomacy and who is skillful in using expedient means. When in another country on a mission, he knows it would be better to lose his life than do anything that would prevent the king's message from reaching its destination. Wise people are also like this, for they do not begrudge their own lives in working among ordinary people to fulfill the imperative to disseminate what they know...namely, that all living beings possess buddha-nature." If I do not speak out, I will have allowed fear to overcome compassion for those who will suffer if they continue to follow false teachings and neglect the true teaching. By keeping silent, I will have failed to repay my debts of gratitude, become an enemy of Śākyamuni Buddha, and inevitably fall into the Hell of Incessant Suffering even if I should escape punishment in this life.'

Troubled as he was by the consequences associated with both of these prospects, and after many vacillations during that long night, he came at last to his decision. 'Nevertheless, I must dare to speak up, without fearing anyone, because of the heavy debt of gratitude that I owe to the Buddha.'

When the sun rose, Renchō was standing atop a steep forested hill behind Seichōji overlooking the Pacific Ocean. He put his hands together upright palm-to-palm before his heart in the gesture of veneration known as the *añjali* mudra and chanted "Namu Myōhō Renge Kyō" ten times as the rays of Amaterasu Ōmikami illuminated

123

the land. Before that morning, he had only recited the sacred title of the *Lotus Sutra*, or *daimoku*, as just one of a litany of invocations included in more complex repentance rites and esoteric ceremonies. Now he let the *daimoku* sound forth as the only necessary invocation that included all else.

At noon he spoke to a small gathering at the southern side of the Buddha-hall in Dōzen-bō's quarters. Gathered there, along with his master, were his former tutors, Gijō-bō and Jōken-bō, and others with whom he had practiced as a boy. After he had mounted the preaching platform and the preliminary invocations had been completed, he began his talk. The confident and resonant tone of his voice reverberated out into the crowd, filling the hall with its sound.

"Today, as of this moment, it is no longer the student Renchō who speaks to you. As of today, I will strive to uphold the *Lotus Sutra* just as the Great Master Tiantai and the Great Master Dengyō did. To do that I must be like Superior Practice Bodhisattva and the other bodhisattvas who emerged from the earth. The Buddha says of them in the *Lotus Sutra*, 'Anyone who understands why the Buddha expounds many sutras, who knows the position of this *Lotus Sutra* in the series of sutras, and who expounds it after my final nirvana according to its true meaning, will be able to eliminate the darkness of the living beings of the world where he walks about, just as the light of the sun and the moon eliminate all darkness.' Maitreya Bodhisattva says of them, 'They are not defiled by worldliness just as the lotus-flower is not defiled by muddy water.' I will take my name from these passages. By speaking out against the slanderous teachings that denigrate the *Lotus Sutra* and by spreading the practice of its *daimoku* I will strive to be like the sun and eliminate the darkness. I will not let myself be swayed by worldly fears or ambitions. I will strive to be like the lotus flower that is not tainted by the muddy pond water it grows in. My name will henceforth be Nichiren, the Sun-Lotus."

Hearing this, Dōzen-bō knitted his brows in concern. A low murmur issued from the gathered monks. It was not unusual for a monk to take on a new name in light of some momentous event in their life or to represent a new understanding or position. However, with this new name, he seemed to be identifying himself with the most exalted figures in the *Lotus Sutra*, aside from the buddhas. This kind of hubris could be dangerous. And what did he mean about "slanderous teachings"? The murmuring quieted down as Nichiren continued. What he said that day was to be repeated many times over the next three decades in his speeches and writing, sometimes briefly and sometimes at greater length. Though the exact words of that first talk were lost to memory, Nichiren, ruminating upon his deathbed, was confident there was no one presently in the shogunate who had not heard or read of the warnings and exhortations he had given since that time.

Refutation of Hōnen's Pure Land Teaching

Nichiren continued to reflect upon what he had said on that day so long ago when he had first spoken out at Seichōji. "Upon reflection, I consider myself fortunate to have been born a human being in this Sahā world in Japan and to have unexpectedly escaped the three evil realms of the hell-dwellers, hungry ghosts, and animals, for our chances of being born in the evil realms are as numerous as the dust particles in all the worlds of the universe, while our chances of being born in the human realm are as small as the amount of soil on a fingernail. This being said, there is no doubt that in my future lives I may be in danger of forfeiting the rare opportunity of being born a human in Japan and instead find myself reborn in the three evil realms.

"The causes for human beings falling into the evil realms after death vary. They go to evil realms for unwholesome deeds committed for the sake of family and relatives; for the grave crime of killing living beings and other brutal acts; for the transgressions of rulers who neglect the sorrows of the people; for taking refuge in depraved teachings without knowing the right or wrong of the Buddha Dharma, or for coming under the influence of wicked teachers. Of those mentioned, even the uninformed are able to discriminate right from wrong when it comes to morality in daily life. It is not easy, however, even for awakened sages to distinguish true from false teachings and teachers. How much more difficult is it for us, ordinary people, in the Latter Age!

"Ever since Śākyamuni Buddha passed away in India and his teachings spread to China, the light of wisdom exalted by commentators in India daily lost its luster and the stream of Buddhism in China transmitted by the masters of the Three Baskets grew polluted month by month. There must be even more mistakes and less truth in the Buddhist schools of Japan than in China. This is because most either practice provisional teachings; or seek refuge in teachings unsuited to the time and capacity of people in the Latter Age of Degeneration; or blindly practice the teaching without knowing whether it is taught by an ignorant teacher or a sage. Many also practice both provisional and true teachings at the same time without knowing the difference between the two; or practice only the provisional teaching, misinterpreting it for the true teaching; or with conceit consider themselves to have reached higher stages of practice. As a result, ignorant people routinely study and practice Buddhism in order to be free of the shackles of samsara, but instead they are accumulating karma causing them to be even more firmly bound.

"About 50 years ago a crafty monk named Hōnen wrote a book entitled *A Collection of Passages on the Nembutsu Chosen in the Original Vow*, in which he maligned the doctrines of all Buddhist schools by advocating only the practice of *nembutsu* for ignorant people in the Latter Age. In the name of the three Chinese masters Tanluan, Daochuo, and Shandao, he divided all the Buddhist scriptures into the gate of the holy way and the gate of the Pure Land way. As a result, provisional sutras were substituted for the true ones, thereby closing the direct way to buddhahood of the *Lotus Sutra* and mantra practices and opening instead the narrow and steep way of the three Pure Land sutras.

"However, since provisional sutras were in fact preached to prepare the way for the true sutras, to choose the former and discard the latter is also against the true intent of the Pure Land sutras. This is an act of slandering both the true as well as the provisional sutras. It is an evil teaching that will forever prevent people from attaining liberation, causing them to fall into the depths of the Hell of Incessant Suffering. Nevertheless, the public at large follows this teaching just like twigs are swayed by strong winds, and his disciples revere this crafty monk just as the gods revere Indra.

"In my studies I discovered that over the years well-known monks of great virtue wrote many treatises with the aim of refuting Hōnen's evil doctrine. Unfortunately, the authors of those works did not fully clarify why Hōnen slanders the True Dharma. Contrary to their intentions, therefore, they only helped to propagate the book, like cowardly soldiers placed in the front line of a battle who only serve to encourage a powerful enemy. Now I would like to examine the truth or falsity of Hōnen's teaching according to the sutras. I will leave it all up to the Buddha whether you believe in my words or call them slander. I will not insist on my own opinion.

"The Buddha's purpose for appearing in this world was to expound the *Lotus Sutra*. In the second chapter of the sutra the Buddha says, 'Now is the time to say it. I will expound the Mahayana definitively.' He also says in that chapter, 'That old vow of mine has now been fulfilled. I lead all living beings into the way to buddhahood.' In chapter 16 the Buddha also tells us, 'To tell the truth, good people, it is many hundreds of thousands of billions of *nayutas* of *kalpas* since I became the Buddha.' Regarding the comparative superiority in doctrine, the Buddha himself declares in the tenth chapter that although he expounded numerous sutras, the *Lotus Sutra* is superior to all the sutras which have already been taught, are being taught, or will be taught. In the eleventh chapter, Many Treasures Buddha appears from underground and testifies, 'What you, Śākyamuni, the World Honored One, have expounded is all true,' while the various emanated buddhas of Śākyamuni Buddha in the worlds throughout the universe stretched out their tongues to reach the Brhamā Heaven, attesting the words of Śākyamuni Buddha to be true. Thus the comparative superiority between the *Lotus Sutra* and all other sutras has been resolved by Śākyamuni Buddha, Many Treasures Buddha, and the buddhas of the worlds of the ten directions. No further comparison between the *Lotus Sutra* and sutras preached before and after it is necessary because they are all preached by the one Śākyamuni Buddha.

"Hōnen and his followers, however, believe that the Pure Land teachings will remain in the world longer than the *Lotus Sutra*, but I say it is certain that the three Pure Land sutras will disappear before the *Lotus Sutra*. In winter, trees appear dead, but pine and oak trees do not wither; grasses die, but chrysanthemums and bamboos remain unchanged. The same is true with the *Lotus Sutra*, which will remain forever helping the people even after other sutras all disappear. The sole purpose of the testimony of Śākyamuni Buddha, Many Treasures Buddha, and the emanation buddhas was so that the Dharma of the *Lotus Sutra* would last forever in this world.

"Reading through *A Collection of Passages on the Nembutsu Chosen in the Original Vow* we see that it slanders the True Dharma. It divides all the holy teachings of the Buddha's lifetime into two: one group called the gate to the holy way, difficult-to-practice way or miscellaneous practices; and another group termed the gate to the Pure Land, easy-to-practice way, or correct practice. The first group consists of all other sutras including the *Lotus Sutra*, whereas the second group refers only to the *nembutsu* preached in the three Pure Land sutras. Criticizing shortcomings of the holy category, Hōnen insinuates that of the ignorant people in the Latter Age only one or two out of 100 practitioners or three or four out of 1,000 practitioners might be able to be reborn in the Pure Land by following it. He also definitely considers those who practice the sutras of the holy way to be bandits, villains, heretics, or men of evil opinions, and evil outcastes. Stating the advantages of the Pure Land way, Hōnen declares that of all those ignorant people in the Latter Age who practice sutras in this category ten out of ten, 100 out of 100 will be reborn in the Pure Land. This is the evil doctrine that slanders the True Dharma!

"Bodhisattva Nāgārjuna and the three Chinese masters divided the sutras preached in the 40 years or so before the *Lotus Sutra* using criteria such as difficult or easy to put into practice, but their division did not include the *Lotus* and *Nirvana* sutras or the mantra teachings and practices. It was Hōnen who took it upon himself to include the *Lotus* and *Nirvana* sutras and the mantra teachings, the true Mahayana and esoteric Mahayana, among the holy way to be discarded for the Pure Land way. This is an arbitrary opinion of Hōnen! Consequently the Japanese people are all convinced that the *Lotus Sutra* and mantra teachings are unsuitable for this time and for the capacity of the people. Furthermore, Tendai and mantra scholars and practitioners, desiring worldly honors and profit, speak ill of their own sutras as unsuitable to the time and capacity of people in order to cater to the whims of the public, reinforcing in effect the evil doctrine of Hōnen. Guided by fleeting self-interest, these so-called scholars are breaking the vows sworn in the Ceremony in the Air of the *Lotus Sutra*.

"Hōnen concluded that uneducated people in the Latter Age are ignorant and always suffering in the sea of birth and death, and so the easy-to-practice way is better than other teachings merely because the *nembutsu* practice of calling the name of Amitabha Buddha seems to be better suited to them. He did not consider whether the Pure Land teaching is provisional or true, or whether or not it is profound. However, saving the evil and ignorant depends on the profundity of the teaching. It does not matter whether or not the teaching is easy to practice. The more grievous a transgression is, the more profound the teaching must be to save the transgressor.

"Aside from the *Lotus* and *Nirvana* sutras, other sutras deny that buddhahood can be attained by the voice-hearers and private-buddhas, who followed the Hinayana, or by the *icchantika*. On the contrary, the *Lotus* and *Nirvana* sutras do allow such people to attain buddhahood. This is because the *Lotus Sutra* alone teaches the doctrine of the 3,000 realms in a single thought-moment, and specifically that the ten realms mutually possess one another. Because the *Lotus Sutra* teaches the One Vehicle whereby all can attain buddhahood, this means that the nine realms of the hell-dwellers, hungry ghosts, animals, *asura*s, humans, gods, voice-hearers, private-buddhas, and bodhisattvas all possess each other and most importantly the realm of buddhahood within themselves. Likewise, because the *Lotus Sutra* teaches that Śākyamuni Buddha attained buddhahood in the remote past but nevertheless remains in the world to teach the way to buddhahood, this means that the realm of the buddha embraces the other nine realms of un-awakened beings.

"We, the ignorant and *icchantika* of the Latter Age, always drowning in the sea of birth and death, long to take faith in this teaching of the *Lotus Sutra* because it forecasts our inherent buddha-nature being revealed. Great Master Miaole explains this in his *Annotations on the Great Calming and Contemplation*, fascicle four, 'Unless the buddha-nature in each of us develops gradually to fill our minds, how can we attain buddhahood? It is this wonderful power of the buddha-nature in each of our minds that awakens us. Therefore, we call this wonderful power of the buddha-nature our teacher-protector.'

"The doctrine of the mutual possession of the ten realms is not explained in any sutra expounded during the first 40 years or so of the Buddha's teaching but only in the *Lotus Sutra*. Since this doctrine is not taught, believers of those sutras do not know about the buddha-realm inherent in their minds. Unaware of the realm of buddha in their minds, they do not know of other buddhas outside of their minds either. Even if they speak of seeing buddhas, they merely imagine buddhas in other worlds, not real buddhas.

"Practitioners of the two vehicles, the voice-hearers and private-buddhas, are unaware of the buddha within their own minds, so they are unable to attain buddhahood. Bodhisattvas who are unaware of the mutual possession of the ten realms because they follow provisional sutras deny that those who follow the two vehicles can attain buddhahood, but by doing so they are unable to fulfill their vows to save all beings so they are also unable to see the buddha or attain buddhahood. Likewise, ordinary ignorant people do not know the mutual possession of the ten realms, so the buddha-realm inherent in them is not revealed. As a result, even Amitābha Buddha will not come to welcome them at the last moment of life, and buddhas will not come to help them upon request. They are like the blind that cannot see their own shadow.

"Now in the *Lotus Sutra*, it was clarified that the buddha-realm is inherently possessed by even those in the un-awakened nine realms, enabling those who had listened to the prior provisional teachings to all see for the first time the buddha-realm in themselves. It was the first time that bodhisattvas, voice-hearers, and private-buddhas were able to attain buddhahood and ignorant people were able to be reborn in the Pure Land. Regardless of whether it is during or after the lifetime of the Buddha, the true, trustworthy good friend of all the people is the *Lotus Sutra*. Tendai scholars in general assert that one can achieve awakening through the sutras prior to the *Lotus Sutra*, but I, Nichiren, do not accept this.

"In sum, those Mahayana sutras taught before the *Lotus Sutra* do not recognize the attainment of buddhahood by the followers of the two vehicles or the *icchantika*. From this viewpoint, the difference between the *Lotus Sutra* and those sutras taught before it is as clear as fire and water. The Buddha himself distinguished expedient from true teachings. His criteria for making this division was whether or not the attainment of buddhahood was allowed to the followers of the two vehicles, whose attainment of buddhahood was considered an impossibility, and to the *icchantika* who seemed to have no buddha-nature. In studying the sutras and commentaries I found that the distinction between expedient and true teachings was plainly explained by the Buddha. Therefore, I revere those scholar-monks, such as Great Master Tiantai and Great Master Miaole, who follow the doctrine defined by the Buddha and bodhisattvas, and I do not accept the opinions of those who contradict it. I have never judged right and wrong at my own discretion; I have just pointed out the difference between the views of later teachers and those of the Buddha.

"Therefore I say that the *nembutsu* of the Pure Land school is the expedient of expedients. It is like having a dream within a dream. It is absolutely just words without substance. It is of no use for anyone to pray for salvation in this way. The lord of the Pure Land of the west, Amitābha Buddha, is also without substance. How can this buddha be superior to the *Lotus Sutra* which preaches the eternal truth? When Amitābha Buddha, whom they depend on, is proven to be just a name without substance, will it make any sense to claim that the doctrine of rebirth in the Pure Land of Utmost Bliss is as high as Mt. Sumeru or say that it is as deep as the ocean? Even if they claim that they have scriptural proof in some sutras and commentaries by the patriarchs, they are mere expedients in which no truth has been revealed."

Refutation of Zen Buddhism

On that long ago day at Seichōji, Nichiren continued, "At around the same time that Hōnen was teaching, the Zen school, taught by monks such as Dainichi Nōnin, proclaimed that Buddhism is not transmitted by words but perceived by sitting in meditation, what they call *zazen*. In other words, the state of awakening has never been explained by the Buddha or any patriarch because there can be no way of putting it into words that can adequately express it. This implies that what is taught in the sutras is nothing more than a finger pointing at the moon, and that our body is itself already the body of the Buddha. Thus they claim not to use words, nor to rely on the Buddha, nor to study his teachings, nor even to venerate portraits and statues.

"Let me then ask why they highly venerate 28 patriarchs of Buddhism in India and six patriarchs in China as the transmitters of Buddhism while claiming that no patriarch has ever explained buddhahood? What about the claim that Mahākāśyapa showed his realization at Eagle Peak by smiling when the Buddha held up a flower? How do we know such a thing even happened if it did not come down to us in words? How can the people of the Zen school venerate Bodhidharma while denying the need for patriarchs? Why do they utter mantras and read and recite sutras mornings and evenings if no word written in the sutras is useful? Why do they chant their devotions to the Three Treasures in their daily rites when they do not believe or respect any buddha or bodhisattva?

"There is no Dharma that has not been expounded by various buddhas of the past, present, and future. If the Zen school insists that the Zen doctrine has not been transmitted by any of the buddhas or patriarchs, is this not a doctrine given by heavenly devils, those who seem lofty but are just filled with pride and arrogance like Māra, who dwells in the sixth heaven? They speak of transmissions and patriarchs but then deny that any teaching has been expounded or transmitted. Isn't this like the non-Buddhists who deny cause and effect or who hold such extreme views that all they say comes to nothing? The doctrine that no buddha or patriarch has ever transmitted the Buddha Dharma is what Zen advocates mention often, but when carefully questioned on this matter they cannot answer convincingly. Nevertheless, as it is said, those who neglect their studies never admit to losing when faced with reason. They do not accept or understand reason. This is why they are said to be irrational. Trying to reason with them is as futile as trying to draw pictures on running water.

"The Zen school teaches people not to cling to anything. This doctrine lacks stability because whether one says 'right' or 'left' it is taken to be clinging to a wrong view that obscures the truth. If you think about it, though, they are telling people not to cling to anything while they themselves are attached to erroneous views that shut them off from the world of common sense. They do not even realize it. Why don't they stop clinging to their own false views instead of blaming others for holding false views?

"As to their doctrine concerning the identity between our bodies and that of the Buddha, they have yet to prove this is true. If they continue to assert this doctrine without providing the basis for it, then it is nothing more than a doctrine taught by heavenly devils. It seems to me that this doctrine is stolen from the Tendai teaching of becoming a buddha in our present form. Is their teaching the same or is it different than the Tendai teaching? If they speak in such a way without understanding the underlying meaning as it is taught in the Tendai school, then isn't it just idle talk? It is like a commoner declaring himself king of a country. No one can be prevented from saying anything. Yet whatever he says, he remains a lowly commoner after all. He is no different from a person who calls a piece of tile a jewel. No stone or tile can ever be a jewel. The same is true with this doctrine that 'our body is nothing but the body of the Buddha.' They are mere words with nothing to back them up, spoken by those without shame.

"What about the doctrine of the Zen school claiming that the Buddha Dharma can be realized without words? What must they think of the written word to establish such a doctrine? The written word reflects the mind of the person who wrote it. Therefore what people think can be seen in what they write. Because mind and body are inseparable, it is even possible to guess whether a person is rich or poor simply by looking at what the person wrote. That is to say, the written word demonstrates that there is no real duality between mind and body. If Zen proponents insist that they do not use written words, it means that they are denying the non-duality of meaning and expression, of mind and body. One should ask them to recite even a single phrase of their Zen doctrines without using body and mind.

"Does the Zen saying, 'Any sutra expounded by the Buddha is like a finger pointing to the moon' mean that after finding the moon, no finger is necessary? If this is their understanding, are parents also useless? Doesn't a disciple need his teacher? Isn't the earth needed? Isn't the sky needed? According to this view, parents are no longer important after giving birth; a teacher is no longer needed after a disciple has learned everything from him; the sky is no longer valuable after it has rained; and the earth is no longer useful after it has helped plants to grow. This is no different at all from the proverb, 'Once down the throat, the heat is forgotten; a patient is no longer grateful to a doctor after recovery.'

"Sutras, after all, are written words. 'Each word is the very life of the various buddhas of the past, present, and future,' said Great Master Tiantai in his *Profound Meaning of the Lotus Sutra*. Great Master Tiantai is regarded as one of the Zen patriarchs in China. Why do they not respect his words? In addition, words are not only of our own minds and bodies but are also the minds and bodies of all people of the past, present, and future. Why do they say that Buddhism is perceived with no help from literary or verbal means, dismissing true reality? This is like a man who forgot to take his wife when moving to a new home! How can they understand the true Zen doctrine? How fragile the Zen doctrine is!"

The *Daimoku* of the *Lotus Sutra*

Nichiren continued, "According to the three major writings of the Great Master Tiantai and Great Master Miaole's annotations on them, the *Lotus Sutra* is able to save the ignorant, the evil, and also women, whom other sutras are unable to save, as well as the incorrigible, who are eternally drowning in the sea of birth and death. Hōnen and his followers say that the *Lotus Sutra* is too difficult to practice but in fact it is easy to practice because, according to the Great Master Miaole, the ignorant of the Latter Age will be able to meet Universal Sage Bodhisattva, Many Treasures Buddha, and the emanation buddhas of the ten directions by simply practicing the teachings of the sutra. In addition, Great Master Miaole declared, 'You may recite the *Lotus Sutra* inattentively; you don't have to meditate or concentrate; with your whole heart just keep in mind the characters of the *Lotus Sutra* all the time whether sitting, standing, or walking.'

"The aim of this interpretation is solely to save the ignorant in the Latter Age. The 'inattentive mind' means the mind of an ordinary person engaged in daily routines as contrasted with the 'concentrated mind' of those undertaking formal meditative discipline. 'Reciting the *Lotus Sutra*' means to recite either the whole eight fascicles or just one fascicle, one character, one phrase, one verse, or the *daimoku*; it means to rejoice upon hearing the *Lotus Sutra* even for a moment or to feel the joy of the fiftieth person who hears the sutra transmitted from one person to the next. 'Whether sitting, standing, or walking' means regardless of what you are doing in daily life. 'Whole heart' refers neither to meditative concentration nor to conceptual reasoning; it is to use the ordinary inattentive mind. 'Keep in mind the characters of the *Lotus Sutra*' means that each character of the *Lotus Sutra*, unlike those of other sutras, contains all the characters of all the Buddhist sutras and the merit of all buddhas.

"The Great Master Tiantai taught, 'Without opening this sutra, one who believes in the *Lotus Sutra* reads it all the time; without uttering a word, recites various sutras widely; even without the Buddha preaching, always listens to the resounding voice of the Buddha; and without contemplating shines over the entire Dharma-realm.' The meaning of this statement is that those who believe in the *Lotus Sutra* are upholding it 24 hours a day, even if they do not take its eight fascicles in hand; that those who believe in the *Lotus Sutra* are in effect continuously reading all the Buddhist sutras every day, hour, and second, even if they do not raise their voices in reciting the sutras; that, though it has already been more than 2,000 years since the passing of the Buddha, his voice remains in the ears of those who believe in the *Lotus Sutra*, reminding them every hour and minute that the Buddha has always been in this Sahā world; and that without contemplating the 3,000 realms in a single thought-moment those who believe in the *Lotus Sutra* will clearly see all the Dharma-realms throughout the universe. These merits are endowed solely to those who practice the *Lotus Sutra*.

"Some may doubt the efficacy of the *Lotus Sutra* because those who received the seed of buddhahood by hearing it in the past continued to follow the six paths of suffering. The reason why those who had received the seed of buddhahood in the remotest past have been transmigrating among the six paths for as long as 500 million dust particle *kalpas* without attaining buddhahood, and those who had heard the *Lotus Sutra* 3,000 dust particle *kalpas* ago have been similarly transmigrating, was because they abandoned the great teaching of the *Lotus Sutra*, seeking refuge instead in expedient and Hinayana sutras such as those taught during the 40 years prior to the *Lotus Sutra*. Later they gave up faith even in those expedient teachings and so continued to travel the six paths of the lower realms.

"Now I would like to elucidate the merits of the *daimoku* of the *Lotus Sutra*, for saving those whose only practice is to chant it from the three evil realms of the hell-dwellers, hungry ghosts, and animals.

139

The Buddha states in chapter 14 of the *Lotus Sutra*: 'Mañjuśrī! It is difficult to hear even the title of this *Sutra of the Lotus Flower of the Wonderful Dharma* even if you try to do so, walking about innumerable countries.' The Buddha also teaches in chapter 26, 'Your merits will be immeasurable even when you protect the person who keeps only the name of the *Sutra of the Lotus Flower of the Wonderful Dharma*.' In chapter twelve the Buddha says, 'Good men or women in the future who hear this chapter of Devadatta of the *Sutra of the Lotus Flower of the Wonderful Dharma* with faithful respect caused by their pure minds and have no doubts about this chapter, will not fall into hell or the realm of hungry ghosts or the realm of animals.'

"How can anyone escape the three evil realms just be hearing the *daimoku* without understanding its meaning? It is due to the meritorious acts of past lives that anyone happens to be born in a land where the *Lotus Sutra* is known, hears the title of the sutra and has faith in it. Even though such persons are ignorant and wicked in this life, because of meritorious acts in previous lives, they can believe in this sutra upon hearing its name. As a result they will not fall into evil realms.

"Now which pure land should practitioners of the *Lotus Sutra* aspire to be reborn in? The Buddha says in the 16th chapter of the *Lotus Sutra*, the essence of the 28 chapters of the sutra, 'All this time I have been living in this Sahā world, and teaching the living beings of this world by expounding the Dharma to them.' He also says, 'In reality this world of mine is peaceful,' and 'This pure world of mine is indestructible.' According to these statements the Eternal and Original Buddha, the origin of all the emanation buddhas, is always in this Sahā world. Then why should we wish to be anywhere other than this Sahā world? You should know that there is no pure land other than the very place where the practitioner of the *Lotus Sutra* resides. Why should we concern ourselves with seeking a pure land in any other place?"

Driven Out

"You must leave," said Dōzen-bō.

Nichiren had known that it might come to this. The *Lotus Sutra* itself warned the practitioners of the sutra that the ignorant and arrogant " ... will speak ill of us, or frown at us, or drive us out of our monasteries from time to time." This was indeed what had happened after Nichiren had spoken out. The assembled monks had frowned, murmured, and cast sidelong glances at each other. Dōzen-bō had looked distraught. His mouth twitched. He had looked away from his disciple and nervously thumbed his *juzu*. Gijō-bō and Jōken-bō, however, had gazed thoughtfully upon their former pupil, but others such as the monks Enchi-bō and Jitsujō-bō glared at him with reddening faces and clenched fists. After the assembly was brought to a conclusion, these two hastened to the side of Dōzen-bō to voice their disapproval of Nichiren's condemnation of the Pure Land teachings and his strange advocacy of chanting the *daimoku* in place of *nembutsu*. There was no immediate trouble, however, though the monks of Seichōji were divided thereafter between those who were sympathetic to Nichiren, and those who had taken offense at his polemics. Dōzen-bō attempted to stay above the controversy. He refused to make any changes in the temple's routines; neither did his own devotion to Amitābha Buddha falter.

The discord between the two factions, so far private, finally came to a head some months later. The Nun Proprietress, whose estate Seichōji was on, asked Nichiren to help her compose a lawsuit against Tōjō Kagenobu, the local steward appointed by the shogunate. She accused Tōjō Kagenobu of unlawfully hunting deer upon the land belonging to Seichōji. For his part, Tōjō Kagenobu was a Pure Land devotee, and many monks, especially Enchi-bō and Jitsujō-bō, hoped to see Seichōji come under his influence and for Nichiren and his faction to be expelled. Nichiren was certain that the buddhas, bodhisattvas, and protective deities would not allow the steward and his faction to win.

He was so sure of this that he even went so far as to pledge, in writing, to abandon his faith in the *Lotus Sutra* should the temple come under the control of Tōjō Kagenobu. He tied the oath to the hands of Space Repository Bodhisattva and prayed for the success of the lawsuit. Within a year the lawsuit was concluded in Kamakura in favor of the Nun Proprietress and the temple was thereafter free of Kagenobu's control. This, of course, infuriated the steward, so after the conclusion of the lawsuit small bands of armed ruffians were more and more to be seen lingering along the paths from Seichōji to Kominato. On his last visit to Kominato his parents had rubbed their hands together in prayer and begged Nichiren to desist from further antagonizing the steward by continuing to denounce the Pure Land teachings.

It was only after all of this had come to pass that Dōzen-bō, fearful of the repercussions that seemed certain to follow, insisted that Nichiren must go elsewhere.

"I understand," Nichiren replied to his master. "I humbly ask you to forgive me for any trouble I have caused you. I will leave tonight. I hope, however, for your own sake, that you will consider taking faith in the *Lotus Sutra*. Please, set aside the *nembutsu* and take up the *daimoku*. I fear for you otherwise."

"Enough. I have heard you before on this subject. We will continue to practice here as we always have. Those who wish may recite the *Lotus Sutra*, those who wish may recite the *nembutsu*. When we come together in the main worship hall we will do as we have always done. We shall recite the *Lotus Sutra* as well as the *Amitābha Sutra* as we have always done. Even the Great Master Tiantai, not to mention the other patriarchs, have all aspired to rebirth in the Pure Land and chanted *nembutsu*. To chant the *nembutsu* and visualize Amitābha Buddha in the Pure Land of Utmost Bliss is one of the four *samādhis* taught in the *Great Calming and Contemplation*. Objecting to Hōnen is one thing, but what you are saying goes against the teachings and practices of the patriarchs themselves."

"But master, please consider..."

"Enough, Nichiren. I have heard what you have had to say. The time for such talk has passed. I can no longer protect you. You are no longer my disciple. Now, for your own safety, you must go this very evening. Gijō-bō and Jōken-bō are waiting for you outside."

Nichiren felt his face flush with shame. Dōzen-bō had disowned him! He was now without a master, some would say he was a monk without precepts. He thought to himself, 'All know that one who acts against their parents or disobeys their teacher or their ruler is chastised by the heavens for being unfilial. Nevertheless, when the enemies of the *Lotus Sutra* are one's parents, or teacher, or the ruler of the country, then it is an act of filial piety and loyalty not to follow their directions.' Nichiren bowed one last time to his now former master. "Please take care of yourself. Consider my words and consider the words of the Buddha. Farewell."

Without a backward glance, he took his leave.

So it was in the ninth month of the sixth year of the Kenchō era (1254) that Nichiren left Seichōji. By torchlight, accompanied by Jōken-bō and Gijō-bō, he traveled along a little used path through the forest. After several hours they came to Rengeji, an affiliated temple where Nichiren could hide for a few days in relative safety before moving on. He wondered if he would ever be able to return to Seichōji or to Kominato. Would he ever again see his parents or Master Dōzen-bō? Still, he did not regret his decision to preach and to uphold what he was sure was the True Dharma. The *Lotus Sutra* and *Nirvana Sutra* had both told him what he must do and what to expect. In the *Lotus Sutra* the bodhisattvas say to the Buddha, "We will not spare even our lives. We treasure only unsurpassed awakening." In the *Nirvana Sutra* the Buddha says of those monks who speak out against corruption in the Sangha, "Whenever there is a monk who can roar like a lion in this way, the precept breakers who hear him speak will all be consumed with rage and attack that teacher of the Dharma. This Dharma teacher, however, even if his life were to end as a result, would be known as one who keeps the precepts, benefiting himself and others." Nichiren was determined to live in accordance with the Buddha's teachings, and even to die for them, if necessary.

Disasters

As he lay on his deathbed, Nichiren looked out at those gathered around him. Several of them had been with him for years, some almost from the time when he had first dared to speak out. After being forced to leave Seichōji and Kominato he gradually made his way back to Kamakura. His family's longtime benefactor, the Nun Proprietress who lived by the Nagoe Pass in the southeast of Kamakura, set aside some land for him at the bottom of a ravine on the periphery of the city called Matsubagayatsu, the Valley of Pine Needles. There he lived in a small straw hut where he could contemplate the 3,000 realms in a single thought-moment, chant the *Lotus Sutra* and its *daimoku*, continue to study and write about the True Dharma, and most importantly, teach any and all who would listen about the supremacy of the *Sutra of the Lotus Flower of the Wonderful Dharma*.

Since his previous stay in Kamakura, the Pure Land teachings of Hōnen had become even more firmly entrenched in the life of the city. The giant wooden statue of Amitābha Buddha at Kōtoku-in and the hall in which it was enshrined had been destroyed in a storm. Another fund raising campaign resulted in a new hall and an even grander statue of gilded bronze to replace the old one. Monks and laymen artists crafted wooden images of Hōnen or painted his portrait. Wooden blocks were carved to print *A Collection of Passages on the Nembutsu Chosen in the Original Vow* so it could be spread throughout the land. It seemed to Nichiren that people revered only the teachings of Hōnen and gave alms only to his disciples. At some temples and prayer halls the monks went so far as to replace the hands of statues of Śākyamuni Buddha with hands carved to form the mudra appropriate to Amitābha Buddha. Others renovated temples dedicated to Bhaiṣajyaguru Buddha, the Medicine Master Buddha, in order to enshrine Amitābha Buddha. The meritorious practice of copying the *Lotus Sutra* was being replaced by the practice of copying the three Pure Land sutras. Tendai monks were suspending the memorial lectures held for the Great Master Tiantai in order to hold lectures in memory of the so-called Pure Land patriarch Shandao instead.

At the same time, the Zen teachings had continued to receive the patronage of the Hōjō clan. The current regent, Tokiyori, the grandson of Yasutoki, was especially enamored with the Zen teachings. He had commissioned the construction of a new temple on the northern border of Kamakura past the Kamegayatsu Pass called Kenchōji, or more fully, Kenchōji Kōkoku Zenji, the Kenchō Era Zen Temple for the Flourishing of the Nation. Its layout and architecture were modeled on the style of the temples and monasteries in China and around it clustered 49 sub-temples. Absent from this enormous complex were any halls for Tendai or mantra practices. The regent installed as its first abbot a Rinzai Zen monk from China named Lanxi Daolong, or in Japanese Rankei Dōryū. At Kenchōji, Rankei introduced the precepts and methods of Zen training. Tokiyori later took the Zen precepts from a monk named Shōichi. Shōichi was a Tendai monk who had spent six years in China and there received transmission in the Rinzai lineage. Once back in Kyōto, Shōichi had founded a new temple named Tōfukuji, where the Tendai, mantra, and Zen teachings were propagated, though Zen was given pride of place. Shōichi came to Kamakura several times at the request of Tokiyori, and for a time was even put in charge of Jufukuji, another Zen temple in Kamakura.

Around that time, Jōben, a monk whom Nichiren had studied with at Mt. Hiei, came to join him. Jōben had been impressed by Nichiren's dedication to the *Lotus Sutra* and had his own doubts about those teachings that were leading to its neglect. Though Jōben was one year senior to Nichiren, he became the latter's disciple and took the name Nisshō. Nisshō sat by him now, leading the others in chanting the *daimoku*. His eyebrows and the stubble on his head had long since turned white, but his face was still much the same, composed and thoughtful as ever.

At Nisshō's side was Nichirō, his nephew. Nichirō was now well into his thirties, but Nichiren remembered the young boy of nine he had taken under his wing and ordained himself back in those early years at Matsubagayatsu. Nichirō had devoted himself to Nichiren like the most filial of sons, and he had suffered greatly for it at the hands of those opposed to the True Dharma. Over the years he had been beaten, jailed, and subject to all manner of deprivation. Once, he had even almost died of frostbite in his eagerness to serve his master. Due to a beating he had received little more than two decades ago, his right arm still hung crooked and useless at his side. Now it was all Nichirō could do to sit upright and chant with composure. His eyes were swollen and red, his face blotchy and streaked with tears. Nichiren was sorry that Nichirō had to suffer so much, but at the same time he knew that his young disciple had gained immeasurable merit for his sacrifices. So had all of those who had stood by him through all the disasters and persecutions over the years.

With help from Nisshō and Nichirō, and from a growing band of sympathetic monks, primarily from the Tendai school, Nichiren held regular lectures on the *Lotus Sutra* and the works of the Great Master Tiantai, especially the *Great Calming and Contemplation*. His hut was soon filled with lower and middle-ranking samurai from the eastern provinces who had come to Kamakura on official business. Some, like Toki Tsunenobu, came because they were themselves well versed in Buddhist teachings, having been educated in temples. Though they had not become monks themselves, these samurai felt a deep longing to know the True Dharma and resolve the great matter of birth and death. In the case of Toki Tsunenobu, he became an "enterer of the Way," a lay person who took Buddhist vows, received the tonsure, and wore Buddhist robes, but continued to live at home. From then on, he had been known as Toki Jōnin. Other important supporters from the ranks of the samurai who joined him at that time included Shijō Kingo, an irascible but good-hearted warrior well versed in the medical arts; Kudō Yoshitaka, the lord of the Amatsu District in Awa; and the Ikegami brothers. Nichiren cast his eyes further out into the room, past the monks who encircled him. There were the Ikegami brothers and their families, chanting along with the rest. Nichiren smiled, for the two brothers had remained steadfast, even when their own father had tried to turn them against the *Lotus Sutra* and even against one another. In spite of everything they had stood by one another and did not forsake their faith in the *Lotus Sutra*.

The persecutions, however, did not begin until some years after his expulsion from Seichōji. Only his small but growing band of followers knew of his denunciation of Pure Land and Zen. He had not yet spoken out publicly in Kamakura, and so there was as yet no resistance to his message. In those early years, Nichiren had hoped that more and more Tendai monks and followers would eventually rally to him. After all, he was expounding the doctrine of the *Lotus Sutra*, the clear mirror that perfectly reflected the True Dharma of Śākyamuni Buddha, supplemented by the commentaries of the great masters Tiantai, Miaole, and Dengyō. He was trying to show that the *Lotus Sutra* was not meant only for advanced practitioners but for all people, and that all the Buddha's teachings were subsumed within it. Once entering the ocean of the *Lotus Sutra*, the prior teachings would no longer be expedients to be dismissed, for they would all take up the flavor of Namu Myōhō Renge Kyō due to the wondrous merit of the *Lotus Sutra*. There would no longer be any need to speak of *nembutsu*, or the precepts, or mantras, or Zen meditation. He had taught what the Tendai school should have been teaching all along.

In other ways, those years were also very difficult ones, for disaster struck repeatedly. The years of the Kenchō era (1249-1256) were unusually wet and cold. The final year of that era saw excessive rains, freezing temperatures in spring and summer, violent winds, floods, and landslides that caused many deaths and widespread destruction of crops. This was followed in turn by famine, which led to the outbreak of multiple epidemics. Conditions in Kamakura deteriorated to the point where the corpses of oxen and horses lay rotting on the sides of the roads while human skeletons littered the streets. A great many perished and there was no one untouched by grief. Even the high officials of the shogunate were not immune, and the 15-year-old imperial prince who was the current shogun found himself beset with inflamed lesions. At the age of 29, citing ill-health, Hōjō Tokiyori retired from the position of regent in the eleventh month to take the tonsure and become a lay monk, though he continued to maintain his power over the Hōjō clan and therefore over the shogunate from his residence at Saimyōji, one of Kenchōji's sub-temples.

In an attempt to curb the unceasing calamity, the imperial court changed the era name to Kōgen in the tenth month. The following year in the third month they changed the name of the era again, this time to Shōka (1257). By doing this they hoped the evils of the old era would be left behind and that initiating a fresh new era would bring with it a better fortune. The results of these and subsequent era changes were negligible.

In the meantime, some tried to avert disaster by chanting the name of Amitābha Buddha, believing the statement of Shandao that the *nembutsu* is the sharpest sword to cut off evil karma. Some recited the sutra of Medicine Master Buddha who vowed that he would cure all disease. Some put their faith in the "Previous Life of Medicine King Bodhisattva" chapter of the *Lotus Sutra* where it says, "The patient who hears this sutra will be cured of his disease at once. He will not grow old or die." Some held the ceremony of giving 100 lectures on the *Benevolent Kings Sutra* according to the statement in that sutra that seven calamities will transform into seven fortunes if such lectures are given. Some tried to ward off evil by sprinkling water over five vases filled with offerings in accordance with the mantra teachings. Some practiced Zen meditation and concentrated their minds in order to overcome suffering by perceiving the emptiness of all phenomena with the clarity of viewing a bright moon. Some wrote the names of seven fierce gods on paper and posted them on every gate, hoping to escape the epidemics. Others sketched the five mighty bodhisattvas described in the *Benevolent Kings Sutra* on paper to hang in every house, hoping for protection. Sill others practiced exorcism at the four corners of the city and prayed to the gods of heaven and earth. The rulers, out of compassion, took various benevolent measures to reform the government and relieve the burdens of the people: they pardoned criminals, prohibited the abuse of the peasantry, remitted taxes, stopped burdensome work levies, and combated banditry and piracy. All of these efforts, however, were to no avail as the famines and epidemics only grew more rampant. Everywhere people looked they saw beggars and the dead. Corpses were piled high as watchtowers and lined up like planks on bridges.

Of all the disasters that occurred during those years, perhaps the worst of them took place between the hours of the dog and pig (nine p.m.) on the 23rd day of the eighth month in the first year of the Shōka era (1257). Nichiren, Nisshō, Nichirō, and other monks were kneeling before the eight fascicles of the *Lotus Sutra* that they had enshrined as the main focus of devotion or *honzon*. They were chanting the *daimoku* and contemplating the 3,000 realms in a single thought-moment when everything began to shake: tables, sutra boxes, cooking pots, and most alarmingly, candles and lanterns. The walls of the hut began to sway and the roof beams creaked. Though the earth was rocking like a fishing boat, Nichiren quickly got to his feet, scooped up the fascicles of the *Lotus Sutra* and led the others outside before the hut collapsed on them. The shaking didn't stop but only intensified. It seemed to go on forever, though in actuality it probably only lasted a few minutes. When it finally abated, there was not a shrine or temple left standing in Kamakura. Rocks rolled down from the hills as numerous landslides buried hundreds of people. In the darkness they could hear the crashing, snapping sound of collapsing houses commingled with the screams of their inhabitants. The ground cracked open and water gushed forth. Fires flowed menacingly in every direction, consuming the wreckage and making short work of those few buildings that had been left standing by the earthquake. Some of the flames burned with an eerie blue glow. Nichiren and the other monks rushed to join bucket brigades to help put out the fires. Only after the immediate danger of fire and smoke was quelled could they begin searching the wreckage for survivors. Cries of panic, moans of pain, and wracking sobs filled the air. It seemed as though all the land had fallen into the Hell of Incessant Suffering.

Nichiren wondered then, 'How could this be happening?' He looked upwards, into a sky blacked by dust and smoke, and cried out wordlessly, then turned his eyes towards the ground in anguish. He perceived that it had begun to shake again; the first of the aftershocks that would continue sporadically for more than a month. 'The rulers of Japan have commissioned numerous prayer services but none have prevented these calamities, instead they seem to have only intensified the disasters. Why do the gods not respond to our prayers? Why do the buddhas not give any indication of their divine powers? The sun and moon continue to shine brightly and the stars and planets make their regular circuits in the night sky; here in this country the Three Treasures are revered; and the line of a 100 emperors, which the Great Bodhisattva Hachiman had vowed to protect, has not yet come to an end. So why have things deteriorated so soon? Why is Buddhism in this country so powerless? How did this come about? What is the matter with this country?'

Nichiren left Kamakura in the first month of the second year of the Shōka era (1258). He hoped to find some answers to these unsettling questions. He traveled west to a Tendai temple called Jissōji in Suruga Province to make use of its extensive library. There he met Nikkō, who was now one of his six main disciples. He sat beside Nisshō, Nichirō, and the others as they maintained their vigil by their master's bedside. Nikkō was now in his mid-thirties, strict and uncompromising, but Nichiren remembered the impressionable attendant of only twelve who had assisted him with his research and later returned with him to Kamakura to dedicate his life to the *Lotus Sutra*.

A month after arriving at Jissōji, Nichiren learned of his father's passing. Old age and sickness had taken him as it had so many others. Nichiren felt the loss keenly. He longed to recite the Verses of Eternity from the 16th chapter of the *Lotus Sutra* at his father's grave, but he knew his life would be forfeit if he dared return to Kominato so long as Tōjō Kagenobu was still the steward there. He chose instead to remain at Jissōji. His concern as a monk was, after all, not simply to pray for the repose of his father, but to discover and teach the True Dharma for the welfare of all sentient beings. There was still so much suffering throughout Japan. The earthquake of the year before was followed by a typhoon on the first of the eighth month of the second year of the Shōka era (1258), a serious famine in the third year of the same era (1259), and widespread epidemics in the first year of the Shōgen era (1259), which remained rampant throughout the four seasons in the following year, resulting in the deaths of over half the population. Disaffected samurai and nobles murmured against the Hōjō clan. It seemed only a matter of time before the intrigues now taking place behind closed doors would inevitably explode into violent insurrection in the streets. Monks and merchants from China and Korea also spread word of the threat of the Mongols, who had conquered all of northern China as far south as the Yangtze River and reduced Korea to a vassal state. They continued to press hard against the Song dynasty that still ruled the south, and it seemed only a matter of time before the entire known world would be theirs, including the islands of Japan. As if all of that were not bad enough, omens in the skies such as the appearance of a comet in the eighth month of the second year of the Shōka era (1258) and the appearance of a blood-red sun for two days in the third month of the second year of the Shōgen era (1260) promised worse evils to come. Nichiren was therefore determined to repay the great debt he felt to the country of his birth, to find the cause of all these calamities and present his findings to the rulers so that something could be done to put an end to all the suffering around him.

Spreading Peace by Establishing the True Dharma

In his current condition it was hard for Nichiren to remember things that had happened more than two decades ago. Nichiren recalled being ushered into the presence of Hōjō Tokiyori, at that time known as the Lay Monk Lord Saimyōji, in his audience chamber at Saimyōji at eight in the morning on the 16th day of the seventh month of the first year of the Bunnō era (1260). At that meeting hadn't he told Tokiyori that it was nothing but the evil act of a heavenly devil for him to have stopped seeking refuge in the existing Tendai and Mantra temples and to have put his faith in the new Zen temples instead. He had also submitted the *Risshō Anokoku-ron* (*Treatise on Spreading Peace Throughout the Country by Establishing the True Dharma*) to him, pointing out that the practice of the *nembutsu* is an evil teaching that actually leads people into the Hell of Incessant Suffering. How had that meeting actually gone? Drifting out of consciousness, Nichiren began to dream of that long ago meeting and of the dialogue in his *Treatise on Spreading Peace Throughout the Country by Establishing the True Dharma* between a traveler seeking to find out why Japan was undergoing such suffering and his host, a master of the Buddha's teachings who had discovered the cause of the suffering and knew what needed to be done to end it. The half-remembered meeting and the imagined dialogue blended together. His eyes closed and for a moment he forgot his pain, ceased to see his sorrowing disciples and supporters, no longer heard the sound of their chanting. He was back in that audience chamber.

Tokiyori sat upon a dais at the far end of the room flanked by two boy attendants. He was five years younger than Nichiren but he looked wan and grey, much older than a man in his mid-thirties. His head was shaved bare and he wore the robes of a Zen monk. Despite his weakened health he sat upright and at ease. Samurai advisors, functionaries, and guards sat in rows on circular rope mats before him on the left and right sides of the room facing inwards.

Lay Monk Yadoya Mitsunori, Tokiyori's chamberlain, directed Nichiren to where a sitting cloth had been laid out for guests, at the opposite end of the room from the dais. Nichiren bowed, prostrated himself upon the mat, and then sat up. All present turned their gaze upon him. He could not help but feel humbled and self-conscious in their presence. After all, he was an unknown monk of little to no standing dressed in coarse black robes now bleached gray by the sun. Still, Nichiren reminded himself, 'Although I may be a person of no account and little ability, I have been fortunate to have studied the Mahayana. It is said that a blue fly riding on the tail of a fine horse can travel 10,000 miles and a vine of green ivy clinging to a tall pine can climb up to 1,000 yards. Likewise, I was born to be a disciple of the Buddha and I have put my faith in the *Lotus Sutra*, the king of sutras, and the *Lotus Sutra* says that the person who keeps it is superior to any other living being. Therefore, I need not be afraid to speak to even this man, Lord Saimyōji, the actual ruler of our country, of my sorrow over the decline of the Dharma, nor to share even a portion of the Buddha Dharma.' With these thoughts, Nichiren was able to compose himself in the presence of the ruler and his officials and advisors.

The chamberlain took his own seat upon a mat before a small table set in the center of the room, between Nichiren and Tokiyori. "Lay Monk Lord Saimyōji, I present to you the monk Nichiren whom I spoke of before. He has asked me to submit to you this written opinion of his," here he placed a scroll upon the table, "entitled *Treatise on Spreading Peace Throughout the Country by Establishing the True Dharma*."

"Welcome, Nichiren," said Tokiyori. "You must know that I have long been a student of Buddhism, and that the fate of this country is still of great concern to me, even though I am no longer the regent.

You must know, however, that this is not the first time such a treatise has been presented. More than 60 years ago the monk Eisai submitted the *Kōzen Gokoku-ron* (*Treatise on Letting Zen Flourish to Protect the State*) to Emperor Tsuchimikado. In the time of the Emperor Saga, the Great Master Dengyō, the founder of your Tendai school, wrote the *Shugo Kokkai-shō* (*An Essay on the Protection of the Nation*) in which he asserted that only the One Vehicle of the *Lotus Sutra* is the true teaching and that all beings have buddha-nature. Tell me, what does your treatise offer that has not already been said by these previous worthy teachers of the Dharma?"

Nichiren bowed low again and then responded, "I thank you for taking the time to see me." Out of the corner of his eye he saw that Lay Monk Yadoya was giving him a look cautioning him to be brief – and tactful. "As you know, in recent years, strange phenomena have appeared in the sky and natural calamities on earth; famines and epidemics have also spread over all the land. I have been worrying about this deeply. Knowing my limitations, I searched through the sutras and came to the conclusion that the cause of national calamities comes from the people turning against the True Dharma to side with the false. Therefore, protective deities and sages have abandoned the country and will not return. This has allowed various evils and devils to invade, causing disasters and calamities. How can I not point this out! How can I not be afraid of this! Finally, I could not refrain from composing this written opinion that I am now submitting to you. It is nothing but a way for me to repay what I owe my country." He bowed again.

The assembled samurai had already been told about Nichiren and his concerns, so there was no show of surprise at his words. They looked to Tokiyori, eagerly awaiting his response to this audacious nobody of a monk.

Finally, the lay monk spoke, "Of course all the people have been grieving over these calamities of recent years. Now that you are here and presenting your own opinion, I would like to ask you in what sutra is it stated that calamities and disasters occur in succession because the gods and sages have deserted the country. What is your evidence for this?"

Nichiren responded, "Many sutras state this and I have cited some of them in my written opinion. In particular, I have copied out passages from the *Golden Splendor Sutra*, the *Great Assembly Sutra*, the *Benevolent Kings Sutra*, and the *Medicine Master Sutra*. These sutras make it clear that the True Dharma is entrusted to the rulers to uphold if a country is to be safe and secure, but if it is not upheld then that failure will be a source of calamities. Who in the world would doubt it? Nevertheless, the blind and deluded, not knowing what is the true teaching, indiscriminately put faith in false teachings. As a result, the people will abandon the many buddhas and the sutras, having no more intention to uphold them. Therefore, the gods who protect the country and the sages who teach the truth will abandon the country. This allows evil demons and those with false views to move in, causing calamities and difficulties."

Now there was shifting and muttering from among the samurai in the audience hall. It was plain that they had taken umbrage to his words. The lay monk remained calm. Speaking for all of them, he asked, "Buddhism has been firmly established in this country ever since Prince Shōtoku built the Shitennōji temple after putting down the rebellion of Mononobe no Moriya, the leader of those who opposed Buddhism. Since then everyone in Japan from the emperor down to the common people has worshipped Buddhist images and single-mindedly recited the sutras. You know this as well as I, so who would you claim has slighted the Buddha's teachings and destroyed the Three Treasures? If you have proof for your allegations, I would like to know of them."

Nichiren responded, "As you say, Buddhist temples and sutra repositories stand in rows. Monks are as numerous as bamboo stalks and reeds or rice and hemp plants. Outwardly they have been revered year after year and day after day. In reality, however, the monks are flatterers and crooked in mind. They mislead the people, but both the rulers and their subjects are not wise enough to tell right from wrong.

"It is stated in the *Benevolent Kings Sutra*: 'Many evil monks who wish to win fame and material gain will preach false teachings before such men of power as the king, crown prince, and princes, which will eventually destroy Buddhism and lead the country to ruin. Unable to distinguish right from wrong, the king will put his faith in their teachings and promulgate laws counter to the Buddha's precepts. This will ruin Buddhism and destroy the country.'

"The *Nirvana Sutra* also warns of evil monks: 'Bodhisattvas, you should not be afraid of rogue elephants, but you should be afraid of an evil friend. Even if you are killed by rogue elephants, you will not be reborn in the three evil realms, but if your heart is lost to the evil monks, you will be reborn in them without fail.'

"Another passage from the *Nirvana Sutra* describes the corrupt monks in the following words: 'After the True Dharma has disappeared, during the Age of the Semblance Dharma, there will be monks who will pretend to uphold the precepts and will read and recite sutras to some degree. Yet these monks will cravenly delight in food and drink, nourishing their bodies for a long life...Although they will wear the *kesa*, they will nevertheless look like hunters. They will move about with their eyes narrowed, like a cat stalking a mouse. They will continually declare, "I have attained arhatship." ... To the outside world they may appear wise and gracious, but internally they will harbor greed and jealousy. ... Their false views will be pursued actively, slandering the True Dharma.'

"Observing the world today in light of these passages, the state of the Buddhist world is exactly as they point out. How can we accomplish anything worthwhile without admonishing the evil monks who slander the True Dharma?"

The assembly grew even more indignant on hearing these words. Was Nichiren daring to challenge their judgment? Was he casting aspersions on the rule of the shogunate?

The lay monk retorted, "Wise kings lead the people by following the principles of heaven and earth, and sagacious rulers govern the country by discerning good from bad. Today all the people in the country revere the monks. If they were evil monks as you claim, wise kings would not trust them. Were they not saintly masters, they would not be revered by men of wisdom and intelligence. Since wise kings and sagacious rulers revere them, we know that these eminent monks are to be greatly respected. How dare you accuse them so falsely? Who would you say are evil monks? I would like to know exactly."

Nichiren answered, "It was during the reign of the former Emperor Go-Toba, in the Kennin era (1201-1204), that two overly proud monks named Hōnen and Dainichi, possessed by evil spirits, fooled all the people in Japan, high and low. As a result, all the people of Japan became followers of either Pure Land or Zen Buddhism. Imperial patronage of Enryakuji temple decreased unexpectedly while scholars of the *Lotus Sutra* and mantra teachings were abandoned. In order to avoid complication, however, my treatise deals only with Hōnen and his false views that were in turn based upon the false interpretations of Buddhism put forth by the Chinese masters Tanluan, Daochuo and Shandao. I have provided citations from Hōnen's *A Collection of Passages on the Nembutsu Chosen in the Original Vow* so that you may see that he declared that the people should 'abandon, close, set aside, and cast away' all the sutras except for the three Pure Land sutras. He also slandered all the holy monks of India, China, and Japan who did not practice *nembutsu* exclusively, calling them 'a group of bandits.'

"Remember that we now live in the Latter Age of Degeneration. There are no saints. The people are led into a blind alley leading to hell, and are forgetting all about the direct way to buddhahood. How sad it is that no one awakens them! What a pity it is that only false faith grows rampant! As a result, everybody from the ruler down to the common people believe that there are no sutras except for the three Pure Land sutras and that there are no buddhas except for Amitābha Buddha with his two attendants.

"How sad it is that in the several decades since the publication of Hōnen's *A Collection of Passages on the Nembutsu Chosen in the Original Vow* a hundred, thousand, or even as many as 10,000 people have been infatuated by this devilish work and have gone astray from the True Dharma! How can the protective deities not be angry when an inferior teaching is favored and the true one is forgotten? How can devils not take advantage when the one-sided Pure Land teaching is preferred and the perfect true teaching is discarded? Is it not the best way to prevent calamities from overtaking the land to ban the one evil teaching, the source of all troubles, instead of having various devotional services?"

The assembled samurai were now red in the face, snorting in derision. The lay monk quieted them with a gesture and said, "This is terrible! How can you blame the august reign of the past emperor for calamities in recent years? How dare you speak ill of not only such earlier masters as Tanluan, Daochuo, and Shandao but also Hōnen? What you are doing is like blowing back the fur to expose a flaw in the hide or deliberately piercing the skin to cause blood to flow. When one looks for trouble, he will find it. I have never heard such abusive remarks as these. You should be ashamed of yourself. You should watch what you say. You have committed a serious transgression. How can you expect to escape punishment for such words?"

Smiling gently, Nichiren said, "They say that a knotgrass eater gets used to its sharp taste, and an insect living in a privy does not smell

160

its offensive odor. Affected by surroundings, people tend to lose their sense of judgment. So you take good words for bad ones, call the slanderer of the True Dharma a holy man, and suspect the true teacher of being a false one. You are utterly confused and have committed a great transgression. Now listen carefully, I will explain in detail what caused your confusion.

"There were five periods of Śākyamuni Buddha's expounding of the Dharma comprising provisional and true teachings in the following sequence: first the *Flower Garland Sutra*, then the Hinayana teachings of the Āgamas, followed by the Mahayana teachings of the Expanded sutras, followed by the Perfection of Wisdom sutras, and finally the period of the *Lotus Sutra* and *Nirvana Sutra*. He began with provisional doctrines that were easier to understand by unprepared people of lesser capacity. Gradually, the Buddha expounded doctrines progressively closer to the full truth and more difficult to comprehend, as the listeners became better prepared, until finally he revealed the ultimate truth by expounding the *Lotus Sutra*.

"However, the patriarchs of Pure Land Buddhism such as Tanluan, Daochuo, and Shandao took refuge in provisional teachings, which had been taught in the first 40 years or so, discarding the *Lotus Sutra*, the true intent of the Buddha revealed during the last eight years of his teaching. Certainly they did not know the ultimate truth of Buddhism. Especially Hōnen, who followed these masters, did not realize that they had based their doctrine on provisional teachings. Why do I say this? It is because he misled all the people by teaching that they should 'abandon, close, set aside, and cast away' all the 637 Mahayana sutras in 2,883 fascicles as well as all buddhas, bodhisattvas, and gods. This is solely an arbitrary interpretation of Hōnen without any basis in the Buddha's teaching whatsoever. His transgression of having uttered false words and abusive language is very grave and without comparison; we cannot reproach him too much.

"The people of today put complete faith in Hōnen's words and revere his *A Collection of Passages on the Nembutsu Chosen in the Original Vow*. As a result they revere only the three Pure Land sutras, discarding all others; and worship only Amitābha Buddha in the Pure Land of Utmost Bliss, forgetting all others. Hōnen was an archenemy of all the buddhas and sutras, a deadly foe of sagacious monks as well as the common people. Yet this evil teaching has spread all over the country.

"You are horrified that I attribute calamities in recent years to Hōnen's slandering of the True Dharma in years past. My treatise will dispel your fears by citing precedents, showing that I am not without basis. For instance, when Emperor Wuzong of the Tang dynasty ordered that *nembutsu* practice be propagated, the result was not peace but war and disorder. He later severely persecuted Buddhism, destroying many temple and pagodas. As a result, unable to put an end to war and disorder, the emperor died in agony. In Japan, the Retired Emperor Go-Toba, under whose reign Hōnen had spread his false teachings, failed in his attempt to reassert imperial authority in the Jōkyū incident and died in exile on Oki Island. That *nembutsu* is the cause of calamities has been shown in Tang China as well as in Japan. You should not have any doubt of it! In order to avert calamities and disasters in recent years, you must first of all discard the evil practice of *nembutsu* and take refuge in the good teaching of the *Lotus Sutra*, blocking the evil at its source and cutting it off at the root.

"Furthermore, I am not the first to request that Hōnen's exclusive *nembutsu* be rejected. During the Gennin era (1224-1225) the temples of Enryakuji on Mt. Hiei and Kōfukuji in Nara repeatedly appealed to the imperial court to suppress Hōnen's doctrine. By orders of the emperor and the shogun the printing blocks of *A Collection of Passages on the Nembutsu Chosen in the Original Vow* were confiscated and sent to the Great Hall of Enryakuji, where they were burnt as an act of gratitude to the Buddha for his favors received in past, present, and future lives. Bearers of the portable shrine of Gion ordered Hōnen's grave to be destroyed and his disciples were banished to remote provinces. They have never been pardoned."

The assembly seemed mollified. The lay monk said, "It is true that Hōnen abandoned, closed, set aside, and cast away all the sutras, together with all buddhas, bodhisattvas, and gods. This is clearly stated in his writing. Still, I do not know whether you are suffering from delusion, whether or not your actions are wise, and whether or not you are right when you strongly insist that it is Hōnen's teachings that are causing the recent calamities and disasters.

"Nevertheless, peace in the world and tranquility of the nation is what both the ruler and subjects alike wish for. Now, the prosperity of a nation depends on the Dharma, which is revered by all the people. If the nation is destroyed and its people perish, who will revere the Buddha and who will put faith in the Dharma? Therefore, we should first pray for the peace and tranquility of the nation before trying to establish Buddhism. If you know the means to prevent calamities and disasters, I would like to hear about it." The samurai nodded in agreement at the lay monk's words. This seemed most reasonable: first everyone should come together to pray for the nation's welfare; then, after peace was secured, one could wrangle over the Buddha's teachings.

Nichiren replied, "I am ignorant and do not know exactly how to address these issues. I would just like to express my humble opinion based upon the sutras. After contemplating the matter in view of Buddhist teachings, I have come to the conclusion that putting a ban on the slanderers of the True Dharma, and highly esteeming the upholders of the True Dharma, will lead to the tranquility of the nation and peace throughout the world.

"According to the *Lotus Sutra*, slandering the Mahayana sutras is a greater transgression than committing the five grave offenses, such as

163

killing one's parents, countless times greater. Therefore such transgressors fall into the Hell of Incessant Suffering. According to the *Nirvana Sutra*, even if offerings to perpetrators of the five grave offenses is permitted, it is not permitted to give offerings to slanderers of the True Dharma. One who kills even an ant will fall into the three evil realms without fail, but one who eliminates a slanderer of the True Dharma will reach the stage of non-retrogression, and eventually will attain buddhahood. The monk Awakened Virtue, who expounded the Dharma in the past despite persecution by slanderers of the True Dharma, became Kāśyapa Buddha; and King Virtuous, who killed slanderers to defend the True Dharma, was reborn in this world as Śākyamuni Buddha. The *Lotus* and *Nirvana* sutras are the essence of Śākyamuni Buddha's lifetime of teachings taught over the five periods. His warnings in them are of great weight. Who would not obey them?

"It is really sad that the people do not heed the sincere warnings of the Buddha. It is indeed a pity that they are misled by the false doctrine of Hōnen. If you wish to bring about the tranquility of the empire as soon as possible, first of all, you had better put a ban on the slanderers of the True Dharma throughout the nation."

The lay monk asked, "In order to eliminate slanderers of the True Dharma in compliance with the Buddha's warnings, is it necessary to put them to death as taught in the *Nirvana Sutra*? If so, killing will beget killing. What should we do about transgressions then? I can hardly believe that such is the proper course to take. How can it be justified?"

Nichiren stated in response, "What the *Nirvana Sutra* means is not that we should outlaw disciples of the Buddha at all, but that we should chastise slanderers of the True Dharma. Speaking of the previous lives of Śākyamuni Buddha, the *Nirvana Sutra* states that in his lifetimes as King Sen'yo and King Virtuous he killed slanderers of the True Dharma. However, as Śākyamuni Buddha, he taught that it was enough to withhold offerings from slanderers. Therefore, if all the countries in the world and all the monastics and lay followers stop giving offerings to evil monks who slander the True Dharma, putting all their faith instead in the defenders of the True Dharma, how can any more calamities or disasters befall us?"

What did the lay monk say to that? Nichiren could not remember. Perhaps that is when he was dismissed. Had the Lay Monk Lord Saimyōji said, "This sounds more like a remonstration than a written opinion. I think we have heard enough for today. We shall read this *Treatise on Spreading Peace Throughout the Country by Establishing the True Dharma* at our leisure and take it into consideration. We will send you a reply if we believe it merits one. Lay Monk Yadoya will now see you to the gate." Is that what he had said?

If only he had responded as the traveler did in the treatise. The traveler knelt on the floor, adjusted his kimono, and respectfully said to the master, "There are various schools of Buddhism, each with a doctrine hard to comprehend. I had many questions and could not tell which is right or wrong. Now you have clearly shown me what is right and what is wrong by quoting many passages from a wide range of sutras. Thanks to you, I am now free from my earlier prejudices, and can see and hear things clearly.

"After all, peace and tranquility of the nation is what the emperor above and the people below together desire and pray for. Let us immediately stop giving offerings to the *icchantika*, and instead support the many good monks and nuns for ages to come."

The master exclaimed in delight, "They say that a dove will become a hawk, and a sparrow will someday turn itself into a clam. How wonderful it is that you have changed your mind so quickly! It is like going into a house of orchids and taking on its scent or like a mugwort plant growing straight among the flax. If you put your faith in my words in dealing with calamities and disasters confronting us today, there is no question that the winds will settle down, the waves will subside, and prosperity will return before long.

"However, human minds change with time, and matters change in nature according to circumstances. They are like the moon's reflection in water moving with the waves or soldiers on a battleground, afraid of swords. You may believe in me now, but you will probably forget me completely. If you wish to bring about peace in our country and pray for happiness in this life, as well as in the future, then waste no time. Think hard and take the necessary measures to thoroughly deal with slanderers of the True Dharma.

"Why do I say this? It is because five of the seven disasters predicted in the *Medicine Master Sutra* have already taken place. There have already been epidemics, irregularities in the constellations, eclipses of the sun and moon, unseasonable storms, and droughts. This leaves just two disasters still to occur: foreign invasion and revolt. Moreover, two of the three calamities, famine and epidemics, predicted in the *Great Assembly Sutra* have indeed fallen upon us, leaving just one yet to come: war and disorder. And each of the various calamities and disasters that the *Golden Splendor Sutra* predicts have indeed fallen upon us except one: invasion of our land by foreign bandits. At this moment, six of the seven disasters foretold in the *Benevolent Kings Sutra* are seriously confronting us: irregularities in the order of the seasons and the cycles of the sun and moon, stars and comets changing their courses, fires, floods, severe winds, and severe droughts. Only one is yet to come: invasion of our land by foreign armies from the four directions. Moreover the same sutra warns: 'When disorder takes over in a country where the True Dharma is lost, the devils will seize control first. When the devils are rampant, the people will suffer and grow wild!'

"Comparing our present situation carefully with this passage, there is no doubt that the devils are rampant and many people are dying. Some of the predicted calamities have already taken place. How can we doubt the possibility of the remaining predictions all being realized? What will you do if the remaining predictions, revolt and foreign invasion, take place at once as punishment for upholding evil teachings?

"The ruler governs the empire holding his country together, and the people make a living by cultivating their farmlands. However, if foreign armies invade the country and rebels pillage the people's lands, how can there be anything but terror and confusion? Where can the people escape when they lose their country and homes? If you wish to have peace for yourself, you should first of all pray for the peace of the country.

"People in this world are afraid of the next life to such an extent that they seek refuge in false teachings or revere slanderers of the True Dharma. I hate to see them confuse right and wrong, trying to seek refuge in Buddhism in the wrong way. If they are to put faith in Buddhism, why should they revere the words of provisional teachings? Should they refuse to change their minds and cling to false teachings, they will soon leave this world and fall into the Hell of Incessant Suffering without fail. I am sure of this because, by examining many sutras, we can see that they all regard slandering the True Dharma as the most serious crime. How sad it is that people should all wander out of the gate of the True Dharma into the prison of an evil teaching! Such ignorance is causing everyone to be reeled in by the rope of evil teachings and caught forever in the net of slandering the True Dharma! In this life such wanderers are lost in the mist of delusions; in the next life they will sink to the bottom of a flaming hell. How sad it is! How terrible it is!

"You should promptly convert your wrong faith to the true and sole teaching of the *Lotus Sutra*. Then this triple world of the un-awakened will manifest the buddha-land. Will the buddha-land ever decay? All the worlds in the universe will become pure lands. Will pure lands ever be destroyed? When our country does not decay and the world is not destroyed, our bodies will be safe and our hearts tranquil. Believe these words and revere them!"

Finally convinced, the traveler said, "Who will not be careful, since this concerns the possibility of tranquility in this life and the attainment of buddhahood in a future life? Who will not be afraid of making a mistake? Listening to the words of the Buddha carefully taught in the sutras, I now realize how serious an offense it is to have slandered the Buddha and destroyed the True Dharma. It was not due to my arbitrary opinion that I took refuge only in Amitābha Buddha, throwing away all others, revering only the three Pure Land sutras, setting aside all others. I only followed the leaders of the past. Probably other people everywhere must have done the same. It is clearly stated in the sutras and is logically obvious that such people will exhaust themselves to no purpose in this life and they will all fall into the Hell of Incessant Suffering in the next. There is no doubt about it.

"I hope to continue receiving your compassionate instructions so that I may completely eliminate my ignorance, devise the best means to chastise slanderers of the True Dharma at once, and bring about peace in the world soon. Let us first secure tranquility in this life, and then try to attain buddhahood in future lives. I not only believe in this but also will try to lead others in correcting their misconceptions."

Nichiren opened his eyes again. He was back in the present at the home of Ikegami Munenaka. He remembered well that Hōjō Tokiyori had not at all responded as he had hoped. In fact, he received no response from him at all in regard to the *Treatise on Spreading Peace Throughout the Country by Establishing the True Dharma*. There were no further inquiries, nor was his advice accepted. There were many others, however, who were not indifferent. They were outraged. It did not take them long to make their displeasure known.

The Riot at Matsubagayatsu

More rocks thumped against the wall of Nichiren's hut at Matsubagayatsu.

"That's where he lives!" shouted the one of the rock throwers. "That's where the enemy of our lord and savior lives! He's the one who spreads the rumor that chanting *nembutsu* is the way to hell!"

Nisshō, hearing all this, stared mutely at the wall of the hut for a time, shaking his head. Turning to Nichiren he said, "Your *Treatise on Spreading Peace Throughout the Country by Establishing the True Dharma* has roused the people against us."

Nichiren responded, "I have merely cited the sutras. The people should think hard about the cause of the recent calamities. Otherwise, they will only increase. This is my humble opinion. It is up to each person to decide whether to accept my plan to eliminate slanderers of the True Dharma or not."

From outside, the noise of shouted denunciations and threats continued. It seemed as though a mob were gathering in front of the hut. "Come out and face us, Nichiren! Are you afraid to meet with a true monk?"

Nichirō rushed into the room. "Master, there are many townsmen and samurai out front. They have brought monks with them. They said that Dōamidabutsu of the Shinzenkōji temple and Nōan of the Chōanji temple sent them. They want to debate with you!"

Nisshō said to his nephew, "Send them away. Tell them that Nichiren is indisposed and will speak with them at another time when proper arrangements for a debate can be made."

Nichirō was about to head outside when Nichiren stopped him with a gesture. "Wait a moment. They are here at the urging of the leaders of those who would establish the supremacy of Hōnen's teachings here in Kamakura. I am prepared to fend off any attack by such followers of expedient teachings."

Nichiren walked out onto the veranda, the fourth fascicle of the *Lotus Sutra* in hand. He surveyed the mob before him, saw the anger in the faces of the merchants, stevedores, farmers, and samurai gathered just behind a handful of monks. Behind the monks and their followers were others who seemed excited and curious. These did not seem to have any personal stake in the debate that was sure to follow. They were simply there to enjoy the spectacle. Most likely, they hoped there would be a full-blown riot that would give them something to gossip about for days to come. There were still others, however, who seemed calmer and more thoughtful, as though they were genuinely curious about what Nichiren had to say for himself. These were the ones who might actually be open to the Buddha's words if they could but hear them and take the teachings to heart. It was for the sake of these that Nichiren exposed himself to the venomous mob and the wrathful monks who led them.

Nichiren addressed them, "Have you come then to debate with me about the relative merits of the *Lotus Sutra* and the three Pure Land sutras? Or are you only here to hurl abuse – and rocks!"

A couple of the monks raised their hands to quiet the crowd. Once the shouting and heckling had died down, one of them turned to Nichiren and said, "We have been told that you petitioned Lord Saimyōji to withhold alms from those who practice the *nembutsu*. Furthermore, you are trying to sow fear into the hearts of the people by claiming that those who chant *nembutsu* will fall into the three evil realms of the hells, hungry ghosts, and animals. Is this true? How dare you hold in contempt the teaching of Śākyamuni Buddha expounded in the three Pure Land sutras, and slander the 48 vows of Amitābha

170

Buddha? It is you who are going to fall into the Hell of Incessant Suffering! I came here to expose your error and prevent you from taking anyone with you!"

Nisshō leaned close to Nichiren and whispered, "They probably heard of this from the Lay Monk Lord Gokurakuji." Nichiren nodded. It seemed to him that Lord Gokurakuji was almost certainly inciting the people against him. Lord Gokurakuji was Hōjō Shigetoki, the great-uncle of Tokiyori and father of the current regent Nagatoki. He had retired the previous year to Gokurakuji temple and was a devout Pure Land Buddhist. He had also been involved with Tōjō Kagenobu, who was his vassal, in the failed attempt to gain control of Seichōji.

Nichiren responded, "Haven't you and other disciples of Hōnen disseminated *A Collection of Passages on the Nembutsu Chosen in the Original Vow* all over Japan spreading the rumor among ignorant people that Hōnen was a wise man who determined that the *nembutsu* is the true teaching, and that there is no statement in the sutras allowing us to reopen the gate to the teachings of the *Lotus Sutra* and the mantra practices once they have been closed, or to revitalize those teachings and practices again after they have been discarded? This has led to people condemning the *Lotus Sutra* and mantra teachings, saying they are as worthless as last year's calendar or as ill-fitting as a grandfather's shoes on a young grandson. Some have even said that reading the *Lotus Sutra* is less worthy than listening to music. Those who take up the sole practice of *nembutsu* are warned that any association with the *Lotus Sutra* will hinder their chances of rebirth in the Pure Land. This is to slander the True Dharma of the *Lotus Sutra* by turning people away from it. Can you deny this?"

"That is not our teaching," said the monk. "One can attain rebirth in the Pure Land through the miscellaneous practices as well. *A Collection of Passages on the Nembutsu Chosen in the Original Vow* does not refute the *Lotus Sutra* and mantra practices. It is just that

171

people should choose the way according to their capacity. There is no need to argue about this."

Nichiren shook his head. "Insisting that rebirth in the Pure Land is possible through miscellaneous practices while claiming to be a disciple of Hōnen is to go against his teachings. I know that you secretly believe that rebirth in the Pure Land is not possible except through the sole practice of *nembutsu*. Are you not aware of the passages in *A Collection of Passages on the Nembutsu Chosen in the Original Vow* urging the people to 'abandon, close, set aside, and cast away' the *Lotus Sutra* and mantra teachings, likening those who believe in them to bandits, and insisting that not even one out of 1,000 of those who believe in them will be able to be reborn in the Pure Land?"

The monk sighed and said, "You are wrong. We disciples of Hōnen revere all the sutras, including the *Lotus Sutra*. How can you say we are slanderers of the True Dharma?

Nichiren answered, "You may open all the sutras and even the *Lotus Sutra*, but only to make certain that those sutras preach the way of difficult practice so as to better promote Hōnen's teaching. The more you read the sutras and commentaries, the more grievous your slander of the True Dharma becomes. When I compare the *Lotus Sutra* with the three Pure Land sutras, I see that the former is like the sun and moon or a great ocean whereas the latter are like a firefly or a river. The *nembutsu* is a provisional teaching of the Buddha. Wishing to be reborn into the Pure Land is like trying to cross the ocean aboard a boat carved out of a heavy rock or to climb over a perilous pass carrying a big mountain on your shoulders."

The monk fiercely responded, "The teachings of the *Lotus Sutra* are indeed profound, but our capacity to understand and accept the sutra are limited. The sutra is admirable, but not suited to the inferior capacity of we who live in the Latter Age of Degeneration. It is not

172

too late for us to understand the *Lotus Sutra* after we are reborn in the Pure Land of Amitābha Buddha, even though we may be committing the transgression of slandering the True Dharma. We should, therefore, only chant *nembutsu*, be reborn in the Pure Land in the next life, reach the stage of non-retrogression, and attain awakening by listening to the *Lotus Sutra* expounded by Amitābha Buddha and his attendants. Moreover, the Original Vow of Amitābha Buddha does not discriminate between the wise and ignorant, virtuous and evil, and observers and non-observers of Buddhist precepts. If only we single-mindedly chant the name of Amitābha Buddha, he will without fail come to meet us at the moment of death according to his Original Vow. We only temporarily give up our connection to the *Lotus Sutra* in this world in order to attain rebirth in the Pure Land of Utmost Bliss and awaken to its teachings there. If people whose capacity is insufficient to understand the profound teaching of the *Lotus Sutra* spend time on it in this defiled world without chanting *nembutsu* at all, they will neither attain the awakening of the *Lotus Sutra* nor be reborn in the Pure Land, resulting in a double loss. In the end, such people end up slighting the *Lotus Sutra* anyway."

Nichiren said in reply, "Your words sound convincing, but when I contemplate them in detail I am sorry to say that you have committed the transgression of slandering the True Dharma. The reason I say this is because of your statement that the *Lotus Sutra* is unsuitable for us in the Latter Age of Degeneration. Does this mean it is useless for all the people in the Latter Age to put faith in and practice the *Lotus Sutra*? If this is correct, among all the people, those who had faith in the *Lotus Sutra* will abandon the faith, those who plan to put faith in the sutra will abandon the plan, and no one will have the heart of rejoicing at hearing the sutra which brings incalculable merit. This means committing slander of the True Dharma. When all the people become slanderers of the True Dharma, it is impossible for them to be reborn in the Pure Land of Utmost Bliss, even if they practice *nembutsu*."

The monk scowled. "It is impossible to practice the *Lotus Sutra* unless one possesses a high capacity to understand it. It only bewilders evil ordinary people in the Latter Age."

Nichiren said, "You should know that the great masters Tiantai and Miaole both urged ordinary people in the Latter Age of Degeneration to have faith in the *Lotus Sutra*. In chapter 18 of the *Lotus Sutra*, the Buddha expounds the merit of the fiftieth person in succession who hears the *Lotus Sutra* and rejoices. Great Master Tiantai compares this fiftieth person who rejoices to the *nyagrodha* tree that can grow a 33' bud in a single day or to the *kalavinka* bird that sings more beautifully than any other bird even before it is hatched. Their merit is 100,000 billion times more valuable than the merit of a great saint who only upholds the expedient teachings and practices of the sutras prior to the *Lotus Sutra*. Great Master Tiantai likened the long period necessary to practice the expedient teachings to the slow growth of various plants and trees, and the immediate attainment of buddhahood through the practice of the *Lotus Sutra* to the rapid growth of the *nyagrodha*. He also compared the saints of the expedient teachings to various birds, and ordinary people who intently keep faith in the *Lotus Sutra* to the cry of a *kalavinka* bird in its eggshell that is superior to that of other birds. Commenting on this, the Great Master Miaole said, 'Those who misunderstand the *Lotus Sutra* are convinced that the practitioner of the sutra in the advanced stages gains more merit and looks down on the novice practicing the *Lotus Sutra*, without knowing the great merit of beginning practitioners of the *Lotus Sutra*. Great Master Tiantai, therefore, showed that even through the beginners have not practiced the *Lotus Sutra* for long, their merit is so deep that it can reveal the strength of the sutra.'

"Great Master Miaole also cites a passage from the *Heavenly Son Abiding Goodness Sutra* wherein Mañjuśrī Bodhisattva told Venerable Śāriputra, 'It is better to listen to the Dharma, slander it, and as a result, fall into hell than to make offerings to many buddhas. For even though one slanders the True Dharma and falls into hell, his

174

transgression will become an adverse condition causing him to get an opportunity to listen to the True Dharma after he emerges from hell.' Great Master Miaole said of this passage, 'This compares the merit of those who listen to the Dharma to those who make offerings to the Buddha but do so without listening to the Dharma. Listening to the Dharma, even if one slanders it, can be the seed for buddhahood, though in that case, attaining buddhahood will take a long time. Needless to say this does not compare to the merit of those who listen to the Dharma, contemplate it, and strive to practice it.'

Great Master Miaole further said, 'If a phrase of the *Lotus Sutra* fills your heart, you can be sure it will help you to reach the other shore of awakening. If you contemplate and practice the *Lotus Sutra*, it is sure to be a ship that can cross the great ocean of birth and death and reach the far shore of awakening. Rejoice at hearing the *Lotus Sutra* and always expound the sutra by becoming a master of the Dharma or an attendant of such a master. Whether you believe the sutra or abandon it, the *Lotus Sutra* can open the way to buddhahood once you hear it. Whether you follow or disobey the *Lotus Sutra*, you will become a buddha in the end, because of the merit of having heard the sutra.' I think that the phrases, 'Whether you believe it or abandon it' and 'Whether you follow or disobey the *Lotus Sutra*,' are truly impressive.

"These interpretations make it clear that even great bodhisattvas who have thoroughly studied the Mahayana sutras and reached the rank next only to the Buddha are incomparably inferior to those who merely listened to the *Lotus Sutra* and made a connection with it, namely ordinary people like ourselves in the Latter Age of Degeneration who are unable to eliminate the defilements or master even one supernatural power.

"You followers of Hōnen should be ashamed of yourselves for assuming you have the capacity only for provisional teachings and not embracing the True Dharma. The result is that you have merely thought of yourselves in seeking to be reborn in the Pure Land, just like the voice-hearers and private-buddhas who were admonished by the Buddha for selfishness when the Expanded and Wisdom sutras of the Mahayana were taught. Both the masters and the disciples who denigrate the *Lotus Sutra* in favor of *nembutsu* will fall without fail into the burning flames of the Hell of Incessant Suffering!"

The monk, red in the face, shouted, "You, a monk yourself, denounce other monks for committing a transgression! This is a violation of at least two of the ten major precepts of the *Brahmā Net Sutra*! You are speaking ill of other bodhisattva practitioners and slandering the Three Treasures in your statements against Amitābha Buddha, the Dharma of the three Pure Land sutras, and your fellow members of the monastic Sangha. How can you excuse yourself?

Nichiren calmly responded, "The Buddha tells us in the *Nirvana Sutra* that a monk who does not correct a bad monk is an enemy of the Dharma, but a monk who does correct the bad one is a true disciple. Adhering to this admonition of the Buddha, I am predicting that slanderers of the Dharma will all fall into the Hell of Incessant Suffering."

The Pure Land monk was left speechless. He and his fellow monks were obviously not as well versed in the sutras and commentaries of the Great Master Tiantai and Great Master Miaole as was Nichiren, who had mastered the art of scholarly debate on Mt. Hiei. The lay followers and other monks were silent, waiting expectantly for the lead monk to rebuke Nichiren. But he could think of nothing more to say. No sutra passage or comment by the Pure Land patriarchs came to mind. Finally he shook his head and said, "It may be that only the light of Amitābha Buddha can make you understand. You are as yet devoid of sincerity, depth, or the determination for rebirth in the Pure Land. I will pray that Amitābha Buddha shines his light upon you and forgives your transgressions and slander of the Dharma. Know that we will be back once we have had time to consult the sutras and commentaries of the patriarchs. Your vicious lies will be answered." The monk waved the others monks away, and they all departed. Once the monks had dispersed, the lay followers also broke up into small groups and drifted off, mumbling and cursing.

For over a month the harassment continued. People passing by habitually threw rocks or sticks at the hermitage. Sometimes many of them gathered outside the hut, yelling their abuse and insults. People who only knew of Nichiren as the monk who hated Amitābha Buddha and the revered Hōnen looked upon him with disgust and hatred, as if seeing an enemy of their parents, or as wives look upon prostitutes. Sometimes monks would attempt to debate Nichiren and his followers, but they quickly left without anything intelligible to say. Oftentimes it was enough to just ask them upon what sutra they based their beliefs and then to point out that any sutras taught before the *Lotus Sutra* were among those taught during the time when, according to the *Infinite Meanings Sutra*, the "final truth had still not been revealed." In any case the *Lotus Sutra* itself says in chapter ten that it is the most difficult to believe and most difficult to understand, and therefore the most profound, of all the sutras taught at any time by the Buddha.

There were those who came to the hermitage with a genuine spirit of inquiry. Both men and women, monks and laypeople, educated and ignorant, were greeted cordially and allowed to come inside to ask their questions privately. Nichiren knew they were uncertain as to whom to believe. He told them what he himself had come to know, "The Buddha told us to rely on the Dharma and not on people. Accordingly we should not believe in anyone, no matter how great a wise man he appears to be, unless he preaches according to the sutra, isn't that so? The only good friends in the sense of reliable teachers in the Latter Age are the *Lotus Sutra* and *Nirvana Sutra*."

The inquirers would ask, "That is strange. Commonly a 'good friend' refers to a person. Why do you say these sutras are good friends?"

Nichiren answered, "Usually good friends are people. However, true good friends do not exist in the Latter Age, so there is much evidence of the Dharma itself as a good friend. In chapter 28 of the *Lotus Sutra* the Buddha says, 'Anyone who keeps, reads and recites this *Sutra of the Lotus Flower of the Wonderful Dharma*, memorizes it correctly, studies it, practices it, and copies it, should be considered to have seen me and heard this teaching directly from my mouth. He should be considered to have made many offerings to me.' According to this passage, the *Lotus Sutra* is identical to Śākyamuni Buddha. For those who do not believe in the *Lotus Sutra*, Śākyamuni Buddha has entered nirvana and never appears in front of them, but for those who believe in it, he is constantly present as though he were alive in this world."

It was often the case that this answer then led to the question, "So is the way of the *Lotus Sutra* the way of other-power as taught in Pure Land Buddhism, or is it the way of self-power as the Zen Buddhists seem to be teaching?"

Nichiren explained, "The 'self-power' of the *Lotus Sutra* is not what those who do not understand Buddhism think it is. We possess in our hearts all living beings of the ten realms, so we have within ourselves even the realm of buddhas, to say nothing of those of all other types of beings. Therefore, to become a buddha now does not mean that one now becomes one for the first time. The 'other-power' in the *Lotus Sutra* is also not what those who don't understand Buddhism think it is. For other buddhas are contained within each of us by nature. They also manifest themselves in us ordinary people."

For the truly curious, yet another question then arose, "If the buddhas are not generated anew by our own efforts and not truly other than ourselves, then what or whom should a believer in the *Lotus Sutra* regard as the focus of devotion? How should we perform Buddhist rites and what should our daily practice be?"

Nichiren told them, "First of all, the focus of devotion could be the eight fascicles, one fascicle, one chapter, or title alone of the *Lotus Sutra*. This is taught in the 'Teacher of the Dharma' and 'Supernatural Powers of the Tathāgata' chapters. Those who can afford to may have portraits or wooden statues of Śākyamuni Buddha and Many Treasures Buddha made and placed on both sides of the *Lotus Sutra*. Those who can further afford to may make portraits or wooden statues of various buddhas of the ten directions or Universal Sage Bodhisattva and others.

"As for the manner of performing the rites, standing or sitting practices must be observed in front of the focus of devotion. Outside the practice hall, however, one is free to choose any of the four modes of activity: walking, standing, sitting, or lying down.

"Next, regarding daily practice, the *daimoku* of the *Lotus Sutra* should be chanted, 'Namu Myōhō Renge Kyō.' If possible, a verse or phrase of the *Lotus Sutra* should respectfully be read. As an auxiliary practice one may, as one wishes, say a prayer to Śākyamuni Buddha, Many Treasures Buddha, the numerous buddhas of the ten directions, various bodhisattvas, followers of the two vehicles, heavenly kings, dragons, or the eight kinds of nonhuman beings who protect Buddhism. Because there are many ignorant people today, precedence is not given to contemplation of the 3,000 realms in a single thought-moment. But those with the will to do so should by all means study and contemplate it."

To which the truly curious responded, "What are the merits of chanting only the *daimoku*?

Nichiren said, "Śākyamuni Buddha appeared in this world to expound the *Lotus Sutra*, but he kept the sutra's name a secret during the first 40 years or so of his teaching. From the age of 30 until 70 or so, the Buddha solely expounded the expedient teachings to prepare the way for the *Lotus Sutra*. At the age of 72, the Buddha for the first time called out the title of the *Lotus Sutra*. Thus it is incomparably superior to the titles of other sutras. Moreover, the two Chinese characters *myō* and *hō* (Wonderful Dharma) in the title of the *Lotus Sutra* are equipped with the doctrine of the 3,000 realms in a single thought-moment and the doctrine of the attainment of buddhahood in the remotest past, the essence of the *Lotus Sutra* revealed in the 'Expedients' and 'The Duration of the Life of the Tathāgata' chapters respectively. *The Profound Meaning of the Lotus Sutra* by the Great Master Tiantai interprets the five characters *myō*, *hō*, *ren*, *ge*, and *kyō* and maintains that everything including the causes and effects of all buddhas, bodhisattvas, and those in the ten realms, and insentient beings such as grasses, plants, tiles, and pebbles are included in the two characters *myō* and *hō* without exception.

"It is taught in the *Lotus Sutra* that the merits of all the sutras taught during the 40 or so years prior are all stored in the one *Lotus Sutra* and the threefold bodied buddhas in all the worlds throughout the universe are all manifestations of the one Śākyamuni Buddha. Therefore, one buddha equals all buddhas, and the two characters of *myō* and *hō* include all buddhas. Accordingly the merit of chanting the five-character *daimoku* of the *Sutra of the Lotus Sutra of the Wonderful Dharma* is enormous indeed. On the other hand, the titles of the various other buddhas and sutras are expedient teachings, which were opened up to reveal the truth of the *Lotus Sutra*. The five-character *daimoku* of the *Lotus Sutra* is the one that opened them to reveal the true teaching, and therefore we should chant the *daimoku* of the *Lotus Sutra*."

Nichiren answered all such questions and others with ease. He had prepared himself for these interrogations by going over all these points in detail in his studies. It was impossible to out-argue him, especially because he responded so credibly to the lay people who came to ask him these things out of curiosity. Therefore, Pure Land followers determined to bring about his downfall by other means. If they could not succeed in completely disgracing him in the eyes of all, then they must try to destroy him.

It was midnight on the 27th day of the eighth month of the first year of the Bunnō era (1260) when the outraged Pure Land devotees at last made their move against Nichiren and his growing band of monks and lay followers. They might all have died had it not been for the agitated monkeys screeching in the trees. Awakened by the monkeys, Nichiren and the others quickly threw on their robes and rushed out onto the veranda. The glow of dozens of torches progressed steadily up the road towards the hermitage. The great light given off by the flames made it seem as though all the people of Kamakura had risen up against them. There were commoners with clubs and knives, and also samurai with swords and bows.

There was no time to pack their things. They rushed back into the hut. Nichiren grabbed the ten fascicles of the threefold *Lotus Sutra* and headed out the back way up the side of the ravine. Other monks stayed behind to make an attempt to defend the hut, but it was no use. They were only a handful armed with staves against an uncountable number of foes that rushed out of the darkness to beat at them with sticks or slash at them with swords. Then the main body of the mob arrived, cursing and screaming, maddened with rage at the blasphemers who were trying to arouse the shogunate against the merciful teachings of Hōnen upon which they relied for their salvation. They hurled torches onto the thatched roof of the hermitage, even as the last defenders were forced to flee into the nearby pines.

At the top of the ridge overlooking the hillside, Nisshō, Nichirō, Nikkō and the others caught up to Nichiren. He was looking down at the hut below, now engulfed in flames. "Did everyone get out safely?" he asked.

Nisshō checked and saw that no one was missing. They had all escaped the mob and the fire. Some were badly bruised or cut, but there were no life threatening injuries. Nisshō reported this to Nichiren who was greatly relieved, though he could see that they were all quite shaken.

Nichiren said to them, "Do not be surprised by this! It was only to be expected. The Buddha warned us that things like this would happen. Did he not say of the *Lotus Sutra*, 'Many people hate it with jealousy even in my lifetime. Needless to say, more people will do so after my final nirvana.'"

Nichiren laughed. "Now we are like Never Despising Bodhisattva. Remember, he said to the people, 'You will become buddhas,' and so the people struck him with sticks or threw tiles or stones at him. Now, like him, we have had to run away to a safe distance. Like him, we should bow and praise even our persecutors."

Nichiren turned to look back down upon the burning hut and the mob surrounding it. Nisshō, Nichirō, Nikkō, and the other monks moved up behind him. Following his lead they all bowed and repeated the words of Never Despising Bodhisattva from chapter 20 of the *Lotus Sutra*, "I respect you deeply. I do not despise you. Why is that? It is because you will be able to practice the way of bodhisattvas and become buddhas."

The Izu Exile

Looking up at the statue of Śākyamuni Buddha that stood in front of the mandala by his bedside, Nichiren recalled the time more than 20 years ago, when the steward Itō Sukemitsu had given it to him. This gift had been presented during his first exile, decreed and enforced by the shogunate. After the riot and burning of the hermitage he did not return to Kamakura until early spring of the following year, having spent the previous fall and winter at the residence of Toki Jōnin in Shimōsa Province. There he had lectured for 100 days on the *Lotus Sutra* and the *Great Calming and Contemplation* in the Lotus Hall, which was Toki Jōnin's family temple. Upon his return to Kamakura, Nichiren and his followers rebuilt the hermitage at Matsubagayatsu. This did not go unnoticed. On the twelfth day of the fifth month in the first year of the Kōchō era (1261), samurai in the service of the current regent, Hōjō Nagatoki, arrived at the hermitage to arrest Nichiren and his disciples. All of them were marched to the beach where a small rowboat awaited on the shore, surrounded by more samurai and sailors. Out on the bay one of the small ships that hugged the coast, engaging in trade with other provinces, was waiting for them.

The lead official said, "Nichiren, you are under sentence of exile. You will be sent to the Itō district in Izu Province." He turned to the other samurai, "Put him in the boat." Two samurai grabbed Nichiren by the arms and escorted him into the boat while others used polearms topped with gently curving blades, called *naginata*, held crosswise to hold back his disciples.

"How can I be exiled?" Nichiren asked the official. "There has not even been a proper hearing."

The official scoffed. "You are fortunate it is only exile. Many think it is unpardonable to let a speaker of evil such as yourself leave here alive!"

Nichiren sat in the boat but he continued to admonish the official, making sure that his disciples and onlookers could hear him as well. "Do you people possess so much hate that you do not realize you are committing an act of self-destruction?! Are you willing to break the Jōei Code, the law of the shogunate, that has been verified in the names of Brahmā, Indra, the four heavenly kings, Amaterasu Ōmikami, and the Great Bodhisattva Hachiman?!"

The official laughed. "You are the one who has broken the code. Or have you forgotten that there are articles against slander and fighting in the streets? When you speak out against good monks like Dōamidabutsu and Nōan, and speak ill of those who practice *nembutsu* or Zen meditation, saying that they are destined for the Hell of Incessant Suffering, then you are the one breaking the law. When you and your people riot in the streets such as they did last year, causing fires as well, then how can you say you are not a lawbreaker?"

Nichiren responded with outrage in his voice, "These are serious allegations! Why has there been no proper summons to court or any investigation? Even if those accusations were true I should have been given a chance to respond. You know as well as I that the riot and fire was the result of a mob attacking my hermitage at night. As for my teachings, they are unique, so I have been misunderstood. But even if the shogunate cannot comprehend my teaching, I should still have been given a chance to engage in debate with the monks whom they have put their faith in. If this did not clarify matters, then officials should have inquired into the teachings of the scholar-monks of India or China. If that still did not resolve things, they should have waited for a while and considered that I might have a good reason for the things I have said. Nevertheless, without grasping the details and

184

without realizing the danger of self-destruction, you are unreasonably breaking the all important vow of the Jōei Code with these illegal proceedings."

"I am no magistrate," said the official. "I am not interested in your arguments. I am only interested in getting you onto that ship, out of Kamakura, and on to Izu. Now keep quiet!"

Nichiren put his palms together and bowed. His disciples cried out to him, some in tears. The guards kept back all but one. Nichirō, now a strong young man of 16, would not be cowed. He slipped past the guards and ran down to the boat just as it was being pushed off into the surf.

"Get back!" screamed the official.

But Nichirō would not get back. Crying for his master as he reached out to him, he waded out into the bay after the boat. Nichiren exhorted him to be calm, but his disciple was too overwrought and would not listen. "Take me with you!" He shouted again and again. Exasperated, the official took an oar and struck the young monk with bone shattering force. Clutching at his broken right arm, Nichirō finally backed away, his face white with pain.

Tears fell from Nichiren's eyes as he saw his faithful disciple so brutalized. "Nichirō! Calm yourself. Is this how a disciple of the Buddha should act? From now on, when you see the sun setting in the west behind Izu, think of me. When I see the sun rising from the sea, I shall think of you."

Nichirō nodded. "Forgive me, master." Becoming faint, he went down on his knees in the water, sweat and tears coursing down his face. One of the guards finally reached him and escorted him back to where Nisshō and the other monks were gathered.

As the boat moved away Nichiren began to chant the final verses from the eleventh chapter of the *Lotus Sutra*, "It is difficult to keep this sutra. I shall be glad to see anyone keeping it even for a moment." The rocking of the waves caused his voice to fade in and out, giving the recitation an odd rhythm. The passage ended with, "Anyone who expounds this sutra even for a moment in this dreadful world should be honored with offerings by all gods and men." From that point on Nichiren knew that he and his disciples had truly become practitioners of the *Lotus Sutra* as its predictions of hardships that would be faced by the teachers of the True Dharma began to be fulfilled in their own lives.

The samurai did not bother to take Nichiren all the way to Itō at the tip of the Izu peninsula. Instead, they stranded him on a desolate shore by the fishing village of Kawana at around four in the afternoon. He looked at the thatched huts of the fishermen and knew that he would find no help from them. They would know better than to offer assistance to an exile, for by doing so they might also incur the displeasure of the authorities. Nichiren walked down the beach towards some nearby cliffs, hoping at the very least to find a cave where he could take shelter.

'So this is Izu,' he thought. 'It was here that Minamoto no Yoritomo had been banished as a boy and languished for over 20 years.' He recalled stories he had heard about the beginnings of the Genpei War. Taira no Kiyomori, the leader of the Taira clan, had beheaded Yoritomo's father, Yoshitimo, and banished the 13-year-old Yoritomo. Full of anguish and bitter resentment against Kiyomori, Yoritomo wondered to whom he could pray for justice. Fortunately for him, he learned to recite the *Lotus Sutra* from a nun named Myōhō who lived on Mt. Izu. On the day he finished reciting the sutra for the thousandth time, the monk Mongaku-bō came to him with the skull of his father and prompted him to revolt against the Taira, enabling him to take revenge for his father's death and become the first shogun.

As Nichiren reflected upon the first shogun's devotion to the *Lotus Sutra*, a fisherman approached and introduced himself as Yasaburō, the local boat-manager. Without even asking Nichiren his name, he invited him to come to his home. "It would be inhuman of me to allow anyone, let alone a disciple of the Buddha, to starve to death on the beach. Please, come with me. We'll have dinner together and see what can be done for you."

"Please, if you could just show me a place where I can stay for the night, I do not want to trouble you or bring down the anger of the steward upon you."

"It is no trouble, and don't worry about the steward. Please, my home is just over here."

Yasaburo's wife proved to be just as kindly. She provided him with water to wash his hands and feet and fed him as though he were a member of the family. That night Nichiren slept by the hearth and the next day Yasaburō and his wife took him to a nearby cave where he could take shelter. They gave him straw for bedding, warmer clothing, and promised to bring food to him in the days ahead.

Nichiren was overcome with emotion. He said to Yasaburō, "What kind of karmic affinity is there between us? You must have been a practitioner of the *Lotus Sutra* in the past, and now you have been reborn in this Latter Age to show mercy to me." Turning to Yasaburō's wife he said, "A man might be generous to a stranger like this; however, I have never met a lady like you. It fills me with wonder." Speaking to them both he said, "You are like my parents reborn. In the *Lotus Sutra* the Buddha says, 'If a teacher of the Dharma expounds this sutra after my final nirvana, I will manifest the four kinds of devotees: monks, nuns, laymen, and laywomen of pure faith, and dispatch them to him so that they may make offerings to him, and that they may lead many living beings, collecting them to hear the Dharma from him. If he is hated and threatened with swords, sticks, tile-pieces or stones, I will manifest men and dispatch them to him in order to protect him.' These verses from the sutra explains that the heavenly gods and benevolent deities will transform into men and women in order to make offerings and help the person who practices the *Lotus Sutra*. There can be no doubt that they must have been reborn as the two of you in order to make offerings to myself, so that I may continue to live and uphold the *Lotus Sutra*."

For weeks Nichiren lived in the cave and survived on the offerings that were brought to him, discretely, by Yasaburō and his wife, even though rice was scarce at that time of year when it had only just been sown. The local steward did not seem to care about him one way or the other, but the people of Kawana had heard about Nichiren and his condemnation of Hōnen's teachings. They looked away from him, even closed their eyes so as not to have to look upon him. If he tried to speak to anyone they would turn away from him with a curse. Finally, after about a month, a messenger came to Nichiren's cave. The local steward, Itō Sukemitsu, had fallen ill and was close to death. Out of desperation he sent for the exiled monk he had been hearing about who claimed that the *Lotus Sutra* was more efficacious than any other teaching or practice. Nichiren hesitated, not sure if he should accept the request. After some consideration he decided that the request was a sign of a certain amount of faith in the *Lotus Sutra* and that it should be honored.

When Nichiren was escorted into the presence of Lord Itō, the steward scarcely seemed to be breathing. Nichiren knelt by his side and immediately began chanting *daimoku*. The sound of the chanting seemed to revive him and he opened his eyes to look upon Nichiren, though he could not lift his head. "Ah, so this is the monk, Nichiren, whom I have heard so much about."

"I have come, Lord Itō. I am sorry that you are not feeling well. I regret that I did not have a chance to visit you before now."

"Yes, I should have called for you before." Lord Itō made a feeble shrug. "I have long chanted *nembutsu* and hoped to go to the Pure Land after death, but I had hoped to not have to make the journey so soon."

Nichiren thumbed his *juzu* and reflected for a moment. Then he said, "This world is impermanent. It is difficult even for healthy people to tend their lives, much less people with illness. However, it is only proper that those with faith should consider matters regarding one's fate after death. However, we cannot determine what happens after death on our own. We can reach a conclusion on such matters only if we base our lives on the teaching of Śākyamuni Buddha, the true teacher of all people."

"Please, is there any prayer that can overcome this sickness?"

Nichiren nodded in affirmation and said, "Even a major illness can be cured and the life span extended if a skillful physician is available to treat it immediately, to say nothing of a minor illness. Even an immutable karma will inevitably disappear when atoned for, to say nothing of a mutable karma. The Buddha says in 'The Previous Life of Medicine King Bodhisattva' chapter of the *Lotus Sutra*, 'This sutra is a good medicine for the diseases of the people of Jambudvīpa. The patient who hears this sutra will be cured of his disease at once. He will not grow old or die.'

"When King Ajātaśatru was 50 years old he suffered from malignant boils appearing all over his body on the 15th day of the second month. Even the renowned physician Jīvaka could do nothing about them. On the seventh day of the third month, he was on the verge of death and about to fall into the Hell of Incessant Suffering. It was as though the pleasures of a luxurious life of more than 50 years were extinguished at once and the sufferings of a lifetime were all concentrated in that 21-day period since contracting the disease. Although the immutable karma of Ajātaśatru had reached its limit, when the Buddha again expounded the *Lotus Sutra*, naming it the *Nirvana Sutra*, and gave it to the great king, the king's illness was cured instantly, and the major transgressions in his mind also vanished at once like dew drops.

"Even extending your lifespan by a single day is more precious than all the treasures in the world, but first of all you must show your sincerity. Like King Ajātaśatru you can overcome your illness by taking refuge in the *Sutra of the of the Lotus Flower of the Wonderful Dharma*."

"I will. What exactly must I do?"

"Simply chant the *daimoku*, Namu Myōhō Renge Kyō. Make a vow that beginning with this body until you attain buddhahood you will strive to uphold Namu Myōhō Renge Kyō."

Lord Itō did so and Nichiren consented to perform prayer services for his recovery. He recited several prose passages, verses, and also *dhāraṇī* from the *Lotus Sutra*. He chanted the *daimoku*. He offered a prayer to Śākyamuni Buddha, Many Treasures Buddha, the emanation buddhas of the ten directions, and also Amaterasu Ōmikami and the Great Bodhisattva Hachiman. He even appealed to the *rākṣasī* Mother-of-Devils and her ten daughters who had once been bringers of disease and death but had been converted by the Buddha into protectors of the Dharma and its practitioners. Nichiren also inscribed and then burned paper amulets so that Lord Itō could drink the ashes mixed in water.

Over the next few days, when Lord Itō sank into despair and expressed doubts about his recovery, Nichiren encouraged him, saying, "Even though a finger might point to the great earth and miss, a person tie up the sky, the ocean's tide cease to ebb and flow, or the sun rise in the west, it could not happen that the prayer of a practitioner of the *Lotus Sutra* would go unanswered. If the various

190

bodhisattvas and other beings I have called upon do not rush to protect the practitioner of the *Lotus Sutra*, they commit the offense of deceiving Śākyamuni and all other buddhas. Thus, they will protect the practitioners of the *Lotus Sutra* without fail, regardless of whether the practitioners are insincere, unwise, impure, or do not observe the precepts, so long as they chant Namu Myōhō Renge Kyō."

Lord Itō's fever finally broke and in the months ahead he regained his strength. One day, when Nichiren called upon him, he said, "I will be forever grateful for your prayers which have made my recovery possible. I am certainly fortunate that you were sent here to Itō. For all your kind efforts, I would like to present to you a gift." Lord Itō called for a servant and sent him out to get the gift he had prepared. The servant returned bearing a box that was then presented to Nichiren. Inside was a statue of Śākyamuni Buddha. Lord Itō explained, "This statue was found in the sea, pulled in with a catch of fish. We cleaned and restored it and wondered why it appeared to us as it did. I think now that it was a happy omen in advance of your arrival. Please accept this as a token of my appreciation."

Nichiren contemplated the statue. He had kept it with him from that time on, always enshrined with the fascicles of the *Lotus Sutra* and later with the mandala he devised. In his eyes, the statue was not the Śākyamuni Buddha who had taught the Hinayana or provisional Mahayana teachings. It was the Eternal Śākyamuni Buddha who revealed his attainment of buddhahood in the remote past in the 16th chapter of the *Lotus Sutra*.

The Five Guides for Propagation

For the rest of his time in Izu, Lord Itō treated Nichiren as an honored guest. He spoke with the steward at length about the Buddha's teachings. One day, in the beginning of the spring of the following year, he asked Nichiren, "Tell me, what makes you so certain that you are teaching correctly? So many say that now is the time for ordinary people to just chant *nembutsu*, or that the way to attain buddhahood in this body is through the mantra practices. Why are you so certain that the *Lotus Sutra* is what should be taught and practiced?"

Nichiren responded, "I have been thinking about this ever since I incurred the wrath of the shogunate. I have realized that those who intend to spread Buddhism must correctly understand five principles for propagation in order to disseminate the True Dharma. They are: the teaching, the capacity of the people, the time, the country, and the sequence of spreading the Buddha's teachings."

"First of all the teaching refers to all sutras, precepts, and commentaries. Among all these there are Hinayana and Mahayana, provisional and true, and exoteric and esoteric teachings. It is best to keep this in mind. These classifications are not the opinions of commentators or teachers who came to prominence after the final nirvana of the Buddha, but stem from the teaching of the Buddha himself. Everyone should realize this when studying Buddhism. Therefore, anyone who disregards this classification is a non-Buddhist."

"When one recognizes the *Lotus Sutra* as the king of all sutras, one can be said to have understood the teaching correctly. What else do you think the Buddha could have had in mind when he said in the *Infinite Meanings Sutra* that for more than 40 years he had not yet revealed the final truth? The Buddha thus invalidated the teachings of all the sutras taught in the first 40 years or so, including the teachings of rebirth in the Pure Land of Utmost Bliss, making them like an outdated will of one's living parents. The Buddha further stated that no one can attain awakening through the previous teachings even if one practiced them for innumerable *kalpas*. In the second chapter of the *Lotus Sutra* the Buddha also taught that he had laid aside all expedient teachings and would henceforth only expound the unsurpassed way. The Buddha therefore teaches us to discard expedient teachings. It means that we should abandon the teachings that were expounded during the first 40 years or so, such as the *nembutsu*. Many Treasures Buddha, seated in his jeweled stūpa, then rose up from underground and declared that this was the truth, and the emanation buddhas of the ten directions gathered together and approved this as the truth by stretching out their long, broad tongues to the Brahmā heaven. The whole assembly present where the Buddha expounded the *Lotus Sutra* witnessed them. Thus, only those who thoroughly discern the difference between the *Lotus Sutra* and the other sutras can truly be said to have understood the teaching."

"In the second place, those who propagate Buddhism should know the capacity of the people to understand the Dharma and accept it. The venerable Śāriputra tried to teach a blacksmith the practice of contemplating decomposing corpses in order to realize the impurity of the body, and a launderer the practice of stabilizing the mind by counting breaths. In three months, neither of these men made the least progress in their practice. Instead, they developed wrong views and became *icchantika* and lost the ability to attain buddhahood. Then the Buddha taught the blacksmith, who worked with a bellows, the practice of counting breaths and to the launderer he taught the practice of contemplating impurity, and they were both able to understand the Dharma immediately. Even Śāriputra, who was reputed to be the wisest of the Buddha's disciples, made a mistake in teaching people according to their capacities. Needless to say, it is not easy for ignorant, ordinary, and unenlightened teachers in the Latter Age of Degeneration to discern a person's capacity. Now, an ordinary teacher who cannot discern an individual's capacity should just teach the *Lotus Sutra* to his disciples."

Lord Itō interrupted to ask, "But doesn't the Buddha say in the third chapter of the *Lotus Sutra*, 'Do not expound this sutra to people of no wisdom'?"

Nichiren answered, "That applies to wise teachers, who are able to discern the capacity of people, not to ordinary teachers in the Latter Age of Degeneration. The latter should do as Never Despising Bodhisattva did when he bowed to everyone he met saying, 'I do not despise you because you can become buddhas' even though he was persecuted for it by those who refused to believe that buddhahood was attainable."

Lord Itō knit his brows and shook his head, "I do not understand. Why is it that the Buddha says in the 'A Parable' chapter of the *Lotus Sutra* that the teaching should be withheld from the ignorant, but in the 'Never Despising Bodhisattva' chapter he insists that it should be forcibly spread among people who slander it? What is taught in these two chapters is as different as fire and water!"

Nichiren nodded in agreement. "Yes, it is difficult to understand. The Great Master Tiantai explained in his *Words and Phrases of the Lotus Sutra* that people during the lifetime of the Buddha had already formed a connection to the *Lotus Sutra* by having heard it in a past existence. Some of them were finally ready to accept it but others were not. In order to keep any of them from slandering it again, the Buddha prepared them all, using the skillful methods of the provisional sutras, until the seeds planted in the past had matured and they could finally hear the *Lotus Sutra* once more, accept it, and attain buddhahood. Those in the lifetime of Never Despising Bodhisattva, however, had not heard the *Lotus Sutra* before and were lacking in virtue, so Never Despising Bodhisattva taught the *Lotus Sutra* to them directly in order to sow the seed of buddhahood in their minds.

Because he caused them to hear it, even though they slandered it, they eventually attained buddhahood in the future through the merit of a reverse relationship.

"According to this interpretation, many people in this Latter Age of Degeneration never had a chance to listen to the *Lotus Sutra* in a past existence and are lacking in any good roots. Thus, there is no doubt that almost all people today will fall into evil realms. If they are going to fall into evil realms anyway, they should be forced to listen to the *Lotus Sutra*. This will cause them to slander the True Dharma, but in the end they will attain buddhahood eventually through a reverse relationship with the sutra."

Lord Itō asked, "What is this reverse relationship exactly? How can having a reverse relationship with the *Lotus Sutra* enable anyone to attain buddhahood?"

Nichiren answered, "It means that even an adversarial relationship with the True Dharma at least creates a connection that can eventually lead to awakening. Have you never heard the analogy of the poison drum? In the *Nirvana Sutra* the Buddha says, 'Good man, imagine a man who painted a great drum with a medicine made up of a mixture of poisons. When he pounded the drum in a crowd, even those with no inclination to listen would nevertheless hear it, and all who did would die. But there would be one exception: a person who unexpectedly did not die from this. This Mahayana scripture, the *Great Nirvana Sutra* is like that. It produces an audible sound everywhere, and those living beings that do hear it will find their greed, anger, and stupidity completely destroyed. Among them there will even be some who do not otherwise think about these things yet will notice that the causal power of the *Great Nirvana Sutra* has destroyed their defilements, and their fetters have disappeared by themselves. And when it comes to those who have transgressed by committing one of the four offenses of defeat or five grave offenses, upon hearing the sutra they, too, will create the causal conditions that lead to the highest awakening, gradually losing their defilements. The exception will be the *icchantikas*, who are excluded from those who will experience such an unexpected death of their defilements.'"

Lord Itō raised his eyebrows, "Ah, I think I see. So a reverse relationship means that any relationship, even one that is initially adversarial, is better than no connection at all. The True Dharma of the *Lotus Sutra* awakens people even if they reject it, just as the people who hear the poison drum still die from it even though they did not wish to hear it. So those who abused Never Despising Bodhisattva were eventually able to take faith in his teaching, expiate their transgressions, and be reborn in the presence of Śākyamuni Buddha. The Buddha had been Never Despising Bodhisattva in the past, and so once again these people were able to hear the True Dharma from him and at that time attain buddhahood."

Nichiren replied, "That is correct. Because those who were the disciples and followers of the Buddha had already received the seed of buddhahood in the past and therefore had the capacity to develop wisdom, the Buddha helped them cultivate the seed by teaching them with the Hinayana sutras to begin with, then the provisional Mahayana sutras, and finally the true Mahayana sutra, the *Lotus Sutra*. On the other hand, in this Latter Age there are few who are prepared to accept the True Dharma, and so they need to form a connection with it for the attainment of buddhahood in the future. Such ignorant people should be taught the *Lotus Sutra* from the start, as it can sow the seed of buddhahood in both believers and slanderers."

Lord Itō said, "So you are saying that the ordinary teacher in this Latter Age of Degeneration is unable to discern the capacity of the people, but that in any case the people of this age have no capacity for the provisional teachings that develop wisdom anyway. Instead, the ordinary teacher should just teach the *Lotus Sutra*. so that even if it is rejected, the seed of wisdom and of future buddhahood will be sown, if only through a reverse relationship."

Nichiren nodded. "Exactly! Furthermore, for 400 years, since the reign of Emperor Kammu, the capacity of all the people in Japan has been suited exclusively to the *Lotus Sutra*. Their capacity to understand the Dharma is similar to those who heard Śākyamuni Buddha expound the *Lotus Sutra* on Eagle Peak for eight years. Even Genshin recognized this, for he wrote in his *Essentials of the One Vehicle Teaching*, 'The people in Japan all have the capacity of receiving the perfect teaching of the *Lotus Sutra*.' Those who perceive this correctly understand the capacity of the people. Those, however, who insist that people can only be saved by the *nembutsu* are like Śāriputra, who did not understand the capacity of his disciples and caused them to become *icchantika*."

Nichiren pressed on with the next three criteria. "Third, those who wish to spread Buddhism should know the right time. For example, if a farmer cultivates a rice field in fall or winter he will not have any harvest, but if he cultivates in spring or summer he can have a bountiful harvest. The same thing is true with Buddhism. If we spread the Dharma at the wrong time, it is not only ineffective, but also causes us to fall into evil realms.

"Although the Buddha appeared in this world to expound the *Lotus Sutra*, he did not preach it until 40 years or so had passed, because the time was not right, even though there were some people with the capacity to understand and embrace the sutra. It is now 2,210 years or so since the Buddha entered final nirvana. We are in the fifth 500-year period that begins the Latter Age of Degeneration, and it is time to spread the *Lotus Sutra* widely, as it is taught in the sutra. For instance, in 'The Previous Life of Medicine King Bodhisattva' chapter the Buddha says to propagate the sutra throughout the world in the fifth 500-year period after his final nirvana so that it will not be lost. Therefore, if you understand the principle of the correct time in which to teach the Dharma then you will know that the Latter Age of Degeneration is the right time for the *Lotus Sutra* to spread.

"In the fourth place, those who propagate Buddhism should understand the country and its inhabitants. There are cold and hot countries, poor and wealthy countries, countries located in the center and those in remote regions, large and small countries, and countries with lot of thieves, killers, or unfilial children. There are also countries where Hinayana teachings are spread exclusively, countries where Mahayana teachings are spread exclusively, and countries where both teachings are spread together.

"Japan is a country suited exclusively to Mahayana teachings. Of the Mahayana teachings, the true Mahayana of the *Lotus Sutra* should especially be spread in Japan. Many past teachers have confirmed this. Thus, if you understand the principle of correctly assessing the country, then you will know that Japan is a country where the *Lotus Sutra* should be spread.

"In the fifth place, we should realize the sequence of spreading the Dharma. We should be aware of the teachings previously spread, if any, then spread the teaching that is one step above it. If Hinayana or provisional Mahayana teachings have previously been taught, then true Mahayana should be spread. If the true Mahayana teaching has been taught, neither Hinayana nor provisional Mahayana should be spread. We should abandon the rubble and pick up the gold and gems. Do not give up gold and gems to get pieces of tile and pebbles.

"During the reign of Emperor Kimmei, Buddhism began to be transmitted from Paekche to Japan. For 240 years or so, until the reign of Emperor Kammu, only the Hinayana and provisional Mahayana teachings were spread in Japan. Although the *Lotus Sutra* had been brought to Japan, its true meaning had not yet been revealed. During the reign of Emperor Kammu, Great Master Dengyō appeared, refuted the teachings of Hinayana and provisional

Mahayana, and revealed the true meaning of the *Lotus Sutra*. Thereafter, no one raised any objections to him and the people all believed in the *Lotus Sutra*.

"During the last 50 years or so since the Kennin period, however, Dainichi Nōnin spread Zen Buddhism, and Hōnen established the Pure Land school. They despised the true Mahayana teaching of the *Lotus Sutra* and expounded provisional doctrines, or they abandoned all the sutras of the Buddha, establishing the doctrine of the special transmission outside the sutras. Their teachings are like abandoning a jewel for a worthless rock, or leaving the earth to fly in the sky. They didn't realize the proper sequence in propagating the Buddha Dharma.

"These are all important points in propagating Buddhism. If one understands these five principles of propagation for spreading the Dharma, one will become a teacher for the nation, leading the people of Japan on the right path."

The Three Kinds of Enemies

Lord Itō considered all that Nichiren had said about the *Lotus Sutra*.
One day he asked, "All that you say about the *Lotus Sutra* seems to
be in accord with the Buddha's own words in the sutras, and yet
perhaps your way of teaching is too harsh. Is it necessary to condemn
others in the way that you have, saying that they are devils or that
they are going to the Hell of Incessant Suffering? By doing so you
have provoked the wrath of the shogunate and now find yourself here.
Surely there is a gentler way of propagating the *Lotus Sutra* in this
age so that you do not have to undergo such persecution?"

Nichiren nodded. "It would seem that there ought to be, and yet the
Buddha himself predicted that anyone who forthrightly teaches the
Lotus Sutra will meet with resistance. Even in the 'Peaceful Practices'
chapter, the Buddha said, 'This sutra leads all living beings to the
knowledge of all things. I did not expound it before because, if I had
done so, many people in the world would have hated it and few
would have believed it.' In the chapter 'Encouragement for Keeping
this Sutra,' we are warned that three kinds of enemies will appear
against those who spread the *Lotus Sutra*." Nichiren unrolled the fifth
fascicle of the *Lotus Sutra* and began to read the verses recited by the
bodhisattvas to the Buddha as a vow to spread the *Lotus Sutra* in the
Latter Age of Degeneration.

"Do not worry!
We will expound this sutra
In the dreadful, evil world
After your final nirvana.

"Ignorant people will speak ill of us,
Abuse us, and threaten us
With swords or sticks.
But we will endure all this.

"Some monks in the evil world will be cunning.
They will be ready to flatter others.
Thinking that they have obtained what they have not,
Their minds will be filled with arrogance.

"Some monks will live in secluded forest dwellings,
And wear patched pieces of cloth.
Thinking that they are practicing the true way,
They will despise others.

"Being attached to worldly profits,
They will expound the Dharma to men in white robes.
They will be respected by the people of the world
As the arhats who have the six supernatural powers.

"They will have evil thoughts.
They will always think of worldly things.
Even when they dwell in forest retreats,
They will take pleasure in saying that we have faults.

"They will say of us,
'Those monks are greedy for worldly profits.
Therefore, they are expounding
The teachings of those outside the way.
They made that sutra by themselves
In order to deceive the people of the world.
They are expounding that sutra
Because they wish to make a name for themselves.'

"In order to speak ill of us, in order to slander us
In the midst of the great multitude,
In order to say that we are evil,
They will say to kings, ministers, and priests,
And also to householders and other monks,

'They have wrong views.
They are expounding
The teachings of those outside the way.'
But we will endure all this
Because we respect you.

"They will despise us,
Saying to us ironically,
'You are buddhas.'
But we will endure all these despising words.

"There will be many dreadful things
In the evil world of the *kalpa* of defilements.
Devils will enter the bodies of those monks.
And cause them to abuse and insult us.

"We will wear the armor of endurance
Because we respect and believe you.
We will endure all these difficulties
In order to expound this sutra.

"We will not spare even our lives.
We will treasure only unsurpassed awakening.
We will protect and keep the Dharma in the future
If you transmit it to us.

"World Honored One, know this!
Evil monks in the defiled world will not know
The teaching that you expounded with expedients
According to the capacities of all living beings.

"They will speak ill of us,
Or frown at us,
Or drive us out of our monasteries
From time to time.

But we will endure all these evils
Because we are thinking of your command.

"When we hear of a person who seeks the Dharma
In any village or city,
We will visit him and expound the Dharma to him
If you transmit it to us.

"Because we are your messengers,
We are fearless before multitudes.
We will expound the Dharma.
Buddha, do not worry!

"We vow all this to you
And also to the buddhas who have come
From the worlds of the ten directions.
Buddha, know what we have in our minds!"

In the margins of the sutra, Nichiren had copied a passage from the *Commentary on the Words and Phrases of the Lotus Sutra*. "Here is what the Great Master Miaole said: 'This citation from the 13th chapter of the *Lotus Sutra* can be divided into three parts. The first part refers to the evil people as a whole, that is, the so-called self-conceited lay people. The next part refers to self-conceited monks, while the following part refers to those arrogant monks who consider themselves sages. Of the three, persecution by the first group of arrogant people is endurable. That of the second group is harder to endure, while that of the third group, self-styled sages, is most difficult to endure. The second and third groups are more cunning and less likely to reveal their faults.'"

Nichiren rolled up the fascicle and continued, "The time at hand matches exactly the Latter Age of Degeneration referred to in the *Lotus Sutra* as the fifth 500-year period after the final nirvana of the Buddha. As I consider whether or not the Buddha's words have proven to be true, it seems that the three kinds of enemies must surely exist today. If I denied the existence of the three kinds of enemies and spread the *Lotus Sutra* in a gentler manner so as to avoid persecution, then I could not claim to be a practitioner of the *Lotus Sutra*. Having taken into account what is taught in the *Lotus Sutra* and the *Nirvana Sutra* I realized that one cannot be a true practitioner of the *Lotus Sutra* unless one is confronted by the three kinds of enemies while spreading the Dharma. He who spreads the Dharma in such a way as to cause the three kinds of enemies to appear is the true practitioner of the *Lotus Sutra*. If he does, however, he is almost certainly bound to lose his life. He will be like the patriarch Āryasiṃha, for example, who was beheaded by King Dammira."

Lord Itō put his palms together and bowed in admiration. "I am not a scholar such as you, but it certainly seems as though you have correctly understood what the Buddha intended. You are certainly the bravest monk that I have ever had the honor to meet. Furthermore, by your prayers you have saved my life. I think that what you teach must be true, and so I vow never again to follow the Pure Land teachings but only the *Lotus Sutra*."

It was remarkable how many memories came to mind, both painful and pleasant, at the sight of that statue of the Buddha by his bedside. In time, Lord Itō, like many others, had fallen away and renounced any connection to Nichiren for fear of his own position and prestige. He had, however, made an initially positive connection to the *Lotus Sutra* and for a time had been Nichiren's supporter. Perhaps in time, Nichiren reflected, after expiating the transgression of abandoning the *Lotus Sutra*, Lord Itō and the others who had lost faith would finally bring to fruition the seeds of their initial faith and be guided into the Pure Land of Eagle Peak. Then they would see for themselves the Eternal Śākyamuni Buddha, of whom the statue Lord Itō had bestowed upon Nichiren was but a rough, though precious, image.

The Komatsubara Ambush

Nichiren recalled his pardon and the return to Kamakura that followed it. He arrived on the 22nd day of the second month of the third year of the Kōchō era (1263).

The main instigator of his exile, Hōjō Shigetoki, had died on the third day of the eleventh month of the first year of the Kōchō era (1261). It seemed to Nichiren that Hōjō Tokiyori had known all along that the charges brought against him were baseless and felt somewhat guilty for the part he had played in the exile of an innocent man. Still, time was needed for things to settle down, so he delayed granting the pardon for over a year. Nichiren hoped that eventually he would be called upon to meet with the former regent once more, but no invitation came. Nine months to the day after his pardon, Hōjō Tokiyori also passed away, though only in his late 30s. With the death of Tokiyori, the only person in a position of power who might have understood him, Nichiren knew that it would be more difficult than ever for his proposals to be adopted by the shogunate.

Seeing no point in remaining in Kamakura, Nichiren visited the homes of his lay supporters in the surrounding provinces, giving lectures and teaching the practice of *daimoku*. He told them, "Even if a person does not understand the meaning of the *Lotus Sutra* it is possible to avoid falling into the evil realms and eventually proceed to the stage of non-retrogression and even become a buddha by chanting the *daimoku* in earnest, just once in a day, month, year, or even lifetime. This is because it is faith that matters most. The basic way to buddhahood lies in faith."

To those lay people who were literate, he taught that recitation of any part of the *Lotus Sutra* was meritorious, but in particular he recommended reciting chapters two and 16 for daily services, as those were the most worthy chapters, the trunks of the Trace Gate and

Original Gate respectively, while the other chapters were like branches or leaves. For memorial services he and his disciples and lay followers recited the Verses of Eternity. He told his disciples and lay followers, "It is the 'expanded' practice to uphold, read, recite, and defend with delight the entirety of the *Lotus Sutra* consisting of 28 chapters in eight fascicles. It is the 'abbreviated' practice to uphold and keep important chapters of the *Lotus Sutra* such as the 'Expedients' and 'The Duration of the Life of the Tathāgata' chapters. It is the 'essential' practice to chant only a four-phrase verse of the 'Supernatural Powers of the Tathāgatas' chapter or the *daimoku* or to protect those who do so. Of these three kinds of practices to chant only the *daimoku* devotedly is the most essential of all."

He also made sure to instruct his female followers that they should not be fooled by teachings wherein one must first be reborn as a male in a pure land after death nor be discouraged by passages in provisional sutras that made it sound as though women could not attain buddhahood. He taught them to seek buddhahood only through the *Lotus Sutra*, wherein the daughter of the dragon king was able to attain buddhahood in her very body without first having to change into a male, though she did make an appearance of doing so to satisfy the doubts of monks like Śāriputra. Furthermore, they should not let taboos about impurity keep them from their daily practice. Nichiren pointed out that menstruation, for instance, wasn't a form of impurity. It was simply a physical phenomenon particular to women that was indispensable for procreation. In this way he taught women that the attainment of buddhahood through the *Lotus Sutra* was as open to them as it was to men and that they need not have any doubts or become discouraged so long as they maintained their faith.

While spreading the teachings among his lay followers and instructing his disciples, Nichiren never forgot the danger faced by all Japan if the warning he gave in his *Treatise on Spreading Peace Throughout the Country by Establishing the True Dharma* was not heeded. His fears only deepened after sunset on the fifth of the seventh month in the first year of the Bun'ei era (1264) when a comet appeared in the northeastern sky. At first, only the tail appeared. As the night deepened and the constellations wheeled above the land, the tail stretched itself from one end of the sky to the other until its brilliant head rose up over the horizon. The comet shone more brightly every night, until by the end of the eighth month it was even visible in the morning sky, its tail covering the heavens. It finally faded from the skies by the beginning of the tenth month. It was the worst omen anyone had ever seen. No scholar, Buddhist or otherwise, could say what had caused it or even remember a comet of such size and brilliance ever having been recorded. Nichiren was perhaps the saddest of all, as he felt it to be an omen foretelling the foreign invasion of Japan.

It was during that time when the great comet of the Bun'ei era still loomed over Japan that he received a message that his mother had fallen ill and was close to death. Nichiren had been unable to visit his home for ten years because of the threat against his life posed by the steward, Tōjō Kagenobu. He had not even been able to return home to perform the memorial services for his own father. This time, however, he was determined to take the risk. With only a handful of disciples he stealthily made his way back to Kominato.

The sight of his mother after an absence of ten years was a shock. She had not been young when he had last seen her. Her hair was white by then, but she had been robust and in good spirits, except when it came to her worries over the controversies her son had become embroiled in. Entering his family home he found that he could not reconcile his memory of her with the wizened figure that seemed drained of all life and hope. As she lay on her deathbed, barely conscious, she seemed scarcely able to draw a weak breath. 'Can this really be my mother? How can she have changed so much? Have I arrived too late?' He rushed to kneel at her side. He knew what he must do. He directed his attendants to bring him paper and a brush and also to fetch water from a pure source. As the attendants hustled away, he began to recite the

Lotus Sutra and its *daimoku*. When the things he had asked for were brought to him he inscribed on the paper the 28-character passage from the 'The Previous Life of Medicine King Bodhisattva' chapter of the *Lotus Sutra* wherein the Buddha promised that anyone who heard the sutra would be cured of their disease at once. He then burned the paper and mixed it with the pure water. He took the cup it was in and spilled a little into his mother's mouth. She revived at once.

After a fit of coughing, Nichiren's mother opened her eyes. She gazed up at him and smiled faintly. "You have come home. My son..."

Tears coursed down Nichiren's cheeks as he recalled his mother's awakening. She had lived for another three years after that. Soon now he would be reunited with her once again, this time in the Pure Land of Eagle Peak. What a joyous reunion that would be!

While his mother recovered, Nichiren was lodged at Rengeji temple, where he had found sanctuary so many years before. Around the beginning of winter he at last received a visit from his old master, Dōzen-bō. It was an awkward meeting. To begin with, it was an embarrassing violation of protocol that he, the disciple, had not visited his master at Seichōji; though both knew that to do so would be a fatal mistake. There were too many monks at Seichōji, such as Enchi-bō and Jitsujō-bō, who would happily race down the mountain to report his presence to Tōjō Kagenobu. In addition to that, Nichiren knew that he must try once more to convince his master to turn away from his slanderous attachments to provisional teachings and take up the practice of the *Lotus Sutra*. How could he so presume? And yet, how could he leave his beloved master to his fate?

Dōzen-bō, hands still thumbing his *juzu*, had asked, "I do not pretend to be a sage, and at my age I no longer have any hopes of becoming one, nor have I studied with any of the revered masters of the Pure Land teachings. All I know is that the practice of *nembutsu* and the

208

carving of statues of Amitābha Buddha has long been seen as meritorious, even in our own Tendai school. What need is there to question their merit? I can understand condemning the extreme views of Hōnen or even Shandao, but why must you condemn all those who practice *nembutsu* or revere Amitābha Buddha? Do you really believe that those of us who practice the *nembutsu* are going to the Hell of Incessant Suffering? How can you be so heartless as to believe that?"

Nichiren sighed. "These are not my own opinions but the teaching of Śākyamuni Buddha. Please allow me to show you." He reached for the second fascicle of the *Lotus Sutra* and unrolled it until he reached the second chapter, 'A Parable.'

"Here is what the Buddha said to Śāriputra:
'The triple world is not peaceful.
It is like the burning house.
It is full of sufferings.
 It is dreadful.
There are always the sufferings
of birth, old age, disease, and death.
They are like flames
raging endlessly.
I have already left
the burning house of the triple world.
I am tranquil and peaceful
in a bower in a forest.
This triple world is my property.
All living beings therein
are my children.
There are many sufferings
in this world.
Only I can save
all living beings.'

"These statements mean that Śākyamuni Buddha is the parent, teacher, and ruler of the people. For us, Amitābha Buddha may be a ruler, but not a parent or teacher. Only Śākyamuni Buddha is the compassionate buddha who possesses the three virtues of ruler, teacher, and parent. Those who refuse to abandon the provisional sutras taught during the first 40 years or so of the Buddha's teaching or practice them along with the *Lotus Sutra* are not following the wishes of our ruler, teacher, and parent. If people are against the Buddha's teachings, the gods of heaven and earth will abandon them. They are most undutiful. That is why the Buddha laments in the very next verse, 'I told this to all living beings but they did not believe me because they were too much attached to desires and defilements.' You have chanted millions of *nembutsu*, but have you yet chanted the *daimoku* of the *Lotus Sutra*? You have carved five statues of Amitābha Buddha that I know of, but have you ever once carved a statue of Śākyamuni Buddha?"

Now it was Dōzen-bō's turn to sigh. "You are as obstinate as ever. Still, perhaps there is something to what you say. I will think it over. In the meantime, please be careful. I know you have come here to care for your mother, but Lord Kagenobu still wants your head and he is sure to have already heard rumors that you are back here in Awa."

On the evening of the eleventh day of the eleventh month of that year, Nichiren was invited to the home of Kudō Yoshitaka, a longtime supporter and the steward of the Amatsu district in Awa. It was dusk when he set out from Rengeji on that frosty winter night, accompanied by ten people, mostly monks who were disciples of his but also a couple of messengers sent by Lord Yoshitaka. He remembered seeing his breath turn to vapor as they hiked along the road to Lord Yoshitaka's manor, little more than a mile away.

As they passed beneath the pines at Komatsubara they heard the snapping of bows and then arrows began to fall upon them like rain. The monk Kyōnin-bō threw himself in front of Nichiren and fell with an arrow in his chest. Nichiren and the other members of his entourage ran for the cover of the pines, but Lord Kagenobu's men were there waiting for them, their swords flashing like lightning. There seemed to be hundreds of them, some on horseback, chasing them beneath the pines. In the confusion, at least, the arrows had ceased to fall. Of Nichiren's companions, only three or four were strong enough to fight back, but they did so with a will. With sword and staff they fended off Lord Kagenobu's retainers, allowing Nichiren and the other monks to slip past.

Horses could be heard coming down the road at speed, from the direction of Amatsu. Now there was hope. No doubt this was the sound of Lord Yoshitaka and his retainers. He must have been warned that Lord Kagenobu had set up an ambush. In the lead, Lord Yoshitaka led his men in a battle cry as they approached, "Ei-ei-ō! Ei-ei-ō!"

Lord Kagenobu's men looked to the road, and those who were mounted rode out to meet the newcomers. There was no time to call out personal challenges as the bands of mounted samurai charged towards one another, spitting arrows. Just as it seemed they were about to collide, they wheeled their horses off the road into the trees. Then the battle became very confused. They drew their *tachi*, long gently curving cavalry swords, each side stalking the other through the darkening forest.

None of the warriors on either side were armored, as Lord Kagenobu and his men had not expected an actual fight. They had probably imagined they could inflict mortal wounds on Nichiren and many of his companions with their first volley of arrows. They had not counted on a general melee, nor that Nichiren would survive long enough for help to arrive. As for Lord Yoshitaka and his retainers, they had received word of suspicious activity near the border of their estate and had rushed out as quickly as they could, pausing only long enough to string their bows and strap on their swords while servants hurried to saddle their horses and bring them from the stables. Consequently, with both sides unarmored, all the warriors realized that any blow that landed or arrow that struck could easily be fatal. Lord Kagenobu's retainers began to reconsider their leader's vendetta. They had come to kill the evil monk who had thwarted their lord and slandered the Pure Land teachings, but they were not so eager to go to the Pure Land that evening. It was also getting too dark to tell friend from foe. They began to hang back.

Lord Kagenobu, however, was not about to withdraw. His skills honed by years of hunting in that same forest, he kept his eyes fastened on the fleeing monks and guided his horse expertly through the gaps between the trees. Keeping his distance from any would-be attackers, he scanned the area for his real target, the reason he had come here. He waited for just the right moment and angle that would assure an easy kill.

Nichiren turned to see Lord Kagenobu bearing down on him, *tachi* raised to strike. There was no time to jump for cover. Nichiren called upon the power of the protective deities and spirits of the *Lotus Sutra*. With his left hand, he raised his *juzu* up as the blade came down. He heard the horse scream, felt the searing pain as the hilt of the sword struck his left wrist and the blade slashed his forehead. Something struck a nearby rock with a sickening thud.

Nichiren lowered his hand. His wrist felt broken, and he had to catch his *juzu* with his right hand before it slipped to the ground. Sweat clouded his vision and he wiped it away. No, it was not sweat. It was blood. The horse was galloping away without a rider. Tōjō Kagenobu lay nearby. He had fallen from his horse. It was his head that had struck the rock. He stirred and groaned. So Kagenobu was alive, if only barely. Nichiren fell to his knees. He felt sick. Strong arms lifted him up. Lord Yoshitaka's men had found him at last.

One of the mounted warriors lifted Nichiren up onto his horse and held him around the waist for the ride back to Lord Yoshitaka's manor. The rest of Nichiren's companions were anxiously awaiting him on the veranda. Aside from Kyōnin-bō, they had all survived the fight, though two had suffered serious wounds. Nichiren was taken to a room where his own injuries could be cleaned and dressed. When that was done he was taken into Lord Yoshitaka's private chambers, and there learned with sorrow that he had received a mortal wound during the fighting. Nichiren thought of King Virtuous in the *Nirvana Sutra* who had died defending the monk Awakened Virtue and thereby attained the indestructible Dharma-body and was reborn as Śākyamuni Buddha. Kyōnin-bō and Kudō Yoshitaka had both attained buddhahood in the same way. Lord Kagenobu, on the other hand, died three days later, delirious and raving.

In the years ahead he was asked whether his faith had been shaken at that time, when he had come so close to being killed and when two of his followers had in fact been murdered. "Not at all," he answered them. "In fact, my faith in the *Lotus Sutra* has been strengthened as I experienced persecutions such as this. The Buddha said, 'Many people will hate the *Lotus Sutra* with jealousy even in my lifetime. Needless to say, more people will do so after my final nirvana.' The Buddha also said, 'I did not expound the *Lotus Sutra* before because, if I had done so, many people in the world would have hated it and few would have believed it.' There are many people in Japan who read and study the *Lotus Sutra*. Many people are punished because they steal or commit adultery, but no one has been punished due to his faith in the *Lotus Sutra*. Therefore, none of the followers of the

Lotus Sutra in Japan have practiced the sutra as it is taught. Only I have truly read it. In the sutra the bodhisattvas state: 'We will not spare even our lives. We treasure only unsurpassed awakening.' I alone have encountered the great trials that the sutra predicts. Therefore, I, Nichiren, am the foremost practitioner of the *Lotus Sutra* in Japan."

The Great Mongol Empire

Now as his life neared its end, Nichiren feared for those around him. Though he felt that he would soon drift out of consciousness, this premonition regarding the fate of his disciples, and of Japan itself, concerned him the most. The threat of invasion by the Mongol Empire still loomed. Everyone in this room might be massacred or enslaved by the barbarians who had already conquered China and Korea and brought so much havoc in the past few years to Kyūshū and the smaller islands of Iki and Tsushima. What would become of his followers and disciples? He had to trust that their devotion to the *Lotus Sutra* would protect them.

He looked with fatherly concern at his six main disciples. Nikō, Nitchō, and Nichiji were the last of the six who had joined him. They were now in their early thirties, but Nikō and Nitchō had only been in their teens when they had become his disciples in the years before the letter had arrived from the Mongol Empire. Nikō's father, a samurai in the village of Mobara in Kazusa Province, had summoned Nikō back home from his studies on Mt. Hiei in the second year of the Bun'ei era (1265) so that he could become a disciple of Nichiren. Nitchō was the stepson of Toki Jōnin and he had become Nichiren's disciple in the fourth year of the Bun'ei era (1267). Nichiji was originally an attendant of Nikkō, but when he became a monk at the age of 20 in the seventh year of the Bun'ei era (1270) he took Nichiren as his teacher with Nikkō's permission. Besides these six there were others who had joined him at that time whom he had previously had so many hopes for, but it was these six main disciples who had stuck with him through the worst of the persecutions.

As he had feared, on the 18th day of the first month of the fifth year of the Bun'ei era (1268) a letter came from the Mongol Empire. Hearing of the letter, he realized that things had turned out exactly as he had predicted in the *Treatise on Spreading Peace Throughout the Country* by *Establishing the True Dharma*. It was like matching two halves of a tally! The letter was from the emperor of the Great Mongol Empire, addressed to the king of Japan. It boasted of having reduced Korea to the status of a subject nation. It also asked why it was that Japan had not so far sent an envoy with even a single cart of tribute. It requested an exchange of greetings and the beginning of friendly relations as all countries should be as one family, but ended on an ominous note, saying, "As for using soldiers and weapons, who would want that?" It seemed to many that this was not just a polite diplomatic request to officially recognize the sovereignty of Kublai Khan over China and Korea but rather an ultimatum to either peacefully submit to being a vassal nation of the Mongols or else face the threat of invasion.

Once the arrival of the letter became known, Nichiren submitted a new copy of his treatise along with a cover letter to the newly installed regent, Hōjō Tokimune, the son of Hōjō Tokiyori, to whom he had submitted it eight years earlier. Tokimune had become the regent on the fifth day of the third month. He was only 17, though as regent he could rely upon the guidance of his co-signatory, a position now held by his great grand-uncle, Hōjō Masamura, the elder statesman who had held the position of regent for the last six years. During those years Masamura had trained Tokimune to the best of his abilities while Tokimune held the position of co-signatory. Nichiren hoped that the young regent would be more receptive than his father.

He also met with a monk named Hōkan-bō who knew many officials in the shogunate. Nichiren explained things to him as well. Later he wrote Hōkan-bō a letter in which he said, "Having witnessed a severe earthquake, a typhoon, and famine in the Shōka era (1257-1259), and wide-spread epidemics in the first year of the Shōgen era (1259), I predicted that these were omens foretelling the invasion of Japan by foreign troops. I may sound as though I am singing my own praises, but I dare say this because, should this land of Japan be destroyed, there is no doubt that Buddhism also will be destroyed.

216

"Eminent monks these days, however, are of one mind with slanderers of the True Dharma, or they do not even know the exquisite doctrine of their own schools. I suppose those eminent monks will probably receive an imperial decree or shogunal directive ordering them to offer prayers for repulsing foreign invaders, but as long as they are not based on the *Lotus Sutra*, I am afraid that such prayers will only intensify the anger of the gods and buddhas, resulting in the destruction of the land of Japan.

"I know how to repulse the impending foreign invasion. Except for those at Mt. Hiei, I am the only one in Japan who knows. This is because two sages will not appear at the same time, just as there never will be two suns or two moons. If this is a lie, I will receive the punishment of the ten *rākṣasī* guardians of the *Lotus Sutra*, which I uphold. It is solely for the sake of the country, the Dharma, and the people; not for myself that I say this to you. I am writing you about this now to clarify what I said when I was able to meet with you earlier. If you do not accept my words, you will regret it."

That had been in the fourth month of the year. Neither his resubmission of his treatise nor his appeal to Hōkan-bō had enabled him to receive an audience with the regent. Four months later he sent the first of several letters to the Lay Monk Yadoya, who had helped him submit his treatise to Tokiyori eight years previously. He received no reply, however. Though national disaster seemed imminent, no one was listening to him or even giving him the courtesy of a response. He could not help but feel in low spirits as his letters to Yadoya seem to have been forgotten or considered not important enough to warrant a reply.

Seeing that he had not been called upon for advice, requested to join any war councils, or instructed to perform prayer services to repulse the Mongols, in the eleventh month Nichiren sent out eleven letters to the political and religious leaders of Kamakura. Letters were sent to Hōjō Tokimune, Yadoya Mitsunori, and Hei no Saemon Yoritsuna, the Deputy Chief of the Board of Retainers. A letter was sent to Hōjō Yagenta, a member of a branch of the Hōjō family who had become a follower of Nichiren. Another letter was sent to Rankei Dōryū, the Zen master who was the abbot of Kenchōji. Yet another letter was sent to Ryōkan, also known as Ninshō, who had been installed as the abbot of Gokurakuji the year before. Ryōkan was a monk of the Mantra school, and yet he and his master Eison in Kyōto were trying to revive precept observance and insisted that Buddhist monks in Japan should once more take up the early precepts that Great Master Dengyō had dismissed as "Hinayana." In addition to being a master of esoteric rites and the precepts, Ryōkan also promoted the practice of *nembutsu*. Letters were also sent to the abbots of the major temples of Kamkura that were teaching Zen or Pure Land Buddhism or had come under the influence of Ryōkan. No reply was forthcoming.

The shogunate also did not deign to send a reply to the Mongol Empire either. In the following year another letter from the empire arrived, and that too received no response. In the meantime, Nichiren conducted prayer services for peace in the present and good rebirths in the future, as well as memorial lectures in memory of the Great Master Tiantai. He also sent another round of letters to those in positions of authority reiterating his warnings. To the Lay Monk Ōta Jōmyō, an important supporter in Shimōsa, he had written a letter summarizing his feelings towards the end of that year.

"I believe that whether or not the teaching of the *Lotus Sutra* will spread depends on the prediction of civil war and foreign invasion that I made in my written opinion, *Treatise on Spreading Peace Throughout the Country by Establishing the True Dharma*, being proven true or not. Last year, when the letter from the Mongol Empire arrived foretelling the coming of foreign invasion, I wrote letters to various people, leaders in the political and religious worlds in Japan, demanding a public debate without receiving any answer, negative or affirmative. As another letter from the Mongol Empire came this year, I again wrote letters to various people around the eleventh month with

218

some of them responding. It seems that the feeling of the people in general has calmed down so as to make them think that I might be right. Or it may be that those letters of mine caught the eye of the ruler.

"At any rate, as I ventured to speak up on such a grave matter, which seemed unreasonable to most of the people, I fully expected to be punished by death or banishment. I feel it indeed strange, however, that nothing has happened to me till today. Does it prove that what I insisted upon was quite reasonable?

"As the scriptural predictions of foreign invasion have proved true, the remaining prediction of civil war will not fail to occur. I hear that the monks of Enryakuji on Mt. Hiei have been stirred up a hundred, thousand, ten thousand, and 100 million times more than in the past. This is not a trivial matter; there must be a reason.

"As China and Korea were converted to Zen and Pure Land Buddhism, protective deities abandoned those countries, leaving them to be conquered by the Mongols. In Japan, too, as these evil teachings of Zen and Pure Land spread and the Tendai-Lotus school has been neglected, Mt. Hiei is being shaken to the roots. As both Buddhist clergy and their followers in Japan have become slanderers of the True Dharma, I am afraid, chances are eight or nine out of ten that this country will be conquered by the Mongols, as China and Korea were.

"Fortunately, I have already been born into the human world without being misled by an evil teacher. For the sake of the *Lotus Sutra*, I was sentenced to banishment to Izu, but regrettably I have not been executed yet. Hoping that such a thing will happen so that I may offer my life for the sake of the *Lotus Sutra*, I have exerted myself to write strongly worded letters to various people.

"I am almost 50 years old, and do not know how many more years I will be able to live. I pray that I may sacrifice my body, which otherwise will be abandoned in a wild field, for the sake of the One Vehicle teaching of the *Lotus Sutra*; that I may follow the examples of the young ascetic in the Himalayas, who was willing to sacrifice his own life in search of the Dharma, and Medicine King Bodhisattva, who burned his own arms in offering to the Buddha and the *Lotus Sutra*; and that I may live up to the example of the kings Sen'yo and Virtuous, defenders of the True Dharma, leaving my name in future lives so that the future buddha will mention my name when he teaches the *Lotus* and *Nirvana* sutras. Namu Myōhō Renge Kyō!"

Ryōkan of the Mantra-Precepts School

Nichiren wanted to save Ryōkan from falling into the Hell of Incessant Suffering by helping him to free himself from his self-conceited, misleading, and deceiving ways. He said as much to his disciples and lay followers gathered at his hut in Matsubagayatsu.

Shijō Kingo, one of the leaders among his lay followers in Kamakura, said, "Your compassion shows truly the mercy of a practitioner of the *Lotus Sutra*. However, all the people of Japan revere Ryōkan. Hōjō Tokimune, the Lord of Kamakura, especially looks up to him. It could be risky for you to undertake such an endeavor."

Nichiren nodded. It was true. Ryōkan always wore the three robes of a Buddhist monk, carried a begging bowl, was said to have never broken the 3,000 rules of deportment, and always firmly upheld the 250 precepts. He was looked upon as though he were Earth Repository Bodhisattva or Mahākāśyapa, the first patriarch after the final nirvana of the Buddha. Consequently, he was constantly being showered with honors, and at every bridge, temple gate, and barrier-station along the roads travellers were solicited by monks gathering contributions for some road, bridge, or hospice that Ryōkan was sponsoring. Nichiren saw that Ryōkan must be one of the fraudulent sages, the third of the three kinds of enemies who would appear in the Latter Age of Degeneration as predicted in the *Lotus Sutra*. Who else but he so perfectly matched the description of the false arhats in the *Nirvana Sutra*, who outwardly wore the *kesa* and observed the precepts but inwardly harbored greed and jealousy?

The Hinayana precepts had long since been rejected by the people of Japan back when the ordination platform of the perfect and sudden Mahayana precepts had been established at Enryakuji on Mt. Hiei. That was as it should be. Hadn't the layman Vimalakīrti told Pūrṇa

221

that the Hinayana precepts and teachings were like rotten food served in a jeweled bowl? Didn't the eighth of the 48 minor Mahayana precepts prohibit turning away from the Mahayana to take up lesser precepts? Hadn't Great Master Dengyō who had petitioned for the establishment of the Mahayana precepts platform, compared the Hinayana precepts to donkeys' milk, which is inferior in taste and nourishment to cows' milk, or to a toad, who stays at the bottom of a well and is unable to see the outside world? In spite of all this, Ryōkan and his master Eison in Kyōto had recently revived the Hinayana precepts that had long been rejected and were promoting a Mantra-Precepts movement.

Since returning to Kamakura, Nichiren had been quite vocal in his criticism of this new movement. Speaking of their attitude, he had said, "They, who cannot observe even a single precept, much less 250 precepts, are deceiving the imperial court and the shogunate, calling themselves teachers of the nation. In addition, believing themselves to be perfect, they despise others, abusing Mahayana practitioners for breaking precepts or for not having precepts. This is like a dog barking at a lion, or a monkey, a retainer of Indra, despising its master.

"The Hinayana precepts were meant to be eradicated in Mahayana temples after the first 500 years of the True Dharma. In Japan they were spread as a preparatory step for establishing the perfect and sudden Mahayana precepts platform. Great Master Dengyō refuted the Precepts school and took its masters into the Tendai school as disciples. Thus the Precepts school ceased to be as a separate Buddhist school. Great Master Dengyō had his disciples learn the Hinayana precepts only in order for them to know what they were, not because they were still considered valid. Nevertheless, scholars today do not know the true reason and think that the six schools of Nara have never been refuted, though actually Great Master Dengyō had already refuted them. What a pity!

"Those of the Precepts school realized the immaturity of their own school and so they gradually converted to the Mahayana precepts of the *Brahmā Net Sutra*. In the end, they even claimed the perfect and sudden precept of the *Lotus Sutra* as their own teaching. Then they accused others of breaking precepts. Having no idea of the actual circumstances and deceived by their venerable outward appearance, the rulers of the country took back the fields that had been donated to Tendai temples, donating them instead to temples of the Precepts school.

"Therefore, many people lost faith in the temples of Mahayana precepts, converting to the Precepts temples of Hinayana. Though men of the Precepts school themselves do not set the fires, they caused the Mahayana temples to burn down all over Japan. They were not eye plucking birds, but they did pluck out the eyes of the people. They are what the Buddha referred to in the *Nirvana Sutra* as '*icchantika* who look like arhats.' A country which keeps faith in the Precepts school as taught by such evil monks as Ryōkan cannot remain in peace and tranquility."

There were monks, nuns, and lay Buddhists who found the arguments between monks such as Ryōkan and Nichiren fascinating. They happily reported Nichiren's refutation to the monks of Gokurakuji, eager to hear their reply or perhaps even get a response from Ryōkan himself. These same people would then hasten to Matsubagayatsu to tell Nichiren what Ryōkan had said in a talk to his followers, "I intend to have all the monks in Japan keep the 250 precepts, all the nuns keep the 500 precepts, all the laymen and laywomen keep the five precepts and eight precepts of abstinence in order to stop them from killing living things and drinking liquor, but Nichiren stands in my way, blocking my wish with his slander."

So now, Nichiren was determined to save Ryōkan and his followers by including the Mantra-Precept movement of Ryōkan and his master Eison among the targets of his refutations, along with Pure Land and

Zen. At the very least, he would be able to establish them in a reverse or "poison-drum" relationship with the *Lotus Sutra*. He also knew that time was running out for them all. It would not be long before the Mongols would tire of receiving no replies to their demands. They would take up arms eventually, overrunning Japan. It would not be long before the unhappy factions in Kyōto and Kamakura rose up against the shogunate.

And once again there was drought, and with it the threat of more famine and epidemics to follow.

On the 18th of the sixth month of the eighth year of the Bun'ei era (1271), at the height of the drought, Ryōkan was ordered by the shogunate to perform a ceremony to pray for rain in order to save the people. Having heard the news, Nichiren declared: "This may be a very small matter, but it's best that I inform the public of the divine power of the *Lotus Sutra*."

The monk Suhō and the lay monk Irusawa had come to Matsubagayatsu on occasion to hear Nichiren's discourses, though they were disciples of Ryōkan and practitioners of *nembutsu*. Was it because they had begun to have doubts about Ryōkan's teachings? Or was it because they enjoyed controversy? Nichiren was wary of them, but it was to them he entrusted a message for their teacher, Ryōkan.

The message read, "This is the best chance for you to defeat me, Nichiren, of whom you have been complaining. If you pray for rain and have success in causing even a drop of rain to fall within seven days, then I will become your disciple, observe the 250 precepts, and apologize to you, admitting that I was utterly wrong for insisting that the *nembutsu* is a teaching that causes people to fall into the Hell of Incessant Suffering. If I surrender to you, my disciples as well as all the people in Japan will seek refuge in you. If, however, you should fail, it will be clear that you are, in fact, a man who misleads and

224

deceives the people, though you look like a sincere follower of the precepts. There have been many such challenges in which prayers for rain decided the superiority of doctrines, as for instance the competition between Gomyō and Great Master Dengyō and the one between Shubin and Kōbō in the Heian period."

Before dispatching them, Nichiren said to Suhō and Irusawa, "Until this moment I have not considered the two of you believers in what I teach. This is therefore the best opportunity for you to determine which is the true teaching. If it rains within seven days, you should continue to have faith in the teaching of the *nembutsu* and the eight precepts of abstinence that you have upheld so far as a means of rebirth in the Pure Land. If it does not rain, however, it behooves you to embrace the *Lotus Sutra* earnestly, keeping in mind that the eight precepts of abstinence and the *nembutsu* are useless for rebirth in the Pure Land."

As a result of this exchange, Suhō and Irusawa eagerly made their way to Gokurakuji to pass the message to Ryōkan. They later reported to Nichiren that Ryōkan was pleased to receive Nichiren's message and had begun to pray for rain, with more than 120 disciples. Those who observed them saw that the heads of the praying monks dripped with sweat in the mid-summer heat as they chanted the *nembutsu* and recited the *Prayers for Rain Sutra* and the *Lotus Sutra* in voices loud enough to reach heaven. In between the ceremonies they taught the eight precepts of abstinence to their lay supporters and officials of the shogunate. However, after four or five days no rain fell at all. Quite at a loss, Ryōkan gathered several hundred disciples from Tahōji and prayed with all his might, but still it did not rain at all. In seven days, not a single drop of rain fell.

Nichiren sent his messengers to Ryōkan three times over the course of those seven days to tell him, "Even Izumi Shikibu, a licentious poetess, and Prince Nōin, a depraved monk, succeeded in making rain fall in an instant by composing 31 syllable poems, though the poems were censured for being frivolous, did they not? On the contrary, you, Ryōkan, foremost upholder of the precepts, master of the true teaching of the Mantra school and the *Lotus Sutra*, who is admired for being the most merciful monk at present, prayed for rain with 100 and 1,000 monks who firmly uphold the 250 precepts but have only caused strong winds to blow. Why is it that you were unable to cause rain to fall in seven days? You should know from this that none of you are capable of being reborn in the Pure Land.

"Consider thoroughly: how is it possible for those who cannot jump over a six-foot wide canal to jump over a 20 or 30' wide canal? If you cannot cause even a little rain to fall by using the mantra practices, then how can you succeed in the more difficult task of helping people to be reborn in the Pure Land of Amitābha Buddha? If you would consider your future existence, you would relinquish your evil hatred of Nichiren and come to see me as agreed. Let me teach you how to make rain fall and to attain buddhahood."

Not only did no rain fall in seven days, the drought grew more severe. Stormy winds blew more ferociously and the people grew more desperate. In the evening of the seventh day, messengers from Nichiren told Ryōkan to stop his praying immediately lest greater disasters fall upon them all. Doubtless, Ryōkan had shed tears of disappointment and embarrassment and both his disciples and followers must have cried loudly in vexation.

Nichiren reflected back upon that time. When he had been condemned by the shogunate later that year, he had hid nothing when responding to their interrogation. Ryōkan and his followers, however, had tried to cover up what had happened by spreading countless lies to the widows of the late Hōjō Tokimune and Hōjō Shigetoki and leveling false charges against Nichiren in the hopes that the shogunate would order him executed. If Ryōkan had really aspired to buddhahood and wanted to maintain his self-respect, he should have retired to the forest, or become Nichiren's disciple as he had promised. Nichiren found it hard to believe that such a person still continued be admired and even looked upon as a living buddha.

Hei no Saemon Yoritsuna

A month after Ryōkan's failed attempt to end the drought, a monk named Gyōbin sent a letter to Nichiren saying, "Although I have never met you, I take the liberty of addressing you in customary fashion and wish to ask some questions. If the rumors are true, your doctrines are indeed dubious. First of all, you hold that all sutras expounded before the *Lotus Sutra* are false and do not lead to buddhahood. Secondly, you insist that Mahayana and Hinayana precepts confuse people, causing them to fall into evil realms. Thirdly, you maintain that the *nembutsu* is a karmic cause for falling into the Hell of Incessant Suffering. Fourthly, you also assert that Zen is a teaching of heavenly devils and if people practice it, their wrong views will only be strengthened. If you have claimed all this, you are indeed the loathsome enemy of Buddhism. Therefore, I would like to meet you and refute your wrong views. However, if these are not your thoughts, it is a shame that you have received such a notorious reputation. At any rate, kindly reply in detail regarding the truth or falsehood of the above."

Nichiren replied, "In regard to your questions, I do not think we should have a private debate, as that would be meaningless. If you are inclined to a public debate, however, you should appeal to the shogunate to sponsor one and then, in compliance with their order to hold a formal debate, the rights and wrongs of the matter can be investigated. As far as I am concerned, I sincerely hope you will make such a proposal."

Gyōbin, and whoever else put him up to his initial challenge, did not take Nichiren up on the offer to petition the shogunate for a public debate. Instead, Ryōkan and two second-generation disciples of Hōnen who were active in Kamakura, Nen'amidabutsu and Dōamidabutsu, sent a petition to the shogunate listing a variety of complaints against Nichiren and demanding that a public debate be held to refute his erroneous views. Nichiren welcomed the opportunity to engage in such a debate with Ryōkan and the others, and in the meantime he submitted a response to Ryōkan's petition. In reply to the accusation that he claimed that there is only one right teaching and all others are wrong, he simply pointed out that this is what Hōnen himself had been teaching when he said to "abandon, close, set aside, and cast away," all other teachings and rely only on the *nembutsu*. In reply to the accusation that he was attached only to the *Lotus Sutra* and slandering all the other Mahayana sutras, he pointed out that it was the Buddha himself in the *Lotus Sutra* who praised only the *Lotus Sutra*, as well as Many Treasures Buddha and the emanation buddhas of the ten directions. In reply to the accusation that he insisted that the sutras preached before the *Lotus Sutra* were all false, Nichiren only had to point to the statement in the *Infinite Meanings Sutra*, "For more than 40 years I have expounded the Dharma in all manner of ways through adeptness in skillful means, but the final truth has still not been revealed." In reply to the accusation that he asserted that chanting *nembutsu* leads to the Hell of Incessant Suffering, he pointed out that practice of Pure Land Buddhism was causing people to turn away from the *Lotus Sutra* even though the Buddha had warned, "Those who do not believe this sutra but slander it will destroy the seeds of buddhahood of all living beings of the world." In reply to the accusation that he insisted that Zen deludes people and disturbs their practice of Buddhism, he pointed out that the Buddha said in his final teaching, "Anyone who insists that the True Dharma exists outside the sutras is a heavenly devil." In reply to the accusation that he insisted that Hinayana and Mahayana precepts delude people, he pointed out that in the past the Great Master Dengyō had already received letters of submission from the six schools of Nara and transmitted the perfect and sudden Mahayana precepts to them, thus making all other precepts obsolete. In reply to the accusation that he burned and threw away statues of Amitābha Buddha and World Voice Perceiver Bodhisattva, he asked if there were any witnesses and accused Ryōkan and his fellow petitioners of lying. In reply to the accusation that he was inciting mobs at his hermitage, he accused them of slandering him just as the *Lotus Sutra* said the three kinds of enemies would do. In reply to the accusation that he was storing weapons, he pointed out that the Buddha allowed for the use of weapons for defense of the True Dharma as he had taught in the *Nirvana Sutra*, "I now allow those who keep the precepts to rely on the companionship of those in white robes who wield weapons. Though kings, high officials, and merchants may take up weapons as lay followers in order to protect the Dharma, I declare this to be entirely in keeping with the precepts. However, though one may take up weapons in defense of the Dharma, he should not take another's life."

No debate ever took place, however. Instead, the monks of the schools he had criticized waged a campaign of rumor and gossip, slandering Nichiren to the magistrates, top officials, and also the wives of the Hōjōs and the widows of the late Tokiyori and Shigetoki. The outcry grew so great that Nichiren was summoned to appear before the Council of State on the tenth of the ninth month of the eighth year of the Bun'ei era (1271) to respond to a series of accusations brought against him. His questioner was Hei no Saemon Yoritsuna, Deputy Chief of the Board of Retainers, second in command to Hōjō Tokimune.

Once Nichiren was shown his seat, he glanced up at the council members ranged before him. Most looked on impassively, though a few could not hide the hostility and contempt they felt for the rabble rousing lowly monk who clearly did not know his place and who had dared to criticize the teachers and teachings that they revered and depended upon for rebirth in the Pure Land. Hei no Saemon looked at Nichiren with nothing but disdain all throughout the preliminaries of the inquiry.

Hei no Saemon took up a scroll handed to him by an aid and addressed the other members of the council, "This monk, Nichiren, who sits before us, is accused of a variety of offenses." He opened the scroll and began to read from it. "It is said here that you declared that the late Hōjō Tokiyori and Hōjō Shigetoki had fallen into the Hell of Incessant Suffering; that such temples as Kenchōji, Jufukuji, Gokurakuji, Chōrakuji, and Daibutsuji should be burned down; and that such monks as Dōryū and Ryōkan, whom the late lords Tokiyori and Shigetoki revered, must be beheaded. How can we fail to exile or execute anyone who dares say such things? You have been summoned here today so that you can tell us whether or not you in fact made such derogatory statements."

In response, Nichiren said, "They are all true, but..." He waited for the astonished gasps and cries of outrage to die down, "It is not true that I insisted that the late lords Tokiyori and Shigetoki had gone to hell after they died. I had warned them that they were heading to the Hell of Incessant Suffering for following false teachings when they were still alive.

"In short, I made all those statements for the sake of this country. If you wish for this country to remain at peace, you should give me the chance to meet those monks in debate, so that a decision can be reached as to whose teachings and practices are correct. If you should listen only to their false charges and unreasonably punish me, in the end this country will surely encounter serious problems. If you exile or execute me, it would mean that you have failed to heed a messenger of the Buddha. In that case, I am certain that within 100 days, or at most within seven years after I am exiled or executed a revolt will erupt, in which struggles among the branches of the Hōjō family will ensue due to the divine punishment of Brahmā, Indra, the gods of the sun and moon, and the four heavenly kings, who are all protectors of the *Lotus Sutra*. Thereafter, this country will be threatened by foreign invasion from four directions, especially from the west. It will then be too late for you to have regrets."

Hei no Saemon was enraged. His face reddened and his eyes bulged as he shouted at Nichiren as though there were no one else in the

231

room. "How dare you say such things! Do you have any idea how much trouble you are in? Have you no shame! Do you really mean for us to burn down temples and execute the most respected monks of Kamakura just because a nobody like you has the temerity to make such demands? For you to even make such a suggestion is a violation not only of the Mahayana precepts against taking life but a violation of the Jōei Code that prohibits slander and provocation! And why do you say there will be a revolt? Are you privy to any plots? If so, you had better tell us what you know immediately."

Nichiren sat still and calm. "I think you misunderstand me. I will be happy to send you a copy of my written opinion, *Treatise on Spreading Peace Throughout the Country by Establishing the True Dharma*. That work will explain things in more detail. The offense of slandering the True Dharma is truly grave and perhaps deserving of execution. However, Śākyamuni Buddha does not teach that we should execute slanderers. He does teach that offerings should not be given to them. Is this not reasonable? Please read my treatise and you will see the clear statements from the *Nirvana Sutra* outlawing slanderers of the True Dharma. What the *Nirvana Sutra* means is not at all that we should outlaw disciples of the Buddha, but that we should only chastise slanderers of the True Dharma. Also, I know nothing of any plots. I am only repeating the predictions in the sutras. All of the disasters predicted have already come true in the last few years, except for revolt and foreign invasion, and so it is inevitable that they will occur as well. Again, I have cited all the relevant passages from the sutras in my treatise."

Hei no Saemon glared at Nichiren, hatred burning in his eyes. Of the other council members, some became angry and even furious, while others were simply amazed at the audacity of this monk who had no standing speaking in such a way, and some of them even began to wonder if there might be something to what Nichiren was saying. Hei no Saemon removed the weights used to hold open the scroll of petition on the desk before him. He handed it back to his aid and then dismissed Nichiren. "We have heard enough, I think," he said as he looked around at the others. "You are dismissed."

Nichiren left. He had been unable to face his accusers in public debate, and now his fate would be decided behind the closed doors of the Council of State. The submission of the *Treatise on Spreading Peace Throughout the Country by Establishing the True Dharma* in response to the impending Mongol invasion would be his second remonstration with the shogunate. This time, however, he was not being met with indifference from the rulers but outright hostility. It seemed that the time had come for him to live the verses of chapter 13 of the *Lotus Sutra* wherein the bodhisattvas vowed to the Buddha: "We will not spare even our lives. We will treasure only unsurpassed awakening."

The Tatsunokuchi Persecution

It was a surprising eventuality to be dying in bed at the age of 60, surrounded by disciples and lay followers. As a much younger man, he had been certain that he would be spared the agonies of old age, starvation, and illness. If he had been asked how he had pictured the end, his best guess would have been by the sudden stroke of an executioner's blade. Would he have felt the cut? Would there have been a moment of searing pain and disorientation as his head fell away? Would his eyes have been able to look back at his body lying upon the beach, his ears hear the cries of his followers, his mind understand that his sacrifice for the sake of the *Lotus Sutra* was complete before his spirit fled? Or would he have instantly found himself among the assembly of the ongoing Ceremony in the Air at the Pure Land of Eagle Peak?

It was in the middle of the afternoon on the twelfth day of the ninth month of the eighth year of the Bun'ei era (1271), two days after he had been brought before the Council of State, when Hei no Saemon led several hundred foot soldiers clad in *dō-maru* armor, light lamellar cuirasses and skirts, and *ebōshi*, black cloth hats, with *naginata* in hand and *tachi* swords at their sides. As they burst onto the grounds of the hermitage their eyes glared and they shouted angrily for everyone present to submit to arrest. All of his disciples and followers, all of the witnesses in fact, had been astounded at the amount of force arrayed against Nichiren and the dozen or so monks at the hermitage, which was far larger in scale than any previous arrests of suspected conspirators over the past two decades. It was clear that they suspected Nichiren not simply of predicting revolt but of actively fomenting rebellion against the Hōjō regency.

Nichiren and his six main disciples and other monks who had been listening to Nichiren lecture on the sutra presented themselves on the veranda of the hermitage. Nichiren considered the size of the force

234

arrayed against them, so unnecessary, and said to his disciples, "The time has come to fulfill my wish. I am overjoyed. From the beginningless past down to the present, I have sometimes lost my life in vain, but not even once for the sake of the *Lotus Sutra*. Now I shall be beheaded on account of the sutra, succeeding the Venerable Āryasimha, the last patriarch of Buddhism who also gave his life for the Dharma. My merit of propagating the *Lotus Sutra* will be more than that of the great masters Tiantai and Dengyō. My name will be added to the list of the Buddha and the 24 patriarchs of the True Dharma and the list will be changed to include 26 names. My practice will be more meritorious than that of Never Despising Bodhisattva. Śākyamuni Buddha, Many Treasure Buddha, and the emanation buddhas of the worlds of the ten directions will not know how to treat me. How fortunate I am to be able to sacrifice my life for the sake of the *Lotus Sutra*."

Hei no Saemon strode forward, dressed in the formal robes of his office as the Deputy Chief of the Board of Retainers. "You and all those with you here are under arrest. If you are lucky, you will only be exiled." He looked over all the monks present and assured himself that no one was armed or likely to resist; then he called to his vassals, "Take them into custody! Search the grounds!" They did not hesitate to carry out his order. As quickly as the space would accommodate, they charged up the steps to the veranda.

Nichiren tucked the fifth fascicle of the *Lotus Sutra* that he had been lecturing upon into the front collar of his robes and stepped out directly in front of the oncoming warriors. In a firm voice he spoke over their heads to Hei no Saemon, "As we all know, the rulers of Japan are able to do anything they wish. Yet, in a lawsuit, the rulers should call both sides to a meeting in order to listen to what each will say to the other before reaching a judgment. Why is it that only in my case they did not hold such a meeting? Shouldn't I be allowed to meet in debate against the teachers of the other schools before being sentenced to such a serious punishment? This is nothing but a breach in proper conduct! Even if I were a felon, such illegal treatment would throw the administration of our country into chaos, with peace lost."

In a rage at Nichiren's insolence, Shō-bō, a ranking vassal of Hei no Saemon, rushed at him. He snatched the fifth fascicle of the *Lotus Sutra* from out of Nichiren's robes. Like all such scrolls it was wound around a heavy wooden rod. Shō-bō repeatedly struck Nichiren in the face with it, then unrolled it and tore it to pieces. Nichiren was stunned and disoriented, unable to ward off the blows or to take back the scroll. He fell back into the arms of Nisshō and Nichirō. Regaining his senses, he looked down upon the scraps of the fascicle that were now being trod under the sandals of the warriors storming past him into the hermitage. He suddenly realized that the scroll used to beat him was the very one that contained the words, "Ignorant people will speak ill of us, abuse us, and threaten us with swords or sticks. But we will endure all this."

Inside the hermitage, the warriors scattered the remaining nine fascicles of the threefold *Lotus Sutra* that remained on the lecture stand, stepped on them, wrapped themselves in them, and scattered them all over the straw mats and the wooden floor of the house. Seeing this riotous behavior, Nichiren uttered in a loud voice, "How amazing! Everybody, look at Hei no Saemonnojō Yoritsuna losing his head! He is now going to fell the pillar of Japan! I, Nichiren, am the chief support of Japan! When you kill me, you will cut the pillar of Japan! Before long, there will be a civil war, in which the Japanese people will fight among themselves, and foreign invasion, in which many people in Japan will not only be killed but also captured by foreign invaders. Unless all the temples given over to Pure Land and Zen such as Kenchōji, Jufukuji, Gokurakuji, Daibutsuji, and Chōrakuji are burned down and their monks all beheaded at Yuigahama Beach, Japan is bound to be destroyed."

Hei no Saemon and his vassals as well as Nichiren's disciples were all struck dumb and astonished. Nichiren had regained his poise, though it was he who was in disgrace in the eyes of the world. The warriors, on the contrary, went pale. They stopped what they were doing, shamefaced, and now regretting that in their anger they had torn and scattered one of the sacred sutras containing the teachings of the Buddha.

Finally, Hei no Saemon gathered his wits and said, "Still you persist in calling for the burning of temples and the execution of holy monks?"

Nichiren said, "I will never stop repeating this, no matter what the punishment! I had a copy of the *Treatise on Spreading Peace Throughout the Country by Establishing the True Dharma* sent to you, but evidently you did not read it, so you still fail to grasp my true meaning when I say these things."

Finally, the mood became calmer. Nichiren and his disciples were bound around the upper arms and chest and marched like criminals to the government offices, where they were kept under guard in a courtyard until that evening. Nichiren was set upon a mat before the steps leading into the building while Hei no Saemon sat at the top of the steps. He looked down upon Nichiren and interrogated him once more. Nichiren refused to recant any of what he had said in the previous interview. He explained in detail to Hei no Saemon that the Mantra school was an evil teaching that would destroy the country, that Zen Buddhism was a false teaching of heavenly devils, that *nembutsu* leads to the Hell of Incessant Suffering, and that the proof of the lack of power of those who followed teachings other than the *Lotus Sutra* could be seen in the failure of Ryōkan's prayer for rain. While listening to this, Hei no Saemon sometimes scornfully laughed and other times got fiercely angry. Unable to defend Ryōkan's failure, Hei no Saemon ended his interrogation of Nichiren in disgust.

Near midnight, it was announced that Nichiren was to be taken into custody by Hōjō Nobutoki, the Lord of Musashi Province, to await exile to some distant region. Though unbound, he was set upon a saddleless horse. Accompanied by Hei no Saemon and his vassals, both foot soldiers and mounted warriors, he was paraded as a prisoner in front of the Tsurugaoka Hachiman Shrine. In the streets of Kamakura, despite the late hour, the followers of Ryōkan and other slanderers of the True Dharma whom Nichiren had denounced came out to point, laugh, and jeer as the procession passed by.

They had told Nichiren that he was being taken to the home of Homma Shigetsura, one of Hōjō Nobutoki's vassals. However, the road they were taking was not the way to Echi, where Shigetsura's manor was located, but to the execution grounds upon the beach at Tatsunokuchi, the Dragon's Mouth. The public sentence may have been exile, but it was quite evident that Hei no Saemon intended to execute him that night.

When they came to the crossing of the bridge over Young Prince Avenue that passed in front of the Tsurugaoka Hachiman Shrine, Nichiren stopped his horse. This was the place where one would have to dismount in any case to show respect to the Great Bodhisattva Hachiman, but Hei no Saemon's vassals clustered around Nichiren warning him not to cause any trouble. He said to them, "Keep quiet, I have nothing special in my mind except that I want to speak to the Great Bodhisattva Hachiman."

Nichiren dismounted, and turning north to face the shrine he loudly declared, "Great Bodhisattva Hachiman, are you truly a god? In ancient times, when Wake no Kiyomaro was about to be beheaded at the order of the corrupt monk Dōkyō, did you not protect Kiyomaro by appearing as a ten-foot-wide moon? When the Great Master Dengyō lectured on the *Lotus Sutra*, did you not present him with a purple *kesa*? Now I, Nichiren, am the foremost practitioner of the *Lotus Sutra* in Japan. Besides, I have committed no wrongdoing whatsoever. What I have been preaching is the doctrine to save all the people in Japan, who are sure to fall into the Hell of Incessant Suffering for slandering the True Dharma, the *Lotus Sutra*. Yet, I am about to be beheaded because of it. How can you, a bodhisattva, just sit and watch me be executed? When the Great Mongol Empire invades this country after I am put to death, will even such guardian deities of Japan as Amaterasu Ōmikami and Great Bodhisattva Hachiman be safe?

"Moreover, when Śākyamuni Buddha taught the *Lotus Sutra*, Many Treasures Buddha, various buddhas and bodhisattvas from all the worlds in the ten directions gathered together and arranged themselves so that they shone like suns, moons, stars, and mirrors. Then the Buddha asked numerous gods as well as virtuous deities and sages of India, China, and Japan to take an oath to protect practitioners of the *Lotus Sutra*. Each of them wrote such an oath, did they not? If this was the case, you ought to immediately carry out what you swore without any reminders. Why don't you appear right here to prove your sincerity?"

After a pause, he added, "Upon arriving at the Pure Land of Eagle Peak after being beheaded tonight, I will, without hesitation, first report to Śākyamuni Buddha that Amaterasu Ōmikami and Great Bodhisattva Hachiman are two deities who do not keep their pledges. If you think that would be hard to bear, you had better reconsider and act quickly."

Having spoken these things, Nichiren got back on his horse. Hei no Saemon and his vassals were speechless. Who would dare to chastise the Great Bodhisattva Hachiman in such a way? Surely, this monk was not in his right mind. The warriors murmured, fearful of even being in the presence of such a madman and blasphemer, lest the ground crack open to swallow him up, and perhaps anyone else who happened to be standing too close.

239

They proceeded along the beach. In front of Goryō Shrine, Nichiren told the escorting soldiers, "Please stop for awhile. Here, I have a person to whom I want to inform about this matter." A boy named Kumaō-maru was then dispatched to the home of Shijō Kingo, who lived nearby.

Shijō Kingo and three of his brothers rushed to join the procession. Nichiren saw that they were all barefoot, having run out of their home so fast they had not even stopped to put on their sandals. Because of his standing as a samurai who was a retainer of one of the vassals of the Hōjō clan, Shijō Kingo was allowed to accompany Nichiren. He took hold of the bridle of the horse Nichiren rode and led it himself.

"What is happening? What is this?" Shijō Kingo stammered.

Nichiren told him, "I am going to be beheaded tonight. This is what I have been longing for over the past several years. In past lives I was born in this Sahā world many times. Sometimes I was born as a pheasant only to be captured by a hawk; and other times as a rat only to be eaten by a cat. Even when I was born a human being, I lost my life for my wife and children, and to my enemies, more often than the number of particles of the great earth without sacrificing my life for the sake of the *Lotus Sutra* even once. As a result, I was born into this world as a poor monk unable to serve my parents as much as I would like and repay what I owe to my country. This is the time for me to dedicate my head to the *Lotus Sutra* and offer the merit of my sacrifice to my parents and also to my disciples and followers. This is what I have been saying for some time now and it will become a reality tonight."

Shijō Kingo burst into tears. When he could finally speak he said, "If you are to die tonight then I will commit *seppuku* and follow you in death, right here upon this beach."

The procession stopped. They had arrived at Tatsunokuchi. The warriors began to mill around in excitement. Some of them set up a camp curtain around the perimeter of the place of execution. A straw mat was laid down for the condemned monk while a folding chair was set out for Hei no Saemon to sit upon while he observed the execution. A brazier was set in place to provide light. Fierce winds blew in from Sagami Bay, causing the camp curtains to billow. Lightning flashed over the waters of the bay, as the crash of thunder echoed in time with the roaring of the breakers.

Nichiren was taken to the mat and made to kneel. Holding his *juzu* before him he put his hands in the *añjali* mudra and began to chant, "Namu Myōhō Renge Kyō, Namu Myōhō Renge Kyō..." The executioner took up his position behind Nichiren and drew his sword.

Shijō Kingo, standing by the curtain with his brothers and still holding the reins of the horse began to cry, saying, "The last moment has come!"

Nichiren turned to Shijō Kingo and his brothers and said, "How dismayed you all are! You should be laughing at such a wonderful occasion as this when I am going to present my wretched head to the *Lotus Sutra*. It will be like exchanging sand for gold or pebbles for jewels. Why do you break the promise you made to stand firm?"

Nichiren resumed chanting the *daimoku*. The executioner forced Nichiren to lower his head and then raised his sword. The storm was making him nervous. It was not a wise thing to be holding up a naked blade while lightning flashed overhead. Executing a monk, even one as mad as this, was also tempting fate. The executioner looked to Hei no Saemon, waiting for the order to strike. Did the deputy chief really dare to go through with this?

Just at that moment, a great shining sphere flew out from Enoshima Island, describing a path from southeast to northwest. The dawn had

241

not yet broken, and it was still so dark that the faces of those gathered could not be seen clearly. However, that last and darkest remnant of the night was now so brightened by the sudden appearance of this shining apparition that all who were present were able to see one another as if by the light of the fully ascended moon. The executioner dropped his sword and fell to the ground as though blinded. The other warriors became frightened. A significant number ran out of the curtained area in all directions. Some remained motionless atop their horses, as if paralyzed. Others leaped down from their saddles and crouched on the sand.

In chanting the *daimoku*, the power of the whole sutra and all its protectors had been invoked. Who had sent that ball of lightning across the sky at just that moment? Perhaps it had been World Voice Perceiver Bodhisattva, of whom the Buddha sang in the verses of chapter 25 of the *Lotus Sutra*, "Suppose you are sentenced to death, and the sword is drawn to behead you. If you think of the power of World Voice Perceiver, the sword will suddenly break asunder."

Nichiren shouted, "Why do you stay away from a felon like me? Come back here quickly!" None of them, however, were anxious to come near the mad monk who now also seemed to be under divine protection. "Daybreak is coming very soon; what can you do if it gets light? If you have to kill me, do it right away. It would be unsightly if you wait until daylight."

Not even Hei no Saemon dared to respond.

The Sado Exile

"A man called Nichiren was beheaded between the hours of the rat and the ox (one a.m.) during the night of the twelfth day of the ninth month last year. His spirit has come to the province of Sado and is writing this in the midst of snow in the second month of the following year to be sent to his closely related disciples. As such, this writing of mine may sound frightening to you, but it should not. How fearful others will be when they read this writing! This is the bright mirror in which Śākyamuni Buddha, Many Treasures Buddha, and the emanation buddhas of the worlds of the ten directions reflect the future state of Japan through the conditions of Japan today. Consider this as my memento in case I die."

So Nichiren had written to Shijō Kingo and other disciples and lay followers back in Kamakura in a long essay entitled *Kaimoku-shō* (*Open Your Eyes*). It would be one of the most important things he had written in his life, for now he could no longer afford to hold anything back from them. Of course he had not literally been beheaded, but he felt as though he had already given his life at Tatsunokuchi, the Dragon's Mouth. Though he had been sent to the barren and remote Sado Island in the Sea of Japan to die slowly of exposure and starvation, it was also still possible that a messenger could arrive from Kamakura any day, with new orders reinstating the death penalty. To be alive at all seemed like a fantastic dream.

As dawn broke on the 13th day of the ninth month of the eighth year of the Bun'ei era (1271), following the aborted execution attempt, Hei no Saemon had directed his vassals to take Nichiren to the estate of Homma Shigetsura in Echi. Shijō Kingo, overcome and speechless with awe of Nichiren, accompanied them. As they rode away from the beach, Nichiren looked back and said, "How wondrous! There may have been times in past lives when I sacrificed myself for the sake of wife and children, property, and retainers. I may have cast my life away in the mountains, in the oceans, in the rivers, on the shores, or on the streets. However, in not one of those cases did I do so for the sake of the *Lotus Sutra* or the *daimoku* and so they did not contribute to my spiritual awakening. Because they did not contribute to such awakening, the oceans and rivers where I cast myself away were not the buddha-land. This time I face exile and the death penalty as a practitioner of the *Lotus Sutra*. I have been exiled to Izu and have received the death penalty at Tatsunokuchi. Tatsunokuchi is where I have cast away my life, so it should not be considered inferior to the buddha-land. This is because it is there that I faced persecution for the sake of the *Lotus Sutra*, the one true teaching in the buddha-lands of the ten directions. There, where my life remains, is the Pure Land of Tranquil Light."

They arrived at the manor of Homma Shigetsura around noon. Upon arriving, Nichiren requested bottles of *sake* to treat the members of his escort. After a while the escort was ready to leave. The warriors bowed their heads, palms pressed together. The leader of the troop said to Nichiren, "We did not know what kind of person you were until today and simply hated you because we had been told that you were a slanderer of Amitābha Buddha in whom we seek refuge. Having seen what happened last night with our own eyes, we are so awestricken that we have now made up our mind to quit the *nembutsu*, which we had chanted all these years." Some of the warriors took out *juzu* from their flint bags and threw them away. Others swore not to chant the *nembutsu* any longer. When the escort left for Kamakura, the retainers of Homma Shigetsura took over the duty of guarding Nichiren. Shijō Kingo also left for home with the escort. Though Nichiren was a condemned criminal, Umanojō, Shigetsura's deputy, was very circumspect and even reverential towards him, treating him as an honored guest rather than a prisoner.

That evening, a messenger of the shogunate came from Kamakura with an official letter. Shigetsura's retainers were grim. They were expecting a letter ordering them to behead Nichiren. Umanojō ran into the courtyard with the letter and knelt on the ground before Nichiren. He said, "This official letter, which I was afraid might be an order to carry out your execution tonight, turned out to be a lucky one. According to the messenger, around the hour of the hare (six a.m.), Lord Hōjō Nobutoki, who is officially your custodian, had already left for a hot spring at Atami. The messenger feared that if he tried to deliver the letter to Nobutoki first it would not reach this manor in time to prevent a hasty execution. So, the messenger decided to deliver the letter here first, rushing over from Kamakura in only four hours. The messenger has already left for Atami Spa, where Hōjō Nobutoki is staying." Umanojō showed Nichiren the postscript of the letter. It stated, "This person is not guilty and will be pardoned before long. Be careful not to commit hasty mistakes that you might regret later."

That night dozens of samurai were on guard duty around Nichiren's room and in the large garden outside. The moon shone in a clear sky as Nichiren stepped out into the garden at midnight to recite the Verses of Eternity. He recited them several times, and then began to briefly explain the comparative profundity of the different Buddhist schools and to outline the teachings of the *Lotus Sutra* to anyone who might care to listen. The guards became still and silent to give ear to Nichiren's talk. When his discourse was done, Nichiren put his palms together, raised his eyes to the heavens and began to harangue the moon.

"Are you not the Moon God who attended the assembly in which Śākyamuni Buddha taught the *Lotus Sutra*? Are you not the very Moon God who was ordered directly by Śākyamuni Buddha in the eleventh chapter, 'Appearance of the Stūpa of Treasures,' to spread the *Lotus Sutra* and protect its practitioners after his death? Are you not the god who was touched by the Buddha on the head three times and made a great vow to carry out the Buddha's order without fail in the 22nd chapter, 'Transmission'? The vow you made in front of the Buddha would be mere empty words if not for the great difficulties of

Nichiren, who is providing you with a chance to carry out your vow. At this moment I am facing this great trial for the sake of the *Lotus Sutra*. You should be delighted to take the place of a practitioner of the *Lotus Sutra*, carry out the Buddha's order, and make good on your oath. It is quite unbelievable that you have not shown any sign of fulfilling your oath at this very moment when I am being condemned for the sake of the *Lotus Sutra*. Should there be no sign, I will not return to Kamakura even if I am pardoned. What will happen to you, Moon God, if you show no sign but continue to shine carefree in the clear sky? It is taught in the *Great Assembly Sutra*, 'The sun and moon will not shine,' in the *Benevolent Kings Sutra*, 'The sun and moon will lose their brightness,' and in the *Golden Splendor Sutra*, 'The 33 gods will become angry' in the land where the True Dharma is slandered. What happened to you, Moon God? Why do you not respond?"

In this manner, he sternly accused the Moon God of dereliction of duty. When he was finished, a star looking like Venus suddenly fell from heaven, and perched on a branch of a plum tree in the front garden. The guards were all astonished at the sight of it and jumped off the veranda. Some crouched in the garden behind the foliage, while others hid behind the house. Soon the whole sky became dark, strong winds began to blow, and the horrible sound of a howling storm around Enoshima Island echoed in the sky as loudly as huge drums.

It was dawn on the following day when a lay monk called Jurō rushed in from Kamakura and reported, "There was an uproar at the residence of the Regent Hōjō Tokimune last night. A diviner who was called in to divine the future on this matter of Nichiren reported that this was an omen of great disorder in the nation. He went on to say that it stemmed from the punishment of the monk Nichiren, and that unless Nichiren was pardoned at once, he would be unable to predict how serious the chaos of the world might become. Some among the regent's counselors suggested pardoning Nichiren right away, but others insisted it would be better to put off pardoning him until they could discover the truth of his prediction of a war to occur within 100 days as he had predicted when interrogated by Hei no Saemon before the Council of State."

That day, Nichiren wrote to Toki Jōnin of the aborted execution, his impending exile to Sado Island, and his detention in Echi. In the letter he wrote, "I understand that you lament for me, but since I expected this to happen from the beginning, I do not lament for myself. In fact, I regret that I have not yet been beheaded. If I had been beheaded for the *Lotus Sutra* in a past life, I would not have been born as such a lowly man in this present life. As stated in the 'Encouragement for Upholding This Sutra' chapter of the *Lotus Sutra*, 'Practitioners of the *Lotus Sutra* will often be driven out of monasteries.' I have received punishment from time to time for the sake of the *Lotus Sutra*, eliminating serious transgressions committed in my previous lives. As this is the only way for me to attain buddhahood, I am willing to undergo such harsh trials."

In a postscript he added, "Having faith in the *Lotus Sutra* involves suffering and punishment by the shogunate. There is no doubt that the moon waxes and wanes and the tide ebbs and rises. Though at the moment I endure punishment and suffering, they will return to me as merit. Why would I lament a joy such as this?"

He was detained in Echi for almost three weeks after that. In the meantime incidents of arson took place seven or eight times and murders occurred nearly every night in Kamakura. Some made false charges to the shogunate blaming disciples of Nichiren for the recurring arson. Believing that might be the case, Hei no Saemon made a list of some 260 disciples and devotees of Nichiren to be banished from Kamakura. It was rumored that the Council of State deliberated a proposal to banish all of them to distant places or to execute imprisoned disciples of Nichiren. However, it was later found that the arson was the work of precept holders and *nembutsu* believers as a ploy to discredit Nichiren's disciples and lay followers. By then, however, the damage had been done. Nichiren's disciples were banished or imprisoned. Samurai who were known associates of Nichiren incurred the anger of their lords and in some cases were stripped of their fiefs, lost their status as vassals, or were expelled. Those followers who remained steadfast were abandoned by their siblings or disowned by their parents. In the end, all but one out of 1,000 followers lost faith. Among those who abandoned Nichiren were Lord Itō and the Nun Proprietress who had been his benefactors. Some of those who disassociated themselves from Nichiren out of fear of persecution even went so far as to persuade others to give up their faith in the *Lotus Sutra* and return to the practice of *nembutsu* or the teachings of the Mantra school.

Nichiren was especially worried about those disciples who had been arrested along with him but had remained in Kamakura. He knew that they were not being treated as gently as he was. On the third day of the tenth month he sent a letter to five of his disciples who had been imprisoned in a cave in the custody of Yadoya Mitsunori. One of the five was Nichirō, who was no longer a boy but had grown to be a competent and learned monk in his mid-twenties. In the letter he wrote, "As all of you who have been put in prison due to your faith in the *Lotus Sutra* have actually read through the entire *Lotus Sutra* with both body and mind, you not only reap the merits yourself, but extend the merits to the spirits of your parents, brothers, and sisters as well. It is so cold tonight that I am worried and feel sorry more for you in prison than for myself. When pardoned and released from prison, be sure to visit me in Sado next spring. I hope to see you then."

To his lay supporters he wrote letters explaining that, like Never Despising Bodhisattva in the *Lotus Sutra*, by facing persecution he was expiating the transgressions of previous lifetimes and that in any case it was inevitable to face great difficulties when trying to spread the teaching of the *Lotus Sutra*, especially in the Latter Age of Degeneration. He wrote, "When evil kings in ancient times acted tyrannically and oppressed Buddhism, many sage monks were persecuted. I can conjecture from my own experience today how grief-stricken their followers, relatives, disciples, and supporters must have been. Now I, Nichiren, have actually practiced the entire *Lotus Sutra* just as it is taught. Even those who uphold a single phrase or verse are guaranteed to become buddhas in the future. All the more so for those who actually practice the entirety of the *Lotus Sutra* to attain buddhahood. This is most certain. Though it may sound presumptuous, my desire was to save the country, but it is beyond my power in an age when I am not heeded."

On the tenth day of the tenth month, the journey to Sado Island began. Nichiren, escorted by the retainers of Homma Shigetsura, traveled for twelve days to reach the port of Teradomari in Echigo Province. The escort set a grueling pace. Tired and hungry every step of the way, Nichiren began to perceive that his senses were becoming distorted. It was all he could do to shoulder his pack, keep putting one foot in front of the other, and chant *daimoku* for as long as he had breath and voice enough to do so. In every small village and post station it seemed as though formidable enemies were lining up one after another in wait for him, to jeer and curse. All of them were believers in the *nembutsu*. Some were armed with swords, spears, and staves but they kept their peace when they saw the determination of the warriors guarding the prisoner. Even his escort, fearing an ambush, became uneasy as they passed through overgrown fields and traversed the mountain passes. Whenever a gust of wind rattled the bamboo or blew through the tall grasses on the cliffs and plains they reached for their swords in alarm.

Upon arriving at Teradomari, they were forced by unfavorable winds to remain harbored there for six days, after which they were able to cross the Sea of Japan in safety. Nichiren looked across the gray choppy waves to the north, but the fog was too thick to see Sado Island. Nichiren knew that of those who were exiled to Sado, very few returned home alive. It was to Sado that the Retired Emperor

Juntoku had been exiled after the disastrous attempt by the Retired Emperor Go-Toba to overthrow the shogunate, and it was there that he had died some 30 years ago.

Recalling the fate of the Retired Emperor Juntoku made Nichiren recall the Jōkyū Disturbance, and the failure of the mantra rites to bring victory to the imperial forces. That had been their second great failure, the first being the prayers by the Tendai monks of Enryakuji on Mt. Hiei to defeat Minamoto no Yoritomo. Now it was the shogunate that was commissioning the likes of Ryōkan and others to perform prayer services using the mantra practices derived from the *Mahāvairocana Sutra* instead of prayers based on the *Lotus Sutra*. Nichiren decided that it was time to begin expressing the misgivings he had long held about the mantra teachings. He began to write about his concerns in letters he sent to Toki Jōnin and planned to write more as soon as could.

As he reflected upon the errors of the mantra teachings and the inevitable destruction of Japan if the mantra practices were employed to aid the country in defeating the Mongols the skies cleared and the arctic winds died down long enough to set sail. On Sado, true to the character of the northern provinces, strong winds and deep snows had already taken hold. As the long winter gathered force, food became even scarcer than before. The coarse hemp robes he had brought with him were thin and threadbare, though he at least had a straw coat to provide a modicum of warmth. Upon arrival Nichiren was taken to see Honma Shigetsura at his Sado residence. The indifferent deputy constable assigned the exile to stay in a memorial chapel known as the Sammaidō, or Samādhi Hall. It was located in a field called Tsukahara, behind the deputy constable's own residence. Nichiren was taken there and left to his own devices on the first of the eleventh month.

The Sammaidō turned out to be a dilapidated thatched hut of about six square feet. It stood in the midst of a charnel ground covered with eulalia and pampas grass. The roof was full of holes and the four walls had so many holes in them that snow collected in piles throughout the room, which was too cold for it to melt away. Day and night, Nichiren sat on a scrap of fur, shivering in his all but useless straw raincoat. At night it snowed, hailed, and thundered continuously. In the daytime not even a ray of sunshine was able to penetrate the heavy clouds. Apart from the storms, all that could be heard was the moaning of the wind. In the overcast gloom of the day, the only thing to look at was the drifting snow that covered the land. Nichiren felt as though he had entered the realm of the hungry ghosts or fallen, still alive, into one of the eight cold hells.

As he had so often, Nichiren considered the teachings of the *Lotus Sutra* relating the hardships that a practitioner of the sutra must expect to face. It seemed as though he alone had undergone the persecutions that the sutra spoke of, and it seemed that the assurances given in the sutras were being spoken directly to him. He felt more certain than ever that he would attain the perfect and complete awakening of a buddha.

He thought of the story related in the twelfth chapter of the *Lotus Sutra* wherein a king in a past age renounced his throne to seek the True Dharma. The king turned ascetic devoted himself to long and difficult practice under the instruction of a seer named Asita who taught him the *Lotus Sutra* as it appeared in that age. Śākyamuni Buddha revealed that he had been able to attain buddhahood because he had been that king who in a past life had been able to encounter and practice the *Lotus Sutra*, and the seer Asita had been a past life of his treacherous cousin Devadatta. Devadatta, therefore, had actually once been the teacher of Śākyamuni Buddha and had helped him attain awakening.

Nichiren considered that the regent, Hōjō Tokimune, who had forced him to experience the hardships predicted by the *Lotus Sutra* by exiling him was actually a good friend enabling him to achieve the way of the Buddha. Hei no Saemon who had tried to kill him was like Devadatta who had tried to kill Śākyamuni Buddha. Those who chanted the *nembutsu* were like the monks who had left the Buddha when Devadatta had split the Sangha. It was as though the events of the Buddha's lifetime were recurring in the present. All of the events of the past few months suddenly seemed to be filled with great significance. And of course they should be! The gist of the *Lotus Sutra* was that all phenomena are themselves ultimate reality. Both seemingly essential and non-essential things have their reasons to exist and are, after all, equally manifestations of the Dharma.

The Great Master Tiantai had taught in the *Great Calming and Contemplation*, "As understanding and practice advance, the three hindrances and four devils will arise in confusing forms to torment the practitioner of the Buddha Way." He also wrote, "It is also similar to an ocean growing larger with its tributaries flowing in, or a fire increasing the force of its flames as firewood is added." The three hindrances were those things that arise to hinder one's practice. They consisted of one's inner defilements such as greed and hatred, the unwholesome habits motivated by the defilements, and finally the painful consequences of those habitual responses to life's vicissitudes. The four devils likewise worked to distract the practitioner or prevent practice altogether. The first was the devil of the five aggregates, one's own body and mind. The second was the devil of the defilements, one's self-centered desires and wrong views. The third was the devil of death, the fear of which hinders practice and the coming of which cuts off practice. And the fourth, last, and most formidable was Māra himself, the devil king of the sixth heaven. Māra was said to enter the minds of kings, parents, spouses, children, religious devotees, or evildoers. Sometimes Māra would even pose as a fellow practitioner or patron. Working through these people, the devil king would do all he could to seduce or scare the practitioner into turning away from the True Dharma. Those who did turn away and take up provisional or false practices would be cherished by the devil king and find themselves greatly esteemed and given offerings by those who had formerly opposed them when they tried to practice the True Dharma. Nichiren saw that his persecutions at the hands of the rulers of the country were proof that he was practicing correctly. It showed that he had aroused the three hindrances and four devils, a sure sign that he must be a practitioner of the True Dharma.

Nichiren reflected to himself, 'Devadatta, archenemy of Śākyamuni Buddha was the primary good friend who helped the Buddha in his pursuit of the Dharma. It seems that strong enemies, rather than friends, are the ones who help people improve themselves. By the same token, my greatest allies who are helping me to attain buddhahood are Tōjō Kagenobu, who tried to kill me at Komatsubara, the monks Ryōkan, Dōryū, and Dōamidabutsu, who brought false charges against me to the shogunate, Hei no Saemon, who tried to have me executed at Tatsunokuch, and Hōjō Tokimuni who sent me here to this island to die. If not for those people, how could I have become a practitioner of the *Lotus Sutra*?'

Feeling his sincere debt to those who had persecuted him and thereby enabled him to live the sutra in both body and mind, Nichiren put his hands together and bowed deeply in the direction of Kamakura, chanting, "Namu Myōhō Renge Kyō, Namu Myōhō Renge Kyō, Namu Myōhō Renge Kyō..."

Open Your Eyes

Nichiren remembered the many doubts of those who left him once he had been arrested and exiled. Even some of his followers and disciples who stood by him had expressed their doubts. The *Lotus Sutra* promised them peace in their present lives and rebirth in good places, but in the meantime all they saw was the threat of exile or death, not to mention constant ridicule from their neighbors and even family members. If Nichiren, the primary practitioner of the *Lotus Sutra* received such rough treatment, then how could anyone else expect to receive any divine protection, let alone the blessings of continued good health, increasing wealth, happiness in love, or an assurance of rebirth in a pure land after death?

One of these doubters had accusingly said, "This persecution is not some necessary fulfillment of ancient prophecies. It is the result of your having high-handedly set forth a crude doctrine without considering whether or not people would be able to understand the teaching of the *Lotus Sutra* that you advocate."

Another said to him, "What is taught in the 'Encouragement for Keeping this Sutra' chapter of the *Lotus Sutra* about practitioners of the sutra encountering difficulties without fail is applicable to advanced bodhisattvas. Beginners like you ought to practice the tolerant way taught in the 'Peaceful Practices' chapter and not criticize others. You have brought these troubles upon yourself by failing to follow the parts of the sutra that are appropriate for you."

Still others said, "I realize that the *Lotus Sutra* is the Buddha's highest teaching, but why cause trouble for yourself and others by harping on it the way you do?"

Then there were those monks and lay monks who said to him, "You put too much stress on the intricacies of comparing the relative profundity of the sutras, but you neglect the practice of calming and contemplation."

Nichiren took these criticisms to heart and was determined to respond to them. He thought to himself, 'People doubt me, and I myself wonder why the gods have not come to help me despite their vows to protect the practitioner of the *Lotus Sutra*. Does that mean I am not a true practitioner of the *Lotus Sutra*?'

From the time he settled in at the Sammaidō on Sado Island he began to muster passages from the sutras and commentaries and marshal his thoughts in order to write the treatise he entitled *Open Your Eyes*. He did this with the help of those disciples who came to join him in exile, including Nikkō, Nikō, and Nitchō. He also found refuge and encouragement in the support he received from those back in Kamakura and its surrounding provinces who had remained faithful and had not been punished too harshly in the months following his arrest, near execution, and exile. Through messengers they sent food, clothing, paper and ink, and also texts. He had believed then that this treatise for his followers might very well be his last chance to express all that was in his heart.

Open Your Eyes began, "People should respect these three: their ruler, their teachers, and their parents. Everyone should study these three disciplines: Confucianism, the non-Buddhist teachings of India, and Buddhism." By this Nichiren meant that all people should study the teachings of Confucius and other sages of China, the sages of ancient India, and the teachings of Śākyamuni Buddha in order to find a way to repay their debts of gratitude to their ruler, teachers, and parents.

Confucianism helped prepare people to understand the threefold training of Buddhist morality, concentration, and wisdom by teaching filial piety, loyalty to the ruler, the five constant virtues of benevolence, righteousness, propriety, wisdom, and trustworthiness, and also the civilized arts of ritual and music. According to the

257

Practicing the Dharma Sutra, Confucius, his most gifted disciple Yan Hui, and the Taoist sage Laozi were all bodhisattvas who appeared in China specifically to prepare the way for Buddhism. The sages of China, however, did not know anything about past and future lives, and so they could not know what they truly owed parents, rulers, and teachers, let alone repay those debts of gratitude.

In India, the sages who came before the Buddha and those who were his contemporaries did know of past and future lives, but their understanding of the law of cause and effect was incomplete or confused. They did not know the middle way, nor did they know how to escape the six paths of samsara. All they could do was follow ascetic practices or yogic meditation in order to attain the temporary respite of the heavenly realms.

Fortunately for all beings, Śākyamuni Buddha appeared to lead the people along the way to liberation and be their eyes to perceive the truth. He was a bridge enabling people to cross the river of defilements, a captain who sailed them across the sea of birth and death, a fertile field in which they could plant the seeds of merit. For 50 years the Buddha taught, from the time of his awakening at the age of 30 until he passed away at the age of 80. His teachings included Hinayana and Mahayana, provisional and true, exoteric and esoteric.

The Hinayana teachings taught that a dedicated few could escape the six paths of samsara by taking up one or another of the two vehicles of voice-hearers or private-buddhas, but did not recognize that there were any other buddhas or pure lands apart from Śākyamuni Buddha, whom they believed had passed into final nirvana more than 2,000 years ago. Naturally, these teachings also did not recognize that all living beings have the buddha-nature. In addition, the final nirvana attained by the arhats, the private-buddhas, and even the Buddha upon dying meant that their bodies were reduced to ashes and their consciousness annihilated. There were no other Dharma-realms according to these teachings other than the six paths of suffering from which the only escape, for arhats, private-buddhas, or even the Buddha himself, was simply the cessation of rebirth in the six paths.

The provisional Mahayana teachings did, however, teach that there were buddhas abiding in pure lands throughout the ten directions. These teachings chastised the voice-hearers and private-buddhas for not aspiring to attain buddhahood. All people were exhorted by the Buddha in these teachings to take up the bodhisattva vehicle. Though the practice for achieving buddhahood might take ages, it was also possible for aspiring bodhisattvas to be reborn in the pure lands of the ten directions where conditions were more favorable than in the Sahā world for attaining buddhahood. The Buddha did not, however, make it clear in these teachings whether all could attain buddhahood. Though all beings may have innate buddha-nature, they did not necessarily have the wisdom that awakens it or the merit needed to develop wisdom.

Some of the schools based on the provisional teachings, such as the Dharma Characteristics school, actively denied that all beings could attain buddhahood. That school insisted that some had predispositions to attain buddhahood, but that others were unalterably predisposed to attain final nirvana as arhats or private-buddhas. Others with more flexible dispositions might choose to follow the way to buddhahood but might also choose the lesser way of the arhats and private-buddhas. Those who did attain final nirvana as arhats or private-buddhas passed away from the six paths for good, were not reborn into the pure lands, and did not appear in any realm of their own. They were gone, and would never again appear to aspire to buddhahood and take up the practice of bodhisattvas. The Dharma Characteristics school also taught that the *icchantika* were forever unable to attain nirvana. Some passages found in provisional Mahayana sutras likewise denied that women could attain buddhahood, or that at the very least they must cultivate merit so they could be reborn as men first.

Here, was the problem. How could one know for sure that the teaching one embraced could lead one's parents, teachers, and rulers to buddhahood? How could one be sure that one was even repaying one's debt of gratitude to the Three Treasures by following the teachings correctly? In *Open Your Eyes*, Nichiren reminded his disciples and followers, "The 3,000 scrolls of Confucian writings can be boiled down to two important points: the importance of filial devotion and loyalty to the ruler. Loyalty also stems from filial devotion. To be filial means to be high; heaven is high but not at all higher than being filial. To be filial also means to be deep; the earth is deep but not any deeper than being filial. Both sages and wise men become so through filial devotion. How much more should students of Buddhism realize the favors they receive and repay them? Disciples of the Buddha should not fail to feel grateful for the four favors received from parents, the people, the ruler, and Buddhism, and repay them."

The solution was found in the *Lotus Sutra*. In the first half, the Trace Gate, Śākyamuni Buddha taught the One Vehicle that enabled even those who followed the two vehicles of the voice-hearers and private-buddhas to attain buddhahood. This meant that even those who had become arhats or private-buddhas had not disappeared irrevocably into final nirvana but would eventually take up the bodhisattva path and attain buddhahood. At last all ten Dharma-realms were revealed, the six paths corresponding to the six realms of the hell-dwellers, hungry ghosts, animals, *asuras*, humans, and gods, and the four realms of the voice-hearers, private-buddhas, bodhisattvas, and buddhas. All of the beings of the six lower realms could take up the practice of the voice-hearers, private-buddhas, or bodhisattvas, but those practices were really all just skillful means leading to the One Vehicle of buddhahood. All beings, therefore, could attain buddhahood. All beings not only had innate buddha-nature in being part of the same one reality as the buddha, they also had the seeds of wisdom and compassionate action within their lives that would eventually come to fruition as buddhahood. In the Trace Gate this is made evident through the predictions of buddhahood given to the major disciples of the Buddha, to his former wife, his foster-mother, and in the end to all the beings in the assembly and to all who hear the *Lotus Sutra*, take faith in it, and rejoice in it. It is also made clear in his prediction of buddhahood for his cousin Devadatta and in the realization of buddhahood by the daughter of the dragon king.

Nichiren summed up, "Filial devotion taught in Confucianism is limited to this life. Confucian sages and wise men exist in name only because they do not help parents in their future lives. Non-Buddhist religions in India know of the past as well as the future, but they do not know how to help parents. Only Buddhism is worthy of being the way of sages and wise men, as it helps parents in future lives. However, both the Mahayana and Hinayana sutras expounded before the *Lotus Sutra* preach buddhahood in name only, without substance. Therefore the practitioners of such sutras will not be able to attain buddhahood for themselves, not to speak of helping parents attain buddhahood. Now coming to the *Lotus Sutra*, when the awakening of women was revealed, the awakening of mothers was realized; and when a man as wicked as Devadatta could attain buddhahood, the awakening of fathers was realized. These are two proclamations of the Buddha in the 'Devadatta' chapter, and this is the reason why the *Lotus Sutra* is the sutra of the filial way among all the Buddhist scriptures."

Still, what did it mean to attain buddhahood? And how exactly did one attain it? Did one have to be reborn in a pure land after death? Did one have to seek out another buddha to practice with or receive a prediction of buddhahood from, since Śākyamuni Buddha had long since entered final nirvana and was no longer a compassionate empowering presence in the Sahā world? Did other buddhas take precedence over Śākyamuni Buddha whose time as a buddha in the world was a mere 50 years? Did a buddha such as Śākyamuni Buddha, really pass away forever from the world?

These questions were answered in the second half of the *Lotus Sutra*, the Original Gate. Finally, Śākyamuni Buddha revealed that he had actually attained buddhahood in the remote past. His buddhahood had no beginning and would not have an end. All other buddhas such as Amitābha Buddha were his emanations or mere aspects of his totality as the Eternal Śākyamuni Buddha. His buddhahood was not a higher form of annihilation. This meant the Eternal Śākyamuni Buddha and his pure land were ever present. This meant that the causes and effects of buddhahood were ever present.

The seed of buddhahood, therefore, was the principle and actuality of the 3,000 realms in a single thought-moment. It had been dimly glimpsed like the reflection of the moon in a lake in the Trace Gate with the teaching of the One Vehicle, but its actuality was hidden in the depths of chapter 16 of the Original Gate, wherein the Buddha's attainment of buddhahood in the remote past was revealed. To joyfully accept the 3,000 realms in a single thought-moment was to joyfully accept the mutual possession of the ten realms wherein the realm of the Eternal Śākyamuni Buddha embraces and is embraced by the lower nine realms. The patriarchs Nāgārjuna and Vasubandhu were aware of it, but did not speak of it. Though the founders of the Flower Garland and Mantra schools tried to appropriate it from the Tiantai school, it was Great Master Tiantai alone who had perceived it and first spoken of it.

In this way Nichiren explained that the pre-Buddhist teachings prepared the way for Buddhism. Hinayana prepared the way for Mahayana. Provisional Mahayana, in turn, prepared the way for the teaching of the attainment of buddhahood by the two vehicles in the Trace Gate. The Trace Gate, in turn, prepared the way for the Buddha's revelation of his attainment of buddhahood in the remote past in the Original Gate. All of this culminated in the seed of buddhahood for all people that is the realization of the 3,000 realms in a single thought-moment in actuality through the chanting of *daimoku*. Here, then was the way to repay one's debts of gratitude.

Nichiren hoped that he had shown that his teachings were far from his own biased opinions. Rather, he had taught with the *Lotus Sutra* in hand and had followed the teachings of Great Master Tiantai in China, and Great Master Dengyō in Japan, both of whom had followed the *Lotus Sutra* and not their own one-sided views. Furthermore, the *Lotus Sutra* itself had said that its teachings would be "the most difficult to believe and the most difficult to understand" and that it would be "hated with jealousy" even in the lifetime of the Buddha. Didn't the Buddha say to his cleverest disciple, "Even you, Śāriputra, have understood this sutra only by faith"? The problem was not that Nichiren had taught a crude doctrine in an arrogant way to people who were not ready for it. The problem was that the *Lotus Sutra* itself was too wondrous to be understood by anyone other than buddhas. It had to be taken on faith initially, until the wisdom to perceive the 3,000 realms in a single thought-moment could develop. There was no other way to attain buddhahood other than accepting on faith, and not rejecting or slandering, the teaching of the 3,000 realms in a single thought-moment.

To address the question of why he and his disciples and lay followers had not been protected from hardship, Nichiren explained that it was inevitable to meet with the three hindrances and four devils that he had spoken of before. He also explained, once again, that he must be expiating the transgressions of past lifetimes, when he had perhaps been a wicked king who had deprived practitioners of the *Lotus Sutra* of food, clothing, and shelter, or even beheaded them. In addition, perhaps the protective deities had forsaken the country because of the widespread slander of the *Lotus Sutra*. Finally, if the three kinds of enemies had appeared to persecute the practitioner of the *Lotus Sutra*, then who could the practitioner of the *Lotus Sutra* be if not himself? The hardships and persecutions he was facing were predicted in the *Lotus Sutra* and no one else but he was fulfilling those predictions.

Nichiren concluded, "In the final analysis, no matter if I am abandoned by the gods or how many difficulties I encounter, I will uphold the *Lotus Sutra* at the cost of my own life. Śāriputra could not attain buddhahood after having practiced the way of the bodhisattvas for as long as 60 *kalpas* because he could not endure the difficulty presented by a brahman who asked him for his eyes. Those who had received the seed of buddhahood from the Eternal Buddha and Great Universal Wisdom Buddha an incalculable number of *kalpa* ago could not attain buddhahood for as long as 500 million or 3,000 dust particle *kalpas* until they listened to the teaching of the *Lotus Sutra* on Eagle Peak in this world. It was because evil friends had tricked them into abandoning the *Lotus Sutra*. No matter what happens, abandoning the *Lotus Sutra* will cause us to be plunged into hell.

"I have made a vow. Even if someone says that he will make me the ruler of Japan on the condition that I give up the *Lotus Sutra* and rely on the *Meditation on the Buddha of Infinite Life Sutra* for salvation in the next life, or even if someone threatens me saying that he will execute my parents if I do not chant Namu Amida Butsu, no matter how many great difficulties fall upon me, I will not submit to them unless a man of wisdom defeats me by reason. Other difficulties are like dust in the wind. I will never break my vow to become the pillar of Japan, to become the eyes of Japan, and to become a great vessel for Japan."

The Tsukahara Debate

Winter officially changed to spring with New Year's Day of the ninth year of the Bun'ei era (1272). Until that time Nichiren was isolated by the mounds of snow that made it nearly impossible to get to Tsukahara. He spent his days writing *Open Your Eyes*, reading the *Great Calming and Contemplation*, reciting the *Lotus Sutra*, and chanting *daimoku*. At night he lectured on the differences between the various schools of Buddhism and the profound teaching of the *Lotus Sutra*.

Nichiren and his disciples would not have lasted the winter, however, were it not for some of the local inhabitants, especially a man named Abutsu-bō and his wife Sennichi-ama and others like them. At first, these people were greatly angered to learn that the exiled monk was opposed to the practice of *nembutsu*. Once they had a chance to speak to Nichiren they saw for themselves that he was not a demon but a kindly monk who was greatly concerned about the truth of the Buddha's teaching in the sutras. In time, even the relatively uncivilized and ignorant peasants, samurai, and clergy on the island began to become more sympathetic and their offerings of food and clothing enabled Nichiren and his disciples to survive.

As spring came and the snows melted away, travel and communication both within the island and with the mainland resumed. Within days after the beginning of the year, Nichiren was summoned to the constabulary office of Homma Shigetsura. The deputy constable bade him sit. Shigetsura frowned at the exile. He was not pleased to have to deal with such a person. Nevertheless, it was his duty. "I have summoned you here today because there are people here who would like me to behead you. There are those, upholders of the precepts and practitioners of the *nembutsu*, who would be happy to do this themselves, confident that they would not be punished since no exile has ever returned alive from here anyway, and it would seem that your execution was only postponed due the pregnancy of the wife of the regent. I had to deal with a mob of such people yesterday, demanding your head."

Nichiren nodded, "I quite understand. This is hardly surprising. My disciples and I will be watchful. However, I have long determined to give my life for the *Lotus Sutra*. I will not give up nor will I bear any grudges. Instead, I will regard my attackers as good friends who are helping me to live the sutra as it teaches. If I were to be killed for the sake of the *Lotus Sutra* so that I could attain buddhahood, it would be like being robbed of a vial of poison and given a precious jewel instead."

Shigetsura shook his head. "That may be, but it will not happen while I am responsible for you!" He took out a letter and passed it over to Nichiren. "I have received this letter from the shogunate directing me to keep you alive, because you are considered an important prisoner. Therefore, I told your would-be murderers that I will only permit them to slay you in debate."

Nichiren read the letter and looked up. "A debate?"

"Yes, it will be scheduled to occur on the 16th of this month at the Sammaidō. I will be there with my family, brothers, and retainers to ensure that it is done properly and to keep it civil and peaceful."

Shigetsura hesitated for a moment, on the verge of dismissing him. He gave Nichiren an appraising look, and then said, "You are not what I expected. When I was told that you would be coming here as an exile, I imagined that you were some kind of madman. However, sitting here before me you seem quite calm and reasonable. I have heard others say they have found you to be quite compassionate, patient, and gentle. Now, I hear you say you regard your persecutors as good friends. So I can't help but wonder why you belligerently claim that followers of Amitābha Buddha and Zen will fall into the

Hell of Incessant Suffering. Doesn't the *Lotus Sutra* say that those who expound it 'should not point out the faults of other persons or sutras' and they 'should not despise other teachers of the Dharma'? Haven't the gods abandoned you because you have not been following these instructions of the sutra?"

Nichiren smiled and responded, "I must cite the teachings of the Great Master Tiantai in the *Great Calming and Contemplation*. He said, 'There are two opposing ways of spreading Buddhism: *shakubuku*, the way of subduing what is evil, and *shōju*, the way of accepting what is good. When the 'Peaceful Practices' chapter of the *Lotus Sutra* says not to criticize others, that is the way of accepting, but when the *Nirvana Sutra* speaks of taking up arms and beheading those who are trying to destroy the Buddha Dharma, that is the way of subduing.' The Great Master Miaole said, 'Regardless of whether it is the past or the present, when the world is full of danger and the True Dharma is hidden, Buddhists should arm themselves, but if the world is at peace they should observe the precepts. Thus, the means of propagation should be chosen according to the condition of the time, it cannot be said to be one way or another.' Even my own disciples have doubts about my methods and say I am too harsh despite my repeated explanations. That is why I cite the teachings of the great masters Tiantai and Miaole to show that these are not simply my own ideas."

Shigetsura gave Nichiren a hard look. "It sounds as though this way of subduing is in fact a call to war against those who disagree with your interpretation of the *Lotus Sutra*. This would in turn be a call to war against the shogunate that supports the Pure Land and Zen Buddhists that you oppose. How can this be anything but treason?"

Nichiren shook his head. "The *Nirvana Sutra* is speaking of the king and his forces who are responsible for defending the true monks. The responsibility of the true disciple of the Buddha is to remonstrate with those who are slandering the Dharma. It is not a matter of starting an insurrection or oppressing others. In any case, even the *Nirvana Sutra* teaches that bodhisattvas should love all people as one would love one's only child. And though the 'Peaceful Practices' chapter emphasizes the gentle way, in the '*Dhāraṇīs*' chapter it says that 'anyone who troubles the expounder of the Dharma shall have his head split into seven pieces.' So both sutras teach both the way of accepting and encouraging the good in others and the way of subduing evil according to the situation."

Shigetsura said, "I see. So you are not advocating violence. You are appealing to the authorities to do something about this great evil that you fear is destroying the True Dharma. Still, I think you are quite presumptuous to assume that you alone are in the right and should be following the way of subduing evil."

Nichiren nodded. "These two ways of propagation, the way of accepting and the way of subduing, are incompatible, just like fire and water. The fire dislikes the water, and the water hates the fire. Those who prefer the way of acceptance tend to laugh at those who practice the way of subduing, and vice versa. However, when the land is full of evil and ignorant people who know nothing of Buddhism, that is when the way of acceptance should take precedence as taught in the 'Peaceful Practices' chapter, so that the little good and understanding that people do have may be encouraged. But when there are many cunning people who slander and misrepresent the True Dharma, then the way of subduing evil should take precedence, as when Never Despising Bodhisattva in the *Lotus Sutra* tells the other Buddhists of his time that he respects them for they shall become buddhas, even though they respond to this direct teaching of the True Dharma with disbelief and even attack him with sticks and rocks.

"It is the same as using cold water when it is hot or fire when it is cold. Because there are lands of evil people who do not know the Dharma at all as well as lands of slanderers who destroy the True Dharma by misrepresenting it in this Latter Age of Degeneration, there should be both the way of accepting and the way of subduing. Today, we have to discern whether Japan is a land of people who are simply evil and ignorant or a land of slanderers in order to decide which of these two ways should be used.

"The Great Master Zhang'an taught that whether we follow the way of accepting or the way of subduing must be decided according to the condition of the time. Great Master Tiantai said, 'It all depends on the time. Sometimes resort to the way of subduing, and other times use the way of accepting.' For instance, we cannot harvest rice by cultivating rice paddies and planting seeds at the end of autumn.

"Today, the false teachings of Pure Land and Zen have spread throughout Japan. The scholar-monks of the Tendai and Mantra schools fear the followers of these new movements and cater to their whims like a dog wagging its tail in front of its master or mice terrified by a cat. To gain the patronage of the rulers they have themselves begun teaching in a way that will lead to the destruction of Buddhism in this country. This is why I have taken up the way of subduing evil."

Shigetura persisted in his questioning, "But what good does it do to accuse the followers of Pure Land and Zen of slander, thereby making enemies of them? Why not just teach the merits of the *Lotus Sutra* without criticizing others?"

Nichiren responded, "I can only tell you what the *Nirvana Sutra* teaches. A true disciple of the Buddha must speak out against evil. Great Master Zhang'an explained, 'Those who destroy Buddhism are those within Buddhism who work against it. Those heartless people who keep friendly relations with evildoers by overlooking their offences are the enemies of the offenders. Those who are kind enough to try and correct them are the upholders of the True Dharma and true disciples of the Buddha. To prevent a friend from committing evil is a friendly act. Therefore, one who accuses transgressors of harming

Buddhism is the Buddha's disciple, and one who does not purge evildoers is an enemy of Buddhism.' Shouldn't we warn our parents if someone were trying to kill them? Shouldn't we prevent an evil drunken child from killing his parents? Shouldn't we prevent an evil man from setting a pagoda on fire? Should we leave our only child untreated when he is seriously sick? Those who do not reprimand the followers of Zen and Pure Land in Japan are no better than those who do nothing to prevent evil. They are what Great Master Zhang'an meant by 'heartless people.' I am like a compassionate parent for all the people of Japan, wherein everyone in the Tendai school has become their worst enemy because they fail to speak out. I am heeding the words of Great Master Zhang'an who said that an act of true friendship is to prevent another from doing evil."

Shigetsura nodded, though he did not seem entirely convinced. "I think I see what you mean. Well, I look forward to hearing what you and the other monks will have to say for yourselves at the debate."

In accordance with Homma Shigetsura's wishes, the grounds at Tsukahara filled up with *nembutsu* believers accompanied by young monks carrying the three Pure Land sutras, or copies of the *Great Calming and Contemplation*, or the three esoteric sutras, as well as other sutras and commentaries, hung around their necks or tucked under their arms. It seemed as though hundreds of monks and lay monks had come not only from Sado Island, but also from the nearby mainland provinces. It was doubtful that anything so exciting as a debate between an infamous exile and the local clergy over the true meaning of the Buddha's teachings had occurred on Sado Island or in any of the neighboring lands in many years.

The disposition of the mob did not seem at all promising. The *nembutsu* believers cursed and swore at the sight of Nichiren and his disciples. The monks of the Mantra school turned crimson with anger, and even the Tendai monks who came to defend the practice of the *nembutsu* or mantra teachings predicted their own victory before the debate had even started. The lay people who were present derided Nichiren loudly. "There's that infamous shave-pate! There's the enemy of Amitābha Buddha!" The jeers and shouting could be heard far beyond the field, if there was anyone who had not gone to see the debate in person there to hear them.

After waiting patiently for things to calm down to no avail, Nichiren called out to them, "You have all come here to take part in this debate. It is therefore useless for you to utter such abuse, is it not?" This was greeted with more heckling.

At that point, even Homma Shigetsura and his entourage were fed up with the mob. The deputy constable directed his retainers to evict those who would not keep quiet, which they did by seizing the most abusive, drunk, and disorderly ruffians by the neck and forcibly escorting them away from the site of the debate.

Finally the debate began. Sitting on the veranda of his small hut, Nichiren at first listened quietly to their attempts to explain the *nembutsu* practice advocated in the *Great Calming and Contemplation* of the Tiantai school, or the way it was understood and used in the Mantra school. Then he closely questioned them, silencing them in a few words. They were even more hopeless than the monks who practiced the Zen, Pure Land, Mantra, and Tendai teachings in Kamakura. Nichiren had looked forward to the debate, but now that it had begun he found it dull going over the same points he had repeated so many times over the years. Debating with them was like using a sharp sword to cut cucumbers. His opponents became for him like so many blades of grass bowing before the wind. Not only were these monks less knowledgeable about Buddhist doctrine than the monks of Kamakura, let alone Mt. Hiei, but they often made contradictory statements or confused commentaries with sutras and vice versa.

One monk asked, "Who are you, a latter student of Buddhism in Japan, to presume to contradict the Venerable Shandao, who was an incarnation of Amitābha Buddha? He taught that not even one out of 1,000 can attain buddhahood through the *Lotus Sutra* but ten out ten and 100 out of 100 can be reborn in the Pure Land of Utmost Bliss through the *nembutsu*."

Nichiren said, "In knowing the comparative merits of the sutras I am superior to the likes of Shandao because I follow the tradition of Great Master Tiantai who said, 'Adopt whatever agrees with the sutras, and do not believe in that which is not found in the sutras in word or meaning,' and the Great Master Dengyō who stated, 'Rely upon the words of the Buddha in the sutras, do not believe in what has been transmitted orally.'

"Also, you should know that, in his haste to reach the Pure Land, Shandao went insane and tried to commit suicide. He climbed a willow tree and hurled himself to the ground, but he did not die then. He suffered for two weeks in delirium and then died. Isn't his action the inspiration for seeking birth in the Pure Land by committing suicide? It seems that when one chants the *nembutsu* in earnest, one naturally feels the urge to commit suicide.

"Now the 18th of the 48 vows expounded in the *Sutra on the Buddha of Infinite Life*, that Shandao and Hōnen upheld, states that those who commit the five grave offences or slander the True Dharma are excluded from rebirth in the Pure Land. The *Lotus Sutra* teaches that those who slander the Dharma will fall into the Hell of Incessant Suffering. So if those who slander the Dharma are excluded from the Pure Land and will fall into the Hell of Incessant Suffering, then how could Shandao and Hōnen not have fallen into hell? And if they fell into hell, then there is no doubt that their disciples and followers will also fall into hell."

A monk of the Mantra school proclaimed, "Surely you know that the *Mahāvairocana Sutra* is superior to the *Lotus Sutra* because it teaches the practice of concentrating on a mandala to observe all phenomena and the practice of forming mudras while uttering mantras?"

Nichiren replied, "Don't you know that the *Lotus Sutra* says that it is the most excellent teaching of all the teachings expounded in the past, present, or future? If the esoteric sutras were taught before the *Lotus Sutra*, then at best they would be equal to the *Flower Garland Sutra*, but if taught after, then at best they would be equal to the *Nirvana Sutra*. Even if they were taught at the same time, the *Lotus Sutra* alone is the perfect teaching. In the esoteric sutras, the perfect teaching is mixed with expedient teachings. They cannot compete with the *Lotus Sutra*."

The Mantra monk rejoined, "Ah, but the esoteric sutras were taught by Mahāvairocana Buddha and not by Śākyamuni Buddha, who is merely a transient transformation-body that appeared only to accommodate ordinary deluded beings."

Nichiren replied, "Well then, tell me about Mahāvairocana Buddha. Who were his parents? Where was he born? Where did he die? No sutra mentions his parents, or where this buddha was born and died, or where he taught. Mahāvairocana Buddha is just a name without substance."

The Mantra monk asserted, "Mahāvairocana Buddha is the Dharma-body, the reality of all phenomena who has no birth or death. This is what makes him superior to Śākyamuni Buddha."

Nichiren said, "If you think it over, it is not only Mahāvairocana Buddha who is everlasting. All living beings, even insects such as a mole cricket, an ant, a mosquito, or a horsefly in their true nature have neither birth nor death. This idea that only Mahāvairocana

Buddha is eternal and all other beings are impermanent is the same idea embraced by non-Buddhists, isn't it?

The Mantra monk was not sure how to reply to that. This was getting too theoretical for him. He vaguely understood that the true nature of all beings was the buddha-nature, which was unborn and deathless, and possessed of the qualities of purity, bliss, eternity, and true selfhood. He was not about to back down, however. He said, "I do not understand how you can have any doubt of the superiority of the mantra teachings. Great Master Kōbō, the founder of the Mantra school, proved it in his lifetime. When he was about to return to Japan from China, he threw a three-pronged *vajra* towards Japan, praying that it would land where the teachings of the Buddha should be spread. It flew up in the sky and disappeared in the clouds. When Great Master Kōbō arrived at the foot of Mt. Kōya he found the *vajra* there. On another occasion, after returning to Japan, he demonstrated the ability to attain buddhahood in one's very body at the imperial court and transformed himself into Mahāvairocana Buddha. Such incidents displaying the virtue of Great Master Kōbō are too numerous to mention them all. These are just a few. How can anyone not believe in such a virtuous man? That is why I know he can be trusted when he taught that the *Mahāvairocana Sutra* and even the *Flower Garland Sutra* are both superior to the *Lotus Sutra*."

Nichiren replied, "Your question is reasonable. I, too, respect and believe in these stories of Great Master Kōbō. However, there are cases of people who worked wonders in ancient days but were unable to prove the validity of their teachings by virtue of these wonders. Of non-Buddhists in India, a hermit kept the Ganges River in his ears for twelve years; another swallowed up the ocean in a day; still another grasped the sun and moon with his hand, or transformed the Buddha's disciples into cows and sheep. They worked such wonders as these, which made them proud and conceited, piling up the seeds of delusion. So no matter how wonderful Great Master Kōbō was, no wise man should accept his declarations that the *Lotus Sutra* is useless compared to the *Mahāvairocana Sutra* and the *Flower Garland Sutra* or that Śākyamuni Buddha was not awakened compared to Mahāvairocana Buddha.

"Besides, these wonders that you mention are, in fact, too incredible to believe. If he changed into Mahāvairocana Buddha at the imperial court, then in what year and under what emperor's reign did it happen? Why was such an important incident not recorded in the official records? Furthermore, the *Nirvana Sutra* warns that even demons can appear as buddhas in order to destroy the True Dharma. The story about the *vajra* is especially doubtful. How do we know that someone had not been sent to bury it at Mt. Kōya beforehand? Great Master Kōbō could have done it himself. He often deceived people with such tricks. Therefore, we cannot accept such stories as proof that his teachings are in agreement with the intention of the Buddha.

"As for the assertion that the *Lotus Sutra* is inferior to the *Mahāvairocana* and the *Flower Garland* sutra, neither of those sutras teach the attainment of buddhahood by the followers of the two vehicles, or Śākyamuni Buddha's attainment of buddhahood in the remotest past, let alone the doctrine of the 3,000 realms in a single thought-moment. Chengguan, the fourth Chinese patriarch of the Flower Garland school, stole the doctrine of the 3,000 realms in a single thought-moment when he was interpreting the teaching in the *Flower Garland Sutra* that the mind is like a skillful painter. The founders of the Mantra school also stole the doctrine of the 3,000 realms in a single thought-moment when interpreting the *Mahāvairocana Sutra*'s teaching of the reality of mind. They then claimed that while the *Mahāvairocana Sutra* was equal in doctrine to the *Lotus Sutra* it was superior in practice because it taught the practice of mudras and mantras, but really they had already submitted to the doctrine of the Tiantai school, and this matter of mudras and mantras is trivial."

So it went. Unable to reply when their errors were pointed out or their appeals to authority were exposed, his opponents hurled abusive words, became dumb, or turned pale. Some regretted having chanted *nembutsu* once it had been so thoroughly refuted in favor of the *Lotus Sutra*. Others were so disillusioned that they threw off their *kesas* and cast away their *juzu*, swearing never to chant *nembutsu* again. Before long, most of those who had gathered at Tsukahara returned home. Homma Shigetsura and his family and retainers also prepared to leave.

As Shigetsura stood up from his seat, Nichiren called out to him from across the courtyard. "When are you planning to go to Kamakura?" he asked.

Shigetsura replied, "It may be in the seventh month, when my retainers will have finished working on their farms. Why do you ask?"

Nichiren said, "The real work of a warrior is nothing if not to serve his master with distinction at times of great need, so as to be rewarded with a fief. You say that you are busy working on your farm, but a battle is about to occur. Why do you not hurry to Kamakura to distinguish yourself in war and gain additional fiefs? You have been a brave and honored warrior in Sagami Province. It will be a shame for you, an honorable warrior, to keep yourself busy working on your farm and lose your chance of participating in an important battle."

Shigetsura's eyes widened in amazement. He turned and walked away without a word. Those monks and lay followers who had come to debate with Nichiren and were still in the courtyard overheard the exchange and were also taken aback. They looked to one another and murmured about the audacity of Nichiren to speak in such a way, but they also wondered if his prediction would come true.

276

Superior Practice Bodhisattva

When at last the debate was over, and the crowd had dispersed and gone back to their daily lives, there was a period of calm. During this time, Nichiren devoted himself to putting the finishing touches on *Open Your Eyes*. When he had finished, he sent Shijō Kingo's messenger on an errand to deliver it to his disciples and lay followers back in Kamakura. Some of the disciples who had joined him on Sado Island warned him that the new treatise was too strongly worded and might cause trouble, but Nichiren insisted on sending it.

On the 18th of the second month of the ninth year of the Bun'ei era (1272), a boat arrived bringing news that there had been fighting in Kyōto and Kamakura. The boatmen decribed the situation there as so chaotic that it was difficult to put into words, since they had never seen or heard anything like it in recent memory.

Homma Shigetsura arrived breathless at the Sammaidō. He pressed his palms together and said to Nichiren, "Save me with your mercy. I was doubtful of what you told me last month after the debate, but fighting has occurred in Kamakura just as you said. It hasn't even been 30 days! Hōjō Tokisuke, the shogunal deputy in Rokuhara in Kyōto, was discovered to have been plotting to take over the shogunate. He was the older half-brother of Tokimune and had long been jealous of his younger brother. His co-conspirators in Kamakura were found out and killed on the eleventh, and on the 15th Tokisuke was himself killed in the fighting in Kyōto. Now I am sure that Mongol forces will attack Japan as you foretold. Now I am sure that your statement that *nembutsu* devotees will fall into the Hell of Incessant Suffering is also true. I will never again chant the *nembutsu*."

Nichiren replied, "No matter what you swear, unless the regent, Hōjō Tokimune, accepts what I say, the people of Japan in general will not.

277

If people do not trust me, Japan is sure to be destroyed. Although I have little power, I am a messenger of Śākyamuni Buddha. Such deities as Amaterasu Ōmikami and Great Bodhisattva Hachiman are highly esteemed in Japan, but they are merely minor gods compared to Brahmā, Indra, the gods of the sun and moon, and the four heavenly kings. Nevertheless, it is said that murdering a person who serves such minor gods is seven and a half times as evil as killing an ordinary person. Taira no Kiyomori and the former Emperor Go-Toba ruined themselves by murdering those who served the gods. Compared to me, those who serve such deities are insignificant. As I am a messenger of Śākyamuni Buddha, even Amaterasu Ōmikami and Great Bodhisattva Hachiman should prostrate themselves, bowing their heads and pressing their palms together to show respect. Brahmā and Indra should attend the practitioner of the *Lotus Sutra* on both sides, and the sun and moon should light the way before and behind him.

"Even if the shogunate pays heed to me, should it do so improperly, the country will surely be ruined. How much worse it is that people have been turned against me and that I have twice been exiled! There is no doubt that this country will be ruined. As I have been praying for the postponement of national disaster and for the protection of the country, Japan has been at peace until today. However, when the law is violated, punishment cannot be avoided.

"If the shogunate refuses to accept my words one more time, the buddhas and gods in heaven will make the Great Mongol Empire send their forces to destroy Japan. This is nothing else but the very disaster invited by Hei no Saemon. Once the Mongols invade Japan, you, too, will not be safe on this island."

Shigetsura's eyes widened, his jaw worked itself up and down and his lips flapped uselessly, but nothing came out. Once more he bowed deeply, then took his leave without another word. That very night he took the fastest ships available and left Sado, rushing to Kamakura accompanied by his family and retainers.

Abruptly, Nichiren snapped back into the present time. Even now, as his life came to an end, he found himself reflecting on his reasons for daring to speak of himself as a practitioner of the *Lotus Sutra* and the messenger of the Buddha whom even the buddhas, bodhisattvas, and gods were obligated to watch over and protect. Was this merely presumption? He did not think so. Any doubts he may have had ended on Sado Island when he awakened to the truth about his life and the mission he had been given.

In *Open Your Eyes*, he had shown through the sutras and the fulfillment of their teachings in his own life that he was indeed the foremost practitioner of the *Lotus Sutra* who would be confronted by the three kinds of enemies. Who else but he had faced the hatred, jealousy, and disbelief that the Buddha predicted would be directed at the *Lotus Sutra* and those who upheld it? Who else but he had been abused, threatened with swords and sticks, and banished again and again? Who else but he had been struck with rocks and staves as had Never Despising Bodhisattva? Who else but he had tried to spread the *Lotus Sutra* throughout the land when Māra and his hosts had tried to take advantage of the degeneracy of the times by using their wiles to make people slander and neglect it?

Even before arriving on Sado Island, Nichiren had written to Toki Jōnin, his most loyal and insightful supporter, telling him that the story of Never Despising Bodhisattva was a past example of persecution at the hands of the three kinds of enemies. He had said that when future buddhas teach the *Lotus Sutra*, it would be himself, Nichiren, who would be seen as the Never Despising Bodhisattva of the previous age. In a later letter to his followers written during that exile, he stated that just as Never Despising Bodhisattva had approached all the Buddhists of his time with a 24 character greeting assuring them of their future attainment of buddhahood and thus of his profound respect, in the same way Nichiren was now spreading the five character title of the *Lotus Sutra* in the form of the *daimoku*. Although the 24 characters of Never Despising Bodhisattva and the five characters that he spread differed in wording, both were the same in meaning.

To Shijō Kingo he had written, "In 'The Teacher of the Dharma' chapter of the *Lotus Sutra* the Buddha said, 'Know that the good men or women who expound even a phrase of the *Sutra of the Lotus Flower of the Wonderful Dharma* to even one person in secret after my final nirvana are my messengers. They are dispatched by me. They do my work.' He who chants even one word or phrase of the *Lotus Sutra* or explains it for people is an envoy of Śākyamuni Buddha. Therefore, I am the person who has come to this country under the decree of Śākyamuni Buddha, though my social standing is humble. Accordingly, those who speak ill of me, even one word, will fall into the Hell of Incessant Suffering, while those who speak even a word or phrase for me will gain merit superior to that received by supporting numerous buddhas."

Nichiren realized that to say or write these things to others would make him sound self-conceited, but he also knew that aside from himself no one else had fulfilled the Buddha's predictions. He felt so overjoyed when he thought about how these sutra passages seemed to have been taught specifically for him that he could not help but praise himself in his talks and writings. But it was a joy for the sake of the *Lotus Sutra,* because if the events of his life had not borne out the teachings of the *Lotus Sutra*, then those teachings would be rendered false, since no one else had encountered such persecutions for its sake. His life was proof of the truth of the Buddha's predictions.

Reflecting on the past, it seemed that the only true practitioners of the *Lotus Sutra* had been Śākyamuni Buddha in India, Great Master Tiantai in China, and Great Master Dengyō in Japan. Even the Buddha had faced hardships, treachery, and abuse in order to teach the *Lotus Sutra*. The great masters Tiantai and Dengyō had also faced hostility from rival monks. Considering that for more than 20 years he had been exiled twice, first to Izu and now to Sado, wounded on the forehead in the ambush at Komatsubara, and was almost beheaded at Tatsunokuchi, all because he denounced the provisional teachings and upheld the *Lotus Sutra*, Nichiren dared to add himself to their company as the fourth of the four masters in three lands.

There was something deeper though. Who was it that was meant to be the foremost practitioner of the *Lotus Sutra* in the Latter Age of Degeneration? Who was it that Śākyamuni Buddha had entrusted to be his messenger? Who had been given a specific transmission of the Wonderful Dharma?

In the beginning of chapter 15, "The Appearance of Bodhisattvas from Underground," the Buddha had declined the offer of the bodhisattvas from the other worlds to uphold the *Lotus Sutra* in the Sahā world after the Buddha's final nirvana. Instead he called upon the billions of bodhisattvas who had been his original disciples from the remotest past who appeared suddenly from where they had been living in the empty space below the Sahā world. Four bodhisattvas named Superior Practice, Limitless Practice, Pure Practice, and Steadily Established Practice were their leaders. In chapter 21, "The Supernatural Powers of the Tathāgatas," the Eternal Śākyamuni Buddha specifically transmitted to Superior Practice Bodhisattva, and to all the other bodhisattvas who emerged from the earth, all his teachings, supernatural powers, secret lore, and profound achievements that were revealed and expounded explicitly in the *Lotus Sutra*. He charged Superior Practice Bodhisattva and the multitude of bodhisattvas who followed him with the five practices of keeping, reading, reciting, expounding, and copying the sutra.

For almost 20 years Nichiren had been teaching people to chant the *daimoku*. Since the previous year, starting the day before he had left Echi for Sado, he had also begun inscribing calligraphic mandalas that would depict what should be the true focus of devotion for Buddhists in the Latter Age of Degeneration. And yet, according to the Buddha's statements in the *Lotus Sutra*, except for bodhisattvas such as Superior Practice and the other high ranking leaders of the bodhisattvas who emerged from the earth, no one is allowed to appear in the Latter Age of Degeneration to spread the five characters *myō*, *hō*, *ren*, *ge*, and *kyō*, the true aspect of all phenomena. Furthermore, no one else can depict the proper focus of devotion for Buddhism in the Latter Age. This is because the *daimoku* and the focus of devotion are the quintessence of the actuality of the 3,000 realms in a single thought-moment doctrine expounded in the 'Life Span' chapter in the Original Gate of the *Lotus Sutra*, and it should only be spread by bodhisattva disciples of the Eternal Śākyamuni Buddha.

Here is what Nichiren had not dared to consider before the exile to Sado. And yet, it was inescapable. On Sado he had thought to himself, 'I must be the lone forerunner of the bodhisattvas that emerged from beneath the earth. I may even be one of them. I was not at the Ceremony in the Air when the Eternal Śākyamuni Buddha transmitted the Wonderful Dharma to Superior Practice Bodhisattva. And yet I have no doubt about its occurrence when I read the *Lotus Sutra*. Perhaps I had been there but cannot remember because I am still an ordinary deluded person. And yet, it is clear that in the present I am a practitioner of the *Lotus Sutra*. Because of that, it is certain that I will surely visit the place of practice of the Buddha in the future. Considering the past according to the present and future, I must have been at the Ceremony in the Air because the past, present, and future are not separate from one another. Therefore, I am not simply a Tendai monk who has received the teachings of the *Lotus Sutra* from the historical Śākyamuni Buddha down through the lineage of Great Master Tiantai and Great Master Dengyō. I must be Superior Practice Bodhisattva, a practitioner of the Original Gate of the *Lotus Sutra* and a messenger of the Eternal Śākyamuni Buddha who has been sent to the suffering people of the Latter Age of Degeneration!'

Contemplation of the Mind and the Focus of Devotion

Above the statue of Śākyamuni Buddha given to him at Izu, and just behind it, hung the calligraphic mandala that Nichiren had inscribed a couple of years before in the third month of the third year of the Kōan era (1280). He gazed at the mandala with a sense of anticipation; soon he would be seeing for himself the Ceremony in the Air of the *Lotus Sutra*, depicted in Chinese characters and Sanskrit *bīja* or "seed syllables." When, upon reaching the residence of Ikegami Munenaka, he had become too bedridden to travel, he requested that this mandala be enshrined at his bedside along with the statue of the Buddha. In the course of many years he had inscribed scores of similar mandalas for his disciples and followers to enshrine as the proper focus of devotion in their temples and practice halls, but only to those who had proven steadfast in their faith in the *Lotus Sutra*. Unlike statue arrangements or costly portraits, these mandalas were easy to roll up and hide away in times of persecution. Nichiren's thoughts drifted back to the time when he had finally revealed to his disciples and followers what the true focus of devotion should be, and had inscribed the mandala depicting the focus of devotion of the Original Gate of the *Lotus Sutra* for the first time in its most complete form.

After the Tsukahara debate and Nichiren's successful prediction of the insurrection in the second month of the ninth year of the Bun'ei era (1272), his reputation had increased. Many Tendai and even Mantra monks who lived in the area became his disciples. Many people stopped making offerings to practitioners of the *nembutsu* and upholders of the precepts and began to bring their offerings to the Sammaidō instead, in large numbers. The monks who practiced *nembutsu* and those who were followers of Ryōkan's precept revival sent angry reports back to Kamakura claiming that Nichiren must have known about the conspiracy because he had been in on it from the start, that he and his followers were burning statues of Amitābha

283

Buddha or throwing them into the rivers, and that he ranted at the gods and cursed the shogunate from the mountaintops day and night. Hōjō Nobutoki was so alarmed by these stories that on three occasions he sent private directives to his deputy, Homma Shigetsura, to expel from Sado or imprison those who were found to be supporting Nichiren. Homma Shigetsura had no choice but to comply. After the directive was given, the retainers of the local steward, with the help of several *nembutsu* practitioners, kept guard over the Sammaidō in order to prevent anyone from coming to see Nichiren. As a result, people were being imprisoned simply for passing in front of Nichiren's hut, or expelled from the island for giving offerings to him, or having their wives and children taken as hostages to ensure that they stayed away from Tsukahara.

Abutsu-bō, accompanied by his wife, dared to visit him at night, when it was less likely that they would be spotted by sentries. When he came he would bring chests filled with food and other supplies, which he carried on his back. The faithful couple slipped past the guards on several occasions, but their luck eventually ran out. They too were caught, fined, and banished from their home for a certain term. In spite of all that, they never wavered in their faith, and in the years ahead they continued to support Nichiren, visiting him as often as they were able. In the meantime, it seemed as though Nichiren and his disciples would starve to death, even as the cold receded and spring began to revive the land.

New orders came from Kamakura in the fourth month, just after the planting of the sprouted rice in the nursery beds at the end of spring. Nichiren and his disciples were transferred to the village of Ichinosawa in the Ishida District of Sado Island. The village heads treated the exile and his disciples harshly. This was not only because of the orders they were bound to follow but because they personally found those who condemned the practice of *nemubtsu* more hateful than if they had been enemies of their parents or sworn adversaries from a past life. The amount of food supplied by the headman of the village was meager. Nichiren and his disciples ended up with only three mouthfuls of rice each for their meals.

A farmer known as the Lay Monk Ichinosawa was given the odious duty of providing lodgings for the exiles. The lay monk was especially uneasy about this since he was a devout practitioner of *nembutsu*, but he was a kindly man and he was relived when his guests refrained from arguing with him about his Pure Land devotions. On the contrary, Nichiren and his disciples were unfailingly courteous and helpful. In time, the Lay Monk Ichinosawa and the rest of his household began to relax around their unwanted guests. Lay Monk Ichinosawa admitted to himself that he enjoyed hearing the sound of Nichiren and his disciples and followers chanting the *Lotus Sutra* and the *daimoku*. He did not even mind when other members of his family began to attend Nichiren's talks. Seeing that the exile and his disciples were not being given enough to eat, the lay monk began helping them in secret, distributing extra rations from among his own stores.

After one such donation, Nichiren said to Lay Monk Ichinosawa, "I will never forget your kindness. Your generosity has saved our lives. I could not be more grateful to you if you and your wife were my own parents."

The lay monk replied, "It is no trouble. I could not bear it if I were to allow the Buddha's disciples to starve in my own home. As you know, I am deeply concerned about the life to come. That is why I have practiced the *nembutsu* for many years now and have even taken the tonsure and become a lay monk. Some years ago I built that *nembutsu* practice hall over there and donated some of my farmland to the teachers of *nembutsu*. All of this merit I have dedicated to rebirth in the Pure Land of Utmost Bliss. Do you really think that it was all for nothing and that I will be unable to attain buddhahood?"

Nichiren sighed. The lay monk was a kind and pious man, but, truth be told, he had no deep understanding of Buddhism that Nichiren could see. He would have preferred to use gentle words and reassure him, but that would actually be the crueler act because it would leave him in the grip of the slanderous teachings that had caused him to turn away from the *Lotus Sutra*. In a soft, but firm tone, Nichiren replied, "For your own sake, I must speak the truth. Buddhahood is not attainable unless you actively put your faith in the *Lotus Sutra*. Even though you have built a *nembutsu* hall, Amitābha Buddha cannot save an enemy of the *Lotus Sutra*. In fact, by neglecting the *Lotus Sutra* you are going against Amitābha Buddha's 18th vow that excludes those who slander the True Dharma. You are, in fact, becoming an enemy of Amitābha Buddha by chanting the *nembutsu* rather than the *daimoku*."

The lay monk rubbed his chin. "Ah, well, I certainly have no intention of displeasing Amitābha Buddha. Perhaps I should read the *Lotus Sutra* one of these days. But if I become your follower I think the local steward would be very unhappy with me. I may or may not fall into hell in the next life, but he'll certainly make things hellish for me here and now if he finds out I've come over to your way."

Nichiren said, "You worry about the steward, but really all the people in Japan without exception are supposed to be the disciples and subjects of Śākyamuni Buddha. But those who single-mindedly pray to Amitābha Buddha are abandoning Śākyamuni Buddha. Those who cherish Amitābha Buddha, who is not the parent, teacher, or ruler of the people of this world, and conversely abandon Śākyamuni Buddha, who is the parent, teacher, and ruler of this world, are like unfilial children. They are as bad as a young couple who are so in love with each other that they forget about their parents, heating their own bedroom while their parents are out shivering in the cold, or indulging in a banquet while their parents starve. Isn't this a grave offense?"

"Hmm, yes, I see what you are saying. I will give it some thought. In the meantime, I hope that you are comfortable, for as far as I am concerned you are honored guests for as long as you are to stay here."

Despite his fears, the Lay Monk of Ichinosawa did not object when his grandmother took up faith in the *Lotus Sutra*. He also remained supportive, and relations between Nichiren and himself were always cordial. At one time he even lent money to a nun who had come to visit Nichiren from Kamakura and did not have enough funds to get back home. All he asked in return was that Nichiren have a copy of the *Lotus Sutra* inscribed for him so that he could read it for himself, a promise that Nichiren made good on a couple of years later by sending a copy to him in the care of his grandmother.

So it was that Nichiren was able to live more comfortably during the rest of his time on Sado. Back in Kamakura, Nichirō and other disciples were released from prison and, together with Nichiren's more influential lay supporters, they began to petition the shogunate for him to be pardoned. Nichiren did not approve. He wrote to Toki Jōnin telling him, "I believe it is the wish of the gods that I am not released yet, but probably ignorant people will not believe this. It is unfilial of my disciples to go around with anxious faces as though I were wishing to be released. I cannot help such disciples to fare better in the next life. All of you had better keep this in mind."

Once settled in at Ichinosawa, Nichiren began work on a new essay called *Kanjin Honzon-shō (Treatise on the Contemplation of the Mind and the Focus of Devotion)*. It was completed on the 25th day of the fourth month of the tenth year of the Bun'ei era (1273). He sent it the very next day to Toki Jōnin and the other leaders among his lay followers in Shimōsa Province.

In a cover letter to the treatise, Nichiren wrote to Toki Jōnin, "I have written a little on the doctrine of contemplating the mind. This is of utmost importance to me. You should keep this a secret unless you find someone with unshakeable faith in the *Lotus Sutra*, to whom you may show it. Concerning the ultimate teaching of the Buddha for those in the Latter Age, this writing contains many difficult questions with only short answers. Since this is a doctrine never heard of before, it may startle those who hear it. Should you decide to show it to others, you should not have several people read it together sitting side by side.

"In the more than 2,200 years after the final nirvana of Śākyamuni Buddha, nobody has ever explained the doctrine contained in this writing. Since we are now in the fifth 500-year period after the Buddha's final nirvana, the first 500-year period at the beginning of the Latter Age, when the True Dharma should be spread, I have expounded this in the face of public persecution.

"I pray that all my followers who read this writing may feel the joy of visiting, together with me, the Pure Land of Eagle Peak to look up at the faces of the Eternal Śākyamuni Buddha, Many Treasures Buddha, and the countless emanation buddhas of the ten directions."

Treatise on the Contemplation of the Mind and the Focus of Devotion was intended for his most trusted disciples and lay followers. It was intended as a response to those who felt that he had spoken far too often about the comparative superiority of the sutras and not said enough about the practice of calming and contemplation. He had spoken of such things before, but not in full, nor to all of his followers. In a letter written a few months before his exile, he had told a disciple studying on Mt. Hiei the following, "What we should chant all the time as the practice of the perfect teaching is Namu Myōhō Renge Kyō and what we should contemplate is the truth of the 3,000 realms in a single thought-moment. Lay followers of Japan today should just recite Namu Myōhō Renge Kyō. As the name has the virtue of invoking that to which it refers, when one chants Namu Myōhō Renge Kyō, one will not fail to receive all the merit of the *Lotus Sutra*." The new treatise was meant to further clarify the

288

connection between chanting *daimoku* and the contemplation of the 3,000 realms in a single thought-moment. More than that, it would declare what the true focus of devotion should be for such practice.

Nichiren began the treatise with a review of the doctrine of the 3,000 realms in a single thought-moment and its importance. These were things he had learned when had been a student on Mt. Hiei. He stated that the Tiantai teachings were difficult to understand and hard to believe because they not only claimed that all people could attain buddhahood and that Śākyamuni Buddha is actually the Eternal Buddha, but also claimed that, according to the doctrine regarding the contemplation of the 3,000 realms in a single thought-moment, even grasses, trees, and the land itself can manifest buddhahood because even the realm of the environment possesses the mental and physical aspects that are the ten suchnesses of causality and thereby can manifest all the ten realms, up to and including buddhahood. This was the reason why statues and portraits could be enshrined and worshipped as the various foci of devotion. "This is acceptable only through Tiantai doctrine. Unless grass and trees possess both the cause and effect of the buddha-realm in both physical and mental aspects, it does not make sense at all to worship statues and portraits."

Nichiren imagined the dialogue that followed from that. The inquirer would have asked him, "What is the meaning of contemplating the mind?"

Nichiren answered, "Contemplation of the mind means to observe all ten Dharma-realms, from the hells up to the pure lands of the buddhas, within our own minds. Now, just as we cannot see our own faces without a mirror, we cannot see the ten Dharma-reams within our minds without the clear mirrors of the *Lotus Sutra* and the *Great Calming and Contemplation*."

The inquirer was still not convinced. "I do not dare question the *Lotus Sutra* or the Tiantai teachings about the mutual possession of the ten realms, but it sounds like calling fire, 'water,' and black, 'white.' No matter how often we look at each other or gaze upon our reflections, we see only human beings. We do not see these other realms, so how can we believe this teaching that all ten Dharma-realms are within our minds?"

Nichiren responded, "When you look at others, you will notice that they are sometimes joyful, enraged, calm, greedy, ignorant, or overbearing to those weaker than themselves while ingratiating towards those who are stronger. These are the looks of the heavenly beings, hell-dwellers, human beings, hungry ghosts, beasts, and *asura* respectively. Thus we can see all six paths of samsara in people's faces, from the hells to the heavens. We cannot normally see the four realms of voice-hearers, private-buddhas, bodhisattvas, and buddhas, which are hidden. Nevertheless, we might be able to see them as well if we look carefully."

The inquirer still had doubts. "It is not entirely clear to me that all six paths exist within us human beings, but I am beginning to think they seem to as I listen to you. Nevertheless, I cannot see the four realms of the holy ones at all. Can you find them?"

Patiently, Nichiren said, "I shall try to explain as much as possible. We see impermanence everywhere before our very eyes. Therefore, we can understand the principle of impermanence by which the voice-hearers and private-buddhas try to attain awakening, so how can we say their realms are not included in ours? A man, no matter how cruel he may seem to be, loves his wife and children. This shows that even such a person has at least a portion of the bodhisattva realm. The realm that is hardest to see is that of the buddhas, but since we can see the other realms within us, the realm of buddhas must be as well. The reason why we, ordinary people, born in the Latter Age, can put faith in the *Lotus Sutra* is that the realm of buddhas is included in the realm of human beings."

A bit anxious, the inquirer continued to express his doubts, "The Buddha's teaching about the mutual possession of the ten realms may be clear, but it is difficult to believe that the realm of buddhas is contained within our vulgar minds. However, if we do not believe, there is no doubt that we will become *icchantika*. We beseech you, out of your great compassion, please help us to believe in it and save us from falling into the Hell of Incessant Suffering."

Nichiren gently chided the inquirer, "If you cannot believe even the words of the *Lotus Sutra*, then how can those who are ranked below the Buddha save you from non-belief? Nevertheless, I shall try because there were some who could not attain buddhahood under the guidance of the Buddha, but were awakened later under the guidance of the patriarchs like Ānanda.

"The mutual possession of the ten realms is as difficult to believe as it is to see fire in a rock and flowers in wood. However, it is not totally impossible because rocks spark when struck together and a tree blooms in spring. You have come to believe that each of the eight realms is contained in the realm of human beings so why can you not believe that the realm of buddhas is also contained within?

"Ancient Chinese rulers, sages such as Yao and Shun, treated all people equally with compassion, providing evidence that at least a portion of the realm of buddhahood is within the realm of humankind. Never Despising Bodhisattva pressed his palms together in respect and bowed to everyone he met because he saw buddhas in them. Born as a human being, Prince Siddhārtha became the Buddha. These examples should convince you to believe that the realm of buddhas exists in the realm of human beings."

At this point in the treatise, Nichiren warned the reader to keep what was to follow confidential and not reveal it to others.

In the imagined dialogue, the inquirer could still not believe that the Buddha was within the minds of all beings. "How could it be possible that the Buddha, as great as he is, resides in the minds of ordinary people like us? We also come across passages such as in Aśvaghoṣa's *Awakening of Faith in the Mahayana* that says, 'There is nothing but the virtue of purity in the buddha-nature.' So it would appear that when buddhahood is attained ordinary consciousness is eliminated. It would seem that the 3,000 realms in a single thought-moment and the mutual possession of the ten realms is just a biased view of Great Master Tiantai."

Nichiren responded, "The past sages and patriarchs such as Nāgārjuna and Vasubandhu were aware of this essential teaching of the *Lotus Sutra* but they did not reveal it because the time was not yet ripe. The other sutras besides the *Lotus Sutra* fail to teach the three causes of buddhahood inherent in all living beings: the buddha-nature, the wisdom to realize it, and the right actions to develop that wisdom. So how can those who follow those sutras know of the seed of buddhahood established on the basis of 3,000 realms in a single thought-moment? Without the seed of buddhahood, the attainment of buddhahood would only be a name without reality.

"The *Lotus Sutra* is equipped with the Buddha's practices at the causal stage and the merit he achieved as their effect. Therefore, Śākyamuni Buddha's attainment of buddhahood is altogether contained in the five characters of the title of the sutra: *myō, hō, ren, ge,* and *kyō.* Consequently, when we uphold these five characters, the merits that he accumulated before and after his attainment of buddhahood are naturally transferred to us. In the second chapter of the *Lotus Sutra* the Buddha said, 'I once vowed that I would cause all living beings to become exactly as I am. That old vow of mine has now been fulfilled. I lead all living beings into the way to buddhahood.' Does this not mean that Śākyamuni Buddha, who has attained perfect and complete awakening, is our flesh and blood, and all the merits he has accumulated before and after attaining buddhahood are our bones? Śākyamuni Buddha, Many Treasures Buddha, and the emanation buddhas of the ten directions are in our minds, and we, upholders of the *Lotus Sutra*, will follow in their footsteps and inherit all the merits of those buddhas. Śākyamuni Buddha who is within our minds is an ancient buddha without beginning, who manifests himself in the three bodies, and attained buddhahood in the remote past of 500 million dust-particle *kalpa*s ago.

"During the time of his teaching the Dharma, the Buddha revealed many provisional and impermanent pure lands presided over by buddhas who are actually his transformations. Therefore, if Śākyamuni Buddha were to enter final nirvana, then all of these buddhas would also vanish and their lands would disappear. Now, however, when the Eternal Buddha was revealed in the Original Gate of the *Lotus Sutra*, this Sahā world became the Eternal Pure Land, indestructible even by the three calamities of fires, floods, and hurricanes, which are said to destroy the world at the *kalpa*'s end. It transcends the four periods of cosmic change: the *kalpa*s of formation, continuance, dissolution, and reduction to nothingness. Śākyamuni Buddha, the lord and teacher of this pure land, has never entered final nirvana in the past, nor will he be born in the future. All those who receive his guidance are one with this Eternal Buddha. It is because each of our minds is equipped with the 3,000 realms in a single thought-moment, including the three categories of the five aggregates, living beings, and the environment.

"The heart of the Original Gate of the *Lotus Sutra*, Namu Myōhō Renge Kyō, was not transmitted even to the most trusted disciples such as Mañjuśrī Bodhisattva or Medicine King Bodhisattva, and certainly not to lower ranking bodhisattvas. Instead the Buddha summoned forth numerous bodhisattvas from underground, for whom he expounded it during the teaching of the eight chapters, beginning with the 15th and ending with the 22nd, and entrusted them with the task of spreading it in the Latter Age of Degeneration.

"The focus of devotion of this transmission of Namu Myōhō Renge Kyō from the Eternal Buddha to his original disciples is this: Suspended in the sky above the Eternal Śākyamuni Buddha's Sahā world is a stūpa of treasures, in which Śākyamuni Buddha and Many Treasures Buddha sit to the right and left of Myōhō Renge Kyō. The four bodhisattvas such as Superior Practice, who represent the original disciples of the Eternal Buddha called out from underground, wait upon them. Four more bodhisattvas, including Mañjuśrī and Maitreya, take the lower seats as followers. Other bodhisattvas, great and minor, who had been taught by the Buddha in the Trace Gate or who came from other lands, resemble numerous commoners sitting on the ground and looking up at the court nobles. Also lined up on the ground are the emanation buddhas who gathered together from the ten directions to praise the Buddha's teaching and who represent provisional buddhas and their respective lands.

"The focus of devotion such as this was not revealed anywhere else by Śākyamuni Buddha during the more than 50 years that he taught. Though he spent eight years teaching the *Lotus Sutra*, this scene was limited to when he taught in the sky above Eagle Peak as recounted in the eight chapters. During the more than two millennia of the Ages of the True Dharma and Semblance of the Dharma, statues and portraits were made of Śākyamuni Buddha as he taught the Hinayana or provisional Mahayana sutras, but statues and portraits of the Eternal Śākyamuni Buddha of the 'The Duration of the Life of the Tathāgata' chapter of the *Lotus Sutra* were never made. Now in the beginning of the Latter Age of Degeneration, is it not time that such statues and portraits were made for the first time?"

In the remainder of the treatise, Nichiren explained what the Buddha intended for the people of the Latter Age. He began by showing that the Buddha's teaching as a whole can be divided into a prologue, main discourse, and epilogue, wherein all the sutras preceding the *Lotus Sutra* are just a prologue, the threefold *Lotus Sutra* is the main discourse, and the *Nirvana Sutra* is the epilogue. The threefold *Lotus Sutra* itself can be divided into a prologue, main discourse, and epilogue, with everything from the second chapter of the *Lotus Sutra* up to and including the 19-line verse in chapter 17 comprising the main discourse. The Trace Gate and the Original Gate can also be divided into three parts each, with the main discourse of the former being chapters two through nine, and the main discourse of the latter being the one chapter and two halves, consisting of the latter half of chapter 15, all of chapter 16, and the first half of chapter 17. Finally, all the Buddha's teachings can be seen as a prologue to the great Dharma of the five characters of *myō*, *hō*, *ren*, *ge*, and *kyō*, hidden in the depths of the 16th chapter. Nichiren asserted, "The teaching of the Original Gate during the lifetime of Śākyamuni Buddha and that which should be spread during the beginning of the Latter Age are both absolutely perfect. However, the former is for the harvest of buddhahood, whereas the latter is for sowing the seed of buddhahood. While the former is crystallized in the 16th chapter, with half a chapter each preceding and following it, the latter is solely embodied in the five characters of *myō*, *hō*, *ren*, *ge*, and *kyō*, the title of the *Lotus Sutra*."

Nichiren insisted that it was time for the bodhisattvas who emerged from the earth and their four leaders to appear in order to spread the *daimoku*, the seed of buddhahood and the actualization of the 3,000 realms in a single thought-moment, the mutual possession of the ten realms wherein the Eternal Śākyamuni Buddha always and forever embraces all beings and all beings contain within themselves the realm of the Buddha. Nichiren further stated that the recent earthquakes and comets and other disturbances could not be anything other than omens of the appearance of these bodhisattvas.

He ended the treatise with the following words, "When the sky is clear, the land is illuminated, so those who know the *Lotus Sutra* can see the reasons for the occurrences in the world. For those who are incapable of understanding the truth of the 3,000 realms in a single thought-moment, Śākyamuni Buddha, out of great compassion, wraps this jewel with the five characters of *myō*, *hō*, *ren*, *ge*, and *kyō* and hangs it around the necks of the ignorant in the Latter age of Degeneration. The four great bodhisattvas will protect such people just as the sage rulers of ancient China were protected by their loyal subjects."

On Sado there lived a Tendai monk named Sairen-bō. He had also been exiled to the island some time before Nichiren had arrived. He had been very impressed by Nichiren after hearing him successfully debate the other monks at Tsukahara. From that time on he visited Nichiren when he could and the two of them held long discussions about the teaching and practice of the *Lotus Sutra* and Tiantai doctrines. When they could not see each other face to face, they would correspond by letters. One day, not long after writing *Treatise on the Contemplation of the Mind and the Focus of Devotion*, Nichiren wrote to Sairen-bō, "Whatever happens to you, have a firm faith and maintain yourself as a practitioner of the *Lotus Sutra* and join the ranks of my followers. As long as you are in accord with me, you will be one of the bodhisattvas who emerged from the earth. And if you are determined to be a bodhisattva of the earth, there is no doubt that you have been a disciple of the Eternal Śākyamuni Buddha since the remotest past. In 'The Appearance of the Bodhisattvas from Underground' chapter, the Buddha states, 'I have been teaching them since the remotest past.' Among those who spread the five characters of *myō*, *hō*, *ren*, *ge*, and *kyō* in the Latter Age of Degeneration, there should be no distinction between men and women, for it would be difficult to chant the *daimoku* unless they were all bodhisattvas of the earth.

"At first only I started chanting the *daimoku*, Namu Myōhō Renge Kyō, but then two, three, then 100 people, gradually began chanting it. This will continue in the future. Isn't this what emerging from the earth means? When an innumerable number of people emerge from the earth and this Wonderful Dharma spreads extensively, there will be no mistake, just as one who aims an arrow at the earth never misses, Japan will be filled with people chanting Namu Myōhō Renge Kyō. You should therefore establish your reputation as a practitioner of the *Lotus Sutra*, and devote your life to it.

"Tears roll down when I think of the great hardship that I have to endure today, but I cannot stop the tears of joy when I think of attaining buddhahood in the future. Birds and insects cry without shedding tears. Nichiren does not cry but tears keep falling. These tears are shed not for worldly matters. They are solely for the sake of the *Lotus Sutra*. Therefore, they could be said to be tears of nectar.

"Have faith in the most honored focus of devotion, the most venerable one in the entire world. Earnestly endeavor to strengthen your faith, so that you may be blessed with the protective powers of Śākyamuni Buddha, Many Treasure Buddha, and the emanation buddhas of the ten directions. Strive to carry out the two ways of practice and study. Without practice and study, Buddhism will cease to exist. Endeavor yourself and cause others to cultivate these two ways of practice and study, which stem from faith. If possible, please spread even a word or phrase of the sutra to others."

Nichiren still expected that any day a messenger might arrive with new orders for his execution. At the same time, he felt hopeful that eventually slander of the Dharma would be defeated and all would be converted to faith in the *Lotus Sutra*. He wrote to his disciples and lay followers, "When all the people under the heavens and various schools of Buddhism are all converted to the one true vehicle, and when only the *Lotus Sutra* flourishes and all the people recite Namu Myōhō Renge Kyō in unison, the howling wind will not blow on the branches, falling rain will not erode the soil, and the world will become as good as during the reigns of the sage emperors in China's golden age. You will see that such times will come when calamities will cease to exist, people will live long, and both people and the phenomena of life will neither age nor die. There should be no doubt about the *Lotus Sutra*'s promise of tranquility in this life."

On the eighth day of the seventh month of that year he inscribed the great mandala just as he had described it in the *Treatise on the Contemplation of the Mind and the Focus of Devotion*. He used a piece of silk two and a half feet wide by five and a half feet long. Using a wide brush he painted the seven large characters for Namu Myōhō Renge Kyō down the center to represent the stūpa of treasures. Immediately flanking the *daimoku* he wrote the names of Śākyamuni Buddha, Many Treasures Buddha, and the four leaders of the bodhisattvas who emerged from the earth: Superior Practice, Limitless Practice, Pure Practice, and Steadily Established Practice. At the four corners of the mandala he inscribed the names of the four heavenly kings who guard the cardinal directions. On either side of the mandala he inscribed the *bīja* of the two kings of esoteric knowledge, Fudō Myō-ō and Aizen Myō-ō. They were not in the *Lotus Sutra*, but Nichiren had received visions of them in the first month of the sixth year of the Kenchō era (1254) when he was still living at Seichōji and he felt assured that they were guardians of the *Lotus Sutra* and its practitioners. Though more exalted, they were in a way like the two fierce kings that flank the gates of the temples. Beneath the two buddhas and the four bodhisattvas he wrote in the names of the bodhisattvas Mañjuśrī, Universal Sage, Medicine King, and Maitreya. On either side of the bodhisattvas were the voice-hearers Śāriputra and Mahākāśyapa. Flanking them, he wrote in the names of Brahmā, Māra, Indra, and the gods of the sun, moon, and stars. Below the gods of the realms of desire and form could be found the ideal human ruler known as a wheel turning king, a king of the *asuras*, a dragon king, the Mother-of-Devils and her ten daughters, King Ajātaśatru, and even Devadatta. Below them were the gods of Japan, Amaterasu Ōmikami and the Great Bodhisattva Hachiman, and also the past teachers of the *Lotus Sutra*: the patriarch Nāgārjuna, and the great masters Tiantai, Miaole, and Dengyō. Nichiren inscribed his own name at the very bottom, below the seven characters of the *daimoku*. With such a mandala one could see and consider the ten Dharma-realms mutually embracing and embraced. Chanting before it, the practitioner could enter into the true Pure Land of Eagle Peak and meet the Eternal Śākyamuni Buddha, the true focus of devotion, the Buddha who always and everywhere transmits the Wonderful Dharma to all beings who receive it with faith and joy and thereby realize that the purity, bliss, eternity, and authenticity of buddhahood is within. At the bottom right of the mandala was written, "This great mandala was revealed for the first time in the world of Jambudvīpa 2,220 odd years after the final nirvana of the Buddha."

The Final Admonition

From his sickbed Nichiren could no longer see the sky, only the rafters overhead, but he recalled a white-headed bird that had once flown across the sky when he had still been on Sado Island. After seeing this bird, he had thought of an old Chinese story in which the King of Qin took Prince Dan of Yan hostage, and facetiously told the prince that if a bird with a white head should appear and a horn should grow on a horse, he would pardon the prince. The prince prayed for his release so earnestly that finally such a bird and such a horse appeared. He also recalled the poem, "A mountain crow's head/ has turned white./ The time has come/ for me to return home." He wondered if the time was near when he too could return home. Soon after, a letter of pardon was issued on the 14th day of the second month in the eleventh year of the Bun'ei era (1274). It arrived on Sado on the eighth day of the third month, and Nichiren and his disciples left Sado on the 13th day.

The trip home was not without hazard. A gale blew his ship off course as they departed from Sado. Despite this, they still arrived on the main island in two days, though at a different port than had been planned. An angry mob had gathered in front of the Zenkōji, a Tendai temple given over to Pure Land teachings, in Shinano Province along the route back to Kamakura, composed of *nembutsu* devotees, upholders of the precepts, and mantra practitioners who were incensed that Nichiren had been allowed to leave Sado alive. In order to avert a riot, Nichiren and his disciples were supplied an armed escort by the governor's office in Echigo Province. They arrived safely in Kamakura on the 26th day of the third month after a twelve-day trip.

On the eighth of the fourth month, Nichiren was summoned to meet once more with Hei no Saemon at the office of the Board of

Retainers. Unlike the previous meeting three years before, the deputy chief was gracious and courteous.

After the preliminaries, Nichiren declared to Hei no Saemon, "I am, of course, grateful to have been pardoned, but it was unreasonable to have been banished in the first place without a proper trial or a chance to debate with those who are slandering the True Dharma. Because the *Treatise on Spreading Peace Throughout the Country by Establishing the True Dharma* has been ignored, Japan will be destroyed by a foreign country."

Hei no Saemon glanced at the others present, who consisted of high-ranking samurai and samurai who had taken the tonsure to become lay monks. They looked back at him and frowned but said nothing. It seemed that on this occasion they were more willing to give Nichiren at least a polite hearing.

Hei no Saemon said, "We cannot have you riling up the people at this time or speaking ill of others. You know very well that the things you have said are violations of the Jōei Code prohibiting slander or provocation. This is a time when all monks, such as yourself, should lay aside your disagreements and pray together for the protection of Japan from the Mongol threat."

Nichiren replied, "Since I was born in the land under the Hōjō's control, my body must follow your orders. However, I cannot obey you in my heart. There is no doubt that Pure Land practice leads to the Hell of Incessant Suffering and Zen is the work of a heavenly devil. The mantra rites and teachings, especially, are the cause of calamities in Japan. Therefore, you should not entrust the disciples of the mantra teachings to perform prayers for the expulsion of the Mongols. If they are entrusted with this great task, they will only hasten the destruction of Japan."

301

One of the counselors asked, "You are very impertinent. However, we invited you here for your honest opinion, since you seem to have some understanding of the omens and portents that have appeared in recent times. Still, I am surprised to hear that you think it is the mantra teachings that are the cause of calamities. It was my understanding that it was the Pure Land teachings of Hōnen, the Zen teachings of Dainichi Nōnin, and also Ryōkan's teachings that you claimed were the sources of slander. But now you say it is the mantra teachings as well?"

Nichiren replied, "Generally speaking, everyone thinks that I am intent on slandering the Pure Land, Zen, and Precept monks, but these three teachings are not worth mentioning. The main problem is the mantra teachings, a false Dharma that is blighting our beautiful country of Japan. The esoteric teachings established by the great masters Kōbō of the Mantra school and Jikaku of the Tendai school are teachings whose curse is about to destroy Japan. Even if this country has the strength to endure the ravages of war for two or three years, it will be destroyed in a year or only half a year if the monks of the mantra teachings perform their esoteric rites."

One of the lay monks present asked, "Why do you say the mantra teachings ruin the country?"

Nichiren answered, "Although I have previously criticized the Zen, Pure Land, and Precept teachings, it is primarily the mantra teachings and practices that have been so devastating to Japan and China. The three disseminators of the mantra teachings in China, Śubhākarasiṃha, Vajrabodhi, and Amoghavajra, the founder of the Mantra school here in Japan, Great Master Kōbō, and the third and fifth abbots of Enyrakuji on Mt. Hiei, Jikaku and Chishō, all misinterpreted the comparative superiority of the three esoteric sutras and the *Lotus Sutra*, subordinating the latter to the former. You may recall that Emperor Xuanzong of the Tang dynasty lost power because he put his faith in the mantra teachings. Likewise, the country of

Japan is slowly weakening. Great Bodhisattva Hachiman's vow to protect 100 generations of emperors has therefore been abrogated."

Impatiently, Hei no Saemon asked, "All that may be. That is something for you monks to debate among yourselves. What I want to know is this: when, in your opinion, will the Mongols attack Japan?"

Nichiren sternly replied, "A definite date is not indicated in the sutras, but when we consider the mood of heaven, it is glaring in anger particularly at this country. The Mongol attack is certain to come within this year. If they attack us, no one will be able to stand up to them. This will be a heavenly punishment for not listening to me, Nichiren; and it will be impossible to drive them out. Never ask the monks to perform the mantra rites for national protection. If you do, the downfall of Japan will only be hastened."

Hei no Saemon asked, "And what you do your propose we do instead?"

Nichiren responded, "I have already presented my proposal on this matter to you, but you have not heeded it. It is already too late. Just as a man who tries to cure an illness without first knowing its cause will only make it worse, so too if the disciples of the mantra teachings perform esoteric rites to expel the Mongol forces, Japan, on the contrary, will be defeated. You should not have mantra practitioners nor any monks from other schools say prayers for victory. Though you cannot tell right from wrong in Buddhism for yourselves, you still do not take my advice. I do not understand why you do not accept what I propose.

"I am going to tell you one fact, which you can think about later. The Retired Emperor Go-Toba was a Son of Heaven while Lord Hōjō Yoshitoki, who revolted against him, was a subject. Does Amaterasu Ōmikami permit children to treat their parents as enemies? Does

303

Great Bodhisattva Hachiman allow a subject to fight against his lord? It was Hōjō Yoshitoki who should have been punished, but in fact it was the retired emperor who was defeated. What was the reason for this? It was indeed unusual. It was due to the fact that Retired Emperor Go-Toba and his supporters put their faith in the misleading teachings of the great masters Kōbō, Jikaku, and Chishō and had monks of Mt. Hiei, Tōji, and Onjōji perform esoteric rites for the defeat of the Hōjō in Kamakura. As it is taught in the 25th chapter, 'The Universal Gate of World Voice Perceiver Bodhisattva' of the *Lotus Sutra*, the curses recoiled upon their originators. The retired emperor and his supporters who started the curse received what they intended for others and they were defeated. In contrast, the warriors who did not know the esoteric rites did not perform any mantra prayers and won the war as a result. It will be the same this time. If mantra rites are performed to defeat the Mongol forces, Japan will surely be destroyed. I am sure, if you, Hei no Saemon, order monks to perform the mantra rites to defeat the Mongol armies, you yourself will surely encounter serious troubles. Do not say then that Nichiren did not warn you."

With that, the interview was brought to an end and Nichiren was dismissed. Though they maintained their polite demeanor, Hei no Saemon and the Board of Retainers were inwardly furious that Nichiren had told them to their faces that he would not obey them, "in his heart," that he had now begun to attack the mantra teachings and practices of the established Mantra and Tendai schools, and worst of all that he had stated that Hōjō Yoshitoki should have been defeated by the Retired Emperor Go-Toba.

Nichiren returned to his hermitage and related what had been said to his disciples and lay followers. Someone asked him how he could predict such things. He responded, "Although I am unworthy, I am a practitioner of the *Lotus Sutra*. When the people of Japan all slight me, then the earthly gods, who pledged to protect the practitioner at the assembly of the *Lotus Sutra*, tremble with rage and the heavenly gods shine a light that threatens this country. No matter how many times they admonish this country, their admonition is not heeded at all. Therefore, in the end, the gods of heaven and earth enter the people, causing civil war and foreign invasion."

It was evident that Nichiren's third admonition to the shogunate had gone unheeded. Once more, there was drought. This time the shogunate ordered the monk Kaga-hōin of the Amitābha Hall to perform a prayer service to bring rain, to begin just two days after Nichiren had spoken to Hei no Saemon. Kaga-hōin was considered the wisest of all monks in the Tōji, the head temple of the Mantra school in Kyōto. He had taught such abbots as Prince Dōjō of Ninnaji, completely mastered the mantra teachings of both the Mantra and Tendai schools, and was also well versed in the Tendai and the Flower Garland teachings. The day after the prayers began it rained quietly all through the day and night. The regent, Hōjō Tokimune, was delighted and Kaga-hōin was well rewarded for his efforts.

Upon hearing this news, the people of Kamakura all clapped their hands, pursed their lips to laugh at and speak ill of Nichiren, saying, "Nichiren proclaimed his evil doctrine and was about to be beheaded, but luckily for him he was pardoned. He should have kept quiet and behaved properly. Instead, he abused not only the *nembutsu* and Zen teachings but also the esoteric mantra teachings. Now we have evidence of the power of mantra."

Among Nichiren's own disciples, there were some who expressed disappointment and lamented that Nichiren's means of propagation were too aggressive. But Nichiren said to them, "Wait for a while. If the evil teachings of Great Master Kōbō were true and the mantra practices could protect the country, Retired Emperor Go-Toba should have won the war and Prince Dōjō of Ninnaji's beloved attendant, Seitaka, would not have been beheaded.

"It was Great Master Kōbō who wrote in his *Treatise on the Ten Stages of Mind* that the *Lotus Sutra* was inferior to the *Flower Garland Sutra*. He also wrote in his *Jewel Key to the Store of Mysteries* that Śākyamuni Buddha who preached the 16th chapter of the *Lotus Sutra*, 'Duration of the Life of the Tathāgata,' was an unawakened man. Great Master Kōbō, furthermore, wrote in his *Comparison of Exoteric and Esoteric Buddhism* that Great Master Tiantai was a thief, accusing him of having stolen the doctrine of the 3,000 realms in a single thought-moment from the Mantra school. The Mantra school monk Kakuban's *Liturgy for the Ceremony Dedicated to the Buddha's Relics* says that Śākyamuni Buddha who taught the *Lotus Sutra* was not even worthy enough to be a sandal holder for the masters of the mantra teachings. If Kaga-hōin of the Amitābha Hall, a disciple of those monks who made such mistaken statements, is able to defeat Nichiren, a practitioner of the *Lotus Sutra*, the dragon king who causes rainfalls will have become an enemy of the *Lotus Sutra* and will be punished by Brahmā, Indra, and the four heavenly kings. There must have been a reason for a rainfall at this time."

Some of Nichiren's own disciples, however, laughed and said, "What sort of reason could it be? We want to know about it."

Nichiren told them, "It is recorded that the monks who introduced the mantra teachings in China, Śubhākarasiṃha and Amoghavajra, were able to cause a rainfall by their prayers, but soon it was accompanied by strong winds. When Kōbō in Japan prayed for rain, it began raining in 21 days. But we cannot say for sure that his prayer brought the rain, because rain almost always falls within 21 days. Even if it rains in 21 days, there is nothing unusual about it at all. Great Master Tiantai and the monk Senkan of the Konryūji in Settsu Province succeeded in rain making by performing a single prayer service, so they deserve to be admired. There is surely some other meaning behind the rain of Kaga-hōin of the Amitābha Hall other than the power of the mantra rites."

Before Nichiren had even finished speaking, the wind began to blow. It gained in force until finally it began to tear the tiles and thatch off the roofs of houses. Branches were ripped from the trees. Up in the sky, luminous and gigantic, some unknown object flew through the air; while on the ground, ridges and beams were scattered. Over the course of the hurricane many people lost their lives, and even horses and cows were found dead afterwards. It was quite unusual that such a storm had occurred in the fourth month of the year, early in summer, instead of in autumn, when storms typically occurred. Moreover, it seemed to have struck only in the eight provinces of the Kantō District, and to have primarily hit the shogunal palaces along Young Prince Avenue, and the temples Kenchōji and Gokurakuji. No one thought it was an ordinary storm. The people of Kamakura, who had been so pleased just the day before, murmured that the prayers of Kaga-hōin had been the cause. Those who had ridiculed Nichiren were dumbfounded at the turn of events. His disciples were astonished.

Just a month later, Nichiren had his disciples pack up their few belongings. He had presented his case for the final time, and saw no reason to remain in Kamakura. He led the group out of the city on the twelfth of the fifth month, taking the Eastern Sea Road. He had no particular destination in mind.

When asked for his reason for leaving, he said, "It was my thought that in order to repay the debts I owe to my country I should remonstrate with its rulers three times, and if they would still not heed my advice, I would seclude myself in a mountain forest. There's a saying among the sages of China that it's best to retire if one's remonstrations with the ruler is rejected three times. Besides, if the rulers will not listen to me, what is the use of preaching to the people, who do not have the power to govern? It does not seem likely that this country will be saved or that the people will be helped to attain buddhahood."

The Hermitage at Mt. Minobu

As he neared the point of death, there was one thing that Nichiren regretted. He had never been able to return to Kominato and chant the *Lotus Sutra* at his parents' graves. When he left Kamakura for the last time, more than eight years ago, he had headed west rather than east. Nikkō, then in his late twenties, had asked his master why he did not visit his home village or Seichōji.

Nichiren had sighed wistfully before replying, "It is said by both Confucian and Buddhist sages that one should return home in glory. It would be unfilial of me to return home without successfully remonstrating with the government. However, I never imagined it possible to leave Sado alive, so it is still my hope that someday the government might heed my warnings. I will visit my parents' grave then, but not under the present circumstances. Even so, I miss my home and long to return. Whenever winds and clouds come from the east, I feel I must go outside just to feel the wind and see the clouds that have passed over Kominato."

Nikkō responded, "I hope that the day comes when you will be heeded and can return to your parents' graves to report to them your success. In the meantime, perhaps we should go visit Lord Sanenaga. He has long wanted you to come visit him at Mt. Minobu."

Hakii Sanenaga was the steward of the Hakii district in Kai Province. Nikkō had convinced him to follow Nichiren's teachings, back in the sixth year of the Bun'ei era (1269) and he had been a faithful and steadfast supporter.

Nichiren considered this proposition, and, having done so, he nodded in agreement.

308

Because of the drought, more crops had failed and famine had spread across the land once again. Bandits roamed the fields and mountains, and the post-stations had little food. It was difficult to buy even a cup of rice. It seemed that everyone would die of hunger. Nichiren and his band of disciples crossed one mountain pass after another, trudged through deep valleys, and forded rivers. They became delirious and their legs trembled from hunger and fatigue. They finally arrived at Hakii to the warm welcome of Lord Sanenaga on the 17th of the fifth month in the eleventh year of the Bun'ei era (1274).

After arriving, Nichiren wrote a letter to Toki Jōnin saying, "I have not yet decided whether or not to live in Minobu, but the atmosphere of the mountain is on the whole comforting to me, so I intend to stay here for a while. However, I am the one who in the end will be alone and wander around Japan. If I should settle somewhere, I would like to see you again."

By the following month, the small band had left the village of Hakii to follow a thickly overgrown trail, little more than a deer track, northwest into the deep boulder-strewn western valley of Minobu where Lord Hakii had donated land to them where they could build a hermitage. From there, they could see the snow capped Mt. Shichimen rising to the west. In the east one could watch the rising sun as it came slowly up behind the peak of Mt. Tenshi. Mt. Minobu towered over them to the north, and to the travelers' southward side, Mt. Takatori soared. Surrounded by the four mountains, they felt as if they were standing at the bottom of a giant basket, made of rock and earth and snow, its walls so high that they wondered how birds could even fly over them. To the east of Mt. Minobu, the river Fuji raced, and at times raged, along its southerly course. Over the course of time, countless vessels that had attempted to cross it had been reduced to ruins, broken on the rocks that closeted the rapids like folding screens. Though remote, it was not a quiet place. The howling of wolves echoed through the mountains and the cries of monkeys reverberated in the valley. They often heard the dolorous mating call of stags, and the constant shrill of the cicadas soon grew irritating.

By the 17th of the sixth month, a makeshift hermitage, six yards square, had been constructed in an open space at the base of Mt. Minobu. It consisted merely of twelve pillars, a thatched roof, mud walls, and tree bark for a carpet. The end result seemed as shabby as fallen leaves spread at the base of a tree. Still, once it was built, Nichiren found that he had no inclination to leave.

"So, you do like it here?" Lord Sanenaga asked Nichiren several weeks after the work on the hermitage was completed.

Nichiren nodded, "I do. Here I can devote my life to the practice of the *Lotus Sutra*. In my eyes, this place looks like Eagle Peak in India or Mt. Tiantai in China. Though I am neither Śākyamuni Buddha nor Great Master Tiantai, I respectfully recite the *Lotus Sutra* here day and night and expound the *Great Calming and Contemplation* morning and evening. So Minobu looks to me exactly like the Pure Land of Eagle Peak and differs little from Mt. Tiantai."

Though he had not intended to at first, Nichiren stayed at Mt. Minobu for eight years. It was a difficult life. Winters were long and the snowfall was very heavy, making it very difficult to receive visitors or get supplies. Even in the summer, it was difficult to get into the valley because of the thick grasses and weeds. But visitors did come from as far as Kamakura, Shimōsa Province, and Sado Island. His supporters also sent many offerings such as rice, wheat, salt, miso, potatoes, rice cakes, *sake*, straw mats, robes, and strings of coins, and also reference books for Nichiren's continued studies, lectures, and writings. Nichiren had found himself writing hundreds of thank you letters for these offerings, without which he and the scores of disciples and lay followers who came to live with him at Mt. Minbou could not have survived.

At times during this period he became unbearably homesick for Kominato. There was a time when he received an offering of sea laver from the Nun Proprietress, who had once more become his benefactor now that it seemed safe, and her now widowed daughter-in-law, who had also become a nun. In response he wrote to the two widows, "Climbing up to the peak, I looked around at what appeared to be seaweed, but were all new shoots of fern. Going down into the valley, I thought I saw seaweed, but on closer inspection I realized my mistake; it was actually thick growing parsley. Living in the mountain, where things of the ocean are rare, I no longer thought about my hometown. But when I saw this laver you sent, memories filled my heart, making me feel sad. This is the laver I used to see in bygone days at the beach of the Kataumi-Ichikawa-Kominato area. The color, shape, as well as taste are the same. Why is it that only my parents have disappeared, never to return? I cannot hold back the tears that spill in remorse."

Despite hardships and homesickness, in his seventh year at Minobu, Nichiren had written, "Residing here at Mt. Minobu is truly like living in the everlasting land of the gods where blessings come down from heaven. Even uncultured men and women would be attracted to this place. In the forlorn autumn twilight, the dew is deep around my grass hut, and in the eaves it is strung like pearls on spider webs. The leaves deepen into scarlet and are reflected in the water that intermittently flows through the bamboo flumes, and seeing them one would not doubt that it is like the view on the upper Tatsukawa River.

"Also, behind my home the rugged mountains rise up out of the depths, and the treetops ripen with the fruits of the One Vehicle. Below the branches the cicadas sing raucously. In front of my hut, the rushing waters flow by. The moon of suchness that is the true aspect of all things floats overhead in a sky cleared of the darkness of deep ignorance because there are no clouds in the sky of Dharma-nature. In this tranquil setting, inside my hut, we spend all day discussing the Dharma of the Wonderful Sutra of the One Vehicle, and all through

311

the night there is the sound of our recitation of the essential passages. It is as though Eagle Peak, where we have heard that the World Honored One Śākyamuni had lived, moved to this very place in our country. In the rising fog and severe storms I go deep into the mountains to cut firewood. Through the dewy grass I go down into the deep valleys to collect water parsley. In the rapids of the swift mountain streams I rinse vegetables, and as I impatiently wait for my dampened sleeves to dry I think of the old poet Hitomaro, who recited, "At Waka-no-ura,/ the fishermen think of the passing of their lives/ as they wait for the seaweed to dry." When I reflect on this fleeting life of mine, it is no different than that of the Buddha when he was seeking the Dharma."

Though Nichiren had found a safe haven, the outside world had not grown any more peaceful. In fact, the foreign invasion that he had long been predicting finally came to pass in the tenth month of the eleventh year of the Bun'ei era (1274), the year that he had arrived at Minobu, when a Mongol fleet attacked Japan. Reports of what would be called the Battle of Bun'ei reached him by the end of the month. He could only imagine the grief and terror experienced by those samurai and lesser warriors who had been deployed to Kyūshū, the southernmost of the four main islands of Japan. They would have had to leave behind aged parents, very young children, young wives, and cherished dwellings, in order to defend the coastline from the Mongol threat. Anxiously looking out over the sea, they must have mistaken clouds for the enemy's battle flags or taken fright whenever they saw fishing boats, thinking that they must be the ships of the Mongol fleet. They must have felt as though they had entered the contentious realm of the *asuras*.

The true horror began when a fleet composed of 300 large ships and 400 or 500 smaller ships descended upon the islands of Iki and Tsushima. The Mongols, along with Chinese and Korean conscripts, slaughtered the defenders. After that, according to the reports, the male farmers were all murdered or taken as prisoners while female farmers were herded together and tied to the ship through holes drilled in their hands. No one was saved.

When the Mongol ships approached the Kyūshū coast, it was said that the two defense commissioners fled without a fight. The Mongols marched forward in close formations. They cut down the warriors left behind with poison-tipped arrows and ceramic bombs filled with gunpowder fired from catapults. The invaders not only killed and wounded many Japanese soldiers but also burned down the palace of the Great Bodhisattva Hachiman at the Usa Hachiman Shrine and devastated the forces under the command of Dazaifu, the Japanese defense headquarters in Kyūshū. Many towns and villages along the coast were also razed and the inhabitants treated in the same way as those of Iki and Tsushima.

Luckily, a typhoon struck after the Mongol troops had returned to their ships for the night. The fleet fled from the storm but as many as 200 ships were lost. When the defenders looked out upon Hakata Bay as the sun rose they saw only the masts of the survivors, retreating north towards Korea.

Had Japan been saved? Based on these reports, Nichiren did not think so. It seemed to him that the Mongols would certainly try again. If it had not been for the storm, they would certainly have overrun Kyūshū. He said to his disciples and lay followers, "It is very likely that when the Great Mongol Empire attacks this country again, they will not think much of our defenses. What will happen if an innumerable number of Mongol troops should surround and attack Japan on all sides?"

Selecting the Right Time

In the sixth month of the first year of the Kenji era (1275) Nichiren began another long essay called *Senji-shō* (*Selecting the Right Time*). In it he insisted, "To study Buddhism, first of all we must know the right time." He was also reflecting on the unsuccessful, though devastating, Mongol invasion, and the responses he had received to his unprecedented teachings regarding the correct way to practice the *Lotus Sutra* in the Latter Age of Degeneration.

"When the *Lotus Sutra* was taught at Eagle Peak, King Ajātaśatru, the most unfilial man in the world, attended the meeting. Even Devadatta, who had abused the True Dharma throughout his life, was given the assurance that he would become Heavenly King Buddha in the future. Furthermore, a dragon girl, though thought incapable of it, became a buddha without changing her dragon-body. The followers of the two vehicles and *icchantika* were all able to attain buddhahood, something as wondrous as a charred seed germinating, flowering, and bearing fruit. When Śākyamuni Buddha's attainment of buddhahood in the remote past was revealed, the assembly was as astonished as though a 100-year old man had been shown to be the son of a 25-year old man. The 3,000 realms in a single thought-moment doctrine explained that un-awakened beings in the nine realms and awakened ones in the realm of the buddha are one and inseparable, opening the way for the un-awakened to attain buddhahood. Therefore, each letter of this sutra represents a wish-fulfilling gem that pours out 10,000 treasures; each phrase of it is the seed of buddhahood. The expounding of these most profound teachings was not done because of the capacity of the audience, their ability to understand, or their faith in upholding them. It was because the time was ripe. The *Lotus Sutra*, chapter two, 'Expedients,' therefore says, "Now is the time to expound the Mahayana teaching definitively.""

Nichiren explained what he had learned in his early studies about the five 500-year periods that would follow the final nirvana of Śākyamuni Buddha. He pointed out that the present time was the fifth 500-year period when the great pure Dharma of Namu Myōhō Renge Kyō, the heart of the *Lotus Sutra*, should spread among all the people. Citing passages from the sutras, he said, "This has been decided by the Buddha, so we must make it a reality."

However, according to the sutras, the present time would also be a time of crisis. "Suppose a wise man appears. The high-ranking monks haunted by devils would induce the ruler, his ministers, and the populace to speak ill of him, abuse him, beat him with sticks or pieces of wood, throw stones or tiles at him, and banish or even execute him. Then Śākyamuni Buddha, Many Treasures Buddha, and the emanation buddhas of the worlds of the ten directions would call upon the great bodhisattvas who emerge from the earth, who would in turn order Brahmā, Indra, the gods of the sun, moon, and stars, and the four heavenly kings to produce strange phenomena in the sky and natural calamities on earth. If those rulers do not heed the divine punishments, their neighboring countries will be ordered to chastise those evil rulers and monks. This would result in the most terrible war the world has ever seen. Then all the people in the world, desirous of the welfare of their countries or of themselves, would pray in vain to all the buddhas and bodhisattvas. Finally, believing in the poor monk whom they had hated, all the people would prostrate themselves and with hands together in reverence recite Namu Myōhō Renge Kyō."

However, Nichiren clarified, such a time of crisis is also a time of great opportunity. "Those who have aspiration for awakening should be glad to see and hear these comments. Those who care for their future lives should rather be born as common persons today in the Latter Age than as great kings during the first 2,000 years after the final nirvana of Śākyamuni Buddha. How could they not believe this? They should rather be lepers reciting Namu Myōhō Renge Kyō than be revered chief abbot of Enryakuji during the Age of the Semblance of the Dharma."

After reviewing the history and development of Buddhism in India, China, and Japan, Nichiren explained that, since the time of the Great Master Dengyō, no one else but he has been upholding and propagating the *Lotus Sutra*. In fact, the monks who follow the Zen, Pure Land, and Mantra teachings have been leading people away from it. Even Jikaku, the third abbot of Enryakuji, who should have championed the Tendai teachings, became a follower of the Mantra school when he taught that both the *Lotus Sutra* and the three esoteric sutras teach the doctrine of the 3,000 realms in a single thought-moment but that the latter are superior for teaching the practice of mudras and mantras. In effect, because of Jikaku, the Tendai temples all became temples of the Mantra school, leaving no one to uphold the *Lotus Sutra*. The mantra practices that had been used to supplant the *Lotus Sutra* then became the cause of the downfall of Retired Emperor Go-Toba when he relied upon them to defeat the Hōjō regency. These same esoteric rites were now being relied upon to drive away the Mongols.

In light of recent events, Nichiren insisted, "There have been many sages endowed with wisdom and talent in China and Japan, but none has believed in the *Lotus Sutra* as firmly as I, Nichiren, nor has anyone had as many strong enemies in the land as I do. From these facts, you should recognize Nichiren to be the prime practitioner of the *Lotus Sutra* in the world...I have never seen nor heard of any man of knowledge who recited Namu Myōhō Renge Kyō himself and advised others to do so during the 700-year period between the reigns of Emperor Kimmei, when Buddhism was introduced to Japan, and the latest emperor. It is only natural that when the sun rises, stars disappear; and when a wise king rises to power, an ignorant king is destroyed. So when the True Dharma spreads, provisional ones decline; and when a man of knowledge recites Namu Myōhō Renge Kyō, ignorant people follow him, just as a body is followed by its shadow or a sound followed by its echo. Consider what is said above. I, Nichiren, am undoubtedly the prime practitioner of the *Lotus Sutra* in Japan. No one in China, India, or in the whole world is comparable to me."

Nichiren warned his disciples and followers that the founders of the Mantra, Zen, and Pure Land teachings had been like worms in the belly of a lion, for they were consuming Buddhism from within. In the Tendai school, the third and fifth abbots of Enryakuji, Jikaku and Chishō, and also the monk Annen, were also like three worms consuming the teachings of the *Lotus Sutra* and the Great Master Dengyō. Because of this Japan itself was imperiled.

"It is pitiful that all the people in Japan are about to fall into the Hell of Incessant Suffering. It is my great joy, however, that I, although unworthy, have been able to plant in my mind the seed of buddhahood.

"You shall see that a time will soon come when the Great Mongol Empire will attack Japan with several tens of thousands of warships. All the people in Japan, from the emperor down to his subjects, casting aside all the Buddhist temples and Shintō shrines, shall recite in unison "Namu Myōho Renge Kyō, Namu Myōhō Renge Kyō," and pressing their palms together, they will cry, "Please help us, Nichiren, please help us."

Nichiren recounted his three previous predictions of the Mongol invasions: when he first submitted his *Treatise on Spreading Peace Throughout the Country by Establishing the True Dharma* to Hōjō Tokiyori on the 16th of the seventh month in the first year of the Bunnō era (1260), when he declared it again to Hei no Saemon at the time of his arrest on the twelfth of the ninth month in the eighth year of the Bun'ei era (1271), and for the third and final time when he spoke again with Hei no Saemon on the eighth of the fourth month in the eleventh year of the Bun'ei era (1274).

317

"It was not I, Nichiren, who made these three important predictions. I believe it was the spirit of Śākyamuni Buddha, entering my body, who made them. I am overwhelmed with joy. This is because of the *Lotus Sutra*'s important doctrine of the 3,000 realms contained in a single thought-moment. According to it, the mind of any person is equipped with the seed of buddhahood, which can blossom when he upholds the right faith. As a result, his mind can function like that of the Buddha. This is what happened to me, Nichiren, when I made these three predictions. Due to my faith in the *Lotus Sutra*, I was able to see things before they actually took place."

Filled with confidence, Nichiren stated, "Rivers come together to form an ocean. Particles of dust accumulate to become Mt. Sumeru. When I, Nichiren, began having faith in the *Lotus Sutra*, it was like a drop of water or a particle of dust in Japan. However, when the sutra is chanted and transmitted to two, three, ten, a million, and a billion people, it will grow to be a Mt. Sumeru of perfect awakening or the great ocean of nirvana. There is no other way than this to reach buddhahood."

Still, he felt saddened for the sake of Japan. "I am in a great quandary. When my prediction comes true, it will prove that I am a sage, but Japan will be destroyed. I have done nothing to regret. I am only sorry that what I said for the sake of my country and in order to repay the debt of gratitude to my native land was not appreciated. ... Although I am an ordinary man not worth mentioning, in regard to upholding the *Lotus Sutra*, I am the greatest man in Japan today."

Nichiren realized that he could very well be accused of enormous self-conceit. In response he wrote, "When Śākyamuni Buddha claimed to be the foremost in the triple world, all the non-Buddhists predicted that he would soon by punished by heaven or that the earth would split open and crumble. He was not punished, however. Instead he was protected by heaven both on the right and left, and the earth was as solid as a diamond and did not split open. ... Therefore, it is not self-conceit, though it sounds like it, to call something excellent when it is actually excellent. It is an act of great merit."

The greatness of Nichiren and his followers, therefore, was because they upheld the *Lotus Sutra*. In chapter 23 of the sutra, 'The Previous Life of Medicine King Bodhisattva,' the Buddha says, "The person who keeps this sutra is superior to any other living being, just as bodhisattvas are superior to voice-hearers or private-buddhas, this sutra is superior to any other sutra. Just as the Buddha is the king of the Dharma, this sutra is the king of sutras."

Finally, Nichiren exhorted his disciples to follow his example, "Therefore, I urge you, my disciples, to practice Buddhism as taught in the *Lotus Sutra* without sparing your life and put Buddhism to the test once and for all. Namu Myōhō Renge Kyō! Namu Myōhō Renge Kyō!"

Gratitude

Nichiren also regretted not having been able to see Dōzen-bō, his former master, before the latter passed away on the 16th day of the third month of the second year of the Kenji era (1276). His former tutor, Jōken-bō, was now the abbot of Seichōji. Jōken-bō and Nichiren's other former tutor, Gijō-bō, had both become Nichiren's disciples. When he had heard the sad news about Dōzen-bō, Nichiren wrote a long essay called *Hōon-jō* (*Essay on Gratitude*) that he completed on the 21st day of the seventh month. Five days later, he sent Nikō with the essay to Seichōji so that it could be read in the woods atop Mt. Kiyosumi and also before Dōzen-bō's tomb.

Though written out of gratitude to his former master, he also wrote it specifically to clear away any doubts that Jōken-bō or Gijō-bō might still have about the correct teaching and practice of the *Lotus Sutra* in the Latter Age. In the essay, he summarized for his former tutors many of the things he had been teaching to his close disciples and lay followers since his time on Sado Island. In a way, just as the Buddha had held back the ultimate truth for 40 years before teaching the *Lotus Sutra*, Nichiren had also held back many things until the time he had been exiled to Sado Island. Since then, he had decided it would be unwise to hold back the truth any longer from those who had proven faithful.

The essay began, "Old foxes never forget their native home. When they are dying, they lie with their heads turned toward the hill where they had lived. The white tortoise once saved by Mao Bao of Chin in China showed its gratitude to Mao Bao by carrying him on its back when he was defeated in a battle and had to flee across a river. Even beasts express their gratitude! It is needless to say that we human beings should do so.

"Yu Rang, a wise man of Chin in ancient China, pretended to be a leper by painting his body with lacquer and acted like a fool by drinking charcoal, trying to repay his indebtedness to his Lord Zhi Bai. Similarly while Hong Yan of Wei was sent away as an envoy to a distant state by order of the Duke of Yi, his lord was killed. Finding only his lord's liver abandoned on the road, Hong Yan cut open his own stomach and died after inserting his lord's liver inside. Thus, even common people behaved this way. Those who learn and practice the teachings of the Buddha should never forget the kindness of their parents, teachers, and ruler.

"What is the best way for Buddhists to express gratitude for the unfathomable kindness that they have received? The best way is to master Buddhism completely and become a person of wisdom. How can a person guide the blind across a bridge, if he himself is blind? How can a captain, who does not know the direction of the wind, sail his ship to transport many merchants to a mountain of treasure?

"Mastering Buddhism, however, remains impossible without enough time to absorb it. And if you are to devote enough time to studying Buddhism, it will be nearly impossible to obey one's parents, masters, and the ruler as well. Those who aim at attaining buddhahood cannot afford to be obedient to parents, masters, and the ruler until they reach the ultimate way to cut the chain of birth and death.

"Most people consider disobeying one's parents and ruler to be against the morals of society and the wishes of the Buddha. In one of the non-Buddhist writings, the *Classic of Filial Piety*, however, it is stated that one can remain loyal to one's lord and filial to his parents even if he does not obey them and even if he admonishes them. A Buddhist sutra states, 'The true way of repaying indebtedness to parents is to stop obeying them and enter the true way of Buddhism.' For instance, Bi Gan, despite disobeying his lord, King Zhou of Yin, was considered a man of wisdom in Confucianism. In Buddhism, Prince Siddhārtha, who disobeyed his father, King Śuddhodana, became the most filial son in the triple world. Having reached this conclusion, I have been learning and practicing Buddhism without obeying my parents and masters."

The essay then elaborated the conclusions that Nichiren had drawn from his studies regarding the doctrines, history, and development of Buddhism. He recounted his refutation of the false teachings, including those of Jikaku and Chishō that promoted the mantra practices and teachings over the *Lotus Sutra* and thereby turned the Tendai school into the Mantra school in all but name.

Nichiren wrote of his determination to speak out against false teachings and to uphold the *Lotus Sutra* and of the persecutions he had faced over the years.

"No one in Japan says Nichiren may have something reasonable to say. This is quite natural. Everyone chants Namu Amida Butsu, and I declare that those who chant it will surely fall into the Hell of Incessant Suffering. Everyone respects Mantra esotericism, and I declare that mantra is the worst teaching and will destroy our country. Rulers of Japan in Kamakura revere the Zen teachings, and I declare it the work of heavenly devils. I know I brought these difficulties upon myself. Therefore, I do not reproach those who abuse me. Even if I wanted to reproach them, there are too many. Even though some have struck me, I do not feel dispirited, for I fully expected it from the outset. ... I sacrificed my life solely for the purpose of repaying the favors I received from my parents, teachers, the Three Treasures, and my country, but I am still alive."

"This virtue of Nichiren, I am sure, is known to all from the venerable Three Treasures above down to such heavenly beings as Brahmā, Indra, and the gods of the sun and moon. The spirits of my parents and Master Dōzen-bō will be given plenty of help by this virtue of mine.

"However, I have one doubt here... I do not think that the late Master Dōzen-bō hated me, for I was one of his beloved disciples. However, he was cowardly. Moreover, he had a strong attachment to Mt. Kiyosumi. He was fearful of the steward Tōjō Kagenobu. Besides, the monks Enchi-bō and Jitsujō-bō, as evil as Devadattva, were always by his side, intimidating him. He was so frightened that he abandoned his disciples who had followed him for many years, even though he loved them. Therefore, I am not sure about his next life. It was fortunate for him that Kagenobu, Enchi-bō, and Jitsujō-bō died before him. They died because of the condemnation of the ten female *rākṣasī*, guardian deities of the *Lotus Sutra*. If they had lived longer, Master Dōzen-bō would not have had time even to have a little faith in the *Lotus Sutra*. Their deaths enabled him to do so, but it was as useless as brandishing a staff after losing a fight or holding up a lantern in the daytime. Besides, it is quite natural that one feels compassion for his children and disciples under any circumstances. Master Dōzen-bō must have taken pity on me when I was exiled to Sado Island, but he never asked about me, though it seemed possible for him to do so. I do not think, therefore, that he truly believed in the *Lotus Sutra*.

"Nevertheless, I am shocked and sorry to hear of his death. Although I feel like running up at once to his tomb through fire and water to recite a fascicle of the sutra, tapping on his gravestone to help him attain buddhahood, I do not think I should come out of the mountain now. I do not think I am a recluse. Others, however, might think that I am and that it is customary for wise men not to come out of their retreats. If I should leave this mountain for no special reason, people may think that I am a person who cannot keep his vows to the end. Therefore, it is impossible for me to leave the mountain no matter how much I would like to.

"Both of you were my tutors when I was young. Just as Gonsō and Gyōhyō, who had been tutors of Great Master Dengyō, later became his disciples, you two are now my disciples. When I left Mt.

Kiyosumi, persecuted by Tōjō Kagenobu, both of you ran after me in secret to help me. It was the supreme service to the *Lotus Sutra* in this world under heaven. Your attainment of buddhahood in the coming life is without doubt."

Nichiren then explained the great merit of the *daimoku*, the essence of the *Lotus Sutra* and of all the Buddha's teachings. Towards the end of the essay he imagined a short dialogue whereby his former tutors would ask him about the Three Great Secret Dharmas of the *Lotus Sutra* that he had only begun speaking of since his exile on Sado Island.

"Are there any Dharmas that Tiantai and Dengyō did not propagate yet?"

"Yes, there are.

"What are those True Dharmas?"

"There are three. They are what the Buddha bequeathed to those in the Latter Age of Degeneration, namely the True Dharmas that masters such as Mahākāśyapa, Ānanda, Aśvaghoṣa, Nāgārjuna, Tiantai, and Dengyō did not yet spread."

Here, then, were what Nichiren thought of as the three great secret Dharmas that had been entrusted by the Eternal Śākyamuni Buddha to Superior Practice Bodhisattva and the other bodhisattvas who emerged from the earth. It was intended that they would spread these three great secret Dharmas throughout the whole world during the 500-year period at the beginning of the Latter Age of Degeneration. These three great secret Dharmas were the actualization or phenomenal expression of the Buddha's realization of the 3,000 realms in a single thought-moment as revealed in the depths of chapter 16, 'The Duration of the Life of the Tathāgata,' of the *Lotus Sutra*.

"What do they consist of?"

"The first is the focus of devotion. All the people in Japan as well as the rest of the whole world should revere Lord Śākyamuni Buddha of the Original Gate as the focus of devotion. That is to say, the focus of devotion should be Śākyamuni Buddha and Many Treasures Buddha in the stūpa of treasures. The other buddhas standing outside the stūpa and the four bodhisattvas such as Superior Practice Bodhisattva should be their attendants."

In addition to the essay, Nichiren had in fact sent a calligraphic mandala depicting the true focus of devotion for Jōken-bō.

"The second is the precept platform based on the doctrine of the Original Gate of the *Lotus Sutra*."

Here was something truly unprecedented. Nichiren rarely spoke of it or put it into writing, for he knew that it would arouse the wrath of all, including the vast majority of Tendai monks. What he meant was that, just as the Hinayana precept platforms for the conferral of the monastic precepts for monks and nuns had been superseded by the Mahayana precept platform for bodhisattvas at Enryakuji, the Mahayana precept platform should in turn be superseded by a precept platform based on the Original Gate of the *Lotus Sutra*. Nichiren dreamed that such a precept platform of the Original Gate would someday be officially established, where all the people of India, China, Japan, and all throughout the Saha world, could come to repent of their transgressions and take up faith in the *Lotus Sutra*.

"The third is the *daimoku* of the *Lotus Sutra*. All the people in Japan, China, and everyone in the whole world, regardless of being wise or foolish, should chant Namu Myōhō Renge Kyō single-mindedly, forgetting everything else. This *daimoku* chanting has not yet been spread in the world. For 2,225 years after the final nirvana of the Buddha no one had chanted this yet. I, Nichiren, alone have been chanting 'Namu Myōhō Renge Kyō, Namu Myōhō Renge Kyō' without sparing my voice."

Nichiren knew that the *daimoku* had in fact been chanted before, but not in the way he meant, as a practice based upon the inner meaning of the Original Gate. During the ages of the True Dharma and the Semblance Dharma the patriarchs Nāgārjuna and Vasubandhu, and the Great Master Tiantai as well, had chanted it as a personal practice to attain awakening based on the Trace Gate of the *Lotus Sutra*. Never before, though, had it been chanted as a practice for benefitting others as well.

"With Nichiren's boundless compassion, Namu Myōhō Renge Kyō will be heard forever, even beyond 10,000 years. It has the merit of curing the blindness of all the people in Japan, blocking the way to hell. This merit is superior to that of Dengyō, Tiantai, Nāgārjuna, and Mahākāśyapa. Practice for 100 years in the Pure Land is not equal to the merit of chanting the *daimoku* for one day in this defiled world. Spreading the Dharma throughout the 2,000-year period following the final nirvana of the Buddha is inferior to propagation for even a short while in the Latter Age of Degeneration. This is not from my own wisdom; it is solely due to the time in which I live. In spring, flowers bloom; in autumn, fruits ripen; in summer, it is warm; and in winter, it is cold; they all go along with the laws of nature."

Nichiren ended the essay with the following words, "Flowers will return to their roots. The true essence of fruit remains in the earth. To my late Master Dōzen-bō I have now dedicated all the merits I have accumulated in spreading the True Dharma. Namu Myōhō Renge Kyō, Namu Myōhō Renge Kyō."

Letters of Instruction and Encouragement

It would be several years before the Mongols were able to send another fleet. During that time, Nichiren remained at Mt. Minobu, teaching the community of monks who had come to live with him there. He also wrote many letters during this time, while his six major disciples took care of propagating his teachings throughout the country. Nisshō and his nephew Nichirō led the community back in Kamakura and in Shimōsa Province. Nikō took care of the lay followers in Kazusa Province. Nikkō remained closer to Mt. Minobu, teaching in the provinces of Suruga, Kai, and Izu. Nitchō helped his stepfather Toki Jōnin in Shimōsa. Nichiji worked in Suruga Province.

In the third month of the first year of the Kenji era (1275), fires spread throughout Kamakura. In response to Shijō Kingo's report, Nichiren wrote, "A name and its referent correspond to each other. There is a sage nicknamed Ryōka (Two Fires), who slanders the True Dharma, but is revered by everyone in Kamakura, high and low, as a master." Here Nichiren was referring to Ryōkan, who he was sure had schemed behind the scenes to have him executed and, when that failed, exiled. Nichiren was certain that Ryōkan and his disciples were continuing to work for the suppression of his teachings and the persecution of his disciples and lay followers. Nichiren went on to say, "The nickname of Two Fires stems from the fire that burnt his own Gokurakuji, transforming it into a temple in hell, and another fire that spread all over Kamakura, destroying the shogun's palace. These two fires not only razed the country in this lifetime but also foretells the fate of the corrupt masters and their disciples in future lives, when they will fall together into the Hell of Incessant Suffering and be burned by its raging fires. When an ignorant monk does not listen to a man of wisdom, he invites calamity such as this. It is pitiful."

Further on in the same letter he wrote, "Watch what happens, hereafter. If those Buddhist monks who speak ill of me pray for the tranquility of Japan, our country will instead collapse further. In the end, the whole of Japan will be tortured and everyone, from the ruler on high down to the masses, will be forced to become slaves of the pigtailed Mongols and have bitter regrets. I have just entreated Brahmā, Indra, the gods of the sun and moon, and the four heavenly kings to punish those who stand against the *Lotus Sutra* in this life, not to mention what will happen to them in future lives. Judge for yourself from the results of my prediction whether or not Nichiren is the practitioner of the *Lotus Sutra*."

Shijō Kingo was a zealous disciple and even tried to convert his lord, Ema Mitsutoki, to abandon the *nembutsu* and take faith in the *Lotus Sutra*. Perhaps tired of such exhortations and heeding the advice of Shijō Kingo's enemies among his retainers, Lord Ema decided to transfer Shijō Kingo from his current fief near Kamakura to one in far off Echigo Province. Angered by the reassignment, Shijō Kingo considered filing a lawsuit with the shogunate, but Nichiren counseled patience.

In a letter written sometime in the third year of the Kenji era (1277), Nichiren wrote to Shijō Kingo, "You need to consider the matter carefully and be cautious. Your lord is someone from whom you, your father, as well as all your relatives have received favors. Moreover, when I was punished by the shogunate a few years ago and despised by everyone in Japan, my disciples were deprived of their fiefs while many of my lay followers were banished by their lords or deprived of their fiefs. You, however, were not ill treated at all by your lord. This was an especially great favor. As such, you should never hold a grudge against him even if you do not receive any more favors from him. Nevertheless, you are unwilling to accept a new fief assignment. Isn't this the case of you not fully understanding the circumstances?

"It is said that a sage is not affected by the eight winds of gain and loss, fame and infamy, praise and blame, and pleasure and pain. This means that a sage neither takes delight in his crowning hour nor grieves when in the depths of despair. Those who are unaffected by the eight winds are protected by the heavenly deities without fail, but not so for those who carry an irrational grudge against their lord, no matter how hard they pray."

On the ninth day of the sixth month of that same year, Shijō Kingo aroused the wrath of his lord by allegedly behaving disruptively during a lecture given by a Tendai monk named Ryūzo-bō. Ryūzo-bō, as far as Nichiren knew, was a disreputable monk who had supposedly been expelled from Mt. Hiei for cannibalism, and had come to Kamakura where he had become a disciple of Ryōkan. Lord Ema, as it happened, revered Ryōkan and his disciple Ryūzo-bō. Therefore, Lord Ema was very displeased when Shijō Kingo's enemies reported that Nichiren's disciple Sammi-bō had interrupted a lecture being given by Ryūzo-bō to initiate a debate and that Shijō Kingo and other armed samurai had been there as well, acting in a provocative manner. Lord Ema immediately demanded that Shijō Kingo submit a written pledge to the effect that he would abandon his faith in the *Lotus Sutra*. Of course this was unthinkable.

Upon receiving a letter from Shijō Kingo relating his determination never to abandon the *Lotus Sutra* even though he might lose his lands, Nichiren wrote back, "I felt as if I had seen an *udumbara* flower, which is said to bloom only once in 3,000 years." He further wrote, "I myself may be able to endure attacks with sticks and pieces of wood, withstand rubble and debris thrown at me, vilification, and persecution by the ruler of the country, but how can lay believers who have a wife and children and no knowledge of Buddhism bear these difficulties? Wouldn't it have been better instead for such people if they had not believed in the *Lotus Sutra*? I had been feeling sorry for you thinking that if you couldn't carry through with your faith, holding it only for temporary comfort, you would be mocked and ridiculed. However, it was wonderful that you showed the steadfastness of your faith throughout my numerous persecutions, including my two exiles. Though threatened by your lord, you wrote this written pledge swearing to carry through your faith in the *Lotus Sutra* even at the cost of two fiefs in two places. Words cannot describe your commendable aspiration."

Lord Ema followed through on his threats and Shijō Kingo's fiefs were confiscated. However, epidemics had begun to spread throughout the land once again. By the ninth month, Lord Ema himself was bedridden and had to call upon Shijō Kingo's skills as a physician. Despite the murderous jealousy of the other retainers, it seemed as though Shijō Kingo might once again find himself in his lord's good graces, if the latter didn't die of fever.

Nichiren worried. There were so many things that could go wrong. Lord Ema could die. Or Shijō Kingo's many enemies might ambush him and strike him down at night or in a careless moment alone. Shijō Kingo's own angry outbursts could easily lead to his downfall. Nichiren cautioned him to remain humble and calm and to stay on good terms with his younger brothers.

Still, despite Shijō Kingo's flaws, he was a warm-hearted and loyal follower. Nichiren would never forget how Shijō Kingo had accompanied him to the beach at Tatsunokuchi when he was certain he was about to be executed. No matter what, Nichiren would never abandon Shijō Kingo either. He wrote to him, "If by chance you should fall into hell, I will refuse the invitation of Śākyamuni Buddha to become a buddha. Instead, I will go to hell with you. If we both were to go to hell, how could it be possible that we would not find Śākyamuni Buddha and the *Lotus Sutra* there?"

He also told Shijō Kingo to have courage and not despair of the world. "Do not complain to other people about hardship in life. If you abandon everything to become a lay monk because life is too much to bear, you renounce the way of sages...It is not easy to be born as a human being in this world. The chance of this happening, as stated in the *Nirvana Sutra*, is as small as the amount of dirt on a fingernail compared to the immeasurable amount of soil on earth. Life as a human being is as fragile as a drop of dew on the grass. It is important, however, to live to earn honor even for a day rather than to live in disgrace for 120 years. Please endeavor so that the people of Kamakura will praise you saying, 'Shijō Kingo was a good man who served not only his lord and Buddhism, but also ordinary people.'"

Nichiren further cautioned him, "It is useless to stack up a pile of treasure in your storehouse if you are in poor health. Therefore, the value of a healthy body is more precious than treasures in the storehouse. At the same time, however, a healthy body means nothing if your heart is not pure. This is why we can say that our most precious treasure is our heart itself. Upon reading this letter, please try to accumulate the treasure of your heart."

He ended the letter with the following exhortation, "A wise man named Confucius of China is said to have thought over what he intended to say nine times before he uttered a word. It is also said that Dan, the Duke of Zhou, would interrupt washing his hair, or having a meal, as many as three times in order to see visitors without keeping them waiting. How much more you who have faith in Buddhism should take these examples to heart! Otherwise, you will regret it later. Please do not resent this advice I am giving you. This is the teaching of the Buddha. The essence of Buddhism is the *Lotus Sutra*, and the essence of practicing the *Lotus Sutra* is shown in the 'Never Despising Bodhisattva' chapter. Contemplate why Never Despising Bodhisattva stood on the street to bow to passersby. The true purpose of Śākyamuni Buddha appearing in this world was to teach us how to conduct ourselves on a daily basis. Consider this well. The wise are called human beings while the foolish are beasts."

In the end, Lord Ema recovered and Shijō Kingo fortunes were restored, as his fiefs were returned and enlarged.

The Ikegami brothers, the elder Munenaka and the younger Munenaga, also persevered in their faith. In the spring of the twelfth year of the Bun'ei era (1275), their father, Ikegami Yasumitsu, a follower of Ryōkan, demanded that the two brothers abandon their faith in the *Lotus Sutra*. When they did not, he disowned the elder, Munenaka, in hopes that the younger, Munenaga, would abandon the *Lotus Sutra* in order to become the new heir. Both brothers, however, remained steadfast and supported one another. Nichiren wrote to them, "This is an opportunity for you to endure persecution to see for yourselves the blessings of the *Lotus Sutra*." He also wrote, "Without the efforts of the both of you, you will never be able to attain buddhahood. You two are like the two wings of a bird or the two eyes of a person."

Concerned that the wives of the brothers might put pressure on them to give in, he wrote, "What is more, your wives are your supporters. Generally speaking, the woman comforts her partner while receiving his support. When a husband enjoys life, his wife also prospers; when a husband is a thief, his wife also becomes a thief. The marital relationship is not limited to this present life but continues to exist forever, life after life, like the body and its shadow, flowers and fruits, or roots and leaves. Insects eat the wood of the trees they live in, and fish drink the water they live in. It is said that orchids sigh when a field dies, and that an oak is pleased when a pine tree prospers. Even plants are like this. It is said there is a bird called *hiyoku* that has two heads in one body with two mouths feeding the one body. It is also said there is a fish called *himoku* that only have one eye each so that the male and female stay together without separation throughout life so they can help each other see all around. Thus should be the relationship between a husband and wife. In order to accomplish faith in the *Lotus Sutra*, the wife should not regret being with her husband, even if the result is death. If the wife is of one mind with her husband

332

and struggles with him, she will succeed the dragon girl who attained buddhahood in the 'Devadatta' chapter of the *Lotus Sutra* and become an example of a woman attaining buddhahood in the Latter Age of Degeneration."

On that occasion the elder brother was restored as heir before long, but was again disinherited by his father in the third year of the Kenji era (1277). By the fall of the following year, however, he was again restored and in addition their father decided to take faith in the *Lotus Sutra* as well.

In considering all that had happened, upon hearing of the death of their father the following year, Nichiren wrote to Munenaga, "As you and your elder brother were born in the Latter Age of Degeneration in an outlying country and have faith in the *Lotus Sutra*, I was sure that demons would possess the nation's ruler or your parents and persecute you. But as I expected, despite your father disowning you repeatedly, you two brothers held onto your faith. Are you the reincarnation of the princes Pure Store and Pure Eyes, who led their father King Wonderful Adornment to the Buddha Dharma? Or did this happen through the workings of Medicine King Bodhisattva and Superior Practice Bodhisattva? Your father's disinheritance was revoked in the end and you were able to carry through with filial piety as before. Are you not filial sons in the truest sense of the word? I am sure the various heavenly beings will give you joy, and the ten female *rākṣasī*, protectors of the *Lotus Sutra*, will accept your prayers. Moreover, there is something heartfelt about you. When my doctrine spreads as widely as predicted in the *Lotus Sutra*, I hope to share the joy of it with you."

Not all the incidents involving his disciples and lay followers worked out so happily, at least in worldly terms. One of the worst persecutions to befall his followers occurred in the village of Atsuhara in the Fuji District of Suruga Province. Nikkō had originally come from Suruga Province and had great success in converting many monks and farmers there, especially with the help of Nanjō Tokimitsu, the steward of Ueno village. Conflict between those who had become disciples of Nichiren through Nikkō's efforts and those who continued to cherish the Pure Land teachings came to a head in the ninth month of the second year of the Kōan era (1279), when Gyōchi, a lay monk who was the deputy administrator of Ryūsenji temple, accused Nichiren's disciples of forcibly invading the abbot's quarters at Ryūsenji on the 21st and of harvesting rice from fields belonging to the temple. Twenty farmers were arrested and sent to Kamakura. Nichiren's disciples filed a counter petition denying the charges brought against them and in turn accusing Gyōchi of all manner of wrongdoing such as inciting violence, taking bribes, misappropriating roof tiles, allowing farmers to hunt on temple grounds, and even of poisoning the temple's pond in order to collect dead fish to sell in the villages.

In light of the arrest of the farmers, Nichiren wrote a letter to his disciples and followers on the first day of the tenth month and sent it to Shijō Kingo in Kamakura. In it he wrote, "The Buddha revealed his true intent in the *Lotus Sutra* after teaching expedients for 40 years or so, while the great masters Tiantai and Dengyō took more than 30 and 20 years or so respectively to accomplish their purposes. As I have told you, the difficulties they encountered during those years were indescribable. In my case, it took 27 years, and you all know about the great persecutions I encountered during this period.

"As the practitioners of the True Dharma, you will inevitably be protected by various deities. My disciples and lay followers, therefore, should have the mind of a lion king and should not be afraid of any threat. As the lion king is not afraid of any animal, its offspring are the same. Those who abuse Nichiren are like foxes howling at a lion, while Nichiren's followers are like roaring lions...Day by day, month by month, strengthen your faith. If you slacken even in the slightest bit, devils will take advantage.

334

"Now regarding the followers in Atsuhara who are farmers, it is important to encourage them without frightening them. Encourage them to strengthen their determination. Tell them that it would be a miracle to be pardoned as suffering is to be expected. If they complain about hunger, tell them about the worse sufferings in the realm of hungry ghosts. If they grumble that they are cold, tell them about the worse sufferings in the eight cold hells. If they say they are scared, tell them to think about how much worse a pheasant feels upon encountering a hawk or how a mouse feels upon coming across a cat."

At the end of the letter, he cautioned his followers not to respond to violence with violence. "Even if they cause a commotion by taking up arms against my followers, we should not act likewise. If any follower of mine tries to take up arms, please send me his name at once."

What was his wish that had been fulfilled after 27 years? What had happened was that ordinary people were at last becoming practitioners of the *Lotus Sutra*. On the 15th of the tenth month, Hei no Saemon interrogated the farmers. According to Nikkō, Hei no Saemon even had his 13-year-old son, Iinuma Hangan, shoot the bound farmers with blunt arrows until they chanted *nembutsu*, but they would not yield and only chanted the *daimoku*. Exasperated, Hei no Saemon finally beheaded three brothers from among them: Jinshirō, Yagorō, and Yajirō. The surviving farmers still refused to give up their faith. Some time later, they were released.

Upon hearing what had happened, Nichiren wrote to Nikkō, "When Jinshirō and other farmers living at Atsuhara who believed in the *Lotus Sutra* were unreasonably imprisoned, I heard that they single-mindedly chanted Namu Myōhō Renge Kyō without any concern for their own lives. Indeed, this is not a trivial matter. I wonder if the ten female *rākṣasī* possessed Hei no Saemon, who interrogated the farmers, and tested them to see if they were true practitioners of the *Lotus Sutra*."

In the same letter he also wrote, "Nāgārjuna and Great Master Tiantai understood the character *myō* to mean changing poison into medicine. If this interpretation is true, justice will soon prevail and this misfortune will become the starting point for spreading the *Lotus Sutra*."

The Divine Winds

In the third and fourth years of the Kenji era (1277-1278), famine and epidemics were once again widespread. Nichiren wrote a description of the ghastly situation, "The condition of Japan today is miserable. As famine has continued for the last several years, people have no clothes to wear and no food to eat. Domestic animals have been eaten, and now cannibalism has begun to appear. Some cut off the flesh of the dead, infants, or the sick and sell them mixed with the flesh of fish and deer. As a result, people began eating human flesh unknowingly. Thus Japan has unexpectedly become a country of demons.

"Moreover, an epidemic spread all over the country from last spring until the middle of the second month of this year, when five out of ten households perished from illness. Those who did not succumb to illness suffered from anguish even greater than the pain of those who contracted the disease. Even if one happened to survive, can life still have meaning after losing a child who had always been there like one's shadow, or losing a spouse with whom one had been inseparable like a pair of eyes, or losing parents whom one depended on as though they were heaven and earth? How is it possible for any sensible person not to abhor human life? The Buddha taught, 'The triple world is unsafe.' Nevertheless, the condition of Japan today seems too cruel."

In the third year of the Kōan era (1280), a fire consumed the Tsurugaoka Hachiman Shrine in Kamakura. Nichiren was grieved to hear of it. It seemed to him that the Great Bodhisattva Hachiman was being reprimanded by the other heavenly beings for protecting and not punishing the ruler of Japan and his subjects who hated and slandered the practitioner of the *Lotus Sutra*. Either that, or the Great Bodhisattva Hachiman had himself burned down his own shrine and returned to heaven to protest the treatment of Nichiren and his followers. On a deeper level, Nichiren believed that the Great Bodhisattva Hachiman was in reality a shadow or trace manifestation of Śākyamuni Buddha and that his vow to protect 100 emperors was actually a vow to reside in the minds of honest people and protect them, a vow that still held true even if it seemed the emperors were no longer protected. In a treatise called *Kangyō Hachiman-shō* (*Remonstration with Bodhisattva Hachiman*) written shortly after the fire, Nichiren explained his earlier remonstrations against the Great Bodhisattva Hachiman, such as he had delivered on the way to Tatsunokuchi. Towards the end of the treatise he asserted, "Now, the Great Bodhisattva Hachiman's original substance, Śākyamuni Buddha, expounded the sole, true *Lotus Sutra* in India. As he manifested himself in Japan, he summarized the sūtra in two Chinese characters meaning honesty, and vowed to live in the heads of wise persons. If so, even if Hachiman burned his palace and ascended to heaven, whenever he finds a practitioner of the *Lotus Sūtra* in Japan, he will not fail to come down to reside where that practitioner is and confer his protection."

Concluding the treatise, Nichiren exhorted his disciples to not be discouraged by such a seemingly evil omen as the burning of the Tsurugaoka Hachiman Shrine, but instead to do what they could to spread the True Dharma of the *Lotus Sutra* throughout the world, even back to India, its place of origin. He told them, "India is called the country of the moon, where the Buddha appears shining in the world as brightly as the moon. Japan is called the origin of the sun. How can it be that no sage as bright as the sun appears in Japan? The moon moves from west to east. It is the omen of Buddhism in India spreading to the east. The sun orbits from east to west. This is a fortunate omen of Buddhism in Japan returning to India. Moonlight is not as bright as sunlight; therefore the Buddha preached the *Lotus Sutra* for only eight years of his lifetime. Sunlight is brighter than moonlight, an auspicious omen of Buddhism in Japan shining throughout the long darkness of the fifth 500-year period. The Buddha did not save slanderers of the *Lotus Sutra* because there were no slanderers during his lifetime. In the Latter Age of Degeneration, there will be many formidable enemies of the One Vehicle Lotus teaching everywhere. This is the time when we can realize the benefit of Never Despising Bodhisattva's way of subduing evil by sowing the seed of buddhahood. Each of my disciples should exert themselves to spread the teaching of the Buddha, even at the cost of their lives."

In addition to drought, famine, disease, and the disastrous fires in Kamakura, the threat of another Mongol invasion still hung over Japan. The Mongols had sent five envoys in the fifth month of the first year of the Kenji era (1275) to reiterate their demand for tribute. This time the shogunate responded by bringing the envoys to Kamakura, where they were beheaded in the tenth month. Before long, more troops were sent west to defend Kyūshū and a wall was built around Hakata Bay to hamper the landing of an invasion force. By the third month of the second year of the Kōan era (1279), the Great Mongol Empire had defeated the last remnant of the Southern Song dynasty. They were finally ready to turn their full attention back to Japan. In the seventh month they sent five more envoys. Those five were executed in Hakata. In the second month of the third year of the Kōan era (1280), the imperial court ordered all the temples and shrines of Japan to pray for victory over the Mongols, who were sure to send another fleet.

Some speculated that Nichiren was looking forward to the impending invasion, as he had prophesied it. Although his predictions had indeed proven true, this was not how he felt. He wrote several times to his supporters to clarify his position. In a letter to Nanjō Tokimitsu after the first invasion attempt in the eleventh year of the Bun'ei era (1274) he said, "To begin with, most of my thinking is devoted to saving Japan from the impending national crisis, but all of the people of Japan, both rulers and subjects alike, not only refused to listen to me but also have subjected me to frequent persecutions. Though this may be an omen of national destruction, I felt things were beyond my capabilities and decided to retreat into the mountain. Regarding the anticipated invasion of Japan by troops of the Great Mongol Empire, I truly feel saddened, as I believe that a national crisis such as this could have been averted if the people of Japan had heeded my words. I cannot stop tears from rolling down my cheeks when I think of the people in Japan, all captured and murdered just as those on the islands of Iki and Tsushima have been recently."

A little over a year later he wrote again to Nanjō Tokimitsu to say, "As I have always taught that, according to the *Lotus Sutra*, a country in which the True Dharma is slandered will be attacked by foreign troops, some people criticize me saying, 'Nichiren is happily waiting for the Mongols to invade Japan.' This is utterly incorrect. Regarding my prediction of foreign invasion, people all blame me as if I were a sworn enemy. I cannot help it, however, because it is clearly stated in the sutras."

Nichiren could imagine the suffering of the samurai and foot soldiers that had to make the long march to Kyūshū, and the greater sufferings that would fall upon all the people of Japan because of how the shogunate had treated him. Despite his deep sympathy for those afflicted, he took refuge in the thought that there was hope for all those who truly put their faith in the *Lotus Sutra*.

Though Toki Jōnin was not one of those sent, Nichiren wrote the following to his wife, "Leaving Kamakura, the husbands went away through Yuigahama, Inamura, Koshigoe, Sakawa, and Hakone Pass. As the days passed, they were journeying further away from Kamamkura step by step, beyond the river, over the mountains, and through the clouds. Through all this, only tears and sorrow kept them company. How sad they were! While grieving over their misfortune, when the Mongol troops attack, they will be captured somewhere in the mountains or ocean and suffer misery aboard the enemy ships or in Korea.

340

"Those in power are solely responsible for this miserable situation in Japan because they abused me, Nichiren, who is the practitioner of the *Lotus Sutra* that is the father and mother of all living beings. Without just cause they beat me and paraded me around the streets like a criminal. Their acts of sheer madness were punished by the ten female *rākṣasī*, resulting in the current misery facing Japan. Hereafter, there will be sufferings millions and billions of times harder to bear. You may be witnessing such awful scenes before your very eyes.

"However, when we believe in the certainty of attaining buddhahood, is there anything to fear? It is pointless to become royalty and enjoy the pleasures of this life. It is useless to be born in heaven and enjoy its pleasures. Instead, follow the example of the dragon girl, who attained buddhahood in the 'Devadatta' chapter of the *Lotus Sutra*, and align yourself with Mahāprajāpati. How delightful it will be! How joyful it will be! Namu Myōhō Renge Kyō. Namu Myōhō Renge Kyō."

The Mongols came to Japan again in the summer of the fourth year of the Kōan era (1281). This time the invasion force was many times larger. It was said to have consisted of a fleet of 900 ships from Korea and 3,500 ships coming up from China to the south. The total number of sailors and troops was believed to be as many as 140,000. The fleet from Korea arrived in the middle of summer and soon overran Iki and Tsushima. They were successfully held at the wall around Hakata Bay for weeks while they waited for the larger fleet from China. The typhoon season had begun by the time the two fleets were able to combine their forces. On the first day of the seventh month a typhoon struck the fleet and destroyed more than 4,000 ships before it ended two days later. Naturally, the monks who had led special esoteric prayer services for the repulsion of the Mongols eagerly claimed credit for the *kamikaze* or "divine winds" that had miraculously saved Japan.

Nichiren was not fooled. The esoteric rites of the mantra teachings had not saved Emperor Antoku or the Retired Emperor Go-Toba. Why should anyone believe that their prayers and rituals were any more effective against the Mongols? In a letter to Toki Jōnin he pointed out, "After the enemy ships were damaged by waves aroused by autumn winds, the Mantra monks must have spread a rumor attributing the capture of the enemy commander to the effects of the esoteric rites of mantric Buddhism. If this were so, you might ask them whether or not the head of the Mongol Emperor had been taken." The defeat of the Mongols was obviously not the result of the power of esoteric Buddhism, but a result of the Mongols having been caught, once again, by the seasonal typhoons. It was as simple as that. Japan was still in danger. The threat of foreign invasion would never go away so long as the rulers and their subjects continued to slander the True Dharma and rely upon false teachings.

Nevertheless, Nichiren and the 30 or more disciples that were studying and practicing with him at Mt. Minobu did not despair of the world. Instead, in spite of rain and later a heavy snowfall, they set to work in the eleventh month of the fourth year of the Kōan era (1281) building a temple roughly 60 square feet in size, along with stables and residence halls. The temple was dedicated on the 24th of the month, the day of the annual memorial lecture for the Great Master Tiantai. In celebration they performed a ceremonial dance for longevity to their hearts content. That evening they gathered before the altar to copy the *Lotus Sutra*, though they did not finish it at that time, as Nichiren felt it would be wiser to complete it when the prayers of their patron, Hakii Sanenaga, had been fulfilled. It was a grand achievement. The temple thereafter came to be called Kuonji, the Temple of Eternity. Actually, the Chinese characters *ku* and *on* together meant "remote past", but these were the characters used to refer to the measureless amount of time since Śākyamuni Buddha actually attained buddhahood according to chapter 16 of the *Lotus Sutra*, so it was understood to mean "eternity."

Though the life span of the Eternal Śākyamuni Buddha of the Original Gate of the *Lotus Sutra* was without measurable limits, Nichiren felt that he was coming to the end of his own time in the world very soon. Shortly after the dedication of Kuonji, he received a horse load of rice, as well as *sake* and medicinal herbs, from the mother of Nanjō Tokimitsu. In his letter thanking her, he wrote, "Conditions on Mt. Minobu have not changed at all, which I told you about in my previous letter to you. I have not stepped out of this place since the 17th of the 6th month in the eleventh year of the Bun'ei era (1274), when I entered this mountain, till today, the eighth of the twelfth month of this year (1281). During these past seven years, I have been ill almost every year and my body and mind have become feeble with age. This spring, I have become seriously ill and my condition has taken a turn for the worse through this fall and winter. I have eaten very little in these past ten days. Besides, this winter has been very cold and there has been heavy snow. My body is chilled like a stone and my breast feels like ice. At such a moment, I warm up the *sake* that you sent me and swallow it with medicinal herbs. They are like kindling ignited in my chilled breast and warm my body like a hot bath. With drops of perspiration I can cleanse my entire body and warm my feet. Wondering how to express my appreciation to you for sending me such articles of great value, I shed tears of gratitude for your kindness."

Now, on his deathbed, Nichiren strained to remember what it was like to feel young and vigorous. How had it been to have the energy to get out of bed, to be able to hike into the mountains and down into the valleys? How had it been to breath fully and easily? Or even merely to be able to stay warm without keeping tightly covered? He had long since lost his taste for food, and now could barely even keep down *sake*, tea, or even water. No breath was guaranteed. He could feel this now, whereas before he had only known it.

He was surprised that he had not succumbed to his illness sooner. By the fall of the fifth year of the Kōan era (1282) he was sick enough that he was willing to be taken to the hot springs in Hitachi Province rather than risk another winter at Mt. Minobu. On the eighth day of the ninth month, he set out. Hakii Sanenaga lent Nichiren a horse to ride and sent his sons along as Nichiren's escort. Ten days later, Nichiren arrived at the home of Ikegami Munenaka. He was too ill to go any further. On the 19th he dictated a final letter to Hakii Sanenaga.

"I would like to tell you how things have gone. We have arrived safely at Ikegami in Musashi Province. I am very glad to say that, although it was not easy for me to cross the mountains and rivers, I was able to reach here, kindly guarded by yours sons.

"I hope to return to Minobu by the same road I passed through, but I am not sure whether or not I shall be able to return due to my sickness. Regardless, I am deeply grateful to you for embracing me for as long as nine years when everyone else in Japan did not know what to do with me, Nichiren. That being said, I would like to have my tomb erected in Minobu Valley no matter where I die.

"The chestnut-colored horse you lent me for riding is a very good and beautiful one. I did not wish to part from it. At first, I wished to ride on it up to the hot spring of Hitachi, but thinking that it might be stolen there, I decided to leave it in the care of Lord Mobara in Kazusa Province until I return from Hitachi. I would feel sorry for the horse if it had to change its groom, so I have decided to leave him with the present groom until I come back. I hope you will approve my decision.

"Please forgive me for omitting my formal signature due to my illness."

At the Beginning

The rising sun cast a soft diffuse light through the *shōji* screens into the room where Nichiren lay in the Ikegami manor. It was dawn on the 13th day of the tenth month of the 5th year of the Kōan era (1282). Winter had begun less than two weeks before. The morning chill no longer bothered him. His mouth and throat were dry, but he was beyond thirst. Quick shallow breaths were followed by long pauses. These lasted almost a minute. The disciples seated around him tensed, unable to breathe easy until he took another breath. He had stopped thumbing the beads of his *juzu*, as it had become irritating. Everything that touched him seemed too hard and coarse. He looked down at his left hand, the one that held the *juzu*, and was amazed at how pale it had become. He smiled contentedly as his six senior disciples led the others, both clergy and lay followers, in chanting the *daimoku*. He lay on his right side facing west. The statue of Śākyamuni Buddha from Izu and the mandala that hung behind it were placed so that they were directly before his gaze. He could not chant aloud anymore, but the recitation of Namu Myōhō Renge Kyō was something that never ceased in his mind and heart. It was always there, a constant companion.

Nichiren closed his eyes. The characters of the mandala began to shine with a golden light. It was so bright that he could still see them through his closed lids. For the first time in what seemed to be years, he felt light and at ease. The pain had fallen away completely. To his surprise he could see everyone in the room as though he were a cloud floating overheard. They were ranged around him to the east in a semicircle, all facing the mandala. There was a choked cry. The six senior disciples had begun to sob. Why such sadness? Couldn't they feel how at peace everything was? He knew now that his efforts had not been in vain. All of them would carry on his work as best they could. He smiled down at Nichizō, the 13-year old younger half-brother of Nichirō. He had become his elder brother's disciple some eight years ago. A few days before, Nichiren had exhorted him to continue in his practice and studies with his elder brother and to someday go to Kyōto and teach the *Lotus Sutra* to the emperor himself. The boy's eyes had flashed with zeal. He had prostrated himself before Nichiren and vowed to give his life to accomplish the mission entrusted to him. There indeed was another bodhisattva emerging from the earth. They were countless. They included those in the room, and multitudes throughout Japan, China, India, and beyond. Those who had already appeared and those yet to come would all rally around the banner of Namu Myōhō Renge Kyō. They might be many in body, but they would be one in mind. Through their harmonious efforts, the great vow of widely promulgating and spreading the *Lotus Sūtra* would be fulfilled.

Nichiren watched as Nisshō, his old companion from his student days at Mt. Hiei and now the eldest of his senior disciples, left the room and went outside to the hanging bell in the courtyard. He weaved his way through a crowd that had gathered there. They were all whispering to one another. Some had begun weeping. Others covered their faces with the sleeves of their kimonos. Using the beam suspended at its side, Nisshō began to strike the bell. At that signal, bitter wracking sobs issued from all present. The disciples inside composed themselves and began to chant the Verses of Eternity.

"It is many hundreds of thousands
Of billions of trillions
Of *asaṃkhyas* of *kalpas*
Since I became the Buddha.

"For the past innumerable *kalpas*
I have always been expounding the Dharma
To many hundreds of millions of living beings
In order to lead them to buddhahood.

"In order to save the contrary people,

I expediently show my nirvana to them.
In reality I shall never pass away.
I always live here and expound the Dharma.

"Although I always live here
With the contrary people
I disappear from their eyes
By my supernatural powers."

The light cast by the characters of the mandala now outshone that of the sun, but somehow its brilliance did not hurt his eyes. The light surrounded him and he became one with it. He could no longer see the courtyard. There was only the light, its boundless compassionate embrace. The sound of crying and weeping also faded, though in his mind the recitation of the verses continued, but now it seemed that other, more resonant, voices had taken it up. There were so many of them! They were all around him now. The first of the voices were coming from the characters of the mandala that were now resolving into figures of light, but more figures were joining them. It was a vast assembly of golden beings floating high above a mountain peak. They placed their hands palm to palm in greeting, gratitude, and mutual reverence.

"When they see me seemingly pass away,
And make offerings to my relics,
And adore me, admire me,
And become devout, upright, and gentle,
And wish to see me
With all their hearts
At the cost of their lives,
I reappear on Eagle Peak
With my Sangha,
And say to them:
"I always live here.
I shall never be extinct.

I show my extinction to you expediently
Although I never pass away.
I also expound the unsurpassed Dharma
To the living beings of the other worlds
If they respect me, believe me,
And wish to see me.
You have never heard this;
Therefore, you thought that I pass away."

He had spoken and written over the years to so many grieving people. Wives mourning husbands, husbands mourning wives, parents mourning children, sons and daughters mourning mothers and fathers, brothers and sisters mourning their siblings. He told them they would meet again if they maintained their faith. Upon death they would at last see that all things and phenomena in the ten Dharma-realms are manifestations of the ultimate reality. They would realize that all beings possess the three bodies of buddhahood. They would know that the only difference between the ignorant ordinary people of the Latter Age and the awakened buddhas was that the ignorant had not awakened to the true reality of all phenomena. The ignorant had no faith but had instead turned away from the truth and slandered the True Dharma. Those with faith, however, would die chanting Namu Myōhō Renge Kyō, awaken at last, and find themselves in the company of the Eternal Śākyamuni Buddha, Many Treasures Buddha, and the emanation buddhas of the ten directions. Upon death these buddhas would take them by the hand and lead them to the Pure Land of Eagle Peak.

"I see the contrary people sinking
In an ocean of suffering.
Therefore, I disappear from their eyes
And cause them to admire me.
When they adore me,
I appear and expound the Dharma to them.

"I can do all this by my supernatural powers.
I live on Eagle Peak
And also in the other abodes
For *asaṃkhya kalpas*.

"The contrary people think:
'This world is in a great fire.
The end of the *kalpa* of destruction is coming.'
In reality this world of mine is peaceful.
It is filled with gods and men.
The gardens, forests and stately buildings
Are adorned with various treasures;
The jeweled trees have many flowers and fruits;
The living beings are enjoying themselves;
And the gods are beating heavenly drums,
Making various kinds of music,
And raining mandārava-flowers
          on the great multitude and me.

"This pure world of mine is indestructible.
But the contrary people think:
'It is full of sorrow, fear, and other sufferings.
It will soon burn away.'
"Because of their evil karmas,
These sinful people will not be able
To hear even the names of the Three Treasures
During *asaṃkhya kalpas*."

Nichiren was home. It was the home he had never left. For 60 years he had struggled in the Sahā world, the world of endurance, but it had never really been anything but the Pure Land of Eternally Tranquil Light. As Nichiren, he had not been able to see this with his worldly eyes. He had, instead, seen a world ravaged by drought, famine, epidemics, earthquakes, the terror caused by all manner of ill omens, and worst of all the brutality of violent oppression and war. Now he could see and think clearly again. All things were truly at peace, for no thing was ever born and so no thing ever died. He could see that there was nothing that was not true reality. There was not a single sight nor smell that was not the middle way that is forever free of the extremes of being and non-being. There was only a single unalloyed reality, and nothing whatsoever existed outside of it. He saw that all things were by nature at peace, and though peaceful, that same nature was ever luminous.

His three peers among the assembly greeted him and he resumed his place among them. They all smiled upon one another and upon their teacher of old, who in turn smiled upon them. Though still and silent, in a space beyond the world, there was not a moment when they did not emerge into the world to expound the True Dharma.

"To those who have accumulated merits,
And who are gentle and upright,
And who see me living here,
Expounding the Dharma,
I say:

"'The duration of my life is immeasurable.'
To those who see me after a long time,
I say, 'It is difficult to see a buddha.'

"I can do all this by the power of my wisdom.
The light of my wisdom knows no bound.
The duration of my life is innumerable *kalpas*.
I obtained this longevity by ages of practices."

The six senior disciples knew in their hearts that things were not as they seemed, nor were they otherwise. Their master had entered final nirvana and so they grieved; and yet they also rejoiced for his suffering was ended and he now awaited them in the Pure Land of Eagle Peak. Hadn't he told them in the past at times of parting,

"Whenever you yearn for me, Nichiren, look toward the sun, which rises in the morning, and the moon, which appears in the evening. I will inevitably be reflected in the sun and moon." Assured in their faith, they continued to recite the Buddha's words in the Verses of Eternity:

"All of you wise men!
Have no doubts about this!
Remove your doubts, have no more!
My words are true, not false.

"The physician who sent a man expediently
To tell his contrary sons
Of the death of their father in order to cure them,
Was not accused of falsehood although he was still alive.

"In the same manner, I am the father of the world.
I am saving all living beings from suffering.
Because they are contrary,
I say that I pass away even though I shall not.
If they always see me,
They will become arrogant and licentious,
And cling to the five desires
So much that they will fall into the evil regions.

"I know who is practicing the way and who is not.
Therefore, I expound various teachings
To all living beings
According to their capacities.

"I am always thinking:
'How shall I cause all living beings
To enter into the unsurpassed way
And quickly become buddhas?'"

Endnotes

Abbreviations for books listed in Sources: LS = Murano, 2012; HS = Hirai; NG = Hori, 1995; TB = Kanda; WNS 1-7 = Writings of Nichiren Shōnin volumes 1-7, translations compiled by Hori, 2002-2015.

At the End

How Nichiren felt toward the end of his life he describes in NG, p. 294. Masaharu Anesaki believed that the symptoms described in that letter indicated cancer of the digestive organs. See Anesaki, p. 130.

That hearing the *Lotus Sutra* enables people to "know peace in their present lives and rebirths in good places" is from LS p. 109.

Nichiren's ideas on gratitude are expressed in many of his writings but particularly the *Hōon-jō* (WNS 3, pp. 1-2).

Zennichi-maro

There are no references in Nichiren's writings as to the date of his birth. TB says:

"However, after Nichiren Shōnin's demise, the *Hokke Honmon Shū Yōshō* (*The Essential Writings of the Hokke Honmon School*), composed prior to the gathering and compilation of the *Goibun* (*Nichiren Shōnin's Sacred Writings*), the *Tōke Yōbun Shū* (*Collection of this Household's Essential Documents*) written by Nichigyō who lived around the time of Nichiren Shōnin, and other related documents, report that his birth was on the 16th of February."

Takashi Nakao states that inside of a statue of Nichiren Shōnin in the founder's hall of Tanjōji temple is a prayer sheet that may be the oldest document relating to Nichiren's birth.

Inside of this statue, a prayer sheet written by a priest was found. This prayer, written by Nichijō, the 4th abbot of Tanjōji temple in the 81st years after Nichiren Shōnin's passing is showing when and where Nichiren Shōnin was born. This is the oldest record to show the birth year and place of Nichiren Shōnin.

Nichiren wrote about his background in *Honzon Mondō Shō* (WNS 2, p. 267). He referred to his family as *chandālas* or untouchables in *Sado gokanki shō* and *Sado gosho*. He also wrote about the connection between his home and the Sun Goddess in *Niiama gozen gohenji* (WNS 7, pp. 149-150). The true social status of his family is not known. According to Jacqueline Stone:

"Attempts on the part of later hagiographers to furnish Nichiren with illustrious forebears are most likely unfounded. Still his family may not have been altogether as humble as he indicates. Recent scholarship suggests that his father may perhaps have been a manager (*shōshi*) or official (*shōkan*) of the local manor or *shōen* (ST p. 868), perhaps in charge of administering fishing rights held by the *shōen* proprieter." (Stone, p. 243)

Even the names of Nichiren's parents and his childhood names are not known for certain. TB says:

"It is commonly said that his father was Nukina Shigetada and his mother was called Umegiku. His childhood names are said to have been Zennichi-maro and Yakuō-maro, but even these too are not clear."

The conversation between Zennichi-maro and Shigetada is fiction of course, but it is based on Nichiren's statement in his *Shinkoku-ō*

354

Gosho (WNS 1, pp. 174-176) that since childhood he had been pondering the meaning of the drowning of Emperor Ankoku at the Battle of Dan-no-Ura in 1185 and the failure of Retired Emperor Go-Toba's attempt to overthrow the shogunate during the Jōkyū Disturbance of 1221. We do not know how he first heard these stories so I can only imagine that he heard them the way others did in those days before newspapers or cable news. He heard them from family members or traveling storytellers.

For information about the *biwa-hōshi*, the blind lute-playing monks, I am indebted to the discussion of them in McCullough pp. 6-11. I am also indebted to Souyri, pp. 80-83.

Zennichi-maro's imagining of the drowning of Emperor Antoku is based on McCullough, pp. 376-379.

The description of the Jōkyū Disturbance is taken from Nichiren's own writings, in particular the *Honzon Mondō-shō* (WNS 2, p. 269), *Kitō-shō* (WND 4, pp. 69-71), and *Hōon-jō* (WNS 3, p. 46).

For the history of the ascension of Minamoto no Yoritomo and the subsequent rise of the Hōjō clan, I am indebted to Souyri, pp. 48-56 and Sansom, pp. 312-394.

That the Nun Proprietress may have enabled Zennichi-maro to become an attendant and study at Seichōji is perhaps hinted at in a statement Nichiren makes about a favor his parents owed to her in his letter *Seichōji Daishū-chū* (WNS 5, p. 177).

Yakuō-maro

Nichiren wrote that he began his studies at Seichōji (aka Kiyosumi-dera) at the age of twelve in *Honzon Mondō Shō* (WNS 2, p. 267), though in the Western way of counting age he would have been only eleven.

The vignette about the cicada is fictional, but I wrote it to convey a sense of what the journey to Seichōji might have been like, as well as the kind of feelings that the cicadas arouse in many Japanese people to this day.

The years of famine and plague from 1229-1232 are written about in Sansom, pp. 393-394 and Farris, pp. 33-51.

Nichiren wrote about Master Dōzen-bō and also his tutors Gijō-bō and Jōken-bō in several letters, but particularly see *Hōon-jō* (WNS 3, pp. 48-49). The conversations in this chapter are all fictionalized but what I imagine might have been said.

For more information about the life of attendants (J. *chigo*), see the article by Atkins.

The account of the temple's daily schedule and services is a generalization based on the schedules and services of many traditional East Asian Buddhist temples.

The Triple World

This account of Nichiren's studies is based on my estimation of the kinds of things he must have studied in his youth as they form the backdrop of his thinking in adulthood. I especially wished to convey here the Buddhist worldview based upon Abhidharma teachings, such as summarized in the *Abhidharmakośabhāṣya* (*A Treasury of Abhidharma, with Commentary*) of Vasubandhu, that were well known to Nichiren and his contemporaries. Nichiren assumed this worldview in his writings and it also became a part of the mandala he designed later in life.

The Awakening of Śākyamuni Buddha

The passage, "Contemplating his own life, ... the aged and the young." is based upon a statement Nichiren wrote about his childhood studies in *Myōhō-ama Gozen Gohenji* (WNS 4, p. 141).

The account of Śākyamuni Buddha's life is based on typical notions that were current in East Asia at that time. In particular the notions that Śākyamuni Buddha had lived more than 2,000 years ago, that he had left the palace at 19, practiced asceticism on Mt. Dandaloka, attained awakening at the age of 30, and spent 50 years teaching until his passing are all things referred to throughout Nichiren's writings and assumed by most of his contemporaries. These assumptions were derived from works such as *The Record of Wonders in the Book of Zhou* and *Dazhidu lun* (*The Treatise on the Great Perfection of Wisdom*) attributed to Nāgārjuna.

I have also drawn from accounts about the life of the Buddha, his struggles with Māra, his awakening, and his reflections and talks with Brahmā afterwards from Jayawickrama, Johnston, and Ñāṇamoli, The discussion about all buddhas praising the Wonderful Dharma and the simile of the lotus pond are specifically based upon accounts in Bodhi, pp. 231-235. I also worked in a brief statement from the *Flower Garland Sutra*. See Cleary 1993, p. 1003 and p. 1005. Last but certainly not least, I also included the statements from LS pp. 44 and 46.

Māra's daughters and his army of demons represent the mental hindrances that arise during meditation practice. The description of Māra's daughters is derived from the appearance of the *shirabyōshi* who were "high-class courtesans who specialized in dancing." See Souyri, p. 97. They were the Kamakura era predecessors of the *geisha* of the Edo period. They also appear in the *Tale of the Heike*. See McCullough, pp. 30-37. The description of the army of demons is based upon the appearance of samurai in full armor, and particularly the *menpō* or facemask that was part of their helmets.

Renchō

We do not know what Nichiren's ordination was like, so what is presented in this chapter is my own fictional recreation based loosely upon the *tokudō jukai* (attaining the way and bestowing precepts) ceremonies that are used today in Japanese Mahayana Buddhism, in particular Nichiren Shū. See HS, pp. 109-122. The major difference of course is that Nichiren Shū does not administer the precepts of the *Brahmā Net Sutra*, but presumably Nichiren was given the bodhisattva precepts that were used in the Tendai School that he was ordained in. Nichiren refers to the three pure precepts and the precepts of the *Brahmā Net Sutra* in *Ichidai Shōgyō Tai-i* (WNS 3, pp. 74-75). In *Senji-shō* (WNS 1, p. 203), Nichiren discusses the establishment of the precept platform on Mt. Hiei by Grand Master Dengyō for the conferral of the precepts of the *Brahmā Net Sutra* and goes so far as to say that in respect to taking these specifically Mahayana precepts, "In Japan...Buddhist monks who were not disciples of Grand Master Dengyō were either non-Buddhists or villains." See also *Soya Nyūdō-dono-gari Gosho* (WNS 3, p. 164). This leads me to believe that Nichiren too, must have been given these precepts at some point if he regarded himself as a Mahayana monk and (at least for a time) as a Tendai monk and a disciple of Dengyō. A complete translation of that portion of the *Brahmā Net Sutra* containing the ten major and 48 minor precepts and explanations of them can be found online at:

http://www.buddhasutra.com/files/brahmanet.htm.

The passage cited from chapter 27 of the Lotus Sutra can be found on p. 339 of the LS.

The Teachings of the Buddha

The summary of the Buddha's 50 years of teaching and the schools that developed based on the Buddha's different teachings as understood by Nichiren and his contemporaries was based upon passages from Nichiren's *Shugo Koka-ron* (WNS 1, pp. 5-10), *Kaimoku-shō* (WNS 2, pp. 45-47, 64-66, and 78), *Ichidai Shōgyō Tai-i* (WNS 3, pp. 79-81), and *Ichidai Goju Keizu* (WNS 3, pp. 238-244).

For the teachings of the Flower Garland period see Cleary 1993, pp. 451-452. For the teachings given at the Deer Park and other pre-Mahayana doctrines and for an account of how the major disciples became part of the Sangha see Nanamoli, pp. 41-44, 46-47, 52, 64-65, 70-73, 77-84, 102-108, and 206-256. Passages relating the life of the Buddha as well as the Buddha's pre-Mahayana and Mahayana teachings can be found in the anthology *Buddha-Dharma* put out by the Numata Center.

The term Hinayana or "Small Vehicle" for those Buddhists who do not follow Mahayana teachings is of course a derogatory epithet. There is not, and never was, a school of Buddhism that would consider itself Hinayana. There are schools of Buddhism that did not and do not view the Mahayana sutras as canonical and there are certainly points of disagreement between Mahayana teachings and those of the Theravāda, the sole surviving non-Mahayana school. However, Mahayana critiques of those they called Hinayana were actually directed at the specific doctrines of schools of Buddhism, for instance the Sarvāstivāda, that no longer exist today. Mahayana criticisms of Hinayana concepts and attitudes may or may not always be justified in relation to any particular school or individual and on the whole it is better to not confuse Mahayana ideas about "Hinayana Buddhism" with Theravāda Buddhism or any other school that may once have existed. For example, the Chinese Mahayana tradition's characterization of arhats and private-buddhas as trying to reduce their bodies to ashes and annihilate their consciousness is a critique of any who would understand the "final nirvana" achieved at death in a nihilistic manner. There are discourses in the Pāli Canon, however, where the Buddha cautions against such a nihilistic understanding. So does this characterization really apply to Theravāda Buddhism? Did it ever really apply to how the Sarvāstivāda school understood "final nirvana"? I should also point out that the three schools of Buddhism in Japan that Nichiren regarded as Hinayana (Abhidharma Treasury, Completion of Reality, and Precepts) were not actually separate Hinayana schools but more like specialized curriculums followed by Mahayana monks and nuns. The Precepts school in particular argued that they advocated the Mahayana precepts and that the monastic rules that originated with the pre-Mahayana schools were not intrinsically Hinayana. In any case, I will continue to use the term Hinayana in this fictionalized biography because it is the term that Nichiren and his contemporaries used to refer to those whom they believed rejected Mahayana teachings and ideals.

The notion that private-buddhas attained awakening by watching leaves falling or flowers scattering seems to have been a well-known trope. For example see *Kanjin Honzon-shō* (WNS 2, p. 136).

The description of the three ages of the Dharma and the history of Buddhism from the time of the Buddha until its arrival in Japan comes from Nichiren's *Senji-shō* (WNS 1, pp. 191-192 and pp. 197-198). Note that Paekche was one of three kingdoms on the Korean peninsula at that time. That there were eight or ten schools (depending on whether or not Pure Land and Zen were counted) that were looked upon as mirrors reflecting the Dharma by Nichiren's contemporaries is found throughout Nichiren's writings, but in particular see *Hōon-jō* (WNS 3, p. 3). Also see *The Essentials of the Eight Traditions* by Nichiren's contemporary Gyōnen translated by Leo M. Pruden.

The Secret Method For Seeking, Hearing, and Retaining

The description that Dōzen-bō gives of the esoteric rites used by the past emperors and the imperial court to subdue their enemies during the Genpei War and the Jōkyū Incident was based primarily on Nichiren's description of them in *Honzon Mondō-shō* (WNS 2, pp.

269-271) and *Shijō Kingo-dono Gohenji* (WNS 6, p. 139). Also, see WNS 1, pp. 235-236, WN 3, p. 46; and WNS 4, pp. 69-71.

In *Seichōji Daishū-chū* (WNS5, p. 175) Nichiren claimed that Space Repository Bodhisattva had given him the wisdom to read all the scriptures of Buddhism and perceive the relative superiority among them and among the schools based on them. In *Ha Ryōkan-tō Gosho* (WNS 5, p. 60), Nichiren claimed that he had been praying to Space Repository Bodhisattva since the age of twelve (or eleven using our way of counting) and he even relates what his initial vow was. It seemed unlikely to me that such a vow would have been made when he was only eleven and had first become a monk and so would not have even learned much about the many different schools and their conflicting teachings. It does make sense that he might have prayed in the main hall of the temple to Space Repository Bodhisattva for wisdom and guidance in his studies and that later on he might have taken up a more rigorous and formal practice such as the *Gumonji-hō* and at that time he very well may have made such a vow. In his documentary on Nichiren's life, Takashi Nakao believes that the *Gumonji-hō* was the practice Nichiren was referring to in these letters. Dr. Stone also writes that Nichiren's letters may indicate that practice. See Stone pp. 243-244. I based my description of Nichiren's practice of the *Gumonji-hō* on Yamasaki, pp. 182-190 and Saso, pp. 37-56.

The story that Nichiren spat out blood, fell into a swoon, and had a vision on the 21st day of his prayer is related in Christensen, p. 26 and Anesaki, pp. 13-14. Nichiren says nothing about being ill in his letters, but if he was practicing the *Gumonji-hō*, then it certainly seems like something that could have happened and would explain his feeling that the bodhisattva personally appeared to him.

The Pure Land of Utmost Bliss

The conversation between Dōzen-bō and Nichiren after his practice of the *Gumonji-hō* is of course speculation, but based upon the kinds of things I imagine a concerned teacher and Pure Land devotee would say. I should also note that the *Gumonji-hō* is a practice that usually takes 100 days but for some reason tradition says that Nichiren received his vision on the 21st day.

The idea that Śākyamuni Buddha faced nine great ordeals is a tradition that Nichiren refers to in *Hokke Gyōja Chinan-ji* (WNS 5, pp. 14-15).

The story of Devadatta's treachery, Ajātaśatru's palace coup, Vaidehī's despair, and the Buddha's teachings regarding the Pure Land of Utmost Bliss of Amitābha Buddha are recounted in the *Three Pure Land Sutras* translated by Hisao Inagaki, and also the anthology *Buddha-Dharma*, pp. 544-569 put out by the Numata Center. An earlier pre-Mahayana version of the story is found in Ñāṇamoli, pp. 257-272. The reference to the traditional idea that women were hindred by the three obediences and five obstacles can be found in *Yakuō-bon Tokui-shō* (WNS 4, p. 33).

The epistemological concept of the three proofs is referred to in *San Sanzō Kiu no Koto* (WNS 3, p. 205).

The four reliances are found in the *Nirvana Sutra*. See Blum, pp. 193-194. Nichiren talks about them in many of his writings, though I specifically am referencing *Ichidai Goju Keizu* (WNS 3, p. 244)

The Exclusive Nembutsu

Nichiren describes his early studies in *Ha Ryōkan-tō Gosho* (WNS 5 p. 60).

Nichiren said that he was exposed to the teachings of Hōnen and Shandao when he was 17 or 18 (16 or 17 in our way of counting) in

Nanjō Hyōe Shichirō-dono Gosho (WNS 3, p. 145). It is not known for sure with whom he studied during his time in Kamakura. I have based the discussion about the Pure Land teachings upon statements Nichiren made in *Shugo Kokka-ron* (WNS 1, p. 4, 30, 32, 37-38, and 49) and *Risshō Ankoku-ron* (WNS 1, pp. 118-121).

The Way of Zen

Likewise, it is not known with whom Nichiren studied Zen. I make the assumption that it must have been with monks connected with the lineage of Dainichi Nōnin (fl. 1190s) since his later criticisms of Zen's origins in Japan curiously make no mention of Eisai (1141-1215) or of Dōgen (1200-1253). Of course today, Dōgen is very well known as the founder of Sōtō Zen in Japan, but in Nichiren's time he was not as well known and lived far from the political center. He had also passed away in 1253. Nichiren may not have been concerned with Eisai because he never established a purely Zen temple, and remained a Tendai monk. Nōnin, however, was the first to promote Zen as a separate school and even in Nichiren's day it would appear that his movement still had adherents, though it would later be eclipsed by the lineages established by expatriate Zen monks from China, such as Lanxi Daolong (1213-1278). The discussion about Zen is based upon *Shugo Kokka-ron* (WNS 1, p. 74), *Senji-shō* (WNS 1, p. 222 and 229), *Kaimoku-shō* (WNS 2, pp. 101-102), *Risshō Kanjō* (WNS 2, p. 233), *Ichidai Goji Keizu* (WNS 3, p. 24), *Ken Hōbō-shō* (WNS 3, p. 125), and *Shoshū Mondō-shō* (WNS 3, pp. 182-185). The kōans that Nichiren referred to may have been case 99 in the *Blue Cliff Record* (see Cleary 1992, p. 546) and case 87 of the *Book of Serenity* (see Cleary 1998, p 372).

Studies in Kyōto

The statement attributed to the Retired Emperor Shirakawa about the three things that refuse to obey his will is in McCullough, p. 50.

Nichiren's idea that the only "good friends" for the Latter Age are the sutras can be found in *Shugo Kokka-ron* (WNS 1, p. 58)

Nāgārjuna's statement about turning poison into medicine is referred to in *Shokyō to Hokkekyō to Nan'i no Koto* (WNS 2 p. 282).

Vasubandhu's statement that the *Lotus Sutra* is like *ghee* is referred to in *Senji-shō* (WNS 1 p. 227).

The Sutra of the Lotus Flower of the Wonderful Dharma

The citations from the *Infinite Meanings Sutra* are taken from Kubo, pp. 21 and 28.

The citations from the *Lotus Sutra* are from LS, pp. 24, 25, 28, 33, 38, 49, 180, 55, 82, 186-187, 198-199, 246, 247, 249, 255, 292, 300, and 311.

The citation from the *Meditation on Universal Sage Bodhisattva Sutra* is derived from Kubo, p. 71.

The citation from the *Nirvana Sutra* is from Blum, pp. 291-292. The argument based on this citation that the *Nirvana Sutra* is a gleaning after the harvest of the *Lotus Sutra* is found in *Shugo Kokka-ron* (WNS 1 p. 12).

The Three Thousand Realms in a Single Thought-Moment

The 3,000 realms in a single thought-moment doctrine is discussed throughout Nichiren's writings but the most thorough exposition is in *Kanjin Honzon-shō* (WNS 2, pp. 127-137).

The enshrinement of the *Lotus Sutra* and the exoteric and esoteric practices based upon it are referred to in *Honzon Mondō-shō* (WNS 2, pp. 259-260). See also *Zemmui-shō* (WNS 4, pp. 52-53). The mantra expressing the gist of the *Lotus Sutra* is found in *Kaimoku-shō* (WNS 2, p. 67). The Japanese way of pronouncing the mantra is given in Murano 2000, p. 60. Nichiren's qualms about esoteric practices involving sitting or stepping on images of the Buddha can be found in *Senji-shō* (WNS 1, p. 229).

Nichiren

Nichiren frequently stated that he began teaching faith in the *Lotus Sutra* and speaking out against Pure Land and Zen on April 28th, 1253. In particular I have drawn upon the following passages: *Shōnin Gonan Ji* (WNS 5 p. 117) and *Seichōji Daishū-chū* (WNS 5 pp. 175-176). Nichiren also stated that it was later that he began to criticize the Mantra school. This is asserted in the letter *Ha Ryōkan-tō Gosho* (WNS 5 p. 60).

Nichiren also recounts his worries and doubts about speaking out and how he overcame them in *Kaimoku-shō* (WNS 2 p. 53), *Hōon-jō* (WNS 3 p. 8), *Yorimoto Chinjō* (WNS 5 pp. 103-104), and *Ichinosawa Nyudō Gosho* (WNS 6 p. 164).

The passages from the *Nirvana Sutra* are from Blum, pp. 79 and 286.

In no extant writing does Nichiren say that he chanted *daimoku* on the morning of April 28th, 1253 but it is traditionally believed that he did so. TB says, "In the early morning of 28th April 1253, it is said that he faced the rising sun and chanted the *Odaimoku* ten times, and newly determined to establish his school."

The passages in the *Lotus Sutra* that inspired Nichiren's choice for his name are in LS, p. 244 and 302. TB says:

"Just before or after Nichiren Shōnin's declaration of his teachings and the establishment of the school, he changed his name to Nichiren. In the following passage of his letter *Shijō Kingo Nyōbō Dono Gosho*

(*Letter to the Wife of Shijō Kingo*) he wrote, "Is there anything brighter than the sun and the moon? Is there anything purer than the lotus flower? The *Lotus Sutra* is the sun and the moon and the lotus flower. Therefore, it is called Myōhō-Renge-Kyō - the *Sutra of the Lotus Flower of the Wonderful Dharma*). Nichiren is also like the sun and the moon, and also like the lotus flower." The word "Nichi" of Nichiren comes from the following passage from the *Nyorai Jinriki* (21st, *Divine Powers of the Tathagata*) chapter of the *Lotus Sutra*: *Nyo nichi gak-kō myō. Nō jo sho yū myō. Shin nin gyō se-ken. Nō metsu shu jō an.* (Just like the sun and the moon can dispel darkness, such a person practicing in the world can dispel the fundamental darkness of all living beings.) and "Ren" is derived from the *Juji Yujutsu* (15th, *Springing up from the Earth*) chapter of the *Lotus Sutra*: *Fu sen se ken bō. Nyo ren ge zai sui* (They are untainted by the ways of the world, just as a lotus flower in the water). The name of "Nichiren" appears [written] for the first time in (*Fudō - Aizen Kan Ken Ki, Annotations of Sensing and Envisioning Fudō and Aizen*) on 25th June 1254."

Refutation of Hōnen's Pure Land Teaching

Nichiren's refutation of Pure Land Buddhism and Hōnen in particular are taken primarily from *Shugo Kokka-ron* (WNS 1 pp. 3-5, 12-13, 24-25, 31-37, 44-46, 60-61). I supplemented those with a passage from *Shoshū Mondō-shō* (WNS 3 pp. 187-188).

Refutation of Zen Buddhism

Nichiren's refutation of Zen is from *Shoshū Mondō-shō* (WNS 3 pp. 182-185).

The *Daimoku* of the *Lotus Sutra*

The argument for the merits of practicing the *Lotus Sutra* and specifically chanting the *daimoku* are from *Shugo Kokka-ron* (WNS 1 pp. 39-42, 65, 67-68)

The passages from the *Lotus Sutra* that Nichiren cites in regard to its supremacy are found in LS, pp. 36, 38-39, 247, and 187. The passages that Nichiren related to the practice of *daimoku* are found in LS, pp. 227, 336, 203. The passages relating to the pure land of Śākyamuni Buddha are found in LS, pp. 248, 253, 254.

Driven Out

The passage about being driven from the monastery is from LS, p. 214. The passages relating to the determination to speak out even if faced with death are from LS, p. 214 and Blum, p. 95.

Nichiren's difficulties with Tōjō Kagenobu and the monks Enchi-bō and Jitsujō-bō are recounted in the following: *Hōon-jō* (WNS 3 pp. 48-49) and *Seichōji Daishū-chū* (WNS 5 pp. 176). In regard to his being forced out of Seichōji, TB states:

"Just as Nichiren Shōnin had felt might happen, immediately after he began his teachings and declared the founding of his school, a persecution began causing him to flee Seichōji. From outside the temple, Tōjō Kagenobu, and within Seichōji, the priests Enchibō and Jitsujōbō, put pressure on Dozenbō. Dozenbō was not able to shield his beloved disciple, Nichiren Shōnin. Regarding his having to flee, it is said that it occurred on the day Nichiren Shōnin first revealed his teachings and established his school. However, it is thought that this most probably occurred after 3rd September 1254. The reasons for his expulsion are probably due to his religious convictions and criticism of *nembutsu* together with Tōjō Kagenobu's scheming ambitions to enlarge his domination over the area while obstructing Nichiren Shōnin who stood on the side of the vassals."

Nichiren's writing *Ōshajō-ji* (WNS 6, p. 128) states that Dōzen-bō disowned him and that his parents tried to restrain him. His reaction to this is also taken from that letter.

The citations from the *Lotus Sutra* are from LS, pp. 214. The citation from the *Nirvana Sutra* is from Blum, p. 197.

Disasters

The description of people turning to Hōnen's version of Pure Land teachings to the detriment of other forms of Buddhism is taken from *Risshō Ankoku-ron* (WNS 1, p. 134).

The religious trends of Kamakura during the period Nichiren lived there are described in Sansom pp. 424-437. In addition, I found the books and articles by Collcutt, Kasahara, Kashiwahara, Maas, Matsunaga, and Stone extremely helpful in understanding what was happening in Kamakura and Japan at that time and who the major figures were.

The comparison of the *Lotus Sutra* to a clear mirror and the comparison of it to the ocean are both found in *Shoshū Mondō-shō* (WNS 3, p. 176 and 179 respectively).

The Shōka famine of 1257-1260 is described in Farris, pp. 51-59. The disasters and political situation are also described in Sansom, pp. 416-417, and the growing threat of the Mongols is described on pp. 438-439.

The description Nichiren gives of the disasters and their effects can be found in *Risshō Ankoku-ron* (WNS 1, pp. 107-108). See also Murano 2003, pp. 11-12. The reference to the *Lotus Sutra* curing disease can be found in LS, p. 313. Nichiren also discusses the disasters and his motivations for writing *Risshō Ankoku-ron* in *Sainan Kōki Yurai* (WNS 1, *pp. 81-88*), *Sainan Taiji-shō* (Ibid, pp. 89-104),

368

Ankoku-ron Soejō (Ibid, pp. 144-145), *Ankoku-ron Gokanyurai* (Ibid, pp. 146-151), and *Ankoku-ron Okugaki* (Ibid, pp. 154-155).

The various disasters and omens are also described in the historical chronicle known as the *Azuma kagami* (*Mirror of the East*), the entries of which for the years 1254-1260 are translated in Rodd, footnote 46 on pp. 24-25.

Spreading Peace by Establishing the True Dharma

Nichiren frequently mentions submitting the *Risshō Ankoku-ron* (WNS 1, pp. 105-143) through Yadoya Mitsunori. However, in *Ko Saimyōji Nyūdō Kenzan Gosho* (WNS 1 p. 156) it would seem that Nichiren did in fact have a face-to-face meeting with Hōjō Tokiyori. However, what they might have discussed beyond the brief statement in that letter is of course purely speculative. For that reason, I have written of the meeting as a kind of daydream drawing upon the dialogue in the *Risshō Ankoku-ron*. I have also drawn from the *Ankoku-ron Gokanyurai* (Ibid, p. 147-150) and *Shimoyama Goshōsoku* (WNS 5, p. 83).

The statement in the *Lotus Sutra* about the superiority of the person who keeps the sutra is from LS, p. 311.

The *Nirvana Sutra*'s description of the corrupt monks is from Blum, p. 113.

The Riot at Matsubagayatsu

The religious debates, harassment, and the attack by a mob are described in *Rondan Tekitai Gosho* (WNS 5, p. 2), *Ha Ryōkan-tō Gosho* (Ibid, pp. 61-62), and *Shimoyama Goshōsoku* (Ibid, p. 83). The *Rondan Tekitai Gosho* also mentions the involvement of Dōami and Nōan.

The dialogue in this chapter is taken from *Shugo Kokka-ron* (WNS 1 pp. 50-51, 56), *Sainan Kōki Yurai* (Ibid, p. 87), *Sainan Taiji-shō* (Ibid, p. 103), *Risshō Ankoku-ron* (Ibid, p. 124), *Ichidai Shōgyō Tai-i* (WNS 3 pp. 82-84, 91, 95), and *Shō Hokke Daimoku-shō* (WNS 4 pp. 3-5, 7,8, 13, 15, 17, 58-59).

Citations from the *Lotus Sutra* are from LS, pp. 180, 292-293, and 346.

The Izu Exile

The Izu exile is described or mentioned in *Ha Ryōkan-tō Gosho* (WNS 5, p. 62), *Shimoyama Goshōsoku* (Ibid, p. 83), *Shōnin Gonan Ji* (Ibid, p. 118), and *Ichinosawa Nyūdo Gosho* (WNS 6, p. 161).

The Jōei Code was instituted by the shogunate in 1232. It is described in Sansom, pp. 394-399.

The meeting with Funamori Yasuburō is taken from the *Funamori Yasuburō Moto Gosho* that is partially translated in the HS, pp. 367-368. There are no extant copies of that writing.

The citation from the *Lotus Sutra* is from LS, pp. 184

Nichiren talks about Minamoto no Yoritomo in connection with Izu in the *Ichinosawa Nyūdo Gosho* (WNS 6, p. 161) and tells a story that relates Yoritomo's devotion to the *Lotus Sutra* in *Nanjō-dono Gohenji* (WNS 7, p. 20). Yoritomo's practice of reciting the *Lotus Sutra* is also mentioned in McCullough, p. 183.

There is no record of what may or may not have been said between Nichiren and Lord Itō, so I have derived this fictional dialogue from *Nanjō Hyōe Shichirō-dono Gosho* (WNS 3, p. 138), *Kitō-shō* (WNS 4, p. 68), *Ben-dono Goshōsoku* (WNS 5, p. 182), and *Kaen Jōgō*

Gosho (WNS 7, pp. 112-114). The gift of the statue of the Buddha and its origins is told in the *Funamori Yasuburō Moto Gosho*.

The Five Guides for Propagation

The discussion of the five guides for propagation is taken from *Shugo Kokka-ron* (WNS 1, p. 26), *Kyō Ki Ji Koku Shō* (WNS 3, pp. 96-104), *Ken Hōbō-shō* (Ibid, p. 123), *Nanjō Hyōe Shichirō-dono Gosho* (Ibid, pp. 138-144), and *Shō Hokke Daimoku-shō* (WNS 4, pp. 21-24).

The analogy of the poison drum is from Blum, p. 291.

The citation from the *Lotus Sutra* is from LS, p. 313.

The Three Kinds of Enemies

Nichiren's understanding of the three kinds of enemies is mentioned in early writings but it is in *Kaimoku-shō* (WNS 2, pp. 91-93) that he cites the whole passage and also the citation from Miaole.

The citation from the *Lotus Sutra* is from LS, pp. 212-215.

The Komatsubara Ambush

Nichiren's pardon is mentioned in *Ha Ryōkan-tō Gosho* (WNS 5, p. 62), *Shimoyama Goshōsoku* (WNS 5, p. 84), and *Ichinosawa Nyūdo Gosho* (WNS 6, p. 161).

The content of Nichiren's early talks is derived from *Hokke Daimoku-shō* (WNS 4, pp. 36-37, 39) and *Gassui Gosho* (NG p. 36 and 38).

Nichiren's description of the comet of 1264 is taken from *Ankoku-ron Gokanyurai* (WNS 1 p. 149) and *Hōren-shō* (*Letter to Hōren*, WNS 6, p. 60). There is also a Wikipedia entry for the "Great Comet of 1264."

Nichiren's prayer for his mother and her recovery is described in *Hōkikō Gobō Goshōsoku* (WNS 5, pp. 209-210) and *Kaen Jōgō Gosho* (WNS 7, p. 113).

The meeting between Nichiren and Dōzen-bō is described in the *Zemmui Sanzō-shō* (See Yampolsky 1996, pp. 130-133). The dialogue is derived partly from that writing, but also from *Nanjō Hyōe Shichirō-dono Gosho* (WNS 3, p. 140) and *Hōmon Mōsaru-beki-yō no Koto* (WNS 5, p. 142). They are supposed to have met after Tōjō Kagenobu's ambush, but in this case I am exercising literary license and having it occur before the ambush for the sake of narrative flow.

Nichiren describes Lord Kagenobu's ambush in *Nanjō Hyōe Shichirō-dono Gosho* (WNS 3, pp. 145-146) and *Shōnin Gonan Ji* (WNS 5, p. 118).

The story of King Virtuous in the *Nirvana Sutra* can be found in Blum, pp. 96-97.

The citation from the *Lotus Sutra* are from LS, pp. 76-77, 180, and 214. Also see pp. 39, 46-47.

The Great Mongol Empire

Background on the letter from the Mongo Empire can be found in Sansom, pp. 438-440, though he gives a date for the installation of Tokimune as regent that is different from other sources. I found the Wikipedia article, "Mongol invasions of Japan" a helpful starting point for research. I also drew upon the article by Kenneth Chase that includes a translation of the letter sent to Japan in 1268 that is kept at Todaiji.

The *Ankoku-ron Soejō* (WNS 1 p. 144) is believed to have been a cover letter to a copy of the Risshō Ankoku-ron submitted to Hōjō

Tokimune. See also *Ankoku-ron Okugaki* (WNS 1, p. 155) for Nichiren's reaction to the arrival of the Mongol letter.

Ankoku-ron Gokanyurai (WNS 1, p. 149-150) is the letter to Hōkan-bō.

Yadoya Nyūdō Sai-gōjō (WNS 1, p. 152-153) is Nichiren's second letter to Yadoya Mitsunori in which he complains of having received no reply from an earlier letter.

That Nichiren sent out eleven letters is attested to in *Shuju Onfurumai Gosho* (WNS 5, p. 22). Nichiren also wrote about this to Ōta Jōmyō in *Kingo-dono Go-henji* (WNS 1, pp. 158-159).

Nichiren's reaction to the letter from the Mongols is also recorded in *San Sanzō Kiu no Koto* (WNS 3, p. 205) written in 1275. This later writing also mentions a revolt of the Ainu in the year 1268 and Nichiren's misgivings about the Mantra school prayers that were to be commissioned for the protection of Japan. I could find no further information about an Ainu revolt and since it is not so important to the story I have not mentioned it. As for Nichiren's criticism of the Mantra school and its teachings, Nichiren does not begin to voice them (or write them down) in detail in the extant writings from around 1268 and 1269.

Ryōkan of the Mantra-Precept School

Nichiren's challenge to Ryōkan, the prayers for rain, its outcome, and Nichiren's refutation of the Precepts school are recounted in *Shuju Onfurumai Gosho* (WNS 5, pp. 26-27), *Shimoyama Goshōsoku* (Ibid, pp. 71-77), and *Yorimoto Chinjō* (Ibid, pp. 105-107, 111).

For background on Ryōkan and fund raising activities in Kamakura see Matsuo, pp. 101-102 and 105-108. Also see Matsunaga, pp.

281-283 for the history of the Mantra-Precepts (J. Shingon-Ritsu) school.

The citation from the *Vimalakirti Sutra* can be found in Thurman, p. 28.

Nichiren makes a lot of claims about Ryōkan's statements and actions in response to his own refutations and challenges. It certainly does not seem from Nichiren's writings that he was getting this information first hand. So who was reporting Ryōkan's responses to Nichiren? I noticed that Nichiren states in *Yorimoto Chinjō* that disciples of Ryōkan were his messengers. Why were these men on hand to deliver messages? It occurred to me that certain unscrupulous individuals may have been carrying messages back and forth between Matsubagayatsu and Gokurakuji not as a favor to either Nichiren or Ryōkan but simply because they enjoyed the controversy and perhaps were stirring it up in the way they reported what was allegedly said and done by both sides.

Hei no Saemon Yoritsuna

Gyōbin Gohenji (WNS 5, pp. 3-4) records the letter from Gyōbin and Nichiren's response to it.

Nichiren's response to the accusations brought against him by Ryōkan and others is found in *Gyōbin Sojō Goetsū* (WNS 5, pp. 5-9).

The citation from the *Infinite Meanings Sutra* is adapted from Kubo, p. 21.

The reference to "those in white robes who wield weapons" in the *Nirvana Sutra* is from Blum, p. 98.

Nichiren's states his belief that a campaign of rumor and gossip was being waged behind the scenes against him in *Hōon-jō* (WNS 3, pp. 47-48).

The meeting with Hei no Saemon and the Council of State is recounted in *Shuju Onfurumai Gosho* (WNS 5, pp. 25-27). Nichiren's counsels withholding offerings rather than executing slanderers in *Risshō Ankoku-ron* (WNS 1, pp. 136-137).

The citations from the *Lotus Sutra* are from LS, pp. 82 and 214.

The Tatsunokuchi Persecution

Nichiren's arrest and the attempted execution is described in *Shuju Onfurumai Gosho* (WNS 5, p. 26-29). It is also described in *Senji-shō* (WNS 1, p. 243-244). Additional dialogue is taken from *Shimoyama Goshōsoku* (WNS 5, pp. 84-85) and *Kōnichi-bō Gosho* (Ibid, p. 48). Additional references and details are from *Kangyō Hachiman-shō* (WNS 1, p. 268), *Hōon-jō* (WNS 3, pp. 32-33 and 47-48), *Hōren-shō* (WNS 6, p. 59-60), and *Nanjō-dono Gohenji* (WNS 7, p. 21).

The citations from the *Lotus Sutra* are from LS, p. 212, 329

The Sado Exile

Nichiren's statement about having been beheaded is from *Kaimoku-shō* (WNS 2, p. 91).

Nichiren's statement about Tatsunokuchi being a budda-land is taken from *Shijo Kingo-dono Goshōsoku* (HS, pp. 370-371).

The events in this chapter and Nichiren's reactions and reflections are based on *Teradomari Gosho* (WNS 2, pp. 9-14), *Ueno-dono Gohenji* (WNS 4, pp. 112-113), *Nyosetsu Shugyō-shō* (*Ibid*, p. 86), *Shuju*

Onfurumai Gosho (WNS 5, p. 29-33), *Hōren-shō* (WNS 6, p. 58-59), and *Nii-ama Gozen Gohenji* (WNS 7, p. 150).

Toki-dono Gohenji (WNS 5, pp. 10-11) is the letter written to Toki Jōnin from Echi.
Gonin Tsuchirō Gosho (WNS 5, pp. 153) is the letter written to his imprisoned disciples.

The passage from a letter written to his lay supporters about the persecution he was facing is from *Tenjū Kyōju Hōmon* (WNDS 6, pp. 29-31).

Open Your Eyes

The criticisms directed at Nichiren are taken from *Teradomari Gosho* (WNS2, pp. 12)

This chapter is an attempt to summarize *Kaimoku-shō* (WNS 2, pp. 29-117). In particular see pp. 39, 58, 91, 105-106.

The *Lotus Sutra* citations in this chapter are from LS, pp. 82 and 180.

The Tsukahara Debate

The events and dialogue in this chapter are based on *Teradomari Gosho* (WNS 2, pp. 11-12), *Kaimoku-shō* (Ibid, pp. 36, 78-79, 84-85, 89, and 109-115), *Toki-dono Go-henji* (Ibid, p. 119), *Hōon-jō* (WNS 3, p. 41-46), *Kyō Ki Ji Koku Shō* (Ibid, pp. 100), *Shoshū Mondō-shō* (Ibid, pp. 186-187), *Shuju Onfurumai Gosho* (WNS 5, p. 34-37), *Shimoyama Goshōsoku* (Ibid, p. 92), *Yorimoto Chinjō* (Ibid, p. 102), *Hōmon Mōsaru-beki-yō no Koto* (Ibid, p. 146), *Shijō Kingo-dono Gohenji* (WNS 6, p. 116), and *Ueno-dono Gohenji* (WNS 7, p. 5).

Citations from the *Lotus Sutra* are from LS, pp. 83-84, 182, and 222.

Superior Practice Bodhisattva

The events and dialogue of this chapter are based on *Shuju Onfurumai Gosho* (WNS 5, p. 36-38).

The fighting in Kamakura and Kyōto in February of 1272 is discussed in Susumu, p. 137. Nichiren also refers to it in *Kyōdai-shō* (WNS 6, p. 78).

Nichiren's comparison of himself with Never Despising Bodhisattva can be found in *Teradomari Gosho* (WNS 2, p. 13) and *Kembutsu Mirai-ki* (Ibid, p. 174).

The letter to Shijo Kingō cited is *Shijō Kingo-dono Gohenji* (WNS 6, p. 117).

Nichiren's thoughts regarding his identity as a practitioner of the *Lotus Sutra*, an envoy of Śākyamuni Buddha, and even as an appearance of Superior Practice Bodhisattva is based on *Toki-dono Go-henji* (WNS 2, p. 118), *Kembutsu Mirai-ki* (Ibid, p. 175), *Hokke Shuyō-shō* (Ibid, p. 210), *Shohō Jissō-shō* (WNS 4, p. 75, 77-79), *Nyosetsu Shugyō-shō* (Ibid, pp. 81-88), and *Yoritimo Chinjō* (WNS5, p. 105).

For background on the creation of the mandala see Stone, p. 437 footnote 114.

Citations from the *Lotus Sutra* are from LS, p. 177, 180, 212, 214, 228, 234, 292-293, 300, 313

Contemplation of the Mind and the Focus of Devotion

The events and dialogue of this chapter are based on *Shingon Shoshū Imoku* (WNS 2, p. 125), *Sennichi-ama Gozen Gohenji* (WNS 4, pp. 150-151), *Shuju Onfurumai Gosho* (WNS 5, p. 37-38), *Kōnichi-bō*

Gosho (Ibid, p. 49), and *Ichinosawa Nyūdō Gosho* (WNS 6, pp. 163-165).

The text of the cover letter is from *Kanjin Honzon-shō Soejō* (WNS 2, pp. 168-169)

The instruction to chant *daimoku* and contemplate the 3,000 realms in a single thought-moment is from *Jisshō-shō* (WNS 2, p. 4).

The summary of *Kanjin Honzon-shō* is based on *Kanjin Honzon-shō* (WNS 2, p. 127-164).

Nichiren's teaching to Sairen-bō is based on *Shohō Jissō-shō* (WNS 4, p. 78-80) and *Nyosetsu Shugyō-shō* (WNS 4, p. 83-84).

The visions of Fudō Myō-ō and Aizen Myō-ō are recounted in *Fudō Aizen Kanken-ki* (WNS 5, p. 1).

Citations from the *Lotus Sutra* are from LS, pp. 38-39, and 243.

Final Admonition

The events, thoughts, and dialogue of this chapter are based on *Senji-shō* (WNS 1, p. 243), *Misawa-shō* (WNS 2, p. 243), *Hōon-jō* (WNS 3, p. 48), *Shuju Onfurumai Gosho* (WNS 5, p. 38-42), *Kōnichi-bō Gosho* (Ibid, p. 49-50), *Shimoyama Goshōsoku* (Ibid, p. 87), *Hōren-shō* (WNS 6, p. 60-61), and *Takahashi Nyūdō-dono Gohenji* (WNS 7, p. 78-79).

The Hermitage at Mt. Minobu

The events, thoughts, and dialogue in this chapter are based on *Kangyō Hachiman-shō* (WNS 1, p. 269), *Shuju Onfurumai Gosho* (WNS 5, pp. 42, 45-46), *Toki-dono Gosho* (Ibid, p. 18), *Kōnichi-bō Gosho* (Ibid, p. 50), *Ajichi Shūfuku-sho* (*Ibid*, p. 113), *Bōjikyō Ji*

(WNS 6, p. 13-14), *Kyōdai-shō* (Ibid, p. 78), *Hyōesakan-dono Gohenji* (Ibid, p. 102), *Ichinosawa Nyūdō Gosho* (*Ibid*, p. 166-167), *Ueno-dono Gohenji* (*Reply to Lord Ueno*, WNS 7, p. 1), *Nii-ama Gozen Gohenji* (Ibid, p. 147), and *Mushiro Sammai Gosho* (Ibid, p. 187).

Selecting the Right Time

The summary of *Senji-shō* is based on *Senji-shō* (WNS1, p. 189, 193, 196, 237-238, 242-244, 246, 249).

The citations from the *Lotus Sutra* are from LS, pp. 36 and 311.

Gratitude

That Nichiren's teachings were different before and after the Sado exile is his own assertion. It is made in *Misawa-shō* (WNS 2, pp. 241-242).

The summary of *Hōon-jō* is based on *Hōon-jō* (WNS3, p. 1-2, 47-48, 57-58).

The further explanations of the three great hidden Dharmas is from *Sandai Hihō Honjō-ji* (WNS 2, pp. 286-291).

The citation from the *Lotus Sutra* is from LS, p. 311.

Letters of Instruction and Encouragement

The events, thoughts, and written statements in this chapter are based on *Sushun Tennō Gosho* (WNS 4, pp. 122-123, 124), *Yorimoto Chinjō* (WNS 5, pp. 99-112), *Shōnin Gonan Ji* (Ibid, p. 117-20), *Ryūsenji Mōshijō* (Ibid, p. 199-201), *Hendoku Iyaku Gosho* (Ibid, pp. 202-203), *Kyōdai-shō* (WNS 6, p. 78, 83-84), *Hyōesakan-dono Gosho* (Ibid, p. 89), *Hyōesakan-dono Gohenji* (Ibid, p. 92), *Kōshi*

Gosho (Ibid, pp. 103-104), *Ōshajō-ji* (Ibid, pp. 127, 128), *Shijō Kingo-dono Gohenji* (Ibid, p. 138), *Shijō Kingo-dono Gohenji* (Ibid, p. 142), *Fukō Gosho – Intoku Yōhō Goho* (Ibid, pp. 148-149), and *Shijō Kingo-dono Gohenji* (Ibid, pp. 150-151).

See Stone 2014, p. 169, for more on the persecution of Nichiren's followers at Atsuhara.

The Divine Winds

The events, thoughts, and written statements in this chapter are from *Kangyō Hachiman-shō* (WNS 1, p. 257-280), *Jibiki Gosho* (WNS 5, p. 122), *Rōbyō Gosho* (Ibid, p. 124), *Hakii-dono Gohō* (Ibid, p. 132-133), *Chimyō-bō Gohenji* (Ibid, p. 206-208), *Toki Nyūdō-dono Gohenji* (WNS 6, p. 26), *Ueno-dono Gohenji* (WNS 7, p. 5), *Nanjō-dono Gohenji* (Ibid, p. 21), *Ueno-dono Haha-ama Gozen Gohenji* (Ibid, p. 62), *Matsuno-dono Gohenji* (Ibid, p. 69), and *Toki-ama Gozen Gosho* (Ibid, p. 117).

The second attempt by the Mongols to invade Japan is described in Sansom pp. 445-450.

At the Beginning

The thoughts and events in this chapter are inspired by passages from *Shohō Jissō-shō* (WNS 4, p. 76), *Nyosetsu Shugyō-shō* (Ibid, pp. 87-88), *Myōhō-ama Gozen Gohenji* (Ibid, pp. 140-143), *Kō no Ama Gozen Gohenji* (WNS 7, p. 167), and HS, pp. 383, 399-400.

Citations from the *Lotus Sutra* are from LS, pp. 252-255.

Glossary

Abbreviation of word origins:
C = Chinese; J = Japanese; S = Sanskrit

abhidharma: In S., "higher Dharma." A systematization of the Buddha's teachings in the sutras.

Abhidharma Treasury school: (J. Kusha Shū) The Abhidharma Treasury School was based on the study of the *Abhidharma-kośa-bhāshya* of Vasubandhu that was translated into Chinese by Paramārtha (499-569) between 563-567 and again by Xuanzang (602-664) between 651-654. Japanese monks who had gone to China to study with Xuanzang brought this school to Japan in 658. In Japan it was called the Kusha Shū. By 793, the Abhidharma Treasury School was merely a curriculum taught within the Dharma Characteristics School.

Ajātaśatru: The son of King Bimbisāra, who overthrew his father and was for a time a patron of Devadatta. He eventually repented and became a lay supporter of the Buddha and sponsored the first Buddhist council after the passing of Śākyamuni Buddha. He was present among those assembled to hear the *Lotus Sutra*. He is often cited as an example of how Buddhism can save even evil and seemingly incorrigible people.

Amaterasu Ōmikami: The Japanese Sun Goddess and also believed to be the ancestor of the Japan's imperial family. Also called Tenshō Daijin.

Amitābha: (J., Amida Butsu) The Buddha of Infinite Light who resides in the Western Pure Land or Pure Land of Utmost Bliss. An enjoyment-body buddha.

Amoghavajra: (705-774) One of the disseminators of the mantra teachings and practices in China. He was a disciple of Vajrabodhi. He retranslated the *Diamond Peak Sutra*.

Ānanda: One of the ten major disciples of Śākyamuni Buddha. He was a cousin of the Buddha, his personal attendant, and the monk responsible for memorizing all of the Buddha's discourses or sutras, therefore known as foremost in hearing the sutras. It is Ānanda who says, "Thus have I heard..." at the beginning of every sutra.

Aniruddha: One of the ten major disciples of Śākyamuni Buddha. He was foremost in clairvoyant abilities developed through meditation.

Annen: (b. 841) A monk of the Tendai school who studied under Jikaku and later wrote many works concerning both esoteric and exoteric Buddhism.

Antoku: (1177-1185) The 81st emperor of Japan from 1180-1185. He was drowned at the Battle of Dan-no-Ura when the Minamoto defeated the Taira.

arhat: In S., "worthy one." An arhat is a "voice-hearer" (*śrāvaka*), a disciple of the Buddha, who has extinguished the three poisons and broken free of the wheel of becoming, thereby attaining nirvana.

Āryasimha: (c. 6th century CE) According to the *History of the Transmission of the Dharma Treasury* (a text that appeared in 472 CE, alleging to be a Chinese translation from Sanskrit) he was last of the 24 patriarchs who transmitted the Dharma after Śākyamuni Buddha. He was martyred in Kashmir by a king opposed to Buddhism. According to Zen, there were four more Indian patriarchs after Āryasimha.

asaṃkhya: In S., "incalculable" or "innumerable."

asuras: In S., "nongods." The fighting demons cast down from the heavens by the gods.

Aśvaghoṣa: (c. 1ˢᵗ – 2ⁿᵈ century CE) An influential Indian Mahayana teacher and poet in the second century CE. Considered to be one of the 24 (or 28) Indian patriarchs who transmitted the Dharma after Śākyamuni Buddha.

Bi Gan: An uncle of the last king of the Shang or Yin dynasty (c. 1600-1046 B.C.E) who remonstrated with his corrupt and evil nephew, King Zhou. The evil king then ordered Bi Gan executed by having his heart extracted, on the pretext that he wanted to know if a sage's heart had seven openings.

Bimbisāra: The king of Magadha and a patron of Śākyamuni Buddha. He was overthrown, imprisoned, and then starved to death by his son Ajātaśatru.

bodhi: In S., "awakening" or "enlightenment."

bodhisattva: In S., "awakening being." A being dedicated to attaining buddhahood or spiritual awakening for the sake of all sentient beings.

bodhisattvas who emerge from the earth: (J. *jiyū no bosatsu*) The bodhisattvas led by Superior Practice, Limitless Practice, Pure Practice, and Steadily Established Practice, who appear from the space beneath the Sahā world in the 15th chapter of the *Lotus Sutra*. They are the original disciples of the Eternal Shakyamuni Buddha. In chapter 21 they receive the specific transmission from the Buddha to teach the Wonderful Dharma in the Latter Age of Degeneration.

Brahmā: The creator god of the Brahmanistic pantheon. In Buddhism, he is considered a protector of the Dharma.

Brahmanism: The mainstream religion of India at the time of Śākyamuni Buddha. Later developed into what is today known as Hinduism.

buddha: In S., "awakened one." Someone who has awakened to the true reality of all existence and then teaches the Dharma so as to free all beings from suffering.

Buddha Dharma: The true nature of reality; also, the teachings of a buddha.

cause-knower: Another term for a private-buddha. Called such because they awaken to the true nature of reality through the contemplation of causes and conditions.

Chishō: (814-891) The fifth abbot of Enryakuji, and therefore head of the Tendai school. Along with Jikaku, he was also responsible for the development of the mantra teachings and practices in the Tendai school. Also known as Enchin.

Completion of Reality school: (J. Jōjitsu Shū) The Completion of Reality school focused on the study of the *Completion of Reality Treatise* (S. *Satyasiddhi-śāstra*) by an Indian monk named Harivarman (c. 4th century) that was translated by Kumārajīva between 411-412. It is primarily an abhidharma work, but it also teaches the emptiness of all phenomena and so is considered a good introduction to Mahāyāna teachings. The Korean monk Hyegwan brought the Establishment of Truth School to Japan in 625, where it became known as the Jōjitsu Shū. By 806 it had become no more than a curriculum taught within the Sanron Shū.

daimoku: In J., "sacred title." Refers to the practice of chanting the title of the *Lotus Sutra* in the form of Namu Myōhō Renge Kyō.

Dainichi Nōnin: (n.d.) A Japanese monk who founded the Bodhidharma school of Zen Buddhism in the late 12ᵗʰ century.

Daochuo: (562-645) Considered by Hōnen to be the second patriarch in China of Pure Land Buddhism.

Dengyō: (767-822) The founder of the Japanese Tendai school and of the temple Enryakuji on Mt. Hie. Also known as Saichō.

Devadatta: The treacherous cousin of the Buddha. He fell into hell upon death but according to the Buddha's prediction in chapter twelve of the *Lous Sutra*, he too will eventually attain buddhahood.

dhāraṇīs: (S) These are a type of incantation composed of "seed syllables" whose power is in their sound and not their meaning. They are, or originally were, a form of mnemonic device to help retain in memory a longer text and also to hold the power of that text or of the being that bestows the *dhāraṇīs*.

Dharma: (S) In Buddhism it can mean truth, law, reality, or the teachings of the Buddha depending on the context.

dharma: (S) In English, the lower case form of Dharma is sometimes used when the word refers to "phenomena," "realities," "entities," or "events."

Dharma-body: (S. *Dharma-kāya;* J. *hosshin*) The universal body of a buddha, which is reality itself. One of the three bodies of a buddha.

Dharma Characteristics school: (J. Hossō Shū) The East Asian form of the Consciousness-Only school based on the translations and commentaries of Xuanzang (602-664) and his disciple Kuiji (632-682). The Dharma Characteristics School was first brought to Japan by the Japanese monk Dōshō (629-700) who had traveled to

China to study with Xuanzang and then returned in 661. In Japan it is called the Hossō Shū.

Dharma-kāya: In S., "Dharma-body."

Dōkyō: (700-772) A monk who tried, unsuccesffully, to become emperor of Japan.

Dōryū: See Lanxi Daolong.

Dōzen-bō: (d. 1276) The abbot of Seichōji temple and Nichiren's master when he was a young monk.

Eagle Peak: (S. Gridharkūta; J. Ryōju-sen) The small mountain northeast of the city of Rājagriha where Śākyamuni Buddha taught the *Lotus Sutra*.

eighteen elements: (S. *dhātu*) The six sense bases, their six objects, and the six kinds of consciousness corresponding to the six sense bases and their respective objects.

eighteenth vow: See Original Vow.

eightfold path: The middle way consisting of right view, right intention, right speech, right action, right livelihood, right effort, right mindfulness, and right concentration.

eight kinds of nonhuman beings: Eight kinds of beings who appear in the sutras as guardians of Buddhism. They are the gods (S. *deva*), dragons (S. *nāga*, spirits of rivers, oceans, and rain), nature spirits (S. *yakṣa*), heavenly musicians (S. *gandharva*); fighting demons (S. *asura*); giant birds (S. *garuda*); heavenly singers (S. *kiṃnara*); and giant serpents (S. *mahoraga*). Some of these beings are mutual enemies, such as the gods and the fighting demons, and the dragons and the giant birds that prey on them, but in Buddhism they are all reconciled as devotees of the Dharma.

eight precepts of abstinence: Every two weeks on the days of the new moon and full moon when the monks and nuns gather to recite their own monastic precepts the laity may also opt to follow not only the usual five precepts for the laity but also three additional precepts so that their lives are more in line with the monastics. These three are: not to wear perfume or makeup or attend dances or performances, not to rest in an elevated bed or chair, and not to eat after noon.

Eisai: (1141-1215) The first Japanese monk to travel to China and bring back the teachings of Rinzai Zen.

Eison: (1201-1290) The founder of the Mantra-Precepts school.

emanation buddhas of the ten directions: The buddhas of the worlds of the ten directions who are shown to be emanations of Śākyamuni Buddha in chapter 11 of the *Lotus Sutra*.

enjoyment-body: (S. *sambhoga-kāya*; J. *hōjin*) The ideal body of a buddha. It is the buddha's enjoyment of awakening which is shared by the bodhisattvas. This is sometimes translated as "reward-body." One of the three bodies of a buddha.

Enryakuji: The head temple of the Tendai school in Japan on Mt. Hiei. Founded by Dengyō.

Eternal Buddha: (J. *hombutsu*) Also, and more literally, translated as Original Buddha. See Eternal Śākyamuni Buddha.

Eternal Śākyamuni Buddha: The unity of the historical, ideal, and universal aspects of the buddha in the person of Śākyamuni Buddha. Nichiren understood the Tiantai teachings to mean that all three of the three bodies of the buddha are without beginning or end and are possessed by Śākyamuni Buddha as revealed in the 16th chapter of the *Lotus Sutra*. Also called the Original Buddha since all other buddhas are emanations of the Eternal Buddha.

final nirvana: (S) "final extinction." Refers to the death of an arhat, private-buddha, or buddha. In East Asian Mahayana, this was seen derogatorily as "reducing the body to ashes and annihilating consciousness."

five aggregates: The components of a sentient being: form, feeling, perception, mental formations, and consciousness.

five constant virtues: The five basic virtues derived from the teachings of Confucius: benevolence, righteousness, propriety, wisdom, and trustworthiness.

five grave offences: The five worst offenses for which one will immediately fall into the Hell of Incessant Suffering after death. They are: killing one's father, killing one's mother, killing an arhat, injuring a Buddha, and causing a schism in the Sangha.

five kinds of eyes: Refers to five different ways of seeing the world: the physical eye of ordinary people, the heavenly eye that sees the deaths and rebirths of all beings in the triple world, the wisdom eye that sees the emptiness of all phenomena, the dharma-eye that sees the attainments of noble beings and bodhisattvas, and the buddha-eye that sees the true nature of all things.

five precepts: The five precepts for lay people: not to kill, not to steal, not to engage in sexual misconduct, not to lie, and not to indulge in intoxicants.

five principles for propagation: (J. *gogi* or *gokō*) Nichiren's teaching that a teacher of Buddhism must take into account the teaching, the capacity of the people, the time, the country, and the sequence of spreading the Buddha's teachings.

Flower Garland school: (J. Kegon Shū) The Flower Garland school considers the *Flower Garland Sutra* the Buddha's highest teaching. It was established by Dushun (557-640), though its third patriarch, Fazang (643-712) was the true founder of the school. The Chinese monk Daoxuan (702-760) introduced the Flower Garland School to Japan in 736, but its establishment as a school is credited to the Korean monk Simsang (d. 742), a student of Fazang who gave a lecture to the emperor on the Flower Garland teachings in 740.

focus of devotion: (J., *honzon*) The primary buddha, deity, or principle venerated by a particular school of Buddhism or temple and the image depicting it, whether a statue, portrait, or mandala. Sometimes an extra honorific is used and it is called *gohonzon*.

four devils: Four things which distract or scare people away from enlightenment. They are the devil of the aggregates (mental and physical needs), the devil of the defilements (self-centered desires), the devil of death (fear of death), and the devil king of the sixth heaven (fear of the unknown and craving for security).

four great vows: The four great vows of a bodhisattva to save all sentient beings, quench all defilements, know all the Buddha's teachings, and attain the Way of the Buddha.

four heavenly kings: The four kings whose palaces are half-way up the slopes of Mt. Sumeru. They guard the four cardinal directions.

four noble truths: The truth of suffering, the truth of the origin of suffering, the truth of the cessation of suffering, and the truth of the means of ending suffering, which is the eightfold path.

four offenses of defeat: In the pre-Mahayana monastic code for Buddhist monks, the four worst offenses are called offenses of defeat because breaking them means one's efforts to live as a monk have been defeated and one must be expelled for life. The four offenses are to engage in sexual relations to the point of penetration, theft of an item worth enough to be a criminal offense, being involved in killing a human being, and deliberately lying about one's spiritual attainments.

Genpei War: (1180-1185) The war fought between the Taira and the Minamoto clans for control of Japan. The Minamoto won and established the Kamakura shogunate.

Genshin: (942-1017) A Tendai monk who contributed to the development of Pure Land Buddhism in Japan when he wrote the *Ojo-yoshu* (*Essential Collection Concerning Rebirth in the Pure Land*).

Gijō-bō: (n.d.) A disciple of Dōzen-bō and one of Nichiren's childhood tutors. Later became a follower of Nichiren.

goma: (J) The Buddhist esoteric ceremony that is an adaptation of the oblations to the gods practiced in Brahmanism.

Go-Toba: (1180-1239) The 82nd emperor of Japan. He abdicated in 1198. In 1221 he led a short-lived rebellion against the Hōjō regents who ran the Kamakura shogunate but was defeated and exiled to the Oki Islands.

Great Power Obtainer: (S. Mahāsthāmaprāpta; J. Seishi) A bodhisattva who is an attendant of Amitābha Buddha and is present at the preaching of the *Lotus Sutra*.

Gumonji-hō: In the J., the "method for seeking, hearing, and retaining." An esoteric practice focusing on Space Repository

Bodhisattva whose purpose is to enable the practitioner to recall and understand anything see or hear.

Hachiman: The Japanese god of war and harvests. Given the title "Great Bodhisattva" in 781 by the imperial court. Believed to have been a deification of Emperor Ōjin, the 15th emperor who ruled from 270-310. He was considered the 16th emperor in Nichiren's time). He is also supposed to have made a vow to protect 100 emperors. Later regarded as the tutelary deity of the Minamoto clan.

Hakii Sanenaga: (1222-1297) A samurai follower of Nichiren. Donated Mt. Minobu to Nichiren.

Hei no Saemon: (d. 1293) The deputy chief of the Board of Retainers during the regencies of Hōjō Tokimune (1251-1284) and Tokimune's son and successor Hōjo Sadatoki (1271-1311). Also known as Taira no Yoritsuna or Hei no Saemon-no-jō Yoritsuna. Was accused of conspiring to revolt against the regent and committed *seppuku* along with his second son Sukemune in 1293. His first son, Munetsuna, was exiled to Sado Island.

Hell of Incessant Suffering: (S. Avīci) The lowest of the eight hot hells where those who have committed the five grave offenses or who have slandered the Dharma are said to be reborn.

Hinayana: (S. Hīnayāna) "small vehicle." A Mahayana term for those who only wish to attain liberation for themselves and do not try to benefit others by striving for buddhahood.

Hōjo Masako: (1156-1225) Wife of the first shogun who became a nun after his death. As the "Nun Shogun," she became a powerful figure behind the scenes during the early years of the Kamakura shogunate.

Hōjō Masamura: (1205-1273) The fourth son of Hōjō Yoshitoki. He was the seventh regent of the Kamakura shogunate from 1264-1268.

Hōjō Nagatoki: (1227-1264) The sixth regent of the Kamakura shogunate from 1256-1264). His father was Hōjō Shigetoki.

Hōjō Nobutoki: (1238-1323) The constable of Sado Island and lord of Musashi Province.

Hōjō Shigetoki: (1198-1261) The third son of Hōjō Yoshitoki. When he retired from public life to become a lay monk he became known as the Lay Monk of Gokurakuji or sometimes Lord Gokurakuji.

Hōjō Tokimasa: (1138-1215) The father-in-law of the first shogun, Minamoto Yoritomo. He was the first regent of the Kamakura shogunate from 1203-1205.

Hōjō Tokimune: (1251-1284) The son of Hōjō Tokiyori and the eighth regent of the Kamakura shogunate from 1268-1284.

Hōjō Tokisuke: (1248-1272) The younger half-brother of Hōjō Tokimune. He was the shogunal deputy in Rokuhara, Kyōto, from 1264-1272. He was killed when he became suspected of conspiring against Tokimune.

Hōjō Tokiyori: (1227-1263) The grandson of Hōjō Yasutoki. He was the fifth regent of the Kamakura shogunate from 1246-1256. Even after he retired as regent and became a lay monk, he ruled from behind the scenes as the Lay Monk of Saimyōji or Lord Saimyōji.

Hōjō Yasutoki: (1183-1242) He was the eldest son of Hōjō Yoshitoki. He was the third regent of the Kamakura shogunate from 1224-1242.

Hōjō Yoshitoki: (1163-1224) The brother-in-law of the first shogun, Minamoto Yoritomo. He became the second regent of the Kamakura shogunate from 1205-1224.

Homma Shigetsura: (n.d.) The deputy constable of Sado Island.

Hōnen: (1133-1212) The founder of the Pure Land school in Japan. Also known as Genkū.

Hong Yan: Died while putting the murdered Duke of Yi's liver into his own stomach in order to save the duke from the disgrace of having his liver abandoned on the road.

icchantika: In S., "incorrigible disbeliever." It is a term for someone who has no potential for awakening. The *Lotus Sutra*, however, teaches that even an *icchantika* can attain enlightenment.

Ikegami Munenaga: (d. 1283) A samurai follower of Nichiren.

Ikegami Munenaka: (d. 1293) A samurai follower of Nichiren.

Indra: The thunder god of the Brahmanistic pantheon and a protector of the Dharma.

Ise Shrine: The main shrine of Amaterasu Ōmikami.

Itō Sukemitsu: (n.d.) The steward of the Itō district in Izu Province where Nichiren was exiled.

Jambudvīpa: In S., "Island of the Jambu Tree." According to traditional Buddhist cosmology, this is the name of the southern continent upon which we are said to live.

Jikaku: (794-864) The third abbot of Enryakuji, and therefore head of the Tendai school. He taught that the *Lotus Sutra* and the esoteric sutras were equal in principle but that the latter were superior in practice because they also taught the use of mudras, mantras, and mandalas. Also known as Ennin.

Jōken-bō: (n.d.) A disciple of Dōzen-bō and one of Nichiren's childhood tutors. Later became a follower of Nichiren.

Juntoku: (1197-1242) The 84th emperor of Japan. He abdicated in 1221. In that year he participated in Go-Toba's rebellion and was exiled to Sado Island.

juzu: (J) Buddhist prayer beads. They typically have 108 beads for the purification of 108 defilements.

kalpa: (S) An aeon.

Kamakura: The city where the shogunate established by Minamoto Yoritomo was based.

kami: (J) The numinous spirits of the natural world, including some powerful animals and humans and especially those who have died and still have a powerful influence on the living.

Kammu: (737-806) The 50th emperor of Japan who reigned from 781-806. In Nichiren's time he was considered the 51st emperor.

karma: In S., "action" or "deed." Sometimes it is used to refer to the consequences of past actions, though that is technically incorrect as there is another Sanskirt term, *phala*, that is the correct term for the "fruition" of past actions.

kesa: (J) The patchwork mantle, often ochre colored, worn by Buddhist monks and nuns over a black or grey robe.

Kimmei: (509-571) The 29th emperor of Japan from 539-571. Considered 30th emperor in Nichiren's time.

Kōbō: (774-835) The founder of the Mantra school. Also known as Kūkai.

Kudō Yoshitaka: (d. 1264) One of Nichiren's earliest followers among the samurai.

Kyōto: The home of the imperial court and the official capital of Japan from 794 to1869.

Lanxi Daolong: (J. Rankei Dōryū; 1213-1278) A Zen master in the Rinzai lineage who came to Japan in 1246. He became the first abbot of Kenchōji in Kamakura in 1253.

Latter Age of the Degeneration of the Dharma: (J. *mappō*) The fifth 500-year period after the death of the Buddha. During this period the true spirit of the Dharma is completely lost and all that is left is sectarianism and bickering. In Japan it was believed to have begun in the year 1052 CE. Sometimes just called Latter Age of the Dharma.

Lord Gokurakuji: See Hōjō Shigetoki.

Lord Saimyōji: See Hōjō Tokiyori.

Lotus Sutra: (S. *Saddharmapuṇḍarīka-sūtra*) A Mahayana sutra in which Śākyamuni Buddha reveals that all his teachings are part of the One Vehicle that leads to buddhahood and that he actually attained buddhahood in the remote past, thereby making him the Eternal Śākyamuni Buddha.

Mahākāśyapa: One of the ten major disciples of Śākyamuni Buddha. He was foremost in asceticism.

Mahākātyāyana: One of the ten major disciples of Śākyamuni Buddha. He was foremost in explaining the Dharma.

Mahāprajāpati: The aunt of Prince Siddhārtha who raised him after his mother, Māyā, passed away

Mahāvairocana: The Great Illuminator Buddha who personifies the Dharma-body, especially in esoteric Buddhism. Known in Japan as Dainichi, meaning "Great Sun."

Mahayana: (S. Mahāyāna) "great vehicle." The school of Buddhism that emphasizes the bodhisattva path wherein one strives to become a buddha for the liberation of all sentient beings.

Maitreya: The bodhisattva who is destined to become the next buddha after Śākyamuni Buddha billions of years from now. In the meantime, he resides in the Tuṣita Heaven.

mandala: In S., "circle." Diagrams or paintings used to focus the mind and express the ultimate truth.

Mañjuśrī: A celestial bodhisattva noted for wisdom. In Japanese he is called Manjushiri.

mantra: In S., "spell" or "charm." Chants or invocations used to invoke protective powers and the ultimate truth. In J., the term is translated as *shingon* and literally means "true word."

Mantra school: (J. Shingon Shū) Esoteric Buddhism was introduced to China when the Indian monk Śubhākarasiṃha (637-735; C. Shan-wu-wei) came in 716 and translated the *Mahāvairocana Sūtra* with his disciple I-hsing (683-727) in 725. At some point they also translated the *Act of Perfection Sūtra*. In 720, two more Indian masters of tantric Buddhism came to China, Vajrabodhi (671-741; C. Chin-kang-chih) and his disciple Amoghavajra (705-774; C. Puk'ung). Amoghavajra translated the *Diamond Peak Sūtra* in 746. These sūtras were the basis of the Mantra School of esoteric Buddhism that taught the practice of the three secrets of body, word, and thought: the gestures called mudras, the recitation of mantras, and the concentration of the mind by visualizing images from the Womb Realm and Diamond Realm mandalas. Amoghavajra transmitted the Mantra teachings to Hui-kuo (746-805) who in turn transmitted them to Japanese monk Kūkai (774-835; later known as Kōbō). Kūkai had gone to China in 804 and returned to Japan in 806 whereupon he founded the Japanese Mantra school, the Shingon Shū.

mantra teachings: Esoteric Buddhism in Japan was called *shingon*, but that word could refer to either the teachings and practices themselves or to the school founded by Kūkai. The mantra teaching and practices were utilized by monks of all school of Buddhism and not just by those of the Mantra school. The Tendai school, in particular, had its own version of the mantra teachings and practices. When "mantra" is used to refer to these common teachings and practices and not to the school founded by Kūkai, it is not a proper noun and therefore is not capitalized.

Mao Bao: A general in ancient China who once saved the life of a turtle caught by a fisherman, and later was carried across a river by that same turtle when he was fleeing from enemies.

Māra: The devil king of the sixth heaven. He is the entity whose mission is to entice or threaten beings into remaining within the cycle of birth and death.

Maudgalyāyana: One of the ten major disciples of Śākyamuni Buddha. He was foremost in supernatural abilities developed through meditation.

Māyā: The mother of Prince Siddhārtha who passed a way a week after his birth.

Medicine King: (S. Bhaisajyarāja; J. Yakuō) A bodhisattva who appears throughout the *Lotus Sutra* but most prominently in chapters 23 and 27.

Medicine Superior: (S. Bhaiṣajyasamudgata; J. Yakujō) A bodhisattva who is the brother of Bhaiṣajyarāja in chapter 27 of the *Lotus Sutra*.

Miaole Zhanran: (711-782) the sixth patriarch of the T'ien-t'ai school if Tiantai Zhiyi is considered the founder, or the ninth if Nāgārjuna is considered the founder.

middle way: Refers to the middle way of selflessness that avoids self-indulgence and self-denial. Also refers to the right view that avoids the extreme views of existence and non-existence, or being and non-being.

Minamoto no Sanetomo: (1192-1219) The second son of Minamoto Yoritomo and the third shogun from 1203-1219.

Minamoto no Yoriie: (1182-1204) The first son of Minamoto Yoritomo and the second shogun from 1202-1203.

Minamoto no Yoritomo: (1147-1199) The first shogun, or "barbarian subduing general." Ruled as the shogun from 1192-1199.

Minamoto no Yoshitsune: (1159-1189) The brother of the first shogun, Yoritomo.

Mt. Sumeru: The mythical mountain at the center of this world according to Brahmanism.

mudra: (S. mudrā) A "seal." Hand gestures used to signify the ultimate truth.

Nāgārjuna: (c. 150 – 250) The founder of the Middle Way (S. Mādhyamaka) school. He lived in the second and third century. Considered one of the 24 (or 28) patriarchs who transmitted the Dharma after Śākyamuni Buddha.

naginata: A Japanese polearm topped with a gently curving blade.

Namu Amida Butsu: In J., "Devotion to Amitābha Buddha." The practice of chanting this phrase is called *nembutsu*.

Namu Myōhō Renge Kyō: In J., "Devotion to the Sutra of the Lotus Flower of the Wonderful Dharma." The Sino-Japanese pronunciation of the two Chinese characters that are used to transliterate the S. word *namas* which means "devotion" and the five Chinese characters which are used to translated the S. title *Saddharmapuṇḍarīka-sūtra* which means "Sutra of the Lotus Flower of the Wonderful Dharma."

Nanjō Tokimitsu: (1259-1332) One of Nichiren's followers among the samurai. Also known as the Lord of Ueno.

nayuta: In S., "hundred thousand million."

nembutsu: In J., "recollection of the buddha's name." The practice of chanting the name of a buddha, though almost always understood to be Amitābha Buddha in the form of "Namu Amida Butsu."

Never Despising: (S. Sadāparibhūta; J. Jōfukyō) The bodhisattva in chapter 20 of the *Lotus Sutra* who greets everyone he meets with respect because they are all able to become buddhas. He is a past life of Śākyamuni Buddha.

Nichiren Shōnin: (1222-1282) The Japanese reformer and teacher who propagated the *Lotus Sutra* by refuting false teachings and introducing the Three Great Secret Dharmas.

Nichiji: (1250-?) Originally an attendant of Nikkō, he became Nichiren's disciple in 1270. Also known as Renge Ajari or Kai-kō. In 1295 he went to the mainland to spread Nichiren's teachings, thereby becoming the first foreign missionary of Nichiren Buddhism.

Nichirō: (1245-1320) Nisshō's nephew who joined Nichiren around 1254. Also known as Daikoku Ajari or Chikugo-bō. After Nichiren's death he and Nisshō took care of Nichiren's followers in Kamakura. He founded the Hikigayatsu lineage of Nichiren Shū. He founded the temples Myōhonji in Kamakura, Kanagawa Prefecture; Hondoji in Matsudo City, Chiba Prefecture; and Ikegami Honmonji, in Tokyo. Ikegami Honmonji was established at the estate of Ikegami Munenaka where Nichiren passed away. It is currently the location of Nichiren Shū's administrative headquarters.

Nichizō: (1269-1342) The younger half-brother of Nichirō. He became one of Nichirō's nine senior disciples and was the first to spread Nichiren's teachings in Kyōto. He founded the temple Myōkenji in Kyōto. It is considered one of the sacred temples of Nichiren Shū.

Nikkō: (1246-1333) Became Nichiren's follower in 1257. Also known as Byakuren Ajari or Hōki-bō. He founded the Fuji lineage of which several important temples, such as Kitayama Honmonji, are part of Nichiren Shū. He began residing at Mt. Minobu in 1285, but left in 1288 after conflicts with Nikō. He established Taisekiji near Mt. Fuji with the help of Nanjō Tokimitsu in 1290. Less than a year later he left Taisekiji and moved to the nearby town of Omosu. In 1298, with the help of Nitchō, he established Kitayama Honmonji where he remained until his death.

Nikō: (1253-1314) Became a disciple of Nichiren in 1265. Also known as Minbu Ajari or Sado-bō. Considered by Nichiren Shū to be the second abbot of Kuonji at Mt. Minobu after Nichiren. He founded the Minobu lineage and also the Mobara lineage, which are both part of Nichiren Shū. The Mobara lineage head temple was originally called Myōkoji but is now called Sōgenji. It is located in Mobara City, Chiba Prefecture.

nirmāna-kāya: In S., "transformation-body."

nirvana: (S. nirvāna) "extinction." Refers to the extinction or extinguishing of the fire of the defilements of greed, hatred, and delusion.

Nisshō: (1221-1323) A fellow student of Nichiren at Mt. Hiei. He joined Nichiren around 1254. Also known as Ben Ajari and Jōben. After Nichiren's death he and Nichirō took care of Nichiren's followers in Kamakura. He founded the Hama lineage of Nichiren Shū. Myōhokkeji, the temple he originally founded in Hamado, Kamakura, is now located in Tamazawa, Mishima City, Shizuoka Prefecture.

Nitchō: (1252-1317) A stepson of Toki Jōnin who became Nichiren's disciple in 1267. Also known as Iyo Ajari or Iyo-bō. After a falling out with his stepfather, Nitchō went to Kitayama Honmonji in 1292 to assist Nikkō.

Nun Shogun: See Hōjō Masako.

One Vehicle: The one vehicle that leads to buddhahood and subsumes all other vehicles, such as the two vehicles.

Original Gate: (J. *honmon*) The latter 14 chapters of the *Lotus Sutra* in which the Eternal Śākyamuni Buddha reveals that he attained buddhahood in the remote past.

Original Vow: The 18th of the 48 vows of Amitābha Buddha that states: "If, when I attain buddhahood, sentient beings in the lands of the ten directions who sincerely and joyfully entrust themselves to me, desire to be born in my land, and think of me even ten times, should not be born there, may I not attain perfect complete awakening. Excluded, however, are those who commit the five grave offenses and slander the True Dharma."

Precepts school: (J. Ritsu Shū) The Precepts School was founded in China by Daoxuan (596-667) who instituted the Vinaya of the Dharmaguptaka school based on the *Fourfold Rules of Discipline* translated in the early 5th century. From that time on, Mahāyāna monks and nuns in China, Korea, and Vietnam have all been ordained in the Dharmaguptaka precept lineage. The Precept school was brought to Japan by Jianzhen (688-763) in 753 where it was called the Ritsu Shū. In 755, Jianzhen established a precept platform to confer the Dharmaguptaka precepts upon monks and nuns at Tōdai-ji temple in Nara, and two more precept platforms were established in 761 at Yakushi-ji temple (in present day Tochigi prefecture) and Kanzeon-ji temple (in present day Fukuoka prefecture). The Ritsu Shū's popularity declined after the 8th century. In Nichiren's day, Eizon (1201-1290) revived the school in conjunction with esoteric Buddhism, thereby establishing the Mantra-Precept School (J. Shingon Ritsu Shū).

private-buddha: (S. *pratyekabuddha*) Also known as "cause-knower." The solitary contemplatives who attain awakening independent of the Buddha Dharma and who do not try to liberate others.

Pure Land of Eagle Peak: Eagle Peak where the *Lotus Sutra* was taught when seen as the place where the Eternal Śākyamuni Buddha preaches and transmits the Wonderful Dharma for all beings in all times and places. See Pure Land of Eternally Tranquil Light.

Pure Land of Eternally Tranquil Light: The true nature of this world as seen by the Eternal Śākyamuni Buddha.

Pure Land of Utmost Bliss: The pure land of Amitābha Buddha. Also known as the Pure Land of the West.

Pure Land school: (J. Jōdo Shū) Pure Land devotions were known and practiced by members of all schools of East Asian Buddhism going back at least to the time of the monk Huiyuan (334-416) and his White Lotus Society that was dedicated to the practice of chanting the name of Amitābha Buddha and visualizing the buddha and his Pure Land of the West. The practice of reciting the name of Amitābha Buddha was also one of the methods utilized for calming and contemplation meditation by Tiantai. After the persecution of Buddhism by the Emperor Wu in 845, only the Pure Land and Zen schools continued to flourish in China. The Zen school initially held itself aloof from and even criticized Pure Land Buddhism, but in the end Pure Land practice was even incorporated into the Zen school. The Pure Land Buddhism which survived the persecution of 845 and later attained mass appeal throughout East Asia was not, however, the same as that championed by Huiyuan or Tiantai. Rather, it was a form of Pure Land Buddhism inspired by the three Pure Land sutras. This form of Pure Land Buddhism deemphasized the visualization of Amitābha Buddha and the Pure Land of the West, and put much greater emphasis on the 18th vow of Amitābha Buddha, called the Original Vow, and the chanting of the name of Amitābha Buddha to the virtual exclusion of all other practices in order to be reborn in the Pure Land after death. Three teachers of Chinese Pure Land Buddhism in particular spread this kind of Pure Land Buddhism. These teachers were Tanluan (476-542), Daochuo (562-645), and Shandao (613-681). In Japan, the exclusive practice of Pure Land Buddhism was advocated by Hōnen (1133-1212) beginning in 1175. By the Kamakuran era, Pure Land Buddhism had become immensely popular, though it was considered a movement within the Tendai Shū and was not recognized as a separate school until the early 15th century.

Pūrna: One of the ten major disciples of Śākyamuni Buddha. He was foremost in eloquence.

Rāhula: The son of Prince Siddhārtha. He was foremost in inconspicuous practice.

Rājagriha: The capital of the ancient Indian kingdom of Magadha. The Buddha taught outside the city at a place called Eagle Peak.

rākṣasī: A malevolent spirit known to cause illness. Some have been converted to Buddhism and become protective spirits. They are a type of hungry ghost. The group of ten Nichiren refers to are the daughters of the Mother-of-Devils (J. Kishimojin) who appear in chapter 26 of the *Lotus Sutra*.

Rankei Dōryū: See Lanxi Daolong.

Renchō: The name Nichiren had as newly ordained monk. It means "Lotus Eternal." He was also called Zeshō-bō.

Ryōkan: (1217-1303) A monk of the Mantra-Precepts school who became the abbot of Gokurakuji in Kamakura in 1267. Also known as Ninshō. He was a disciple of Eison, the founder of the Mantra-Precepts school.

Sahā: In S., "Endurance." It is the Buddhist name for this world where one must endure many forms of suffering.

Śakra Devānām Indra: See Indra.

Śākyamuni Buddha: The historical Buddha. Also known as Siddhārtha Gautama. Some scholars, notably Hajime Nakamura (1912-1999), estimate that the historical Siddhārtha Gautama, the young man who would become Śākyamuni Buddha, was born in the year 463 BCE. According to the accounts in the Pāli Canon he left home at the age of 29 to practice yoga and asceticism for six years and then attained buddhahood under the Bodhi Tree at the age of 35. He passed away at the age of 80 in the year 383 BCE. Some scholars might push these dates back as far as a century. Nichiren and his contemporaries, however, going by a text called the *Record of Wonders in the Book of Chou*, whose Chinese author wanted to set the date for the Buddha's appearance during the auspicious period of the founding of the Chou dynasty, believed that the Buddha was born on the eighth day of the fourth month of 1029 BCE and died on the fifteenth day of the second month of 949 BCE. Furthermore, Nichiren and his East Asian contemporaries accepted the time line of the Buddha's life taken from the *Treatise on the Great Perfection of Wisdom Sutra* attributed to Nāgārjuna (but possibly written by its ostensible translator Kumārajīva). In that treatise, Siddhārtha left home at the age of 19, spent 12 years practicing asceticism in the Himalayas (counting the year that he was 19) and attained awakening under the Bodhi Tree at the age of 30. He then spent the next 50 years teaching, culminating in the expounding of the *Lotus Sutra*. At the age of 80 he passed away (or attained final nirvana).

samādhi: In S., "concentration."

sambhoga-kāya: In S., "enjoyment-body."

samsara: (S. *samsāra*) "wandering on." Refers to the wanderings of sentient beings within the cycle of birth and death.

Sangha: In S., "Assembly." It is the community of those who uphold the Buddha Dharma.

Śāriputra: One of the ten major disciples. He was foremost in wisdom.

Seichōji: In J., Temple of Clear Luminosity. Seichōji was the temple where Nichiren studied as a body and was ordained as a monk.

seppuku: In J., "belly slashing." In order to safeguard their honor, a samurai might chose to die by slashing open their own bellies, immediately followed by a beheading at the hands of an assistant.

Shandao: (613-681) Considered by Hōnen to be the third Chinese patriarch of Pure Land Buddhism.

Shigetada: Traditionally believed to be the name of Nichiren's father.

Shijō Kingo: (n.d.) One of Nichiren's earliest followers among the samurai. He received many important writings including *Kaimoku-shō*.

Shōichi: (1202-1280) A Japanese Zen master in the Rinzai lineage. Also known as Enni Bennen.

Shōtoku: (572-622) An imperial prince who was the regent during the reign of Empress Suiko. He was a devout Buddhist who was credited with writing commentaries on important sutras, including the *Lotus Sutra*. In 604 he put forth a constitution whose second article states the importance of taking refuge in the Three Treasures.

shōnin: In J., "sage."

Siddhārtha: The Indian prince who became Śākyamuni Buddha. The name means "Aim Accomplished."

six kinds of sense consciousness: The forms of consciousness corresponding to each of the six sense organs.

six paths: The six paths of suffering that refers to ways of living that lead to and are reflective of rebirth among the hell-dwellers, hungry ghosts, animals, *asuras* (fighting demons), humans, and gods.

six perfections: The six practices of a bodhisattva consisting of generosity, morality, patience, energy, meditation, and wisdom.

six senior disciples: On the eighth day of the tenth month of 1282, Nichiren designated the six senior disciples to carry on his work after his death. They were: Nisshō (1221-1323), Nichirō (1245-1320), Nikkō (1246-1333), Nikō (1253-1314), Nitchō (1252-1317), and Nichiji (1250-?).

six sense bases: The eyes, ears, nose, tongue, body, and mind which are all sensitive to various phenomena.

six sense objects: The forms, sounds, odors, flavors, tangibles, and mental objects (concepts and emotions) that are the objects of the six sense bases.

skillful means: (J. *hoben*; S. *upaya*) The various means or methods that the Buddha uses to teach the Dharma. Sometimes called "expedients" or "expedient means."

Space Repository: (S. Ākāśagarbha; J. Kokūzō). Space Repository Bodhisattva was the "focus of devotion" at Seichōji temple when Nichiren was a student there.

Śubhākarasimha: (637-735) One of the disseminators of the mantra teachings and practices in China. He translated the *Acts of Perfection Sutra* and the *Mahāvairocana Sutra*.

Subhūti: One of the ten major disciples of Śākyamuni Buddha. He was foremost in understanding emptiness.

Śuddhodana: The father of Prince Siddhārtha.

Sun Goddess: See Amaterasu Ōmikami.

Superior Practice: (S. Viśiṣṭacāritra; J. Jōgyō) One of the four leaders of the bodhisattvas who emerge from the earth. Nichiren believed that he was the appearance of this bodhisattva, though frequently he more humbly referred to himself as the forerunner of this bodhisattva.

sutra: In S., "thread of discourse." A Buddhist scripture.

tachi: A Japanese cavalry sword with a long and gently curving blade that preceded the appearance of *katana*.

Taira no Kiyomori: (1118-1181) The leader of the Taira clan (also known as Heike) who dominated the imperial court in the middle of the 12th century.

Taira no Tokiko: (1126-1185) Wife of Taira no Kiyomori and the grandmother of Emperor Antoku. She was known as the Nun of the Second Rank.

Taira no Tomomori: (1152-1185) A fourth son of Taira no Kiyomori. He was one of the chief commanders of the Taira during the Genpei War.

Tanluan: (476-542) Considered by Hōnen to be the first of the Chinese patriarchs of Pure Land Buddhism.

tathāgata: In S., "thus come one" or "thus gone one." Another title for a buddha. It refers to one who comes from and goes to ultimate reality.

ten courses of wholesome conduct: The ten forms of good conduct which lead to a heavenly existence and are descriptive of the ethical dimension of the eightfold path. They are: not to kill, not to steal, not to engage in sexual misconduct, not to lie, not to engage in malicious speech, not to engage in harsh speech, not to engage in idle chatter (or gossip), not to give in to covetousness, not to give in to ill will, not to hold wrong views. Also called ten good acts.

Tendai Shū: The Japanese version of the Tiantai school. The Tendai school after the time of Dengyō increasingly put more emphasis on esoteric teachings and practices, esp. after the time of Jikaku.

ten Dharma-realms: The six paths or realms of suffering within samsara and also the four realms that transcend suffering of the voice-hearers, private-buddhas, bodhisattvas, and buddhas.

ten good acts: see ten courses of wholesome conduct.

ten suchnesses: The ten factors or aspects of reality enumerated at the beginning of chapter two of the *Lotus Sutra*. They are: appearance, nature, entity, power, activity, causes, conditions, effects, consequences, and the equality of all phenomena despite apparent differences. All ten of these are empty of substantial existence, yet provisionally existent in accordance with changing causes and conditions, and all manifest the middle way between being and non-being.

three ages of the Dharma: Refers to the Former Age of the True Dharma, the first millennia after the Buddha's passing; the Middle Age of the Semblance Dharma, the second millennia after the Buddha's passing; and the Latter Age of the Degeneration of the Dharma, the 10,000-year period that follows the the second millennia after the Buddha's passing.

three baskets: (S. tripitika) The three collections of the sutras, the vinaya, and the abhidharma that respectively record the Buddha's discourses, the precepts and procedures for the Sangha, and the systematization of the teachings.

three bodies: (S. *trikāya*) The Dharma-body, enjoyment-body, and transformation-body of a buddha.

three categories: Part of the teaching of the three thousand realms in a single thought moment. The three categories are the five aggregates of beings (forms, feelings, perceptions, mental formations, and consciousness), the lives of sentient beings as nominal individuals who interact with other individuals, and the environments of those beings.

three esoteric sutras: The three sutras most revered by Tendai monks practicing the esoteric or mantra teachings. They are the *Mahāvairocana Sutra* (S. *Mahāvairocanābhisaṃbodhi Sūtra*; J. *Dainichi Kyō*), the *Act of Perfection Sutra* (S. *Susiddhikara Sūtra*; J. *Soshitsuji Kyō*), and the *Diamond Peak Sutra* (S. *Vajraśekhara Sūtra*; *Kongōchō Kyō*).

threefold *Lotus Sutra*: The *Lotus Sutra* combined with the *Infinite Meanings Sutra* (J. *Muryōgi Kyō*) as a prologue and the *Meditation on Universal Sage Bodhisattva Sutra* (J. *Kan Fugen Bosatsu Gyōbō Kyō*) as an epilogue.

threefold training: The eightfold path broken down into threefold training of morality (right speech, right action, right livelihood), concentration (right effort, right mindfulness, right concentration), and wisdom (right view and right intention).

three hindrances: The defilements, unwholesome habits, and painful consequences of those habits which can prevent one from attaining enlightenment.

three kinds of enemies: Three kinds of people who will oppose the teachin of the *Lotus Sutra*: ignorant laypeople, evil monks, and false arhats

three poisons: Greed, hatred, and delusion. Alternatively: greed, anger, and ignorance.

three Pure Land sutras: The three sutras of most revered by the Pure Land school of Hōnen. They are the *Buddha of Infinite Life Sutra* (S. *Sukhāvatīvyūha Sūtra*; J. *Muryōju Kyō*), the *Meditation on the Buddha of Infinite Life Sutra* (S. *Amitāyurdhyāna Sūtra*; J. *Kanmuryōju Kyō*), and the *Amitābha Sutra* (S. *Sukhāvatīvyūha Sūtra*; J. *Amida Kyō*). In Sanskrit the *Buddha of Infinite Life Sutra* and the *Amitābha Sutra* both have the same name, but the latter is shorter.

three thousand realms in a single thought-moment: (J., *ichinen sanzen*) The Tiantai teaching, based upon the *Lotus Sūtra*, that all modes of existence are present in every single moment of conscious awareness. The three thousand realms consist of the ten Dharma-realms that mutually possess one another, the ten suchnesses, and the three categories.

Three Treasures: The Buddha (the awakened teacher), Dharma (the teaching and practice and reality itself), and Sangha (the community of those who uphold the teaching and practice and pass it on) that every Buddhist takes refuge in.

Three Treatises: (J. Sanron Shū) A Mādhyamaka school based on the study of three treatises translated by Kumārajīva. In 404 Kumārajīva translated the *One Hundred Verses* attributed to Nāgārjuna's disciple Āryadeva. In 409 he translated the *Middle Way Treatise* (a translation of Nāgārjuna's *Root Verses on the Middle Way*), and the *Twelve Gates Treatise* attributed to Nāgārjuna. Jizang (549-632) is considered the founder of the Three Treatises School because he was the one who systematized and refined its teachings. The Korean monk Hyegwan (the same monk who brought the Establishment of Truth teachings in Japan) was a disciple of Jizang and he brought the Three Treatises School to Japan in 625, where it was called the Sandron Shū. The Sanron Shū died out as an independent school by the mid-12th century.

Tiantai Zhiyi: (538-597) The founder of the Tiantai school.

Tiantai, school: (J. Tendai Shū) Mahayana Buddhist school founded in China in the 6th century CE by the Great Master Tiantai. Tiantai Buddhism considers the *Lotus Sutra* the Buddha's highest teaching. It was established in Japan in 805 by Dengyō, where it was called the Tendai school.

Tōjō Kagenobu: (d. 1264) The steward of the Tōjō district where Nichiren grew up.

Toki Jōnin: (1214-1299) One of Nichiren's first supporters among the samurai. He received several important writings, most notably *Kanjin Honzon-shō*. Also known as Toki Tsunenobu. He took the name Jōnin when he became a lay monk. After Nichiren's death he ordained himself, took the name Nichijō, and founded the temple Nakayama Hokkekyōji. He is the founder of the Nakayama lineage of Nichiren Shū. Nakayama Hokkekyōji is in Ichikawa City, Chiba Prefecture.

Trace Gate: (J. *shakumon*) The first 14 chapters of the *Lotus Sūtra* in which the historical Śākyamuni Buddha teaches the One Vehicle.

transformation-body: (S. *nirmāna-kāya*; J. *ōjin*) The historical body of a buddha. This is the body that is manifested in order to teach the Dharma to other beings.

trikāya: In S., "three bodies." Refers to the three bodies of a buddha.

triple world: The desire realm, form realm, and formless realm. The world of desire extends from the hells up to the more concrete heavens. The worlds of form and formlessness include the higher heavens of increasing refinement.

Tsuchimikado: (1196-1231) The 83rd emperor of Japan. He abdicated in 1210. After Go-Toba's rebellion in 1221 he voluntarily went into exile to Tosa and later to Awa province.

Tsurugaoka Shrine: The shrine of Hachiman in Kamakura. In Nichiren's day it also functioned as a Tendai temple.

twelve-fold chain of dependent origination: The twelve links that describe the process of birth and death over many lifetimes. The twelve links are: ignorance, volitional formations, consciousness, name & form, six sense bases, contact, feeling, craving, clinging, becoming, birth, aging & death.

two vehicles: The teachings for the voice-hearers and private-buddhas that lead to individual liberation but not to buddhahood. It is another term for Hinayana Buddhism.

Umegiku: Traditionally believed to be the name of Nichiren's mother.

Universal Sage: (S. Samantabhadra; J. Fugen) A bodhisattva known for awakened activity. He features prominently in Chapter 28 of the *Lotus Sutra* and in the closing sutra of the Threefold Lotus Sutra, the *Meditation on Universal Sage Bodhisattva Sutra*.

Upāli: One of the ten major disciples of Śākyamuni Buddha. He was foremost in upholding of the precepts.

Vaidehī: The queen of Magadha, wife of King Bimbisāra, and mother of Ajātaśatru.

Vairocana: Another name for Mahāvairocana. However, sometimes he is understood to be the enjoyment-body of Śākyamuni Buddha, in which case he is considered to reside in a pure land called the Lotus Matrix World. In East Asia, Vairocana is sometimes called Lochana to indicate the enjoyment-body, esp. when the name Vairocana is being used to indicate the Dharma-body instead of Mahāvairocana.

vajra: In S., "diamond pounder." A kind of club made of prongs curling in to form a ball. Represents a thunderbolt, the weapon of Indra.

Vajrabodhi: (671-741) One of the disseminators of the mantra teachings and practices in China. He translated the *Diamond Peak Sutra* into Chinese.

Vasubandhu: (c. 320-400) Co-founder of the Consciousness Only (S. Vijñānavāda) school along with his older brother Asanga. He lived in the fourth century CE. Considered to be one of the 24 (or 28) Indian patriarchs who transmitted the Dharma after Śākyamuni Buddha.

Verses of Eternity: The verses of chapter 16 of the *Lotus Sutra*. In Japanese, Buddhist verses in sutras are called *ge*, and the first two characters of the verses of chapter 16 are "*Ji ga*," so in Japanese the verses are known as the *Jigage*.

voice-hearers: (S. *śrāvaka*) The disciples of the Buddha who were able to hear his teachings.

Wake no Kiyomaro: (733-799) An official in the imperial government who spoke out against the monk Dōkyō, who was attempting to have himself enthroned as emperor.

World Voice Perceiver (S. Avalokiteśvara; J. Kanzeon or Kannon) World Voice Perceiver Bodhisattva is the bodhisattva known for compassion who takes on many forms. The bodhisattva is an attendant of Amitābha Buddha and also features prominently in Chapter 25 of the *Lotus Sutra*.

Yadoya Mitsunori: (n.d.) The chamberlain of the Hōjō Tokiyori. He also served Tokiyori's son Tokimune.

Yakuō-maro: Traditionally said to be Nichiren's second childhood name given to him at Seichōji. Yakuō is also the Japanese name of Medicine King Bodhisattva.

Yaśodharā: (n.d.) The wife of Prince Siddhārtha.

Yu Rang: A retainer who disguised himself as a leper and acted foolishly in order to get close to the rival lord who had murdered his own liege so that he could assassinate him.

Zennichi-maro: Traditionally said to be Nichiren's first childhood name. It means "Splendid Sun."

Zen school: Bodhidharma is credited with establishing the Zen school in China in the early 6th century. Bodhidharma was the legendary 28th patriarch of Indian Buddhism and the first patriarch of the Zen school in China. Zen is actually the Japanese pronunciation of the Chinese word Chan, which is in turn a transliteration of *dhyāna*, the Sanksrit word for meditative absorption. Zen, however, refers to the unity of *dhyāna* and *prajñā* (wisdom) and not meditative absorption alone. According to the Zen school the Dharma has been transmitted from person-to-person (or mind-to-mind) from Śākyamuni Buddha through his successors all the way to the present day Zen Masters. In this way the true meaning of the Buddha's teachings has been passed on through the actual awakening of these successors and not just in the written teachings. By the 10th century there were Five Houses of Zen, but only two have survived: the Linji founded by Linji Yixuan (d. 866) and the Caodong founded by Dongshan Liangjie (807-869) and his disciple Caoshan Benji (840-901). Zen was actually brought to Japan before the Kamakura period, for instance Saichō was given transmission in the Ox Head lineage while in China, but it was never promulgated. A monk named

Dainichin Nōnin tried to establish a Bodhidharma School in 1189 after receiving a certificate of Zen transmission with a correspondent in China, but he was regarded as a fraud. Eisai (1141-1215) succeeded in introducing Linji (J. Rinzai) Zen to Japan in 1191, after spending four years in China training with the Zen Masters there. Dōgen (1200-1253) introduced Caodong (J. Sōtō) Zen to Japan after studying in China from 1223-1227. After the Sung dynasty fell to the Mongols, Zen Masters from China such as Lanxi Daolong (J. Rankei Dōryū; 1213-1278) came to Japan and helped to spread Rinzai Zen.

Zhang'an Guanding: (561-632) The second patriarch of the T'ien-t'ai school. He was the successor to Tiantai Zhiyi, and the compiler of Tiantai Zhiyi's lectures.

Sources

Anesaki, Masahuru. *Nichiren the Buddhist Prophet*. Gloucester: Peter Smith, 1966.

Atkins, Paul S. "Chigo in the Medieval Japanese Imagination," *The Journal of Asian Studies* vol. 67, No. 3 (August) 2008: 947-970.

Bodhi, Bhikkhu. *The Connected Discourses of the Buddha: A Translation of the Samyutta Nikaya*. Boston: Wisdom Publications, 2000.

Blum, Mark L., trans. *The Nirvana Sutra (Mahāparinirvana-sutra) Volume I*. Berkeley: Bukkyō Dendō Kyōkai America Inc., 2013.

Chase, Kenneth. "Mongol Intentions towards Japan in 1266: Evidence from a Mongo Letter to the Sung." *Sino-Japanese Studies Journal* vol. 9, No. 2 (1990)

Christensen, J.A. *Nichiren: Leader of Buddhist Reformation in Japan*. Fremont: Jain Publishing, 2001.

Cleary, Thomas and Cleary, J.C. *The Blue Cliff Record*. Boston: Shambhala, 1992.

Cleary, Thomas, trans. *The Flower Ornament Scripture: A Translation of the Avatamsaka Sutra*. Boston: Shambhala, 1993.

Cleary, Thomas, trans. *Book of Serenity*. Boston: Shambhala, 1998.

Collcutt's, Martin. "The Zen Monastery in Kamakura Society." In *Court and Bakufu in Japan*, ed. by Jeffrey P. Mass, pp. 191-220. Stanford: Stanford University Press, 1982.

Deal, William E. *Handbook to Life in Medieval and Early Modern Japan*. New York: Oxford University Press, 2006.

Dolce, Lucia. "Criticism and Appropriation: Nichiren's Attitude Toward Esoteric Buddhism," in *Japanese Journal of Religious Studies* 26:3-4, 1999: 349-382.

Dunn, Charles. *Everyday Life in Traditional Japan*. Boston: Tuttle Publishing, 1969.

Farris, William Wayne. *Japan's Medieval Population: Famine, Fertility, and Warfare in a Transformative Age*. Honolulu: University of Hawai'i Press, 2006.

Hirai, Chishin, and McCormick, Ryuei, trans. *Shutei Nichiren Shū Hōyō Shiki*. Hayward: Nichiren Buddhist International Center, 2013.

Hori, Kyotsu, ed. and comp. *St. Nichiren's Nyonin Gosho: Letters Addressed to Female Followers*. Tokyo: Nichiren Shu Overseas Propagation Promotion Association, 1995.

Hori, Kyōtsū, comp. *Writings of Nichiren Shōnin: Doctrine Volume 2*. Tokyo: Nichiren Shū Overseas Propagation Promotion Association, 2002.

_____. *Writings of Nichiren Shōnin: Doctrine Volume 1*. Tokyo: Nichiren Shū Overseas Propagation Promotion Association, 2003.

_____. *Writings of Nichiren Shōnin: Doctrine Volume 3*. Tokyo: Nichiren Shū Overseas Propagation Promotion Association, 2004.

_____. *Writings of Nichiren Shōnin: Faith and Practice Volume 4*. Tokyo: Nichiren Shū Overseas Propagation Promotion Association, 2007.

_____. *Writings of Nichiren Shōnin: Biography and Disciples Volume 5*. Tokyo: Nichiren Shū Overseas Propagation Promotion Association, 2008.

_____. *Writings of Nichiren Shōnin: Followers I, Volume 6*. Tokyo: Nichiren Shū Overseas Propagation Promotion Association, 2010.

_____. *Writings of Nichiren Shōnin: Followers II, Volume 7*. Tokyo: Nichiren Shū Overseas Propagation Promotion Association, 2015.

Inagaki, Hisao, trans. *The Three Pure Land Sutras*: Revised Second Edition. Berkeley: Numata Center for Buddhist Translation and Research, 2003.

Jayawickrama, N.A., trans., *The Story of Gotama Buddha (Jataka-nidana)*. Oxford: Pali Text Society, 2002.

Johnston, E.H. trans., *Asvaghosa's Buddhacaritra or Acts of the Buddha*. Delhi: Motilal Banarsidass Publishers, 1998.

Kanda, Akira, ed. *Bukkyō no Oshie: Shason to Nichiren Shōnin*. Tokyo: Shunshūsha, 2005.

Kasahara, Kazuo. *A History of Japanese Religion*. Tokyo: Kosei Publishing Co., 2002.

Kashiwahara, Yusen & Sonoda, Koyu. *Shapers of Japanese Buddhism*. Tokyo: Kosei Publishing Co., 1994.

Kubo, Tsugunari, trans., et. al., *Tiantai Lotus Texts*. Berkeley: Bukkyō Dendō Kyōkai America Inc., 2013.

Mass, Jeffrey P., ed. *Court and Bakufu in Japan: Essays in Kamakura History*. Stanford: Stanford University Press, 1982.

Matsunaga, Alicia & Matsunaga, Daigan. *Foundation of Japanese Buddhism Vol. I & II*. Los Angeles: Buddhist Books International, 1988.

McCullough, Helen Craig, trans. *The Tale of the Heike*. Stanford: Stanford University Press, 1988.

Montgomery, Daniel B. *Fire in the Lotus: The Dynamic Buddhism of Nichiren*. Hammersmith: Mandala, 1991.

Murano, Senchu, trans. *Kaimokushō or Liberation from Blindness*. Berkeley: Numata Center for Buddhist Translation and Research, 2000.

_____. *Two Nichiren Texts*. Berkeley: Numata Center for Buddhist Translation and Research, 2003.

_____, trans. *The Lotus Sutra: The Sutra of the Lotus Flower of the Wonderful Dharma*. Hayward: Nichiren Buddhist International Center, 2012.

Nakao, Takashi. *Nichiren Shōnin: Hokkekyō no Gyōja*. Kyōto: Dōhōsha Media Plan, 2005. DVD and booklet.

Nanamoli, Bhikkhu, *The Life of the Buddha*. Kandy: Buddhist Publication Society, 1992.

Numata Center for Buddhist Translation and Research Editorial Staff. *Buddha-Dharma: The Way to Enlightenment (Revised Second*

420

Edition). Berkeley: Numata Center for Buddhist Translation and Research, 2003.

Petzold, Bruno. *Buddhist Prophet Nichiren: A Lotus in the Sun*. Tokyo: Hokke Journal Inc., 1978.

Pruden, Leo, trans. *The Essentials of the Eight Traditions*. Berkeley: Numata Center for Buddhist Translation and Research, 1994.

Rodd, Laurel Rasplica. *Nichiren: Selected Writings*. Honolulu: University of Hawai'i, 1980.

Sansom, George. *A History of Japan to 1334*. Stanford: Stanford University Press, 1958.

Saso, Michael. *Homa Rites and Mandala Meditation in Tendai Buddhism*. New Delhi: Aditya Prakashan, 1991.

Souyri, Pierre François. *The World Turned Upside Down: Medieval Japanese Society*. Translated by Käthe Roth. New York: Columbia University Press, 2001.

Stone, Jacqueline. *Original Enlightenment and the Transformation of Medieval Japanese Buddhism*. Honolulu: Kuroda Institute, 1999.

_____. "The Atsuhara Affair: The *Lotus Sutra*, Persecution, and Religious Identity in the Early Nichiren Tradition." *Japanese Journal of Religious Studies* 41/1 (2014) pp. 153-189.

Susumu, Ishii. "The Decline of the Kamakura Bakufu." Trans. Jeffrey P. Mass, and Hitomi Tonomura. In *The Cambridge History of Japan Volume 3: Medieval Japan*, ed. John W. Hall, Marius B. Jansen, Madoka Kanai, and Denis Twitchett, pp. 128-174. New York: Cambridge University Press, 1990.

Thurman, Robert A., trans. *The Holy Teaching of Vimalakirti: A Mahayana Scripture*. University Park: The Pennsylvania State University Press, 1988.

Yamamoto, Kosho, trans. *Mahaparinirvana-Sutra: A Complete Translation from the Classical Chinese Language in 3 Volumes*. Tokyo: Karinbunko, 1973.

Yamasaki, Taikō. *Shingon: Japanese Esoteric Buddhism*. Boston: Shambhala, 1988.

Yamasaki, Taikō. *Shingon: Japanese Esoteric Buddhism*. Boston: Shambhala, 1988.

Yampolsky, Philip B., ed. *Selected Writings of Nichiren*. New York: Columbia University Press, 1990.

Websites:

"Great Comet of 1264." *Wikipedia*. Wikipedia, n.d. Web. 21 September 2014.
(https://en.wikipedia.org/wiki/Great_Comet_of_1264)

"Mongol invasions of Japan." *Wikipedia*. Wikipedia, n.d. Web. 21 September 2014.
(https://en.wikipedia.org/wiki/Mongol_invasions_of_Japan)

The Brahma Net Sutra: Bodhisattva Mind-Ground Chapter. *BuddhaSutra.com*. n.p., n.d. Web. 21 September 2015. (http://www.buddhasutra.com/files/brahmanet.htm)